RAISING HELL
for JUSTICE

RAISING HELL
for JUSTICE

The Washington Battles of a
Heartland Progressive

DAVID R. OBEY

THE UNIVERSITY OF WISCONSIN PRESS

The University of Wisconsin Press
1930 Monroe Street
Madison, Wisconsin 53711

www.wisc.edu/wisconsinpress/

3 Henrietta Street
London WC2E 8LU, England

5   4   3   2   1

Printed in the United States of America

Library of Congress Cataloging-in-Publication Data

Obey, David R.
Raising hell for justice : the Washington battles of a
heartland progressive / David R. Obey.
p.   cm.
Includes index.
ISBN 0-299-22540-2 (cloth : alk. paper)
1. Obey, David R. 2. Legislators—United States—Biography.
3. United States. Congress. House—Biography.
4. Politicians—Wisconsin—Biography. I. Title.
E840.8.O225A3   2007
328.73092—dc22   2007013249
[B]

to Joan
who has put up with it all

Contents

Acknowledgments

No public figure can be truly successful without the help of so many others who work behind the scenes. I have been blessed with working partners (staff), in Wisconsin and in Washington, who have helped me to learn what I needed to know and how to put that knowledge to effective use on behalf of my country and my constituents. I want to acknowledge their absolutely crucial help and support.

At home, three men, Jerry Madison, Larry Dahl, and Doug Hill, have run my district office and served as my eyes and ears with incredible competence and dedication, ably assisted by so many others. People like Martin Hanson, Don Garner-Gerhardt, Rene Daniels, Jeff Burhandt, Terry Shulta, Melissa Schroeder, Sandi Kinney, Evie Pellet, Josh Zepnick, Kevin Shibilski, Annmarie Blume, Nate Myszka, Vonnie Solomonson, Cathy Coffey, Marlys Matuszak, Bob Jauch, Amy Sue Vruwink, Matthew Rudig, Jolene Plautz, and for so many years the irrepressible and effervescent Win Spencer have given me the best team of public servants the Seventh District has ever known.

In Washington Carly Burns, Norma Monahan, Ruth Barnes, and Kathy O'Hara, and in Wisconsin Nelda Madison and Rene Daniels, have served me with incredible loyalty and dedication as all-purpose alter egos, personal secretaries, office managers, gatekeepers, and mother confessors. They have seen me at my very worst moments and have stuck with me. Most especially, Carly has been there for me at any hour, for any problem. I hope that she and the others can know the depth of my appreciation and gratitude.

With the exception of Scott Lilly, I have in recent years leaned on Christina Hamilton for her advice and judgment more heavily than on anyone else. As my chief of staff, she has been steadfast in her dedication to keep me focused on what is most important.

Likewise, Lyle Stitt, Al Katz, Joe Crapa, Elliot Fiedler, and Will Stone have given me thoughtful guidance for thirty-six years.

No one has worked harder, given more speeches in my stead to visiting groups from home, or kept me pointed right on a broader range of complicated issues than Paul Carver. And no one has given more dutiful service in my legislative shop than Will Painter. Working with them along the way have been Jason Barnett, Tim Barnicle, Kori Bernards, Carol Cockrill, Jennifer Collins, John Deeken, Sue Economou, Jennifer Eloranta, Anne Georges, Dennis Glavin, Michelle Guanari, Kris Hurley, Elizabeth Kohl, Bea Larson, Molly Lepeska, Geralyn Lobel, Sara Mailander, Kathy Martin, Andy Meisner, Michelle Montgomery, Tim Morrissey, Betsy Nelson, Neal Neuberger, Sue Pascal, Amy Pennington, Rick and Diane Pollack, Tom Powell-Bullock, Judy Robinson, La Donna Seely, Rachel Spector, Elizabeth Spears, Floyd and Dena Stoner, Gerry Sturges, Andy Tantillo, Peggy Taylor, and Melissa Vetterkind.

No Appropriations Subcommittee chairman ever had a more able or dedicated staff than I did when Mike Marek, Terry Peel, Bill Schuersch, and Mark Murray, assisted by Jim Cheek, Carol Lancaster, Genta Hawkins, and Al Romberg (the last four all superb career State Department foreign service officers) and many others, guided my work as Foreign Operations Appropriations chairman for ten years.

For the last fourteen years Mike Stephens, Mark Mioduski, Cheryl Smith, and David Reich worked incredibly hard to help me deal with the issues about which I cared the most: education, health, and the rights of workers on the Labor, Health, Education, and Social Services Subcommittee. Before that, Henry Neil, Nick Cavaracchi, Fred Pfluger, and Bob Knisley taught me the ropes in my early years on the subcommittee.

Today in my personal office I am also ably served by Ellis Brachman, Jon Wheeler, David Frey, Connolly Keigher, Andrew Tyler, Brendan Rose, and Katherine Sydor. They are representative of the many talented people who have served with distinction during my career.

On the Appropriations Committee I have also received such dedicated help from Bob Bonner, Jade Brennan, Kirstin Brost, Michelle Burkett, Melody Clark, Dixon Butler, Greg Dahlberg, John Daniel, Del Davis, Sally Chadbourne, Nisha Desai, Sandy Farrow, Chris Fitzgerald, Martha Foley, Tom Forhan, Alex Gillen, Rebecca Greenberg, Kate Hallahan, Heidi Hanneman, Dave Helfert, Beth Houser, Di Kane, Dave Kilian, Nancy Madden, Mike Malone, Dave Morrison, Carol Murphy, Donna Needham, Dale Oak,

Linda Pagelsen, Beverly Pheto, David Pomerantz, Lee Price, Michael Pruden, Sue Quantius, Jaclyn Sobocienski, Pat Schleuter, David Sirota, Mandy Swann, Lesley Turner, and Heather Wilson.

Dick Conlon served me with uncommonly shrewd and skilled dedication in the two years I served as chairman of the Democratic Study Group (DSG) and in all the years he served the House.

Steve Quick, Don Terry, Bill Buechner, Jamie Galbraith, Kent Hughes, Richard Kaufman, Colleen Healy, Mike Musto, Glen Rosselli, Rick McGahey, and many others were invaluable in my work on the Joint Economic Committee (JEC).

Joe Cooper, Al Katz, Tom O'Donnell, Carolyn Cheney, Don Terry, and many others helped to fashion the reform recommendations and the code of ethics changes made by the Commission on Administrative Review.

Above all others, Scott Lilly has helped me to do a far better job than I would otherwise have done to meet my responsibilities, first in my personal office then at the JEC, then as the keeper of the flame at DSG after Dick Conlon's death, and finally as my Appropriation's staff director. He has broadened my understanding and elevated my standards, and in the process made me a far more effective advocate than I ever expected to be when I walked into the halls of Congress as a rookie.

And when Scott left I could not have done better than I did when I selected Rob Nabors to succeed him. I am proud, and I know Rob is, that he is, to my knowledge, the first African American to serve as the Democratic chief of staff for an exclusive committee in the House of Representatives; but that is not why he got the job. He was simply the best person, and he demonstrates that on a daily basis.

On the political side of my life, I have been blessed to have the help of Fritz Albert, Louis Hanson and Martin Hanson, Jerry and Nelda Madison, Marlys Matuszak, Jack Spencer, John Slaby, Joe Wilson, Tom King, Geoff Garin, Frank Greer, Kim Haddow, Jim Lauer, Mike Fraioli, Mickey Hart, and my wife, Joan, who has a wonderfully textured understanding of politics and people. All of these people and more have made me much better than I otherwise would have been. I thank them all for their help, their friendship, their acceptance of my failings, and my sometimes excessive passion. I have been truly blessed by their abilities, their judgment, their loyalty, their friendship and love.

As I acknowledge their help and support, I would like to also acknowledge one fact about this manuscript. In writing this book I have also used quotations to describe conversations and events. Those quotes are produced from notes, newspaper accounts, or memory. They may not always be the exact words uttered at the time, but they represent the best approximation that it is possible to produce.

I also want to acknowledge and thank my good friend Dr. James Lorence for his help and assistance in editing this manuscript.

RAISING HELL
for JUSTICE

Prologue

During April and May, the usual trickle of constituents coming to Washington, D.C., to lobby turns into a torrent. Most do not come on their own. They come as part of an effort of one organized group after another to bend Congress's collective ear. They want different things, but with few exceptions they have two things in common. First, what they want (tax cuts or spending programs) will cost money. Second, almost all want their causes to be put at the front of the line.

A long time ago I learned one thing about most people from home who walk into my office . . . and about those people who don't. Most who don't are those with the biggest problems, like the woman I met in Rhinelander who, because she was on Medicaid, could not find a single dentist to remove the braces from her son's teeth; she finally gave up and held her son down while her husband removed the braces with a pair of pliers. People like her cannot afford to come to Washington to plead their case. They struggle in the shadows of their neighborhoods, trying to hang on, trying to get through the day, happy if they don't find themselves farther behind at day's end than they were at the beginning.

Some who do make it to Lake Wobegon on the Potomac have problems just as big. So many have stories that go right to the heart—teenagers who are afraid of dying fighting catastrophic diseases, workers afraid of being cheated out of their pensions, parents worried about losing their health insurance and their kid's chance of getting a decent education if they lose their jobs. Most are reasonable people. They make their case, they try to learn, they are examples of representative democracy at work. But it seems that at least once a day someone walks in who is so self-centered, so selfish, so hell-bent on being in the first car on the gravy train, so blind to the problems of others, that it

makes you want to scream. That's why, when groups come into my office
to ask me for something, before we begin to talk, I have them read—out
loud—two signs that are hanging on my office wall. The first reads, "If what
you want costs money, are you willing to go home and tell your friends that
we need to cut back on the size of the president's tax cuts so there is room
for it in the budget?" The second asks, "Is there anything you want me to
do for somebody else that is more important than whatever it is you want
me to do for you?"

I ask those questions because I hope they will make at least one person a
day think about the broader obligations of citizenship. While what democracy can do for each of us as individuals is important, what it can do for all of
us as a nation is fundamental. The right question for citizens of a democracy
to ask is not Ronald Reagan's question of 1980, "Are you better off than you
were four years ago?" The better question is this: "Is the country better off
than it was yesterday and will it be better off tomorrow than it is today?" In
the Judeo-Christian tradition that lies at the core of American democracy and
Western civilization, we are called on to think about the legitimate needs of
others at least as often as we think about our own.

But there is a second reason I ask those questions and that is to remind
myself why I got into politics and public service in the first place. I believe
passionately in the idea of public service as a calling, just as strong as the calling to be a priest, minister, or rabbi.

I am a politician and proud of it. A comment to me by my wonderful Irish
friend, John Hume, illustrates why. John is from the city of Derry in Northern Ireland. He received the Nobel Peace Prize several years ago for his lifelong leadership of the peace movement in Northern Ireland. In the 1960s,
to protest the oppression of the Protestant government in Northern Ireland
that had denied jobs to almost 70 percent of the men in that country, John
led a series of peaceful marches out of Derry's Catholic neighborhoods. His
efforts were met by brutal force from the British-backed Protestant Unionist
forces. He was arrested numerous times, beaten bloody twice. During one
brutal assault by government forces, John lay down in front of a tank. His
wife, Pat, was watching from a few feet away and thought he was a dead man.
The tank stopped; the brutality did not.

But the violence directed against him did not just come from the Protestant side; it came from the Catholic side, too—from the Irish Republican
Army, who wanted John eliminated because he denounced their violent, mur-
derous tactics and insisted that only peaceful action would bring the moral
force to bear that would, in the end, produce the needed change. They tried

to assassinate him numerous times. They firebombed his house twice—once with his family in it.

Several years ago John was driving the countryside and came to a stop sign. He looked in the rearview mirror and saw a car about to smash into him at breakneck speed. He told me later that the first thought that flashed into his mind was, "The fuckers got me at last." They didn't. The cars exploded, but miraculously John stepped from the wreckage with no apparent injury. A week later he collapsed from post-traumatic stress reaction and almost died. When I asked him in a pub one evening, "John, how do you stand the physical stress?" He answered, "What do you mean, I'm fifty-two and nothing works anymore."

Visiting me in my office several years ago, he began to comment on the state of American politics. "David," he said, "I'm astounded to see the viciousness of the rhetoric against government and politics in America. Don't your countrymen understand that, no matter what the problem, politics is the democratic substitute for violence? Don't they understand what a priceless luxury democratic politics is in this world? If they don't, all they have to do is to look at what has happened to my country." I remember that statement every day of my life.

I have been interested in politics ever since the seventh grade, but I never really thought that I would have a chance to live a life of public service. In college I thought that I would probably wind up teaching Russian government in a small college somewhere. But life takes funny bounces, and I have been given opportunities I never dreamed possible. This is my story about how it happened, how I came to be who I am and believe what I believe, some of the things I have seen and learned, some of the battles I have fought along the way, and some of the unfinished challenges.

PART I

FOUNDATION YEARS

CHAPTER I

ᐁ

Roots

My father was the only person in America to move to Oklahoma during the Great Depression to get a job. That's why I was born in Okmulgee, Oklahoma, on October 3, 1938. But my family's roots have been in the Wisconsin River Valley for more than a century. My father, Orville John Obey, was born on November 2, 1915, to a French-Irish railroad worker, John, and a Scotch-English mother, Perle (Kimball). John Obey's father had emigrated from Ireland to Canada, from there to Tripoli, Wisconsin, and then to Tomahawk, Wisconsin. As a young man in search of opportunity, John moved to eastern Marathon County.

Perle Kimball's family brought her to Wild Rose, Wisconsin, from the White Mountains of New England. She was a tall, imposing, strong woman, and she needed to be. By the time my dad was five and his younger brother David was four, she was a single mother. John had pulled up stakes and left her high and dry to support two rambunctious boys on her own. He moved to Chicago after a divorce and later remarried.

My grandmother supported her two boys by working at the Pied Piper shoe factory on Wausau's west side—now long gone as are so many other companies of that era. After her divorce, she began to date Chuck Kuchera, a broad-shouldered Bohemian farmer turned auto mechanic and auto parts salesman. When she and Chuck began to talk marriage she became so fearful about how his family would feel about his marrying an older woman—she was five years older—that she decided to lie about her age. But her conscience fought her every step of the way, and in the end, she finally shaved only one year off her real age. We never knew about it until she finally admitted, on her seventy-fifth birthday, that she was actually seventy-six.

Chuck had been a hell-raiser as a young man. He raced cars, became a
fine "one-armed auto mechanic," as he described himself, and put in more
than twenty-five years as an auto parts salesman for Northern Auto Supply.
He loved fishing, hunting, and Mercury automobiles. An avid angler, he
always cast with his left hand because his right hand had been blown away in
a hunting accident when he was seventeen. Chuck had the strongest arms of
any man I ever knew. He would do carpentry work as well as any two-handed
man, holding nails in his left hand and pounding them in by holding the
hammer inside the folded elbow of his stubbed right arm. He loved to drive
faster than the law allowed and enjoyed the frequent rebukes his driving
would tease out of Grandma Perle. He and my grandmother provided a real
anchor for me in my childhood.

My dad went to Grant School on Wausau's northeast side but dropped
out of high school and drifted into the CCC camps set up to provide public
works jobs for young men in the Depression era. He always felt he became a
man in those camps. After that experience, persuaded by a favorite teacher, he
went back to high school and graduated two years later.

My mother was born Mary Jane Chellis on January 21, 1915, and her story
is more complicated. She grew up on a dairy farm southwest of Wausau in
the town of Rib Mountain on Highway N. Her father, Walt Chellis, was a
handsome raw-boned man of French ancestry known for both his gentle-
ness and his integrity. He served in town government and worked his farm
until his back gave out. When he was nearly fifty-five, he moved to South
Third Avenue on Wausau's southwest side and spent the rest of his work years
breathing sawdust at Curtis and Yale lumber factory. It's gone now, too. Walt
was married to Lydia Stork, a hard driving, forceful, talkative, take-charge
woman of German stock.

My mother grew up a happy girl. A hard worker, she learned to drive a
tractor when she was nine. When she was about twenty, her world turned
upside down when her favorite "uncle," Guy Chellis (Walt's brother), was
killed when his car crashed into an unlighted box car in a moving train. It
was then that she learned that her favorite "uncle" was really her father, the
"parents" she had grown up with were really her aunt and uncle; the "sisters"
she had grown up with, Ruth and Ellen, were really her cousins; the "cousins"
she thought she knew, Ruth, Mae, and Annette, were actually her sisters; and
that her real mother, Guy's wife, Minna (Andreis), had died bringing her into
this world. Guy, distraught at his wife's death, had feared he could not raise
an infant when he was on the road so much as an insurance salesman; he
asked Walt if he and Lyd would take care of Mary Jane. They said they would,

provided they could raise her as their own. Guy consented, and Mary Jane's life was changed forever.

There is no doubt in my mind that from the day she discovered her real identity, my mother never really felt that she could be sure about anything in her life. I have always believed that experience so shattered her that she was plagued by doubts about whether she really was loved by—or belonged with—anyone. Her convoluted family history meant that my Grandpa Walt may not have technically been my grandfather, but to me he was Grandpa. And Grandma Lyd was a human dynamo. Years later, when I ran my first race for the legislature, she phoned every friend she had in Wausau and asked them to vote for me—and she had a lot of friends.

Mary Jane met my dad through Cliff Schuette, who married Walt and Lydia's youngest daughter Ellen. The week my parents married, my dad learned that he was losing his job because the creamery he worked for was closing. At the wedding, my mother's uncle, P. J. Ney, who managed a J. C. Penney store in Okmulgee, Oklahoma, said to him, "Orv, if you need a job, I've got an opening in the shoe department. If you want it, it's yours." My dad took it in a flash, and that's why I was born in Oklahoma. I remember only two things about Oklahoma—eating dried apricots on the back porch and dropping my dad's harmonica off the porch into the bushes. He didn't find it till spring.

My folks were able to work their way back to Wisconsin because the Penney Company allowed its employees first crack at any job that opened up around the country. My dad used that transfer system to move back to Wisconsin—first to Marshfield, a town forty-five miles southwest of Wausau, and then back to Wausau. I was baptized at St. John's Catholic Church in Marshfield. The church still stands across the street from a lovely tree-lined neighborhood square.

And I remember only two things about life in Marshfield. We lived in an apartment above Normington's Laundry on Central Avenue—the building is gone now. I used to press my nose to a window to watch parades pass by on the street below, and I remember a tiny tabletop Christmas tree in front of the window, decorated with plain red balls and blue lights.

When my folks moved back to Wausau, they rented the first of many houses we would live in—on the west side of town on South Sixth Avenue, just three blocks from Grandma and Chuck Kuchera. Within a few months my dad went to work for the 3M Company in the color quartz lab making roofing granules used by the military in World War II for camouflage. He stayed with them for almost fifteen years. My sister Kathleen was born after we moved back to Wausau, my brother Dean followed in 1943, and Diane arrived after the war in 1949.

My dad was never drafted because his job in the lab at 3M—making sure those camouflage roofing granules were baked in kilns at just the right temperature for just the right length of time to create perfect color matches—was considered essential to the war effort. He wanted to earn more than he could make at 3M, so he began buying and remodeling houses while we lived in them, selling them, and then doing it all over again with another house.

The first house I really remember was across the street from the power plant on Harrison Boulevard (now First Avenue) that runs along the west side of the Wisconsin River, which divides Wausau. I have a vivid memory of peeking out the window from our darkened house during the World War II evening blackouts. Seeing the silhouette of the power plant and the power lines, I often wondered if the Germans would come that night to capture the plant. In the middle of the war we moved from Harrison Boulevard to Emerson Street on the southeast end of town.

The first thing I can recall about politics was FDR's death. Almost all the news on the radio during the war was war news. When the radio announced that Roosevelt had died, I was impressed by people in the neighborhood crying openly. I remember being surprised at my mother's reaction. I knew my dad admired him and that my mother thought that he had too much power, but when he died, she cried. I would often sit at my grandfather Kuchera's house and listen to Jack Sloan, his best friend, constantly berate Roosevelt. Jack started out in life poor, but he worked hard and wound up being quite well off. My grandfather used to say that Jack was for Roosevelt until he made so much money he could afford to think like a Republican.

The day the war ended, my mother came running out of the house saying, "My God, the war is over." Everybody poured into the streets and began pounding on kettles or anything else that made noise. One of my next door neighbor friends was Jimmy Ryan. Jimmy and I grabbed a galvanized washtub and began to beat the bottom out of the thing as we marched down Emerson Street and around the neighborhood. By the time we were finished, we had left a trail of galvanized specks all around the neighborhood. Jimmy and I didn't know quite what it all meant, but we understood that it was good to have the war over. I knew that it meant that my uncle, who was in the navy, would be coming home. That evening I asked my mother, "Does that mean there won't be any more news programs?" "No," she said, "but it will mean a lot of changes."

The end of the war meant many things to my family, including the end of the wartime ration coupons and tokens. I had an old scooter with balloon tires that I had bought for a quarter from a neighborhood kid. The first day I had it the tire went flat. You couldn't get any new tires in those days because rubber was needed for the war effort, so I was stuck with a dead scooter. Imagine my delight when my dad told me that the end of the war meant the end of rationing—and with that the possibility of getting a new tire.

We did not have a car during the war, but shortly after it was over, when I returned from school one afternoon, my mother smiled and told me to go two doors down to a neighbor's garage. "Your dad has something to show you." I ran down the street and found my dad working on an old 1937 Chevy. He, the neighbor, and Grandpa Kuchera repaired it, sandblasted it, and repainted it a dark bronze. That car lasted until my dad bought a 1947 torpedo-backed Oldsmobile in 1952.

I began my schooling in the first grade at St. James Catholic School. On the first day my mother took me to the first-grade room. Terribly shy, I headed right for the back seat in the middle row and tried not to attract any attention. A plump nun bounced into the room with a warm smile on her face and barked an order that made my heart sink. "I want everyone in the room to change seats," she said. "Those in the front row move to the back seats; those in the back seats move to the front." She understood that the shy kids would burrow into the back row, and she wanted to shake that out of us right away. I understand it now, but it terrified me at the time. Sister Climacus was a warm, wonderfully reassuring woman who constantly injected doses of confidence into the shyest of her students. I was delighted many years later when, out of the blue, a letter arrived in my congressional office from her. Forty-five years after I had last seen her, she had retired. She sounded like the same giving person who helped me so much so long ago.

Shortly after my dad acquired the car, he went to the hospital for an emergency appendectomy, and he came home with his arms paralyzed. To this day I don't know what happened—the doctor thought it might have been caused by the anesthetic. That was back in the days before people sued for things like that. We were terrified. We thought we had no future at all. Even the simplest task was a challenge for him. Herb Franke, my dad's barber, would come over to the house and shave him. But we were lucky. Gradually he started to regain the use of his arms. While they continued to bother him for a long time, he eventually regained their full use. That experience taught me at an early age what a tenuous grip most working families have on security. My dad was just a working man. He had no fancy retirement program and no golden parachute. Only the good fortune of his recovery separated us from a life of poverty.

When dad began to feel better, we moved again. This time, he bought a tiny, two-bedroom house with an adjoining empty lot. Located southwest of town on Highway NN, the lot was at the foot of Rib Mountain, a 1,946-foot-high hill that until the late fifties was thought to be the highest point in Wisconsin. The house was three doors from a tiny, one-room country school, but I continued to attend St. James.

I started the third grade at St. James, but an incident with my teacher unexpectedly landed me in that country school. During the first week of classes, Sister Norma sent me home with a note to my parents telling them that I could not come to school in jeans. My dad exploded. We were always close to the edge financially, always under money pressure. The only trousers I owned were jeans. "To hell with them," my dad said, "if your clothes aren't good enough for St. James then we're not good enough for St. James." The next day my mother enrolled me in the one-room school down the road. I was upset; because I was still very shy, it was hard to make new friends and I wanted to be back with my old ones.

About a week later Sister Norma called. She wanted to know where I was. "You seem to be more interested in what he wears than in what he learns," my dad said. "You must understand, it's against our policy to allow any child to wear jeans. Their brass fittings scratch the seats," she replied. "Well, you have to understand that that's all he will wear because it's all he has," my dad told her. The next day someone from St. James called and told my mother that we could forget about the problem and I could wear anything I had. I was embarrassed by it all. I didn't want anybody thinking we were poor, and I was afraid that if I went back that everybody would know about it, but I did return and was glad that I did.

My favorite teacher in grade school was Sister Margaret, who taught a combined class of fourth and fifth graders. She was a warm, cheerful, and intelligent woman who conveyed to every student that each of us mattered and that we could do anything we put our minds to. Many years later I encountered her again. During the 2002 campaign, I stopped at a truck stop in Edgar to grab a sandwich. As I walked over to a booth, a white-haired woman stood up and said, "Oh my goodness, you're Dave Obey." It was Sister Margaret, whom I hadn't seen since the fifth grade. She told me she had just retired as a school principal in LaCrosse. We talked for quite a while, and she was just as warm and wise as I had remembered her.

My first school conversations about politics occurred during my late grade school years. During the 1948 presidential election my mother was all for Dewey, and my dad was neutral. I remember the discussion we had in class the day after the election. Everybody had thought that Dewey was going to win, and because I was influenced by my mother's opinions I had a vague feeling of disappointment. But I kept thinking, "Gee, just think how good Truman must feel when everybody says you are a loser and then, whammo, you knock it to them."

Meanwhile, my dad continued his perpetual house-building plans. He was planning to build and then sell a new home on the vacant lot next to our house. He got the basement dug but ran into money troubles. He finally decided to finish it, cover it with roofing tar paper, sell the house we lived in, and move into the basement. I hated it; it was depressing, and it felt like we were living like moles and going backwards in life.

Two years later we moved again. A friend of Lyd and Walt Chellis, Ed Henschel, agreed to lend my dad the money to buy a small house on Highway 29 in the town of Stettin, west of town. To this day when I think of home during my childhood, that's the house I think of. I lived the most unhappy part of my childhood there, but we were there longer than any other place, almost four years, and we weren't living like moles anymore.

TROUBLED YEARS

Until the seventh grade, I had always been a good student, but starting in the sixth grade, things began to fall apart. During seventh grade I was skipping school two days a week, and I hated everybody and everything. My parents were under terrific money pressures again, and their marriage was falling apart. When we first moved to Highway 29, we had a lot of work to do. About seventy-five feet from the house there was an old chicken coop and a rundown attached garage. My dad remodeled the chicken coop, turning it into a tiny but cute one-bedroom house that he rented to a young couple. I was truly amazed that my father could see such possibilities in a dilapidated chicken coop, but he could always look at a house and see in his mind's eye how it could be remodeled.

This was also about the time I learned to play the harmonica. In those days, Larry Adler and the Harmonicats were well known around the country. My dad loved their music and played the 64 Chromatic beautifully. He and two friends, Fritz Kroeplin and Artie Feck, used to play together. Buck Leverton, who was a radio celebrity and later a television celebrity doing a local farm show, would appear as an emcee at local talent contests around the Wisconsin River Valley. My dad and Fritz appeared in those contests in Antigo, Wausau, and Marshfield. They even made a 45 rpm single-play record, which they were able to place on a number of jukeboxes around town. I used to sit in the kitchen watching them play together. When I was about ten, my dad taught me to play "Silent Night" on the harmonica as a Christmas present for my mother.

The Dalsky family had a farm across the road. They had a flock of kids, and one of them, Anthony, was about my age. He and I would often walk the cows out to pasture in the morning and bring them back in the evening. I liked to play softball, but it was hard to find anybody to play ball with until the Dalsky kids finished their chores, so many a day I helped to pick beans, plant potatoes, or do other chores so that Anthony and I could toss a ball around later. We had no diamond to play on like the city kids, but there was a hayfield behind our house, where Anthony and I used our family hand-push lawnmowers to cut the hay down for the infield and mow the left and right field foul lines. We planted old, worn kiln brick from 3M for home plate and the three bases. Summers were great, but I began to hate the rest of the year.

I especially hated the fact that my mother and dad were not getting along. My dad was having trouble making the mortgage payments, and Ed Henchel, who held the mortgage, was getting nervous. One Saturday when Ed, Walt, and Lyd came over to our house, Ed was talking foreclosure. I was shocked to think that we might lose our house. The kitchen table conversation between my dad and Ed was getting more and more tense when my sister Kathy broke the tension. She had been sitting on the porch when she noticed that our male dog was doing to our female dog what male dogs do to female dogs. She didn't understand and came running into the kitchen screaming, "Quick, quick somebody do something; the dogs are stuck together." It took a few seconds for everyone to realize what Kathy was referring to. Ed let out a roaring laugh, and after that the conversation seemed to take a turn for the better.

Seventh grade was the beginning of the two worst years in my life. I hated what was happening to our family; I hated my life; I hated school. My mother would push me on the school bus in the morning. At least twice a week, as soon as I got off the bus at school I would turn around, walk the three miles back home, find my dog, and hide out in a little shack I had built in the neighboring woods. In spring and fall there was a little creek that ran right by it. I played a lot of harmonica there and read a lot of books.

During those years I formed some strong opinions about President Truman and Douglas MacArthur. During the early stages of the Korean War when our troops were being pushed down the Korean peninsula by the invading North

Koreans, our hometown newspaper, the *Record Herald,* would print daily maps showing where the combat line was that day. I remember watching it recede farther and farther down the peninsula until, in the end, we held just a small rectangular area in the southeast corner of Korea around Pusan. Then MacArthur engineered an audacious amphibious landing far to the north behind enemy lines at Inchon. Suddenly, that shrinking black line outlining what territory we controlled moved all the way back up north to the 38th parallel and beyond. MacArthur was mopping up those "damn commies" and everyone felt good. Then the Chinese poured across the Yalu River, and within weeks that combat line on the newspaper map was right back at the line that had divided North and South Korea before the war. I remember thinking, "My God, what has all of this been worth? Why didn't we listen to MacArthur and use the Chinese on Formosa to attack Mainland China." Then Truman fired MacArthur. I was so upset at Truman that I fired off a letter of protest to him. I didn't have any stamps so I took three pennies and attached them to the envelope with a piece of scotch tape, stuck it in the mailbox, and waited for an answer from the White House. I never got one. Years later I learned that my mother had gone out to the mailbox and had taken the letter out because she didn't want me to get into trouble.

Not long thereafter, my seventh grade teacher, Sister Tecla, did something that was to change my life. On one of the few days that I attended school, she announced that we were going to have a debate. The debate was going to be on Joe McCarthy, the junior senator from Wisconsin who was just beginning to make a name for himself by denouncing "commies" in the State Department. Sister Tecla gave us some reading material on the subject and assigned me to defend him. I took the reading material home, and I remember thinking, "Gee, this is really interesting." I remember nothing about the debate, but as a result I started to read everything I could get my hands on about politics. It was one of the few things in life that I really found interesting enough to take my mind off troubles at home.

Sister Tecla seemed to be a very unhappy woman. She would often say things that were hurtful to other kids in the class. We had a very nice guy in the class who was not very verbal. Often, when she got angry at someone in the class, she would say, "Good grief, you're dumber than Tom." Imagine how that must have made him feel, and it didn't make the rest of us feel very good either. She was frustrated with me because of my school skipping, and I'm sure I frustrated her because she couldn't get through to me.

One spring day when she asked me a question in class, I honestly did not hear what she asked. When I asked her to repeat the question, she exploded.

She walked back to my seat and said, "I'm sick of your inattention, stand up." When I stood up, she hauled off and backhanded me across the face. Her ring split my lip. I was shocked and angry. Instinctively, I swung back and nailed her right on the jaw. I was as surprised as she was because I was the runt of the class, and she was bigger than I was. She marched me to the office of the principal, Sister Rose Francis. To make a long story short, I was "conditioned" to the eighth grade. The condition was that I go to another school. This was bad news for me because I had felt at home at St. James up until the seventh grade. Many years later, after I was elected to Congress, I received a warm note from Sister Tecla, who had left teaching and had become involved in antipoverty work. I was glad that she appeared to be happy in what she was doing. Four years ago I received a letter from a member of her family telling me that she had been killed in a hit-and-run accident in California.

After my parting of the ways with St. James, I moved to the public junior high school, where I was almost expelled again because my attendance was even worse. I disliked all of my classes, except for the civics class taught by Lowden Schlaegel. Much as I liked the class, I still hated school and kept skipping.

Finally Russell Slade, the junior high principal, called my folks to inform them that he was going to expel me, and if my parents wanted to challenge it, they could come to a conference in his office the next day. My dad was working, but my mother went. I found out afterwards that Schlaegel had interceded with Slade one last time. Slade then came to me and to my parents and said that he would allow me to remain in school the rest of the year, but I had to get all of my grades out of the failing category or they would make me repeat every subject. I finished the year, got my grades up just enough to avoid disaster, and never saw Schlaegel again. I do not know what happened to him, but he left town that summer. Without his concern and attention, I would have remained a total loser. He was the person who began to pull me out of the emotional dumps—an example of how one dedicated teacher can make all the difference in someone else's life.

High School Turnaround

In the ninth grade, things finally turned around for me. I wound up getting nothing but As and Bs, except for gym. That was also the year when I really started to get deeply involved in politics, and I think that made all the difference. On weekends I took my sister's wagon, filled it with literature, and hand-delivered it to fully one-third of the ten thousand households in Wausau. I eagerly put posters for Eisenhower, Joe McCarthy, and congressional candidate Mel Laird in our window during the general election.

About a year after that election, I first laid eyes on Joe McCarthy. One of my mother's friends, Barb Lemke, was the wife of a local Republican, Chuck Lemke, who was corporate treasurer for WSAU, Wausau's first TV station. The Lemkes knew of my interest in politics and enthusiasm for Joe McCarthy, so they asked if I would like to come with them to a Republican dinner at the Elks Club to hear McCarthy speak. I jumped at the chance.

I will never forget that evening. After the dinner, the lights were dimmed and the spotlight was turned on the head table. The room was filled with swirling cigarette and cigar smoke. When McCarthy was introduced, I remember thinking, "My God, his five-o'clock shadow is so black." He looked more like Humphrey Bogart on a bad night than a United States senator. In his speech he ridiculed an inventory of Democratic and State Department officials, like Dean Acheson and Owen Lattimore. He gave nicknames to most of them and then laughed in a strange, chilling, panting way that resembled a hyena. I came away impressed by his powerful personality, yet disquieted by the pleasure he took in savaging individual reputations, including Eisenhower's.

My interest in politics continued to grow as my family situation became more chaotic. We moved four more times between ninth grade and the time that I graduated from high school. My mother and dad finally split after one trial separation, and I immersed myself even more in everything that I could find at school in order to avoid going home at night. Fortunately, I had some teachers I really liked. One was Joan Bartz, my homeroom teacher, who often took the time to talk to me when I was trying to find any excuse to avoid going home. Another was Cliff Westlund, an English teacher, who was probably the closest friend I had on the high school faculty until Art Henderson came along in my junior year. Westlund was a Republican, but it was clear that he thought McCarthy was a bad actor and he made his feelings quite clear outside of the classroom.

I remember watching the Army–McCarthy hearings in snatches, always rooting for McCarthy. I was sure he would vindicate himself, but he never did. He just kept looking meaner and meaner. I recall the debates about executive privilege. One day I would be on McCarthy's side, and the next day I would have doubts. Then came the infamous day that McCarthy engaged in a vicious personal attack on a young legal assistant to Joseph Welch, who had been retained as the legal counsel for the secretary of the army, Bob Stephens. I watched while Welch finally said to McCarthy, "Sir, at long last have you no sense of decency?" And I thought, "My God, that's it, he doesn't." At that moment I knew I just couldn't support him anymore.

About that time I attended a county Young Republican's meeting. The guest speaker for the evening was Mary Connor, wife of Gordon Connor, who owned Connor Lumber and Land, and, as I later learned, an aunt of Mel Laird, our new congressman. In her speech she attacked unions and rejected the very idea that government should be involved in mitigating any economic problems faced by working people. She gave what I later came to understand was the standard Ayn Rand–argument about morality being best served when people pursued their own self interests, even if it meant crushing individuals. I walked out of that meeting thinking to myself that if that was what the local Republican Party believed, there was no room in it for a working-class kid like me.

By this time, I was a junior in high school and had encountered the greatest teacher I ever had, Arthur Henderson. On the first day of class, I walked into room 152 and saw this man with an incredibly pale complexion. He had a massive head, square jaw, twinkling eyes, hair that was gray on the side and sandy red on the top. The very first day he gave us a quiz. During the quiz a fire truck went by, and Henderson walked over to the window, put his hands behind his back, leaned forward from the waist, looked out the window again, and said, "Well, the wife must be cooking dinner again." It was my first exposure to his Scandinavian sense of dry humor.

He encouraged debate on every subject in his class, and when you took a position he would not argue with you. He would simply agree with you and then extend your position logically until you said, "Good grief, I really don't believe that." He tried to make us see what we really believed and constantly challenged us by giving us books that contradicted our points of view, no matter which side of the question we took. And he was tough!

I remember his asking us to do a paper on how Harding, Coolidge, or Hoover felt on several subjects—capitalism, organized labor, government involvement in the economy, and government regulation of business. I thought he said Harding, Coolidge, *and* Hoover, so I went to the Wausau Public Library and dug into reference books. When the day came to turn in the paper, I had a twenty-one-page report. I looked around the class and saw that everybody else had six, seven, or eight pages. At that point I realized that Henderson had asked us to research *one* of the three presidents, not all of them. "Well," I thought, "at least he will give me an A for extending myself." But when I got the report back, he had given me an A-minus because I hadn't followed directions.

I learned a lot about that man, and what I learned taught me a lot about politics in my hometown. I discovered that several years earlier several Republican members of the school board had tried to have him fired for being a "Bolshevik." What that really meant is that Henderson had the temerity to teach that the United States Constitution and the platform of the United States Chamber of Commerce did not necessarily coincide. The pressure on him got so bad that his wife, who had been teaching in the Wausau system, said "Forget it," quit her job, and took one in Clintonville, some forty-five miles away. That incident, when I learned about it, taught me more about academic freedom and the value of courage than all the books in the world. It also made me realize that if you believed in those things—in those days of Joe McCarthy and in that community—you could not be a Republican. His experience taught me about the power of politics run amuck. It showed me what political frenzy could do to good people, and I have never forgotten it. To this day, whenever I am dealing with a tough issue and am tempted to take the easy road, I imagine Art Henderson looking over my shoulder—and then I usually know what I should do.

During my high school years, I earned money on the side working with my father in his new part-time job. My dad had taken a short trade-school course offered by Armstrong Flooring Company in Lancaster, Pennsylvania, to learn how to install linoleum and carpet, and he began a floor-covering business to augment his salary at 3M. Dad and his partner, Tommy Smith, usually worked different shifts at 3M, so sometimes I would work with Tommy and sometimes with Dad. On the weekends we would all work together.

On one Friday night after the stores closed at nine o'clock, we started the job at Wrights Music Shop and worked through the night so the new floor would be ready for the opening of business the next day. I earned enough that night to buy my first three long-play albums: *Pictures at an Exhibition* by Mussorgsky, a record of Hungarian and Romanian rhapsodies by Enesco and Liszt, and Harry Belafonte's *Calypso*. Years later, I enjoyed getting Belafonte to autograph that album when he testified before my subcommittee on behalf of UNICEF.

That same year, our YMCA group put on an April Fool's Day dance. Cliff Westlund, my English teacher, was the faculty advisor for the group, which ran a series of dances at the old Y. Most kids danced the jitterbug at the time, and rock and roll was just becoming popular. I never learned to dance anything but the basic slow dances. Because I was shy, I was more comfortable running the dances than actually going through the pain of having to ask a girl to dance and being turned down.

Ralph Hintz, Bill Hanna, Jim Backus, and I used to serve as the disc jockeys at those record hops. We played music, sold the tickets, and in general ran the operation. For the April Fool's dance we needed some posters, and Cliff Westlund suggested that I ask Pat Lane, a blond pony-tailed sophomore, who was quite an artist, if she would help out. I told him I was reluctant to ask her because I really didn't know her. He said, "Why don't you ask her to the dance and then ask her to do the posters." I didn't think that was such a smooth suggestion, but it did put a bug in my ear. I introduced myself to her and asked her if she would be willing to help us out by making some posters. After she agreed, I then asked her to go to the dance and, much to my surprise, she accepted. We were steady dates for over a year until we broke up the week of graduation.

Her father was one of the most impressive people I have ever met. He worked at the paper mill in Rothschild. An accomplished artist who loved classical music, he often set his radio and reel-to-reel tape deck to record music on the "state station," as public radio was known in those days, so he could listen to it when he got home from work. Often encouraged by management to take a job in the front office, he always refused. His reasoning was clear: "I like my life now. I have time for my family, my art, and my music." And he said something that I will never forget: "You know, making a living is not the same as living. I work so that I can earn a living for my family, but there's more to life than work, and if you are not careful, your job can make you forget that." I have thought of that statement thousands of times since then. But like most people, I have not followed his advice enough.

Although the class that had the most profound impact on my life was Henderson's history class, the hours that gave me the most useful skills later in life were those I spent in George Rosenhauer's journalism class. Rosenhauer also served as the faculty advisor to the yearbook. At the end of my sophomore year I signed up to work on the staff of the *Wahiscan*—*WA* for Wausau, *HISC* for high school, and *AN* for annual. As a junior I served as the class editor, which meant that it was my responsibility to organize the section of the annual devoted to the sophomore, junior, and senior classes. In journalism class, Rosenhauer pounded into us the importance of putting into the lead paragraph of every story the five Ws and H—who, what, when, where, why, and how. The idea was to punch as much information into the first paragraph as you could, in descending order of importance so that if you have to cut the story you will always be left with the most important points. In later years when I wrote my own press releases, in the legislature and afterwards in Congress, I put that advice to use many, many times.

As a teaching exercise, the journalism class was given the responsibility of publishing the Christmas edition of the *Skyrocket,* the high school newspaper. The *Skyrocket* office was right next to the journalism classroom where the *Wahiscan* staff worked, and I was the editor of the Christmas edition. Traditionally, the *Skyrocket* carried a "Mr. and Miss Student" column, biographical sketches of a male and female student. I decided to have the Miss Student column written about Joan Lepinski, the regular editor of the newspaper who published every edition of the newspaper except the Christmas edition. She was a year ahead of me in school.

The day after my junior year ended and Joan had graduated, I needed to go over some preliminary plans for the new book and went to the *Skyrocket* office, which was used by the yearbook staff over the summer. Looking out the window, I saw Joan walking out of the building on the sidewalk directly below, and I leaned out the window and talked to her for a few minutes. I remember thinking after our conversation that she was a very nice person. I had no idea that within six years she would become my wife.

My predecessor as yearbook editor had been Gerry Beck, a person I grew to greatly admire. Toward the end of our junior year, George Rosenhauer came to me and said, "Dave, I would like you to be editor next year." I was thrilled. It was the first time I had gotten significant recognition, and I really believe it was an important turning point in my life because it was a real confidence builder.

At the end of the year, during our staff party, Gerry called me aside and said, "Dave, Rosy and I went back and forth about who should be editor and finally picked you because we thought you would be the most innovative and decisive." He then said something I have remembered all of my life, "Dave, lots of times next year you will have decisions to make and you will be criticized for them. Just remember, it's your name on the book as editor. It is you who will get the credit and the blame. So when you have to make a big decision, get as much information as you can, ask as many questions as you can think of, give the people whose advice you trust or people who have to implement your decisions a chance to have their say. But when you have to decide, decide. Do what you think is right, even if everybody disagrees, because it's your responsibility. And remember, sometimes there is no right decision. Sometimes the important thing to remember is to simply decide and then move on." I have received a lot of advice through the years, but none has served me better than those words Gerry Beck said to me before we had even entered adulthood.

Everyone in high school used to call me "Senator." Anyone looking at my yearbook and reading the messages from my friends will notice that everybody began their notes to me by saying "Hi, Senator." I remember the story about me in the "Mr. Student" column in my senior year. I always used to say "Blast it!" when something angered me. The column began: "The year is 1970 and the place is the Capitol in Washington, D.C. A voice can be heard in loud forceful tones in the Senate chamber saying, 'Blast it!'—This is the voice of the youngest senator in the Senate, Dave Obey." The article was off by one year, and it had placed me on the other side of the Capitol building, but in 1969 I did become the youngest member of the U.S. House of Representatives. Not a bad bit of predictive reporting, a lot more prescient than many of the predictions of today's political pundits. That column was amazingly prophetic, but at the time I had a long way to travel before making reality out of that high school fantasy.

∾

Money was getting tighter and tighter, which was nothing new for us. We would be okay at the beginning of the month, but by the last week we were short. Almost every month we would take something we owned to Izzy Etskin. Izzy owned a combination secondhand store and pawn shop, and we were able to get a few dollars to help us through the end of the month. My mother was truly one example of the working poor, somebody who had a job but couldn't make enough money to keep afloat. It was a terrible feeling, and I will never forget it until the day I die.

My most painful recollection of those years came from an act of kindness by my mother's friends, the Lemkes. The week before Christmas in 1955, Barbie Lemke knew that my mother was having an especially tough time financially. My folks had finally split and my dad was late with his support check; we had some unexpected bills and the cupboard was bare. Barbie found out and went with her husband, Chuck, and bought a hundred dollars worth of groceries. I was in the upstairs bedroom doing some ironing (ironing the kid's clothes was one of the chores my mother had assigned to me). I was good at it, and to this day I enjoy watching an old movie on TV while I'm ironing my shirts. I find it relaxing, and I kid my wife that I'm better at it and faster at it than she is. She agrees. That evening, when I heard the Lemkes come in the front door, I went to the top of the stairs and saw them carrying in bag after bag of groceries. My mother was so grateful she started crying. I was grateful, too, but my feelings of gratitude were overpowered by an acute sense of embarrassment and shame.

I remember my face burning with embarrassment at being forced to accept someone else's charity. As I stood in the upstairs hall watching it all, my mother turned and said, "Dave, come down and thank the Lemkes. Look what they've done." I just couldn't do it. I was so mortified by our need for charity that I walked into the bedroom and closed the door. My mother sent my sister Kathleen up to get me, but I just couldn't come down. I hated that moment. It seemed that we would always be living on the edge, never being able to get both feet on solid ground. I knew my mother was bright and caring. I knew she worked hard. I knew my dad worked like a dog, and I couldn't understand how people could try that hard and still be so screwed up that we were still living on the edge. I felt that there ought to be some place that my mother could go to get some help, some advice, or some training for a decent job that paid enough to keep her from relying on groceries from friends. The little money that I made working with my dad hardly made a dent in our needs.

Today, I still feel that frustration and anger when I run into people who are in that same circumstance and especially when I see homeless people. And part of me just gets a little bit scared thinking of how little it takes—bad luck, sickness—to be pushed back to that awful edge. And I cannot help but feel that, in terms of helping families meet their needs, this country has in many ways gone backwards since those days. I know that there are people on welfare today who take advantage of the system, but I also know from personal experience that there are many poor and near-poor people who hate it, who desperately want help and will work to earn that help if somebody would just help to show them how.

As I neared graduation, my mother began to think that the way out of our financial hole would be to pull up stakes and move. She decided to transfer to her employer's headquarters in Minneapolis in July. She told me that I could go to school at the University of Minnesota, but I knew I could not afford that. I had decided on my own that I would stay in Wausau, find a room of my own, work with my dad and try to earn enough to start college the second semester at the two-year University of Wisconsin branch campus in town. After his divorce my dad had moved in with Gram and Chuck Kuchera. When my dad found out about my mother's plans, he insisted I move in with him and start college in September. My mother, brother, and both sisters moved to Minneapolis in July, and I did finally move in with my dad and grandparents, feeling guilty all the way.

In one way I was relieved because, since my dad had left, I had really been the disciplinarian in the family. My mother played on a table shuffleboard team for recreation and at night would often go out with "the girls," as she called them. It was her way of letting off steam, having a little fun, and escaping her troubles and loneliness. That meant that we were home alone a lot, and I wound up being the overbearing ogre who tried to see to it that my younger brother and sisters were in at night, hitting the books. Because they resented big brother bossing them around, it affected our relationship. While I was happy, in a way, to be rid of that responsibility, I also felt guilty about not being around to help.

CHAPTER 2

ᕝ

College Years

UW–Marathon County

I enjoyed the two years at the UW Center in Wausau. It was the fall of 1956, and politically I had come a long way from the 1952 campaign when I had distributed literature for the Republican ticket. I only half kiddingly told people that McCarthy made me an Independent, Stevenson made me a Progressive, and Eisenhower made me a Democrat. I say Progressive because by then I had become aware of the rich Wisconsin Progressive tradition under Robert La Follette's leadership and really felt at home with that school of politics. It stood for government action on behalf of working people, and that's what I believed in. I tried to organize a Young Democrats Club on campus, but the state party rules required us to have at least ten members, and I could find only eight other students willing to say that they were Democrats.

I gained a great deal of confidence during those two years at the UW–Marathon County. At that time, the University of Wisconsin had eight small two-year branch campuses around the state. About 260 students attended the Wausau Center, and about one-quarter of them were returning Korean War vets. These were no-nonsense guys who were serious about life, focused on getting a good education, and determined to get on with their lives. They had a maturing influence on those of us just out of high school.

On weekends I joined three other students, one of whom was Steve Miller, a Korean War vet who later became my college roommate, in sponsoring college dances in the basement of the Tic Toc Club—a tavern on the southwest side of town—in order to supplement what I earned by working part-time in my dad's floor covering business.

I usually laid floors one or two nights a week and all day Saturday and used the rest of the time to study. On the nights I wasn't working I would grab a hamburger after class at Steck's bar—a block from campus—and then walk to the Marathon County Library just across the river on the east side of town. I would go to the desk, check out some quiet long-play classical albums— usually some Chopin played by Artur Rubinstein—sit in an easy chair in the music-listening area, put on the headphones, and study until the library closed at nine o'clock. That was the only way I could concentrate. The music not only screened out the sounds of people whispering in the library but kept me awake if I was tired. To this day I do my best studying if I have a TV set on with some program that I glance at from time to time. The background noise keeps me awake and keeps me from feeling bored or alone. When the library closed at nine, if my dad was working the second shift from three to eleven at 3M, I would go across the street to the post office and stand at a table in the lobby reading until he picked me up a little after eleven. I never dreamed that years later that post office would be converted to a federal office building and the postmasters office would become my congressional district office.

Most days become fuzzy in our memories as time passes, but there are certain moments that never fade. One that stands out in my memory was the day the Soviet Union first put their Sputnik satellite into orbit. Shortly after I heard the news, I ran into the campus dean, Dr. Henry Ahrnsbrak, and we talked in amazement about how the Russians had beaten us into space. America was used to being first, just as we had been used to winning wars until the Korean standoff. Because the Russian triumph had come on the heels of the first war since 1812 that had not been a clear victory for America, concerns abounded that America might be losing its edge, that the Soviet Union might indeed be becoming a colossus. It shook the country's confidence to the roots. I remember Dr. Ahrnsbrak saying two things. First, he speculated that "maybe this will remind us all that it is not inevitable that America will always finish first." Then he said something else, something I did not realize at the time would have a direct effect on my life: "This will shock America and it will change American education. Math and science will get much more attention, and the country will have a whole lot better idea ten years from now than it does today about what we are up against with the Russians." I didn't think that had much to do with me. I had no idea that, as a response to Sputnik, Congress would pass the National Defense Education Act, and that within four years I would finance my postgraduate education studying Russian government under the law that was a direct legislative response to the shocking events of that day.

❧

In my sophomore year I edited the student newspaper. One week, I had written an editorial criticizing a statement that Mary Conner had made about an issue that had been before the university Board of Regents. Jerry Onheiber looked at the editorial and said, "Dave, you can't run that." "Why not," I asked. "It's a legitimate issue." "That's not the point," Jerry responded. "She's an important person to the university, and you just can't do it." "Well, if that's the case, I resign," I said, determined to preserve the independence of the "press." Three days later we resolved our differences, and I went back to work as a member of the "free press."

On Fridays, all classes ended at about 1:25, but some of us took a one-credit choir course that didn't start until a little after four o'clock. The faculty had been looking for a way to use that open time. One Friday, a friendly impromptu debate about U.S. policy in the Middle East took place. Two popular faculty members, Sam Weiner, a Jewish science professor, and Bob Najem, a Lebanese American professor of French and English, started discussing the Middle East, and a number of students began to listen. Soon a crowd gathered, and the discussion went until four o'clock. So much interest had been generated that Weiner and Najem decided to start what became known as Friday Forum, and for the next six weeks they continued the debate. It was absolutely fascinating to me. Their exchanges took headlines in the newspaper and helped us to understand the religious, economic, historical, and cultural differences that were behind them. They gave us an understanding that the world was much more complicated than "Uncle Sam vs. the Russians." And so my lifelong interest in the Middle East began.

That exchange between two good, informed men, both of whom had their own beliefs and respected one another, was a lesson for me that politics was much more than persuading other people that you were right; it was also understanding the complexity and nuances of the human condition and making room in the debate for the reasonable interests and views of the other side. It was dialogue, not mutual monologues. Without that Friday Forum experience, I doubt that years later I would have sought a position on the Foreign Operations Appropriations Subcommittee, which I chaired for ten years, dealing every month with some aspect of Middle East policy. Even today, when I deal with issues affecting this troubled region, I often think about how Sam and Bob would have seen it.

I had some wonderful teachers those two years, especially Bob Najem, Louise Hanley, a tough taskmaster in English, and Val Kolpitzke, who taught economics. I hated to see those two years end. They had changed me. Leaving the UW–Marathon campus, I was a much more confident person than I had been when I left high school. But one monkey wrench got tossed into the gears.

Just as I was preparing to transfer to Madison, my dad, caught in a work-force downsizing, lost his job at 3M. Management didn't like the fact that he had a part-time job on the side, so there I was, going off to Madison with no idea how much help I could get from home. That experience drilled into me the conviction that access to education should be determined by how much determination you had in your heart and how many smarts you had in your head, not how many dollars your old man had in his wallet. But things worked out. My dad simply decided to do floor covering work full time, and I landed a job in Madison hustling tables at Rennebohm's drug store (Oscar Rennebohm had been a Republican governor just a few years earlier). And when my new landlord found out I could install floor tile, I made some needed money putting new floor covering in several of his apartments. I was on my way.

Madison

My first year at Madison I roomed with Bill Steckbauer and Dave Hunt-hausen in a one-room, ground-floor apartment with four built-in bunks hid-den behind a curtain strung across the middle of the room. The apartment, on the shore of Lake Mendota, was next door to a row of fraternity houses. I never set foot in a fraternity house during my years at Madison, but we got a good across-the-fence view of the fraternity lakeshore yards and piers.

The year before, I had visited my high school history teacher, Art Hender-son, and asked him what courses he thought I should take and which teachers I should seek out. When I told him I thought I wanted to focus on political science, he said, "The one man I want you to get is Ralph Huitt. There are a lot of good ones down there, but Huitt is the best." So the first thing I did on campus was to seek out Huitt as my faculty advisor. I was thrilled the moment I met him, and we began a lifelong friendship. I told him that I was pas-sionately interested in politics and in using government to change things to give little people a better deal out of life. "I can't believe I could ever run for office," I added, "but I was hoping I might wind up working as a staffer for a mayor or a legislator." "Well, this is a good place for you," Huitt said. Then he observed, "From the way you talk I presume you are a Democrat?" I told him about my slow conversion, and he told me I should join Campus Young Democrats. "You can make some quick friends. This place won't seem so big to you, and you can learn a lot by simply working in campaigns and rubbing elbows with people in politics. In this state, that's easy." In less than twenty minutes talking with him, I felt like I had a sense of direction.

After registering for classes at the ancient campus armory building on the shores of Lake Mendota, a structure once used by Old Bob La Follette for his inauguration as governor at the turn of the century, I walked next door to the Memorial Union to find out how I could find the Young Democrats. Before I got to the door of the union, I stumbled upon their registration table and signed up. Several nights later I walked into the room in the student union where the Young Dems were meeting. Dominating the meeting was a black-haired, angular-faced guy with a unique laugh (he would rock back and forth at the waist, clapping his hands) named Pat Putzi. Putzi was trying to round up volunteers to peddle literature in nearby Edgerton for state senator Gaylord Nelson, who was running for governor.

I had no idea who Nelson was. I wanted to help Bill Proxmire, who had just won a special election the year before to succeed Joe McCarthy and who was up again in 1958. Putzi explained that we needed to help Nelson because, as the candidate for governor, he would be at the top of the ticket; if he didn't do reasonably well, it would hurt Proxmire, who was listed farther down on the ballot. Putzi said, "Most people disagree with me, but I also think this young guy Kastenmeier has a chance to win the congressional seat here if we have a good night." Two Saturdays in a row we distributed literature on the east side of Madison and in southern Dane County for Nelson and Kastenmeier.

The night before the election, stores were open, and I was standing in front of Woolworth's on Capitol Square in Madison passing out literature for the Democratic ticket. I noticed an attractive woman passing out literature about a hundred feet from me. After about fifteen minutes she walked over to me and said, "We're hitting the same people. Don't you think it would be a good idea if you would move down to the end of the block?" "I'm sorry, lady," I said. "All is fair in love and politics." "I know," she said, "but we're on the same side; I'm Dorothy Kastenmeier." I felt like an idiot and scurried down the street. That was the first time I had ever met a candidate's wife. The next night was a great night. Nelson, Kastenmeier, and Proxmire all won—a landmark night in the history of Wisconsin's Democratic Party.

WISCONSIN'S SECOND PROGRESSIVE REVOLUTION

Wisconsin has been the scene of two Progressive revolutions in the twentieth century. The first was led by Robert M. La Follette Sr. at the turn of the century. The second was led by a cadre of reformists who reinvigorated the

Democratic Party after La Follette's son had presided over the collapse of the Progressive Party founded by his father.

In the late nineteenth century, Wisconsin politics had been like politics in most other places in America. It was owned lock, stock, and barrel by powerful interests, especially the mining, timber, and railroad companies. All that changed when a young rebel named Robert La Follette broke with the Republican machine to begin a ten-year fight to take Wisconsin government away from the old-time party bosses. In those days, many office holders were private—not public—servants, public officials who were supported financially by private-interest clients.

Wisconsin's politics had been in the grip of the GOP stalwarts and the state's corporate elite from the 1870s until La Follette's successful reform movement. In 1900 La Follette-led Progressives finally toppled the industry-owned Republican machine known as the Stalwarts. La Follette, his son Phillip, and other reformers who succeeded them produced decades of progressive legislation that advanced the interests of ordinary working people. Virtually everything that La Follette and his followers did was intended to knock the rough edges off capitalism in order to give the average working family a chance to stand up to the awesome power of corporate interests. He led a sustained crusade, first as governor and then as U.S. senator, to change the rules of the economic game to give the little guy a chance, and the corporate elites hated him for it.

In 1924 he ran for president on the Progressive ticket, pushed for worker-oriented economic and social causes, and fought to limit the influence of big-business money on politics in the same reformist tradition as had Teddy Roosevelt, Woodrow Wilson, and Nebraska's George Norris. When La Follette died in 1925 he was succeeded in the U.S. Senate by his son, Young Bob, who followed in those same footsteps until the Progressive movement collapsed: he was defeated by Joe McCarthy by about five thousand votes in 1946.

"Fighting Bob" was the greatest *political* leader Wisconsin has ever produced, but until Gaylord Nelson came along, "Young Bob" was probably Wisconsin's greatest legislative craftsman. Years later when Nelson was elected to the U.S. Senate, House Speaker Sam Rayburn told him that Young Bob was the most able senator with whom he had ever worked. Young Bob, working from Washington, and his brother Phillip, working from the governorship in Madison, dominated the state and drove a reformist progressive agenda until Phil was defeated for reelection in 1938. That year, many Wisconsin progressives had gone down in defeat in congressional and legislative elections. Young Bob hung on, but stalwart Republicans regained their dominance in gubernatorial and legislative elections. World War II had changed the economic and political landscape of Wisconsin as well as the nation.

In 1946, at its state convention in Portage, the Progressive Party (independent since 1934) faced a crisis of conscience and strategy. Should they try to hold out as a progressive third party, disband and try to take over the moribund Democratic Party, or move back into the Republican Party and try to survive there? They voted to disband. Young Bob La Follette tried to lead them into the Republican Party, gambling that he could survive a primary challenge, but he lost. That same year he also shepherded through Congress the landmark Congressional Reorganization Act of 1946, which created the modern Congress. La Follette neglected to mount an aggressive campaign at home and lost by five thousand votes to the man who has since gone down in history as the worst major public official in the state's history—Joe McCarthy.

Wisconsin's Progressives had been thrown into the wilderness by the 1946 results. Some tried to adjust to life in the Republican Party, but most of their young leaders saw that with McCarthy's ascendancy there was no place for them there. Wisconsin's second wave of Progressive reform began when they decided on an organizational effort to take over and remake the Wisconsin Democratic Party in the early 1950s. For anyone with Progressive leanings, the Progressive Party had been where the action was. The Democratic Party had limped along as a reactionary paper organization, affiliated with the national party organization largely for the purpose of doling out patronage in the form of post office jobs. Its reformation began when a cadre of young progressive idealists met and created the Democratic Organizing Committee—founded for the sole purpose of taking over and transforming the Democratic Party and remaking it into a modern, humane, progressive organization. Committed leaders like Elliott Walstead, Tom Fox, Jim Doyle, Tom Fairchild, Frank Nikolay, Marge Pattison, Bill Proxmire, Bob Kastenmeier, Carl Thompson, Horace Wilke, John Reynolds, and Gaylord Nelson took the first steps to bring the Wisconsin Democratic Party back from spiritual and political oblivion.

Since 1932 when Albert Schmedeman was elected governor in the Roosevelt landslide, no Democrat had been elected to the governorship and Democrats had fared no better in legislative elections. In 1946 Gaylord Nelson, running as a Progressive, lost a race for state assembly from Polk County. Two years later, he ran for the state senate from Madison as a Democrat and was elected. He was only the third Democrat in the state senate—there were twenty-seven Republicans and three vacancies. Rising from such depths to victory that happy evening in 1958 seemed like a dream. Proxmire had won the breakthrough special election in 1957 following the death of McCarthy, but Proxmire's reelection in 1958, Gaylord Nelson's and Philleo Nash's election as governor and lieutenant governor, and John Reynolds as attorney general meant the Progressives were back, even though they were now wearing a Democratic label. And there was more. At the congressional level Kastenmeier had won, and Democrats had taken control of the state assembly. That fall was a buoyant time for a young Democrat to begin his college years in Madison, the state capital, the center of Wisconsin politics.

STATE PARTY

From my first days on campus, my focus was divided between both ends of State Street—the street that ran from the front of Bascom Hill on campus to the state capitol on the downtown square. Standing at the top of Bascom Hill, near South Hall, which was then the Political Science Department, or near the statute of Abe Lincoln, prominently seated in a chair in front of Bascom Hall, I would see that majestic capitol dome and think, "My God, I really want to be a part of that." Only a matter of blocks physically separated the campus from the capitol, but to me it seemed a universe away. I wanted to get from one end of State Street to the other but couldn't imagine how. I had no idea that I had already taken the first steps that would lead me there in just four years.

In those days, Wisconsin State Democratic Party headquarters was housed on the second floor above a movie theater on the west side of Capitol Square. The party was chaired by Philleo Nash, a Wisconsin Rapids cranberry grower and anthropologist who had served in the Truman administration, and then by Pat Lucey—a highly successful, well-organized real estate broker who had worked as field organizer for the Democratic Organizing Committee and had served one term as a state assemblyman from Crawford County. Eunice Gibson, a smart, savvy, young woman in her twenties, was the office manager (Ellen Proxmire had the job before her), and she relied upon a cadre of Dane County Democratic women to do the volunteer work that was needed. This was truly the era when grassroots politics had real roots.

The drill was simple. If you had a mailing to get out, you called five or ten volunteers and got those envelopes stuffed. Young Dems from the campus would come down to help in their spare time. You could read about politics and history in political science texts, but you could meet Bobby Kennedy, Hubert Humphrey, Gaylord Nelson, and a fistful of state legislators just by helping out around party headquarters. The people who really made the Dane County organization go in those days were hard-nosed (but nice), practical, coalition-building women, like Ruth O'Malley and Liesle Tarkow. At least half of what I would need to know to run a state legislative campaign I learned just by listening to them.

In the spring of 1959 I attended my first Young Democratic state convention in Fond du Lac. The organization was split between one faction led by the University of Wisconsin unit and another led by Marquette University, in alliance with the Stevens Point University delegation. That faction was led by Bill Drew of Marquette, who later became staff chief for Milwaukee mayor Henry Maier, and by Jerry Madison, a New London high school teacher who was later to become a lifelong friend and advisor to me.

Pat Putzi was the leader of our UW delegation. Both factions fielded a slate of candidates for leadership slots in the organization. A leader in our UW group, Dave Sheridan, was running for national committeeman—the person who represented the state at all national meetings. His opponent was Jerry Madison, who was finishing a term as state chair and wanted to move to the national committee slot. I knew nothing about Jerry or his ally Bill Drew. I just followed Putzi's lead as did most of our delegation. The convention lasted two days with many caucuses and meetings. Those two nights gave me my first lessons on how to put together coalitions to build a majority . . . and how not to. Saturday at about midnight, Jerry Madison appeared before our caucus in a pitch for votes. When he finished his pitch, Putzi challenged him. "How can you ever think of running for national committeeman when the last year as state chair you had a right to attend the national convention and didn't show up?" Jerry responded, "Well Pat, I think I had a pretty good excuse. I was blind at the time." I couldn't believe it. It turned out that Jerry had developed ulcers on his eyes in the previous year. I couldn't believe our delegation leadership hadn't known that. Pretty dumb. When the votes were tallied, Jerry won handily.

The convention was an embarrassment for our delegation, but it was helpful for me because I got into a well-publicized debate about loyalty oaths. Many of the Marquette delegates supported them. I opposed them as insulting, ineffective McCarthy-era political leftovers. Until that time I had been a fairly quiet and largely anonymous member of the organization, but when we got back to Madison, Bill Whitford, Dave Sheridan, and Tom Eckerle asked if I would like to be treasurer of the UW Young Dems. I accepted, and that's how I began my political road to the legislature.

Shortly thereafter, I saw Adlai Stevenson for the first time and observed, close up, how effectively humor could be used in the hands of the right politician. Stevenson was in town to speak at the Civil War Roundtable. Afterwards he was supposed to come over to the old Park Hotel for a late evening rally with local Democrats. He was scheduled to be there by 8:30, but it was about 9:30 when Gaylord (now Governor Nelson) and Stevenson walked in and swept through the crowd to the waiting microphones. Gaylord, who was notorious for his self-deprecating brassy wit, grabbed the mike and said, "I'm sorry, we're terribly late because the Civil War Roundtable wouldn't stop asking Governor Stevenson questions. It's very late and I have to get him to bed at the governor's mansion, so I'll give one of my typically short speeches." "And I'll give one of my typically long ones," Stevenson interjected. "You do and I'll leave without you," Nelson quipped. "Go ahead, see who the crowd follows," Stevenson rejoined. They both laughed as the crowd roared. It was a great night to be a Democrat and to be in such company.

Of course, politics was not the only thing I did with my hours. I enjoyed the life of a college student, especially football Saturdays. I roomed with Bill Steckbauer and Dave Hunthausen, but my closest friends were Jim Backus, Ralph Hintz, and Pete Bauer, who roomed with another friend, Don Luetschwager. On Saturday we would catch the Badger football game at Camp Randall. Afterwards we would grab some beer and a bottle of ninety-eight-cent wine and go over to their apartment. We would make spaghetti, play poker, and watch *Gunsmoke*.

And, oh yes, I did go to class. I loved the classes with my professors, especially in poli sci and English literature. Ralph Huitt was my favorite. I took his courses on Public Opinion and the Legislative Process. He was a spectacular teacher. A Texan, he spoke with a soft drawl, and he spoke from experience. A nationally recognized scholar, he also knew the system from the inside, having worked for LBJ and for Bill Proxmire. He taught government and politics, not as an academic thought it should be but as an analyst and practitioner knew it really was. He was shrewd, thoughtful, and wise. I had some other great teachers: Selig Perlman for Labor History, Bernard Cohen for International Relations, Leon Epstein for British Politics, John Armstrong for Soviet Politics, George Mosse for European Intellectual History, and David Fellman for Constitutional Law.

I will never forget the second day of Fellman's course. Anyone who remembers John Houseman's portrayal of the law professor in *Paper Chase* will know what Fellman was like—intimidating, tough, clipped, proper, dry, acerbic. The class had just started. About three minutes into Fellman's lecture, the door opened and in walked the Big Man on Campus. Bill Steiger was the rail-thin, blond, smart leader of the Young Republicans on campus. He was also heavy into student government politics. His father was president of the Board of Regents. A bigger man on campus you could not be. But on this day Steiger, clearly chagrined to be interrupting Fellman's lecture, slunk to his seat. Fellman, peering over eyeglasses pulled low on his nose, said icily, "Pardon me, Mr. Steiger. On behalf of the university, allow me to apologize. Ordinarily, we would have an usher escort you to your seat. Unfortunately, our carnations have not yet arrived." He had figuratively reduced Steiger to the size of a pea in his own eyes, and we all felt shrunken with him. Tough guy, tough course, great teacher.

Steiger was one of those people who had his whole life's course already set. In the 1958 campaign, he would take the steps of the Memorial Union to debate the cause of Vernon Thompson, the incumbent Republican governor being challenged by Gaylord Nelson. He and I wound up on the same track—he two years ahead of me. He would be elected to the legislature in 1960; I followed two years later. He would be elected to Congress in 1966 and I came along two years later. Neither of us knew that at the time. All I knew was that he had smarts, political experience, connections, money; and he was a very nice guy. We debated on the student union steps in 1959 and started a lifelong friendship.

In my senior year I organized Hubert Humphrey's presidential campaign on campus and found myself in the middle of a nasty split in the Wisconsin Democratic Party. As the 1960 presidential campaign approached, the party was divided into two-and-a-half camps. Half the party, led by Pat Lucey and the new state party chairman, was for Jack Kennedy. The other half, led by Gaylord Nelson, the sitting governor, favored Hubert Humphrey. In their hearts, though, many of the Humphrey supporters were really for Stevenson, but he was waiting for a draft and was not going to be on the ballot in Wisconsin. The campus Humphrey for President Club was organized in 1959 with me as president, Tom Eckerle as vice president, Judy Vanish as secretary, and Vic Ouimette as treasurer. We recruited people for literature drops, factory gate distributions, and dorm canvassing operations. Early in the campaign, Miles Lord, an old Minnesota friend of Humphrey's who later became a federal judge, came to campus to see how we were doing and discovered I had a roommate named John Kennedy. One hour later we had filed papers for a Kennedy for Humphrey Club on campus with John Kennedy as president, secretary, and treasurer of the organization. Lord then drafted a press release announcing the dog-bites-man story. Two days later, the story was picked up by CBS evening news.

The first time I met John F. Kennedy, I was sitting at a table in the student union running a planning meeting of the Humphrey organization. I knew

Jackie Kennedy was upstairs at a fashion show, but I had no idea that her husband was in town. As I was concluding the meeting, the door opened and in peeked Jack Kennedy. I remember thinking, "He's taller than I thought!" "I understand this is a meeting of the Young Democrats," he said. "Well," I responded, "we're all young Democrats, but this is a meeting of the Humphrey for President Club." He laughed and said, "May I come in anyway." I said, "Of course, happy to meet you." Kennedy grinned, walked around the table, shook hands with us, wished us luck "but not too much," and was gone.

My involvement in the Humphrey campaign gave me an opportunity to meet one of my heroes, Jackie Robinson, the man who had broken baseball's color barrier, but that opportunity turned into a lousy story for Democrats. Governor Nelson called me one afternoon and said, "Jackie Robinson is coming to town to endorse Hubert. Build a crowd for him at the union and you can emcee the program." I thought, "Jackie Robinson, what a coup. This will really turn on students to Hubert." It didn't quite turn out that way. The afternoon of the event we had the room packed. When he was introduced, Robinson gave a strong endorsement of Hubert. So far, so good. Then came the questions from the press. One reporter asked Robinson, "Are you confident Hubert Humphrey can win the primary?" "Yes, I am," Robinson replied. "What happens if Humphrey loses the primary to Kennedy?" the reporter shot back. "Well, then I'll vote for Nixon," Robinson replied. All hell broke lose. Reporters raced for the phones to file their story. I stood on stage dumbfounded. I could not believe that Robinson had turned a media event for Humphrey into a coup for Nixon, but that's what he had done. That experience gave me a good hard lesson about why nobody in politics likes to be surprised.

Another lesson I learned is that when the press referred to the late Hubert Humphrey they weren't talking about Hubert's father. In January or February—I don't remember which—Humphrey made a sweep through Wisconsin and had us set up a rally at the student union. We had the place packed at the appointed time of two o'clock, but Hubert, as usual, was late. After the first forty-five minutes, I said to Tom Eckerle, "If he isn't here by the time an hour has gone by, we're going to lose these kids." But I was wrong. They stayed, thanks to a little entertainment by Joe Glaser, the guitar-playing troubadour who lent his labor songs to Hubert's campaign. Hubert finally showed up almost an hour and forty-five minutes late, and the kids loved him. His energy, his optimism, his good heart made you feel glad to be alive. He won many a student to his side that day. "He wasn't cool but damn, he was real!" I heard my friend Jim Ehrmann say afterwards.

The next time I saw Hubert was on a bone-chilling February morning at the Oscar Mayer meat-packing factory. About a dozen students were on hand to pass out campaign literature as the workers streamed past Hubert into the plant door. It was a bitter cold February morning, and the literature was ice-cold to the touch; every twenty minutes or so the kids would take turns going into the campaign bus to warm their cold, stiff fingers. The cold didn't bother Hubert. When we were walking back to the bus, Hubert kidded, "Dave, you're a softy, warming up your hands." I said, "That's easy for you to say, you were shaking warm hands; that paper is cold." "Well," he said, "that should teach you a trick of the trade. Never leave your literature outside over a cold night. Take it inside and keep it warm, and your fingers won't freeze." We all climbed in the bus to go back to the hotel. Hubert sat down in the second row, put his feet up across the aisle, and said, "Well, young people, what do you want to talk about?" For the entire ride back he answered questions from the students—not the press—the *students*. Teddy White, the famous national reporter, eased over to me and said, "What do you think of that man?" "I think he is about the nicest man I have ever met," I replied. Years later, after talking with Hubert countless times, I still feel the same way. He could make you feel more proud while losing than most people could make you feel by winning. Hubert lost that Wisconsin primary by the narrowest of margins. I never regretted for a moment working for him. To me, he personified what politics is supposed to be—a happy struggle to make this a better country. And he enjoyed the journey as much as he cherished the goal.

A Door Opens

In the spring of 1960, the presidential election wasn't the only important event looming on the horizon. I was only a few months away from graduation and still had no earthly idea what I was going to do next. I had no money and no prospects. I thought about trying to get a job with the party or with the governor's office. I thought about law school. I thought about grad school, but I was adrift.

All that changed when John Armstrong, my Soviet politics professor, walked up to me shortly before class one morning and asked, "Dave, do you have any plans after graduation?" "I don't know," I said. "Do you like this course? Are you interested in the Soviet Union?" he asked. "I certainly am," I said. "I find the whole country, its politics, its history, its culture, its music absolutely fascinating." "Well," he said, "under the National Defense Education Act there are three-year full-cost fellowships available for students in the Russian Area

Studies Program. I think you would have a reasonable chance to get one of those." "I would be ecstatic," I replied. "What does it involve and what do I have to do?" "And how much do they pay?" I added. "$1,800 the first year, $2,000 the second year, and $2,200 the third," he said. It sounds like a pittance today, but in those days it was virtually a full-boat, full-cost package. He told me that the three-year program that would immerse me in Soviet politics, history, and economics. It would involve learning the Russian language, and I would emerge with a masters degree, a certificate of completion from the UW Russian Area Studies Program, and I would have almost all the course work I needed for a PhD. It sounded too good to be true, but I filled out the papers and hoped. I never really expected anything to come of it, but several months later as I was seated in Armstrong's class preparing for a quiz, he came up to me, hands clasped before him, a broad grin on his face and said," You got it!" I couldn't believe it. Just a few weeks earlier I had no idea what I was going to be doing with my life. Now a totally unexpected door had been opened for me, and I had a three-year road map. But one obstacle remained.

When I received the paperwork that I needed to sign for the fellowship, I discovered that in order to receive it I had to sign a loyalty oath. I had known that the National Defense Education Act had previously required a loyalty oath, but I had been told erroneously that that particular requirement had been changed. I thought such a requirement was insulting to any American citizen who genuinely cared about his country. Every instinct within me rebelled against this remnant of the McCarthy era. I believed that American citizens had a right to be assumed loyal citizens unless there was specific evidence to the contrary. I thought the requirement was stupid because anyone who was a subversive could simply sign such an oath without blinking.

I went to Armstrong and told him I was going to turn down the fellowship because of the requirement. Armstrong was horrified. He talked to Ralph Huitt, and both of them sat down with me determined to change my mind. Huitt put it bluntly. "Don't be stupid, Dave," he said. "You don't have any money. This fellowship is your door-opener. For God's sake sign the damn oath. Take the money, get your education, and you'll be in a hell of a lot better position to influence your government on things like this than you will if you make a noble but dumb gesture." I hated to accept reality, but I knew he was right in practical terms. So I swallowed my pride, signed the oath, and got ready to wrap up my undergrad years. The day I graduated, the ceremonies were over at 12:15 and I had to be to work at my summer job at Wausau Paper Mill in Brokaw at three o'clock. There was not even time for a photograph in my graduation gown. I raced to my car, barreled north, and pulled into the paper mill lot at exactly 2:52 p.m. Since the statute of limitations has run out, I will admit that I never drove under the speed limit once. That money was badly needed, and Gib Schreiber, the personnel manager, made it clear I had to be there at three o'clock sharp to begin the job.

I enjoyed my summers at the mill. I worked in the finishing room, stacking reams of trimmer-cut paper, working as a trimmer loader, working on the packaging line, or loading boxcars. Sometimes I would work in the machine room. It was a great way to learn about the paper industry—the backbone of the economy in the Wisconsin River Valley. Often I worked a double shift when a regular mill worker needed to take a day off. I looked for every opportunity to do that because it really made a difference in the old paycheck. I never really minded doubling up the first and second shift. The hard drill was to start at three in the afternoon, keep going on the graveyard shift and finally get home for some sleep at seven thirty in the morning. On those nights, time seemed to run awfully slow after about four in the morning.

In September I couldn't wait to get back to the presidential campaign in Madison and to explore the world of graduate school. When JFK came to campus that fall, I was invited to sit on the stage with him. Earlier I had met Jackie—sat right next to her at an event at the student union—and had met Jack briefly when he crashed the Humphrey campaign meeting I was running. But sitting on stage with a presidential nominee was exciting stuff for a college student. He gave an energizing speech at the Law School, and I remember thinking, "He's as smooth as glass." In fact, his whole operation ran like clockwork. I couldn't help comparing the discipline of the Kennedy operation with the far looser Humphrey organization I had seen earlier that year. "No wonder we lost," I thought, as we were sitting on stage.

The weekend before the election we got word that Nixon was going to touch down at the Madison airport in his last national swing. "Damn," I thought, "that might be just enough to ice the state for him." We tried to figure out what we could do to take the edge off. Somebody—I think it was Bill Whitford—got an idea. We went down to the Republican headquarters and got several dozen Nixon-Lodge signs, took them back to Channing Murray House, the Unitarian student center, cut Lodge's name off the bottom of the sign, moved it above Nixon's name, and added the letters "D-I-S" in front of Lodge's name. The signs now read: Dislodge Nixon. We made about thirty signs like that, working until the early hours of the morning. I went home about 2 a.m. looking forward to our morning effort, but I never made it to the airport. When the alarm rang at 5 a.m., I shut it off and rolled over in bed for "just a minute." I woke up at 7:30 to the horrified realization that I had missed the whole show.

On election night an excited crowd gathered at my house. For the first hour we were joyous. Returns from the East came in with Kennedy smashing Nixon. Mary Doyle, the daughter of Jim Doyle, national chairman of the Stevenson campaign, was at the party. About nine o'clock Jim called to tell her it was going to be a wonderful night, but she replied, "Tell that to Dave Obey here, Dad. He's sucking his thumb because he thinks Kennedy will still lose most of the West, and Nixon could still be president." "Well, Mary," Jim replied, "you tell Dave not to worry. It's going to be a great night." About midnight he called back and told her, "You tell Dave I apologize; it's going to be a long night." And it was, until Illinois finally decided it the next day.

After Kennedy's election, I hit the books to make up for the time I had lost working on the campaign. I especially enjoyed Michael Petrovich's Russian history course. His lecture on the death of Rasputin produced a scene I had never witnessed in any other classroom. In vivid terms, Petrovich described Rasputin's background, his hypnotic personal style, and his ever-growing influence in the life of Tsar Nicholas and his wife. He described the plots and counterplots involving Rasputin. Pacing back and forth, Petrovich physically demonstrated the struggle between Rasputin and his assassins. When the bell rang announcing the end of the lecture period and time for us to move on to our next class, we all sat transfixed as Petrovich demonstrated Rasputin's final agony. At last he finished and dropped to one knee. We sat for a second and then spontaneously and simultaneously leaped to our feet to give him a standing ovation. Only then did we move on to our next class. I have never since seen that kind of reaction to a college lecture.

The next spring I attended another Young Dems state convention in Racine. I had decided to run for vice chair of the organization. I made the usual round of caucuses, made it a point to get to know Bill Drew from Marquette, the state Democratic chair, whom I really liked. My campaign was undistinguished, and so were the results. I lost by almost sixty votes—smashed! As I drove back to Madison I thought, "My political career—crushed before it began." One evening several months later, I got a call from Drew. "Dave, you know John Hayward?" "Yes," I said. John was the administrative rep of the State YDs— which meant that he represented the Young Dems on the Democratic Party state central committee. "Well," Bill said, "John is leaving to go into the Peace Corps." "The executive board needs to find a replacement, and we were thinking of you, but I need to ask a couple of questions. How are you on Pat Lucey?" I didn't really know what Bill was getting at, but I knew Pat and liked him so I said, "Fine, I think Lucey's great." "So you are okay on Pat then?" he said. "Well, sure," not quite understanding what he meant. "Well," he said, "that's all I needed to know. I am going to recommend your name to the board as a unity move, and I think they will approve. There will be a senior party central committee meeting next week in LaCrosse, and you will need to be there." "Great," I said. The next day he called me and said I had been approved, and I was off to the meeting.

What I had not realized was that a huge behind-the-scenes fight had been brewing between Lucey and Nelson over who would be selected for a vacant federal judgeship. I had not known it, but Lucey and Nelson were split about who should get the job, and Lucey forces had planned to push for an endorsement for his candidate at the central party committee meeting in LaCrosse. Lucey wanted Dave Rabinowitz, a Sheboygan attorney, and Gaylord favored Jim Doyle. I had never met Rabinowitz, but I greatly admired Doyle. I did not know the players well enough to know that the real fight was not between Rabinowitz and Doyle; it was between Lucey and Nelson about who was going to control the Wisconsin Democratic Party.

At the LaCrosse meeting Howard Meister, a banker from Milwaukee, made a motion that the board endorse Doyle. Tom Pattison, a Lucey ally, urged support for Rabinowitz. Lucey and Nelson were never mentioned by name, but the debate was furious. I did not much care for Meister. I thought he was awfully slick, but on this day he was roguishly funny and effective in his support for Doyle. And to me, Doyle was a hero. So when the roll call was called I voted for Doyle, who won by one vote. Pattison was enraged. "How could you do this," he raged afterwards, "I thought Pat could count on you." "I think he can if it has something to do with the party, but Jim Doyle is a friend of mine, and I think Jim is a great man and the class of the party," I replied. I realized at that point that Drew's elliptical reference to Lucey was more important than I had understood. But my ignorance of the deep division between the Lucey and Nelson wings of the party had allowed me to vote my conscience—in blissful ignorance of the fact that my ignorance had misled Drew. But life went on.

A few months later another episode gave the Lucey forces another opportunity to doubt my lucidity. A year earlier I had seen Joan Lepinski walking down State Street. We said hello to each other, had a cup of coffee at Rennebohm's Drug Store, and renewed acquaintances. She had graduated from the University of Wisconsin and worked for a year in the Racine school system as a speech therapist. She had then returned to Madison and had taken a job in rural Dane County. I asked her out on a date, but neither she nor I were especially bowled over by the experience. The following year Joan's brother, Dick, moved in with Steve Miller and me. He kept trying to get us together.

In late summer the Wisconsin Democratic Party had its annual fish boil in Door County on the shores of Lake Michigan. Joan accepted my invitation to go, so on a Saturday morning, we climbed into my straight-eight, straight-stick 1953 Buick and drove to Bailey's Harbor on the Door County peninsula. As we were walking onto the grounds, the first people we ran into were Pat Lucey, Jim Buckley, the executive director of the party, and John Reynolds, then attorney general and, later, governor. We walked over to them, and as I began to introduce Joan to them my mind went blank. I had begun, "Fellows, I would like you to meet . . ." My God, I had blanked on Joan's name. After what seemed the longest five seconds in eternity, I blurted out, "Alice." I had never dated an Alice in my life. To save my soul, I cannot think to this day why, of all names, I had blurted out Alice. After I had made a damn fool of myself, Joan's name reappeared in my memory bank. "I mean Joan," I stammered. All three men gazed at me with looks that ranged from bemusement to pity. Great way to make a lasting impression on the state chairman and attorney general, this college kid who couldn't remember his date's name! After my initial mortification, Joan and I did have a good time, and we really enjoyed the trip back. We did a lot of singing and I remember thinking, "She really has a pretty voice." I knew then that I wanted to see her again.

Weeks later, at one of the Dane County Democratic noon luncheons at the Town Club in Madison, Janet Lee, Gaylord Nelson's sister, circulated a petition calling for the abolition of the House UnAmerican Activities Committee (HUAC). The committee had made a name for itself by searching for Communists under every political bed in the land. There was nothing wrong with trying to protect the country from Communist subversion; the problem was that the committee saw ghosts everywhere. HUAC was careless and reckless with people's reputations. It pressured the movie and entertainment industry into denying employment to persons suspected of having impure political thoughts. It employed vicious techniques of guilt by association and innuendo to ruin innocent people guilty of nothing (except perhaps being naïvely romantic about the Russian revolution and the Soviet Union in its early years). In short, the committee's methods were a bigger threat to American freedom than the naïve idealism of many who stood accused. Painting with a broad brush, it found ways to equate a desire for social justice with a lack of love for America. When Gaylord Nelson's secretary, Esther Kaplan, signed a newspaper advertisement calling for HUAC's abolition, the Republican leadership in the state assembly called a press conference to demand that Governor Nelson fire

Esther. Many academics and civil libertarians had demanded that HUAC be abolished, but very few elected politicians had demonstrated such courage.

Paul Alfonsi and Curt McKay, the state assembly majority leader and majority whip, clearly thought they had Nelson in a box. But Gaylord broke out of it with one good-humored press conference. When a reporter asked him whether he was going to fire Esther, Gaylord responded, "You know, Assemblyman McKay is clearly right. Clearly, Esther was out of line. The least she could have done was to bring that petition to me so I could have the privilege of signing it first." The press conference erupted in laughter. The GOP leadership's attempt to use Esther to get at Gaylord had been laughed to death. It was a good lesson to me in how practicing politics with a sense of humor and a sense of abandon could defuse an issue.

It was just after that press conference that Janet Lee had circulated her own anti-HUAC petition, which I had enthusiastically signed. To exploit the issue, the state assembly Republicans held a public hearing on a resolution pushed by McKay that praised HUAC. My friend, Dave Sheridan, put on his ROTC uniform, strolled down to the capitol, and asked to testify. Normally, committee hearings were held in modest-sized hearing rooms in the capitol, but the Republican Party had drummed up a crowd, and the hearing was held in the state assembly chamber itself.

About twenty university Young Democrats squeezed into the seats in the gallery. We watched our friend Sheridan testify against the McKay resolution and for abolishing HUAC. McKay had been saying all along that anyone who opposed HUAC was either a subversive or a dupe. Sheridan ended his testimony by saying, "I'm wearing this uniform today to show that while I may be a dupe, I most certainly am not a subversive." Sheridan was harangued for his statements by the Republicans on the committee, but Frank Nikolay, who had enlisted just before World War II even though he was two years underage, praised Sheridan for his courage.

The next day all hell broke loose. McKay had been outraged by Sheridan's statement and wanted to punish him. He contacted the ROTC program director and demanded that Sheridan be bounced from ROTC for his actions. Technically, Sheridan had violated military rules by wearing his uniform while testifying. Republican legislators were outraged by this breach of protocol, although fewer than ten years earlier they had been moved to ecstasy when Douglas MacArthur did the same thing during his battle with President Truman. Dave Sheridan was in trouble. He talked to Ralph Huitt for political advice, and Huitt put in a phone call to UW professor Carlyle Runge, who had just been named Undersecretary of Defense for Manpower. Runge defused the situation by arranging an official warning to Sheridan for his use of the uniform. Privately, one professor told Runge, "This kid has guts, the military needs more like him, not less," and the issue died down for Sheridan. Little did I know that, years later, I would have the privilege, as a new member of Congress, to be part of an action in the House that effectively abolished the committee. What goes around comes around, as they say.

Shortly after that episode, I got caught in another fight between Pat Lucey and Gaylord Nelson. Gaylord was an easy going charming man, but Pat Lucey really got under his skin. Nelson was legendary for his ability to strike up friendships with almost anyone in politics, including Republicans. In the state senate, he had developed warm friendships with Mel Laird and with Warren and Bob Knowles. Both of the Knowles brothers served with distinction in the state senate, and Warren was to become governor in the late 1960s. But Gaylord and Pat both wanted control over the Democratic Party, and that led to tensions. Lucey was close to Kennedy because he had headed JFK's Wisconsin campaign while Gaylord had privately preferred Stevenson and Humphrey.

Their fight was over both power and policy. Because Nelson did not control the legislature, he was in a box. To eliminate the state's budget deficit, the Republicans demanded he impose a sales tax; Democrats preferred the income tax route. When Gaylord cut a compromise with the Republicans to do a little bit of both, Lucey was less than enthusiastic. Pat also felt that, as the state chair who had stuck his neck out for Kennedy, he should be the Kennedy go-to guy in Wisconsin. Gaylord decided the way to deal with it was to get a new state chairman. He convinced Frank Nikolay to run.

I had become close to Frank because Frank was the key leader of the Humphrey forces in the Wisconsin primary and at the national convention. He was outspoken, tough-minded, and gutsy, and he had a passion for justice for the little guy. Jim Wimmer, Gaylord's special assistant, called and asked me to support Frank, and I readily agreed. The next day I got a call from Jim Buckley, Pat's right-hand man as executive director of the party. He came down to campus to see me. "I understand you are thinking of supporting Frank Nikolay for state chair," he said. "That's true," I responded. "Well, that would be unfortunate," he said. "Frank can't win, and you would be backing a loser." Then he said something that hit my response button. "It would be too bad if you did that," he said. "You have a good future, and it would be a shame to see your career ruined before it got off the ground." His words enraged me. "Jim," I said, "you say Frank has no chance to win. If that's the case, you wouldn't be wasting your time threatening a nobody college student. If you have a case, make it, but don't threaten me. I don't work well with people who threaten me."

Two days later, the contest between Pat and Frank was rudely interrupted. The *Milwaukee Journal* broke a story saying that because of the Berlin crisis, Kennedy was calling up the Thirty-second Army Division to show the Russians he meant business. Because Nikolay was a high-ranking officer in the division, he was suddenly on his way to Fort Lewis, Washington, and could not run for state chair. End of campaign. The announcement came out the same day I had put out a press statement endorsing Frank, who later joked, "It took the White House and a national military crisis for Pat Lucey to beat me for state chair." With Kennedy's call-up, no one had a realistic shot at beating Lucey, and he and Nelson put some patches on their relationship. That made me happy because I loved Gaylord, but I also respected Lucey and disliked opposing him. They were both good Democrats, both had their strengths, and the party and the state needed both of them.

Soon after, I did get involved in another skirmish involving Gaylord. Suzie Gjetson, a local party activist in Marathon County, asked if I could help get a message through to Gaylord. She told me that two candidates, Bill Kaplan and Pat Crooks, were competing for appointment by the governor to the vacant district attorney slot in the county. I was not acquainted with Kaplan, and I knew he had not been active in party affairs. I did not know Pat Crooks either, but I did know his father had been district attorney years earlier and that Pat was widely respected in the Wausau area. Suzie told me the local Democratic Party favored Crooks because he would make a much better candidate in the general election, but that John Evans, the newly elected county party chairman, was falsely telling the governor's office that the local party executive committee had endorsed Kaplan.

I called Wimmer and explained Suzie's call. I asked Wimmer if he would tell John Evans that Gaylord wanted a letter from the local party spelling out what the vote of the local committee had been. He said "Sure," but urged me to go up to Wausau and make sure Crooks would have the votes. I called Crooks to set up a meeting to plan strategy, and he suggested we meet at his father-in-law's house. When I asked him who that was, he said "Joe Lepinski." That was how I discovered that Pat was married to Joan's sister, Rita, and that was also how I met Joan's parents long before I had any idea of marrying her. Evans tried to bluff his way through, but Gjetson insisted on a formal meeting of the local executive committee, and Pat won the vote handily. I discovered later that Evans thought that Kaplan would financially support his own run for office if he got the nod for DA. But with the letter, Nelson happily

appointed Pat, and we knew we had made progress in fielding a good slate of
county candidates in the coming election.

LOVE AND POLITICS

There was also progress in my personal life. I had begun seeing Joan again,
largely because of the matchmaking efforts of her brother, and I liked what
I saw. She was fresh, sweet, smart, and had the right values. Although she
had been thinking of going into the convent, she was now having second
thoughts. I recognized that I wanted to marry her but was afraid that if I
asked, she might not be ready and that it might throw cold water on the
whole relationship.

On homecoming weekend my dad and his new wife, Pat, came to Madison for the Ohio State–Wisconsin football game. Wisconsin lost a close game
in a miserable, gray drizzle at Camp Randall. After the game they drove back
to Wausau. Joan and I went out to eat and walked around the neighborhood.
When we got back to her apartment, neither of her roommates were home.
After some more talk I summoned the courage to ask her to marry me. I desperately wanted her to say yes, but for the longest time she didn't answer
me, parrying my question with questions of her own. I was smoking a cigarette (I smoked three packs a day in those days) and was beginning to think
she would turn me down. Then she finally said, "All right! On one condition—that you put that cigarette out and never touch another one. If you are
serious, I want you around to know your kids." I was ecstatic.

We wanted to tell somebody immediately, so at one thirty in the morning
we drove over to Joan's older sister Audrey's house to tell her. The next morning we went to Mass at St. Raphael's Cathedral, where Joan sang in the choir,
and that afternoon we drove up to Wausau to tell Joan's parents. Just after
dark, we pulled into their driveway and broke the news. I could see Joan's
mother was pleased. Her dad was smiling, low key. We had taken a liking
to each other since the meeting with Pat Crooks. He had a strong social conscience and liked politics. He asked me how we intended to get along financially. I explained my three-year fellowship and told him I expected to teach
Russian government when I was through. That was good enough for him. I did
not know, nor did Joan, that within weeks I would be setting out on a very
different course.

Within days of my engagement to Joan, Pat Lucey asked me to go back to
Wausau to try to convince John Evans, the local party chairman, to run for
the Wausau area state assembly seat occupied by Republican Paul Luedtke.

Luedtke had held the seat for twenty years. He was a former head of the Marathon County Central Labor Council—a nice man with an undistinguished record. Before going to see Evans, I had analyzed the district precinct by precinct. In the previous election, the Democratic candidate Charlie Pauls had been defeated by five thousand votes, but I knew that was an aberration caused by a controversy that had plagued all Democratic candidates that year. Father Duffy, a local Catholic priest, had publicly told Catholics they were committing a sin if they joined the Wausau YMCA.

Jack Kennedy, in 1960, had worked overtime to convince the American Protestant majority that Catholics could be trusted to follow their own conscience and not the dictates of Rome or the Catholic hierarchy on matters of national policy. But Duffy's comments had inflamed the local community and thus resurrected Protestant suspicions about how much freedom Catholic politicians had in following their own judgments. That impacted the Democratic ticket all down the ballot. Kennedy lost the county decisively, and the Democratic candidate for the Wausau area assembly seat lost by close to five thousand votes. But I knew that before the anti-Catholic backlash in 1960, the usual margin of defeat for a Democrat in that seat was between 1,200 and 1,800 votes, and I thought that with the right candidate and the right campaign, it was winnable.

When I made my pitch to Evans, he astounded me with his reply. "No, Dave," he said, "the assembly seat is small potatoes. I have bigger things in mind." "Like what?" I asked. "I'm going to be your next congressman. I'm going to run against Mel Laird." "You're crazy," I said. "Nobody can beat Mel Laird." "Oh yes I can," he said. "I have a plan." Then he lowered his chin, looked me in the eye, and said, "If you think running for the assembly is such a hot idea, you run." I said, "Are you kidding, nobody would elect a twenty-four-year-old college kid." Evans replied, "Well, I'm not going to, so if you want a candidate, do it yourself."

On the drive back to Madison, I rolled it over in my mind, still dubious. When I told Lucey about the meeting with Evans, he replied, "Hell, if he wants to run against Laird that's fine. He sure as hell can't win, but if he wants to be a sacrificial lamb, fine." Then I asked him what he honestly thought about my chances of winning. "Yes," he said, "it's tougher than hell, but with the right combination you could win. If you're interested, you ought to do it; you really have nothing to lose." Next, I went to Ralph Huitt. "I think you ought to do it," he said. "It's in your blood." I told him that I was thinking of serving a couple of terms and using my experience to write a thesis about state government, effectively changing my focus from Russian studies to domestic politics. Ralph Huitt's response was this: "You go down there and it's in your blood, you'll never come back to the UW. Don't let that deter you; that's always been your talent anyway. It's got you hooked. Go after it. You'll either get it out of your system or it will be your life—one of the two. What you do is announce, get your picture in the paper, and then don't be dumb enough to give any other press statements. Don't alert the opposition that you are a good candidate. Just sneak up on them. You just go door to door, house to house, shake as many hands as you can, don't put anything in the paper until after Labor Day. After Labor Day rev it up publicly. But until then, just work, work, work like termites in the wood."

Buoyed and surprised by what Huitt had said, I rolled it over in my mind for a week. I told Joan I wanted to do it, but I also understood that when she agreed to marry me she thought I was going to be a teacher, not a legislator, and if she didn't want me to do it, I wouldn't. She told me she didn't look forward to a political life, but if that is what I really wanted to do, it was okay with her. At the cliff and ready to jump, I broke the news to John Armstrong. I thought he might object, but he said that since the campaign would only eat up nine weeks of the school year, he thought I ought to get it out of my system. "Besides," he said, "there's a fifty-fifty chance you will lose, and you will then be more contented to hit the books." So I took the step that changed my life forever.

In May I wrote the news release announcing my candidacy. On June 9, 1962, Joan and I were married in St. James Church in Wausau. After spending the first two days at a cottage on Summit Lake near Antigo, we slowly made our way around Lake Superior to Thunder Bay, Canada. Concerned that my buddies might do something to my car as a joke on our wedding day, I parked it at Mark Vladek's Texaco Station and placed it in Mark's "protective custody." On the third day of our honeymoon, we pulled into a service station in Ashland to gas up. The attendant said to me, "Newlyweds, huh? Congratulations!" Surprised I asked, "Is it that obvious? How did you know?" "Let me show you something," he said walking to the back of the car. Taped to the lid of the gas tank was a note: "This couple has just been married. Congratulate them, but don't tell them how you knew." So Mark had protected the car, but he hadn't protected us from a practical joke. On our way back from Canada, we went through Minneapolis, where we saw billboards advertising Rep. Walter Judd, a well-known Republican congressman who focused on foreign affairs and who was being challenged by a promising young fellow named Don Fraser. I had no idea that within seven years I would be serving with Fraser in Congress.

First Campaign

After an eight-day honeymoon, Joan and I plunged into the campaign. We often went door to door together. On the legislative ticket with me in Marathon County were two incumbents, state senator Bob Dean and state assemblyman Ben Riehle, a dairy farmer who represented the county's rural assembly district. Only two courthouse candidates were Democratic incumbents: Herb Lambert, the county coroner, and Pat Crooks, the DA. I thought that the county fair afforded me the best opportunity to meet the most people over the shortest amount of time. The Republican Party had traditionally had a booth in the exhibition building, so I persuaded the Democrats to set up a booth outdoors on the midway just at the entrance to the park. I had six thousand blue campaign cards printed, and Joan and I passed them out each day from 11 a.m. until about 7 p.m. . By the last day every card was gone. I knew that had paid off in the weeks after the fair: I would go door to door and women would say to me, "Oh yes, I met you at the fair."

Joan and I were pretty much a two-person band in that campaign. The only campaign workers we had for any organizational help were my two high school buddies, Jim Backus and Dennis Shawl. The campaign also had important volunteer help from Bob Roy, a local podiatrist, and Mary Jo Brzezinski, whom I had dated in college.

Gaylord Nelson was running for Senate that year and attorney general John Reynolds was trying to move up to the governorship. Almost the only issue was taxes. Reynolds, with Pat Lucey as his main advisor, had repudiated Nelson's compromise tax agreement with the Republicans who, as the majority party, had forced Nelson to accept a partial sales tax. Reynolds campaigned on the slogan "Repeal the Republican Sales Tax." That caused a split in the Democratic Party between those who insisted on traditional Democratic anti–sales tax dogma and those who thought the compromise was a reasonable way to work out the differences between the parties in a divided government situation. The split was hard on Gaylord. The GOP was opposed to him on any account, and the sales tax dispute split his political base. And cynically, the same Republicans who had insisted on the new sales tax kept putting out press statements saying, "And Three Cents for Gaylord."

Bob Dean came to me and said, "Dave, you've got to come out against the sales tax compromise or you will lose." I told him I couldn't do that because I was already on record in support of Gaylord's compromise, and I wasn't going to walk away from Gaylord just to win an election. In my view, both politically and substantively, Bob was wrong: politically because promising to

repeal a bipartisan compromise sounded shrill, and substantively because repeal would force us to come up with that money from some other source—
and there wasn't one. So Bob and I went our separate ways on the issue.

Bob was in a tough race with Charlie Smith Jr., the son of a well-respected
lawyer and conservationist. In the last week of the campaign, Smith bought
$2,200 worth of advertising on Channel 7, the only TV station in town. That
may not sound like a lot today, but in those days, in a small start-up market,
it was significant. I had bought fourteen ten-second spots for $168. Bob had
not expected Smith to buy TV—no local candidate did in those days until I
did—and he became concerned about Smith's last-minute buy.

Channel 7 was owned by the Wausau newspaper and several other Wisconsin Valley papers—the heart of the Republican establishment. The news
anchor at Channel 7 was Walter John Chilsen, the son of the owner of the
Merrill paper. Because of complete GOP domination of news outlets, Democrats seldom cracked the news barriers in those days, except for WRIG radio.
Bob tried to buy a fourteen-spot package identical to mine, but the station
would not sell him a dime's worth of time. That was strictly against Federal
Communications Commission (FCC) rules at that time, but the local establishment wanted Dean defeated, and the station was willing to break the rules.
That infuriated me because TV stations were granted licenses by the government to use publicly owned airways for the common good. The station's action
was outrageous, and I never forgot it. It is one reason why, to this day, I remain
fiercely opposed to allowing media corporations to dominate any local market.

The night before the election, we had a large crew of volunteers fan out
across the city to distribute door hangers in the form of a coffee cup to every
household in the city of Wausau. They said, "Good morning! Today is election day. Be sure to vote" and were signed by me. Before that election no local
candidates had used election morning door hangers, and none had used political yard signs.

On election night, Joan and I gathered with other candidates at campaign
headquarters on Scott Street. By eleven o'clock, it became apparent that I
had won, but every other Democrat except for Crooks and Lambert was
going down, including Dean. I was delighted that I had won, but I recall that
my primary emotion was not happiness—it was embarrassment. Everyone at
headquarters was congratulating me, but I was reluctant to show joy while
so many others in the room were disappointed. And I knew Dean must have
felt worst of all because he had loved the job so much.

The phone rang at headquarters. It was Kay Dean, Bob's wife, with a message that Bob wanted me to come over to his house. When Joan and I walked

in, I didn't know what to say. There he was, the Senate minority leader, and he had lost, and I, a rookie, had won. Bob said, "Enjoy yourself down there. I will give you all the help I can." Then he said, "Kid, you ran a better campaign than I did. But remember tonight. In two years the big boys in this town will be gunning for you, just like they were after me tonight. They think that money owns this goddam town, and they think they own your seat and mine. Work with them, but don't turn your back."

I had won by 1,070 votes. My entire campaign had cost $1,160, $550 of it our own money—all the money we had in the world. We found out later that Paul Luedtke had been sitting on a friend's porch one hot August afternoon and had seen me knocking on doors across the street. "That poor young fellow," he said. "He doesn't understand. He doesn't have a chance." Sometimes I had thought the same thing, but we had kept working and it had paid off. At 6:15 a.m. Joan and I went to the Brokaw paper mill plant gate to thank workers for their help and finally fell into bed about 8 a.m.

About 9:30 I woke up to the sound of someone walking up the stairs to our second floor apartment. I answered the door and saw the smiling face of Claude Giles, an insurance salesman who had sung at our wedding. "You told me in June when I asked you about life insurance to wait to see if you were elected. You're elected, so here I am," he said. "You have to be kidding," I said. "For God's sake, we just got to bed. Give me time to catch my breath before I make a decision on something like insurance. Talk to me in a month," I said. "Right now, I'm going back to bed." But I didn't. I was too excited. After a short celebration at my dad's supper club, the Gaslight, I drove down to Madison and made arrangements with the university to cut short my fellowship. Ralph Huitt was as proud as if I had been his own son. Armstrong was all smiles and said, "Well, now you can help us with the university budget. Don't forget your old friends when the faculty salary issue comes around." That afternoon I tied up some loose ends at the university. The next morning, I walked down State Street to the capitol building to attend my first caucus—only a little more than four years after I had first stood next to Lincoln's statue at Bascom Hall, wondering if I would ever make it to the other end of State Street.

PART 2

~

THE OTHER END
OF STATE STREET

CHAPTER 3

Political Baptism

As I walked into my first caucus meeting in the state capitol building, the first question I confronted was this: Who would I vote for in the caucus leadership races? John Reynolds had infuriated the Republicans by winning an election nobody thought he could win. The GOP had been totally convinced that Phil Kuenn would return the governorship to its "rightful" GOP ownership. They unleashed incredible vitriol on Reynolds when he had upset their apple cart. They were about to make Reynolds pay for winning an election they had been confident was in their bag.

Democratic legislators knew the Republican majority would hammer Reynolds every day, and they were looking to beef up our front row leadership. In the state senate, with Bob Dean gone, Dick Zaborski of Milwaukee became leader. The assembly Democratic leader was Bob Huber. Bob was a high school graduate who had never gone to college, but I soon came to understand that he was as shrewd and smart as he was decent. Since the legislature was considered as part-time duty, most members had other jobs. Many served on county boards; many others were lawyers. Bob, who represented West Allis, a Milwaukee suburb, worked part-time for Schlitz Brewing setting up window displays when the legislature was not in session. Norm Anderson, an extremely able legislator from Madison, was the Democrat's lead legislative spokesman on conservation matters. I had known him since the 1960 campaign. When I called Norm shortly before the caucus he told me that there was some thought being given to challenging Huber because he was not liberal enough, but it quickly became apparent to me that Huber was in good shape. Frank Nikolay was challenging Bill Ward of St. Croix County for party whip. I voted for Frank, who won by one vote.

In those days the majority party had absolute power in the legislature.

Committee assignments were decided by the Speaker—not just for his own party, but for the minority party as well. I asked to be assigned to the Education Committee, but Speaker Bob Haase, who represented Marinette in northeast Wisconsin, appointed me to the Public Welfare Committee. What I learned on that committee that term would serve me well several years later when I was appointed to the commission that designed Wisconsin's first Medicaid program.

I was intrigued by one Republican leader—the majority leader, Paul Alfonsi. Alfonsi, who represented Iron, Oneida, and Vilas counties in the far north, was fiercely proud of being the first person of Corsican descent to serve in the legislature. He was strikingly handsome, with a dark complexion and wavy, silver-black hair. First elected to the assembly in 1932 as a twenty-four-year-old La Follette Progressive, he quickly rose to majority leader. He then lost a race for governor in 1940 and had been out of politics until he returned to the assembly as a Republican in 1958. His rise up the leadership ladder had been just as swift in his second stint in the assembly as it had been in the 1930s. My grandfather Walt had admired Alfonsi greatly, and I was anxious to meet him, but the way we met was not the way I had hoped.

In the 1962 election Earl Elfers, a Democrat, had won an excruciatingly close election in the Kenosha district against the incumbent Rusty Olsen. The Republicans moved inexorably to overturn the election. On election night Elfers had been declared the winner by a tiny margin. After two recounts his margin had shrunk. The county judge ordered a third count, and again Elfers's lead held. Then the Republican leadership appointed a select committee to review the results once more. Chairing the committee was my old friend, the GOP wunderkind, Bill Steiger. The committee threw out enough contested ballots to make Rusty Olson the winner. (Years later Steiger told me he was proud of virtually everything he had ever done in public life, but if there were one action in his career that he would like to have taken back, it would have been his involvement in the Elfers case.)

The day the assembly was scheduled to vote on whether Elfers would be ousted, Bob Huber called a caucus. If any newcomer to politics looked at Bob's personal résumé, it would have been easy to underestimate him—no education beyond high school, part-time job setting up beer window displays. He was a big, good-looking man of dignified bearing, jet black wavy hair, silver at the temples. He had an aura that signaled "This is a solid man."

I had already observed that Huber was good at listening, but on this day he wasn't in a listening mode. He was breathing fire. "All right, fellas," he said (there were no women in our ranks at the time):

This is the day they plan to steal the election. We can't stop them, but we have to make them pay a price for their abuse of power. This country was founded by people who said "Enough is enough." It has been defended by people who died to preserve the right of the people's will to rule. They aren't taking Earl's seat today because they have analyzed the voters' intent. They are taking it for only one reason—because they can. We can't stop them today, but I want there to be no doubt that every person in the caucus did everything possible to stop this coup. That means that I want every single person in the caucus to stand up and say No!—from the most senior veteran to the newest freshman. You all owe it to the institution in which you serve.

Bob was passionate, he was eloquent, and he was fierce. The caucus gave Bob a standing ovation, and we walked out of caucus ready to do battle.

My seat was in the back row on the Republican side of the chamber because there were more seats on the Republican side than on our side, and about eight Democrats sat in the back two rows on the GOP side. After several hours of debate I finally stood up, a knot in my stomach, my throat bone dry, to give my maiden speech. As I rose I glanced at Alfonsi, then at the Speaker, and I said:

Mr. Speaker, I had expected my first speech in this body to be a happy occasion, but it isn't. It is a sad day for this institution and this state. I am grateful about one thing—that my grandfather, Walt Chellis, is not around to see the action taken by the Republican leadership because one of my grandfather's heroes had been the Paul Alfonsi who had run for governor in 1940. I know he would not understand this action today because the Alfonsi he had campaigned for was a fighter for justice and fairness and the rule of law equally applied. I thank God that my grandfather did not live to see this day. His heart would have been broken by what his hero is doing today.

When I finished, Huber stood up and began clapping. So did the other Democrats. Alfonsi turned blood red. As the next speaker rose to comment, Alfonsi stormed back to my seat, waggled his finger at me, and hissed, "You cocky little son of a bitch, I know how you got elected; it was a goddam fluke. I'll be up in your district. I'll campaign against you from every street corner. I used to teach in that town. I'll see to it you never come back to this place." I was taken back by his vehemence, but I knew every eye in the place was on the two of us. I thought for a second about how to respond, then stuck out my hand and said, "Hello, Mr. Alfonsi, nice to meet you," and I smiled. Alfonsi's jaw dropped, he sputtered, turned, and strode back to his seat. When the vote to unseat Elfers passed, Elfers packed his briefcase, stood up, and said, "Gentlemen, I bid you leave!" saluted, and walked out the chamber doors. Huber then walked back to my seat and said, "Kid, nice speech. Why don't you move up and take Earl's seat. You can pick up a few pointers sitting next to Toby." So I picked up my things and slipped into the seat between Ray Tobias on my left and Joe Sweda on my right, and my legislative education had begun.

"Toby" was Ray Tobias, Huber's wiry sidekick from Milwaukee's south side. Bob and Toby usually went out to dinner with each other after each day's session, and many times over the next six years Joe Sweda and I joined them. I was delighted to be seated closer to the action—you could hear a lot better in the third row than in the back, but it was also an expensive move. Sweda smoked about twelve cigars a day and Toby was a chain smoker. Toby would take a drag on his cigarette and absentmindedly flick his ashes into his ashtray. But often he would miss. That first week, Toby burned a hole in my suit trousers. I only owned two suits and, making $3,600 a year, I couldn't afford to buy many. In one week, Toby had cut my wardrobe in half.

By June, Joan was pregnant, and we were looking for a small house we could buy in Wausau. My dad, who was doing some real estate work on the side, called me in Madison one day and said, "Dave, I am listing a house tomorrow. I sold it once before about three years ago. It's at 515 North Ninth Avenue. It has two bedrooms, a utility room, but no basement. It's very well taken care of. I know the house, and it will sell in a day. I think you should buy it." I talked to Joan. She withdrew $900 from her teacher's retirement, and we used that as the down payment on the $8,900 purchase price. We bought it sight unseen, and by June we were property owners with a kid on the way.

The week we moved in we saw four or five girls playing badminton in the street. We discovered that the oldest of what we thought was a collection of sisters was actually the mother—Win Spencer. She and her husband, Jack, were to become our closest neighborhood friends. It was the start of a long friendship. Six years later when I was elected to Congress, I would hire Win as office manager and scheduler in my district office. Win worked with me for almost thirty years until she retired. She would make thousands of friends for me because of her cheerful, perky, make-everybody-feel-good personality.

CHARACTERS, COLOR, AND CONTROVERSY

As Joan settled in to make our new home comfortable, I settled in to make my new job more understandable. In my first days in the legislature, as I got to know the players, I soon discovered that it was populated by a host of vivid characters—some dedicated and some rogues.

In the beginning days of any legislative session, very little legislation comes to the floor because committees have just been organized and have not yet reported bills. Typically, the assembly met for routine business for a few minutes and then adjourned for committee hearings. The editor of the *Capital Times* was Bill Evjue, an old-time Progressive who had been a fierce ally of Bob La Follette. He had strong opinions about everything, and he relished using the legislature as a foil. During the second week of the session, Evjue wrote an editorial attacking the assembly for being overpaid (we were paid $300 a month) because we had only "worked" an average of forty-four minutes that week—ignoring the hours we spent in committee (don't hold me to these exact times. I'm working from memory, but they are close).

Evjue's cheap shot was more than Gerry Flannigan, another old-time Milwaukee Progressive, could bear. During morning business, Flannigan, who was as acid-tongued as he was bright, growled into the microphone:

Mr. Speaker, yesterday I noted that the esteemed bloviator in the editorial office of the *Capital Times* has taken another of his habitual shots at this institution. He opined in an editorial yesterday that because the assembly had been in session for only thirty-seven minutes yesterday, that we had only worked for thirty-seven minutes and were therefore grossly overpaid. Well, Mr. Speaker, I counted the number of words in the editorial by that noodle-headed Norwegian on Carroll Street. And assuming that even the village idiot can type thirty words a minute, I have concluded that Mr. Evjue worked a grand total of twelve minutes yesterday. Understandably, his compensation is many times what ours is, but on the basis of my calculations, no matter how fast he types he is overpaid at any speed. For the benefit of public understanding I intend each day to post my estimates of Mr. Evjue's workday on the bulletin board in the assembly lobby.

The next week, most legislators attended the Wisconsin Rural Electric Association annual dinner at the Park Hotel. The main speaker was Drew Pearson, the hard-hitting, nationally known news columnist whose column was taken over in later years by Jack Anderson. Evjue was scheduled to introduce Pearson. Evjue strode to the podium, leaned into the microphone, put his hands above his eyes to shield them from the lights, scoured the crowd with his eyes, and growled, "Where the hell is Flannigan!" The two old warriors roared with delight. It was obvious both enjoyed the game.

Within a few months I began to room with Joe Sweda, a first-term, nattily dressed, cigar-smoking, Buick-addicted farmer from Lublin in western Taylor County. We each had a separate room and a shared bath at the Belmont Hotel. The Belmont had long since seen its best days. Most Democrats stayed at the Belmont because they charged only $5.50 a night, compared to the $7.50 at the Lorraine where most of the Republicans roomed. A $15-a-day expense allowance was stretched awfully thin and that $2-a-day difference in room rates was pretty big to us. Just down the hall from us roomed three of the most colorful men in the history of the legislature—all three from the northwest part of the state.

Bob Barabe, a French Catholic from Ashland County, on the south shore of Lake Superior, had teamed up with Bill Ward, an Irish Catholic from St. Croix County, and Harvey Dueholm, a Danish Lutheran farmer from Polk County. Four years earlier Barabe had been officially named the poet laureate of the Wisconsin legislature. He had once written a poem on a scrap of paper during the middle of a World War II battle in France; he was universally liked. Ward and Dueholm came from western Wisconsin counties that bordered eastern Minnesota. Ward was a man of strong opinions as was Harvey, but Ward expressed himself with thunderous lectures; Harvey made his point with rough-hewn humor. Harvey was probably the most feared debater on our side of the aisle because he could deflate the opposition with a line or a story, much the way my congressional colleague Barney Frank does today, only Harvey's humor was considerably more earthy.

In the previous legislative session, Ward had been Harvey's victim. At the end of the session, Gaylord Nelson had reached a tax compromise with the Republican legislative majority and swallowed a new partial sales tax as the price for Republican passage of the state budget. Gaylord visited the Democratic caucus to explain why he had had no choice and to ask for support. The Republicans were demanding that Nelson accept a new sales tax, but they wanted Democrats to shield them from criticism for the new tax by supplying half the votes—and Gaylord was shopping for Democratic votes.

When Nelson finished his pitch and Huber asked for a show of hands, Ward, who was party whip, did not raise his hand. Huber said, "What about you, Bill?" It was well known that Ward, coming from a border county, was reluctant to vote for a sales tax because businesses in his county didn't want to lose retail sales to Minnesota and were banging hard on Ward. Ward rose slowly, looked at the governor, and said, "Gaylord, I love you like a son, but when I go over to the Belmont Hotel at night, and I take my clothes off, and put my pajamas on, when I climb into bed, put my head on the pillow, and put my false teeth in that glass of salt water, my *conscience* won't let me vote for a sales tax!" The caucus groaned because they knew Bill's reluctance was not rooted in such high-mindedness. Then Dueholm stood up and asked the caucus chairman, Kenosha's George Molinaro, for recognition. "Mr. Chairman," Harvey began, "I have one suggestion for the gentleman from St. Croix. The next time you go over to the Belmont Hotel, take your clothes off, put your pajamas on, and crawl into bed, and put your head on that pillow . . . leave those false teeth in your head, put that *conscience* in the glass of salt water, and everybody will be better off." The caucus erupted in knowing laughter, and Gaylord won the day.

Dueholm, Ward, and Barabe loved to debate anything and everything, and would do so deep into the evening. Sweda and I would often be in our room late at night when a knock would come at the door, and Harvey standing in his pajamas would say, "Boys, come on over, I need your help. I'm knee-deep in Catholic blood." Sometimes the subject of the debate was religion, but often it was about political strategy for the bills coming up the next day.

Harvey was perhaps the funniest and most courageous man I served with during those days in the legislature. A retired farmer, first elected in 1958, he needed that sense of humor each and every day of his life because he fought a twenty-year battle with cancer and was often on chemotherapy. In one election, Harvey debated his opponent before a crowd of farmers (I believe it was at a local Rural Electric Association meeting). At one point his opponent said, "Look folks, everybody likes Harvey, but we all know he's sick, and you deserve somebody who will give you full time representation." The crowd gasped. Slowly, Harvey rose to his feet to respond. Harvey had a long, rugged, deeply lined face that often looked as sad as a basset hound on a bad day. Harvey rubbed his jaw. A melancholy look spread across his face. He rubbed his stomach, snapped his suspenders with his thumbs, and said, "It's true, I've got cancer. It could well be terminal. That bothers me a whole lot more than it bothers anybody else in this room. But you know that job in Madison is awfully important to you. It affects you and your kids in a lot of ways. I just ask one thing of you. When you go into that ballot booth to cast your ballot, just ask yourself one thing. Who would you rather have representing you, a guy you know is going to die . . . or a guy you wish would?" Everybody in the room split a seam laughing, and Harvey had vanquished another foe. If he could look the big C in the eye and laugh at life and death, he didn't need any help to handle a mere political opponent in the election.

One summer's day, Dueholm was engaged in a toe-to-toe floor debate on a bill out of the Agriculture Committee. He was being challenged by Gervase

Hephner, a young conservative Democrat from Calumet County. When the assembly recessed for a caucus, everybody strolled into the caucus room, and Hephner jumped all over Harvey. "Dammit, Harvey, you think you have all the answers when it comes to agriculture. Well, I've farmed long enough to have manure under my fingernails, too." When the floor debate resumed, Harvey gave a pitch for the bill being debated and triggered another Hephner retort. When Hephner finished his speech and sat down, Harvey rose to his feet and said, "Mr. Speaker, I don't blame the gentleman from Calumet for that outburst. I think I understand his problem. He's just been chewing his fingernails again." The Democratic side of the aisle roared, but the Republicans looked on in puzzlement. They had no idea what had been so funny because they hadn't been in our caucus. On another occasion the legislature was debating a mining bill, and Harvey had a strong difference of opinion with Tom Harnish, a southwestern Wisconsin legislator. Tom was a good, gutsy guy, but Harvey perceived him to be soft on mining-company regulation. Harvey and Tom were standing in the lobby just off the assembly floor, and Tom was complaining about a pain his knee. "It's your own damned fault," Harvey blurted. "Your knees would be in a hell of a lot better shape if you didn't put so much strain on them by continually genuflecting to the mining companies."

Nothing got under Harvey's skin more than politicians who covered themselves with false piety. Several legislators often got together at the Lorraine in a pick-up jazz band. Two members of that band, one male and one female, were sometimes the picture of piety and religiosity whenever subjects like teenage sex, family planning, or abortion were concerned, and Harvey often clashed with them on the floor. But on the nights they were playing, after a few drinks had been consumed, they would take a break from playing music and dance to a few jukebox tunes. On one such evening when Bob Huber walked in, Harvey was sitting at the bar. Harvey nodded his head in the direction of the two dancing legislators who seemed to be holding each other as close as the law allowed. "Hey, Bob," he whispered, "do you suppose they're thinking about *God?*"

Bob Barabe was no slouch at teasing people. He had a keen sense of humor that enabled him to get along with almost every major player on the Republican side of the aisle, but his style was much more droll than Harvey's and he loved to get under people's skin. Early in my first year, I saw Barabe perform political water torture on Alfonsi, one of the few people Bob did not like. Alfonsi was immensely able, but he had a reputation in some circles for being more cozy with certain lobbyists than he should have been.

Everyone knew that revenue in the form of forest crop payments to counties was one of Paul Alfonsi's top priorities: he represented several low-income

counties, which badly needed the state money. Even on a good day, Alfonsi
was wound up tight as a spring. He hated long drawn-out conflicts. He worried daily that something might happen to upset whatever apple cart he was
pulling. A month before the bill was called up to renew the forest crop payments, Barabe started playing Alfonsi's high-strung nature like a Stradivarius.
He started telling legislators in both parties, "You know, I was with Paul the
last time forest crop was up, but I've watched that program, I've watched the
way Alfonsi has been handling this, and I've got some information that's going
to blow the lid off the capitol. When I get through with him on the floor, I
don't see how anyone will be able to vote for that bill. Poor Paul, I don't want
to devastate him, but in the name of good government, I have no choice but
to reveal certain information to the House!"

Barabe's comments got around to everybody—just as he intended. A number of the Republicans went to Paul and asked him if he had done anything
on the bill that would make them look at all shoddy. Were there any hidden
provisions that would make them look bad or beholden to any lobby group?
Alfonsi went to Barabe and tiptoed around the issue, asking Bob if there was
anything Bob wanted to change in the bill. Bob said no, he just had a duty
to relay certain information to the assembly, and if Paul brought the bill to
the floor he would have to do it. Alfonsi delayed the bill for about two weeks,
and Barabe was clearly driving him nuts. Finally the bill was scheduled, and
at the appointed hour Alfonsi gave an impassioned speech asking for renewal
of the payments "to help the low tax base counties who live or die by these
payments." All during his speech Alfonsi's eyes kept darting over to Barabe.
He was visibly sweating.

When Alfonsi finished and sagged into his seat, for a few seconds no one
asked for recognition. The chamber went silent as everyone's eyes turned to
Barabe. Barabe slowly rose, pulled the mike from its holder, and asked for
recognition. "Mr. Speaker, as you know, last time this legislation was considered it had my full support. But in the meantime a piece of information has
come to my attention that forces me to change my mind. The last time around
the Bayfield County Board was for it. This time they passed a resolution
against it. And it's my duty to so inform the House that I will act accordingly."
With that he placed the mike back into the mike stand and slowly sat down.

For a few seconds no one moved or said a word. Then, those of us in the
front within easy earshot of Alfonsi heard him mutter under his breath, "Is
that it? For Christ sake, is that all there is?" Then Barabe broke out in a
slow, long-repressed grin, slapped his knee, licked his lips, and slowly started
to chuckle. Slowly, comprehension washed across the chamber. Bob had used

Alfonsi's own corner-cutting reputation and tightly wound personality to drive Paul to distraction. God knows what actions Paul thought Barabe might reveal, but Bob had Alfonsi going for weeks. It had been a month-long put-on.

The state senate also had its share of characters. One who stood out was "Packy" McFarland, the veteran Democratic caucus chairman, who had been a Golden Gloves Milwaukee boxing champion in his youth. Packy was of good heart, but every few months or so he would succumb to his liking for scotch in spectacular fashion. Dick Zaborski would tell the story about how Packy single-handedly held up the budget compromise one year. As usual, part of the deal for passing the budget was that both parties had to produce the votes from about half their caucus for the bill. Senate party leaders compared notes to be sure each party lived up to the bargain. But when the Senate vote came, Packy, who had been counted as a yes vote, allowed a bottle of scotch to change his mind. The roll was called by the clerk; when Packy who had been expected to vote "Aye" instead answered "Nay," the Republican floor leader sensed a double cross, and his troops voted to bring down the deal. Zaborski explained to the GOP leadership that he tried to sober Packy up with coffee, but Packy was "over the hill" and no power on earth was likely to bring him back in line. Finally the GOP leadership said, "Okay, if you can just get rid of Packy so he doesn't vote, that will be good enough." So Zaborski tried a different approach. He called Packy down to his office and offered him a scotch, then another, and yet another. Finally Packy said to Zaborski, "Dick, I got to take a leak." Zaborski said, "Here, Packy, use my facilities." Packy got up to accept Zaborski's offer, Dick opened the door to his closet, shoved Packy in, locked the door, and raced to the Senate floor. The question was put and the bill passed with Packy in absentia. All it had taken was a little planning and perhaps one wet closet floor.

Norm Sussman was a stocky, gruff but warm-hearted, blue collar state senator from Milwaukee who had only a passing familiarity with the King's English. The usual manner of addressing the chair in the assembly was to say, "Mr. Speaker," and Norm could never get used to the fact that in the Senate the presiding officer was addressed as "Mr. President." Norm was the kind of guy who was clearly more comfortable in a T-shirt than a suit. One day Norm was speaking on the Senate floor, and no one was paying particular attention. Several members were skimming through newspapers. Becoming more and more agitated, Norm finally blurted, "Mr. Speaker, we've got a problem in this chamber! We ain't got no decorum! I was in Canada last year visiting the Parliament and if there is one thing they got, they got decorum!" "What do you mean by decorum?" one member asked loudly enough to be heard by the gallery. "Well, for one thing," Norm said, "they dasn't turn their ass on the Speaker." The exchange did not move anyone to launch an effort to name Norm "Officer in Charge of Decorum." He was the all-time Wisconsin master of malapropism and mixed metaphors. One of his favorites, "Ah, that's a lot of water under the river." Another, "You can ride a horse, but you can't make him bark."

Sussman was an old-time, big-city politician to the core. One cold winter evening Governor Reynolds had given a speech in southside Milwaukee. As his chauffeur was driving through the dark neighborhood streets, he stopped at a stop light. The governor looked out the car window and saw a bulky figure crossing the street with his coat collar pulled up around his neck, carrying a small bucket of coal. "My God," Reynolds inquired of his staff assistant, "isn't that Norm Sussman?" Indeed it was. A constituent who had run out of coal on that cold winter night had called Sussman asking for help, and Norm had scurried to oblige.

The Senate also had its share of class acts. Zaborski was one. Another was Lynn Stalbaum from Racine. Stalbaum was the Senate Democrats' expert on taxes. He knew so much about the tax code that in later years he taught H&R Block trainees how to do tax returns. He was witty, decent, and thoughtful. Aldric Revell, a widely respected political reporter for the *Capital Times* with an H. L. Mencken personality, once wrote of Stalbaum, "Stalbaum is a first-rate legislator, but he has the maddening tendency to expect reason to dominate legislative debate."

Zaborski, Stalbaum, Sussman, McParland, Dueholm, Ward, Barabe, Flannigan, Alfonsi, Sweda, Nikolay, and Huber were just some of the personalities who made life in the legislature not just vivid and unpredictable but also interesting and enjoyable to go to work each day.

LEARNING THE ROPES

Three controversies kicked off my first session in the legislature. The first was the Republican Party leadership's hatred of John Reynolds and their determination to bring him down. They had expected to recapture the governorship with Phil Kuenn, the former GOP state chairman, and their sense of entitlement was shattered by Reynolds's upset victory. From day one it was apparent that the Republican leadership had bet the farm on their belief that John Reynolds—unlike Gaylord Nelson, who could charm any legislator or voter in the room—had a more reserved personality, and that they could bring him down if they could create enough turmoil. They also believed that Reynolds as governor was the most visible figure on the political landscape, and as such he would take the heat for whatever chaos they manufactured.

From the first day, the Republican leadership demeaned Reynolds to the press and did everything they could to perpetuate the split between the Nelson and Lucey/Reynolds factions of the Democratic Party. When Reynolds appointed Frank Zeidler, the former Socialist mayor of Milwaukee, as chief of industrial development, the GOP had a statewide heart attack. Zeidler was really more of a European-style social democrat, but even though he was highly regarded for the good, clean efficient government he had brought to Milwaukee, the word "socialist" drove the GOP up the wall and gave them a hammer to pound Reynolds with, every day of his tenure. Despite the fact that Zeidler was a brilliant public servant with a good relationship with the Milwaukee business community, the GOP leadership told the statewide business community that the fact that Reynolds appointed a *socialist* as head of business development clearly demonstrated that Reynolds was antibusiness. Milwaukee business leaders, who had worked with Zeidler in the past, knew better but for political reasons kept quiet, and the outstate, small-town business leadership—not knowing Zeidler—swallowed the line.

The second attack the GOP launched against Reynolds came on the mental health issue. Two years before, Gaylord Nelson had tried to civilize the state's system of mental institutions. His effort preceded the national movement for de-institutionalizing the mentally ill. Wisconsin had a sad network of county mental institutions and three state institutions. I personally knew how inadequate some of them were because I spent one summer installing floor covering in the Marathon County facility and witnessed firsthand the neglect experienced by some of the patients. Nelson met major GOP opposition in his efforts to increase funding in order to reduce overcrowding and strengthen staffing, and, in the end, had won only modest increases. Reynolds asked the Republican leadership, which dominated the state building commission, to approve more funding but was met with the same foot-dragging opposition encountered by Nelson. Because he knew he didn't have the votes to overcome the GOP majority on the commission, Reynolds appealed over their heads to the public: he invited the press on a tour of the state system so they could see and report the conditions for themselves.

At the outset Reynolds ran into spectacularly bad luck. On his first visit, he moved around the institution grounds and began talking with the patients. Reynolds went up to one of the first inmates he saw and struck up a conversation. The press gathered around and began to take notes and pictures. It was at that point that Reynolds's staff discovered the identity of the person

Reynolds had approached. It was Ed Gein, a notorious figure who had been institutionalized after it was discovered that he had killed and skinned several people and used their skin to make lampshades. Poor John! Instead of headlines being "Reynolds Exposes Conditions at Mental Institutions," the public was treated to front-page stories about Reynolds chatting with Gein—probably the worst media event experienced by a politician in the history of Wisconsin politics. The Republicans had a field day. One GOP legislator later told the press that the caption should have been, "Which One Is the Looney?"

But Reynolds slogged on with his tour, and soon the storyline changed to the miserably inhumane and overcrowded conditions witnessed by the press, and opinion on the issue began to turn. Reynolds told one reporter that legislative opposition to added funding was "heartless." That comment set off Curt McKay, the Republican whip. When the building commission met again after that statement, in full view of the press, McKay snarled at Reynolds, "Governor, I would like to reach across this table and punch you in the nose." Reynolds calmly stood up, leaned across the table, smiled gently and said, "Curt, if that will get more money for these poor souls, go ahead!" That exchange tipped the PR battle in Reynolds's favor in the eyes of most of the working press even as GOP foot-dragging continued. GOP resentment that Reynolds had been able to salvage the issue made them even more obstructive. In the end, Reynolds won only modest funding increases for the program, but without his effort virtually no added support would have been forthcoming.

But the issue that really dominated the session was the budget/tax fight. It was clear the Republican majority was determined to drag out the debate on the budget as long as they could so Reynolds would appear weak and ineffective. The Republicans controlled the assembly 54 to 46 and the Senate 19 to 14. Our party was still split on the sales tax, and Reynolds's public stand was being hurt. After months of delay, Republicans rammed a sales tax expansion through the legislature, and the governor faced the key moment of his governorship. He had campaigned on his intention to abolish the sales tax imposed by the GOP on Nelson in the previous session, but Reynolds had not brought a Democratic legislature majority into power with him and he had no way out. In those times, if no budget was passed by July 1, government stopped, payless paydays occurred, and the pressure was immense. Reynolds conferred with Huber, Nikolay, and a number of other Democratic leaders. I was included in the meetings at Huber's request. Reynolds decided to veto the bill, but the way he did it virtually killed him.

Reynolds's press secretary, Stan Williams, and his legal counsel, Len Zubrensky, and other top staffers worked out a veto message that ended with the statement to the Republicans: "You'll have to beat me to get a sales tax!" Huber went up the wall when he saw it. "Damn it," he told the governor's staff, "of course, you had to veto it, but the GOP will not give in; they control the legislature, and in the end you will have no choice but to take some of their sales tax demands. When you do, they will take that 'you'll have to beat me' statement and wrap it around your neck in TV ads and the blue collar boys on the southside and in every working class neighborhood in the state will think you caved. You raised the stakes rather than lowering them, and you will pay a terrible price." Within two weeks, Huber's concerns were borne out. The legislature passed a new compromise budget with added sales taxes, and Reynolds reluctantly signed it.

With the budget behind us, the legislature took a break until fall and the Republican message machine went to work. They quoted Reynolds's original veto message in every newspaper in the state. They said the governor was either a demagogue when he issued the statement or a wimp when he backed down. "Either way, he was a weak leader," they claimed. The next weeks were depressing. Reynolds's popularity sank out of sight. In September and October we returned to Madison for some clean-up work. After a final round-the-clock marathon, we wrapped up the fall session at about 5 a.m. on Friday, November 22. I had developed a bad cold and acute laryngitis, and was on complete vocal rest. I carried a tablet of paper around with me so I could communicate.

I got home to Wausau about ten in the morning with no sleep, had breakfast, and went to bed. Early afternoon, Joan shook me from my sleep and said, "Dave, something terrible has happened; the president has just been shot." I was still bone tired, fuzzy, groggy, and sick. I thought she was just trying to shake me out of my sleep. "That's not funny," I croaked. I rolled out of bed, went into the living room just in time to see Walter Cronkite take his glasses off and announce that President Kennedy had died. Anyone alive that weekend remembers how it was: the 24/7 news coverage, the throngs filing past the casket in the rotunda of the Capitol, the Kennedy family touching the casket and following the caisson down Pennsylvania Avenue to Arlington Cemetery, John John saluting. All I could remember was Nehru's comment about the death of Gandhi in India, "The light has gone out of our world."

The last months of 1963 were as shattering for the country as they were for us. But January 1964 brought great joy to Joan and me. Our first child, Craig David Obey, was born on January 27, Joan's birthday. I will never forget how exciting it was to rush Joan to St. Mary's Hospital on that cold January morning and to return home four days later with a new person in the house. Next to the day I married Joan, it was the most thrilling day of my life.

Our happiness at Craig's birth pushed our sadness at Kennedy's death into the background, as did the surprising actions of the nation's new president, Lyndon Johnson.

In the first months of his presidency, I was as amazed as the rest of the nation at how well Lyndon Johnson moved to fill the vacuum in people's hearts as well as their minds. He quickly demonstrated his understanding of everyday life symbols. Johnson was publicly struggling to keep his federal budget total from breaking through the $100 billion mark for the first time in American history. Stories hit the news about Lyndon personally flipping off light switches in the White House to save on the electric bill. Johnson's "Let Us Continue" speech to the Congress soon made it clear that Kennedy's death would not be the death of his agenda but its launching pad. Even as far away as Wausau, Wisconsin, it was obvious to me that LBJ was to be as much a happy surprise to progressive Democrats as Pope John XXIII's papacy had been to progressive Catholics. But the picture for the Wisconsin Democratic Party looked quite different.

A wounded John Reynolds, battling back from a disastrous fall and winter, had developed a three-pronged program in an attempt to seize the momentum back from the GOP. On the higher education front, he announced a proposal to provide tax credits to help families pay the cost of sending their kids to any college. He asked for volunteers as cosponsors, and I was happy to oblige. Next, he proposed a property tax credit for senior citizens to help retired people on fixed incomes stay in their homes. I cosponsored that legislation as well and was happy to see it win passage. The Senior Citizen Property Tax Credit was one of the first in the nation. It was later expanded to include tax-payers of all ages, and it remains a key element in Wisconsin's tax code today. The third initiative was a blockbuster. Reynolds proposed to raise the gas tax two cents a gallon and use that tax to underwrite a bonding program that would upgrade Wisconsin's highways 41, 51, 29, 53, and 2 from two- to four-lane status by 1966. Reynolds's program, Project '66, was stunning in its bold-ness. It was unheard of for a politician to propose a gas-tax increase going into an election, but Reynolds was gambling that frustration with traffic congestion and the business community's interest in the economic development impact of a modern transportation system would make it a winning package.

Paul Alfonsi was known to feel strongly that four-lane roads would be a boon to northern Wisconsin's tourist industry by putting all of Chicago within driving distance of the Northwoods' fifteen thousand lakes. Reynolds had sounded Alfonsi out before he unveiled the package, and his initial public comments were tentatively favorable. But the Republican Party establishment quickly brought Paul to heel. Many of them had never quite taken Alfonsi as one of their own because of his early Progressive history, and Paul was always eager to stamp out any conservative doubts about him that might block his rise to power in his newfound political home.

In those days candidates for governor and lieutenant governor ran separately, and Warren Knowles, a Republican, had been elected lieutenant governor in the same election that had elected Reynolds governor. The older of the two Knowles brothers, Warren was widely expected to be John Reynolds's challenger in the 1964 election. Alfonsi and other Republican leaders conferred with Knowles about how to handle Project '66. The powers in the GOP were in a near panic, fearing that Reynolds's plan had a lot of initial public support that might resurrect an otherwise shaky bid for reelection. They were determined to block Reynolds's plan at all costs, but they didn't quite know how to attack it. Knowles's solution was to place on the ballot, in a statewide referendum in April, the stand-alone question of raising the gas tax by two cents without an explicit tie to the construction plan. They then leaned on their big-money contributors to bankroll a TV ad campaign denouncing the gas tax hike. Reynolds was at a disadvantage because people were being asked to vote only on a tax increase with no specific linkage to highways that would be built with it.

From the moment Reynolds announced his plan, I had decided to be a strong advocate for both political and substantive reasons. Politically, because I believed people would respect a politician more for acting rather than temporizing, and substantively, because under Reynolds's legislation Wausau would become the transportation hub of northern Wisconsin. Under the plan, both Highway 51, which ran north and south up the middle of the state, and Highway 29, which was the main east–west transportation artery in central Wisconsin, would become four lanes, and they intersected in Wausau. I gave an interview on WRIG radio on the issue, saying that I knew the proposition would probably get beat, but that I intended to fight for it anyway, because it was good business for this community and because I was tired of seeing people die on Highway 29, one of the most accident-prone highways in the state.

That evening I got a call from Gordon Connor, president of Connor Land and Lumber Company. Connor was a skilled, shrewd businessman who happened to be Mel Laird's uncle. He was the husband of Mary Connor whose Ayn Rand–style speech before the Young Democrats years earlier had horrified me and had helped drive me out of the Republican Party. "Dave," he said, "I heard your interview on Project '66. I'm with you all the way. These damn

Republicans are putting politics before the welfare of the businesses they say they are for. This plan would be wonderful for Marathon County; it certainly would improve my ability to do business and that's true of every other major business in northern Wisconsin. We got left out by the interstate system, and this would help us catch up," he said. "Why don't we go on the road together? With you as a Democrat and me as a Republican, we are opposites enough to draw attention, and we might be able to cut through the nonsense. The Taxpayers League and the Rotary Club would be good places to start if you are willing." I thought that was a great idea. I had always liked Gordon because, while we disagreed, he was as blunt and honest as a man could be, and he was driven by what worked, not by what was easy. So we teamed up. I gave forty-one speeches in twenty-eight days for the proposition, many of them at joint appearances with Gordon.

Despite our efforts, when the April election came we were swamped. The trucking industry, which initially had been for Reynolds's plan, was persuaded to abandon it by Alfonsi, who was a close friend of John Varda, their chief lobbyist. Both were from Iron County. The ads they and their allies bought buried us. Statewide we lost 7 to 1. Gordon and I counted it a moral victory that we only lost Marathon County 4 to 1. Thirty-six years later, in August 2000, I would sit on the platform of a flatbed truck with Governor Tommy Thompson and other dignitaries as we cut the ribbon finally completing the new four-lane Highway 29 from Green Bay in the east to Chippewa Falls in the west. On that day, I thought of Gordon Connor, the old Republican warhorse, and the campaign we had waged. If that referendum had passed in 1964, Highway 29 would have been a four-lane reality by 1966. Instead, because of partisanship, it took more than three decades to get the job done.

First Run for Reelection

With the swamping of Project '66 at the ballot box, I went into the 1964 election worried that the campaign for Reynolds's project would be an albatross around my neck, but it would wind up not being any factor at all. In spite of the two-year pounding that John Reynolds had taken, the 1964 election was shaping up as a pretty good one for other Democrats, not just in Wisconsin but nationally as well. The question for me was how to capitalize on the trend and how we could use it to build party strength in Marathon County. Pat Crooks was retiring as district attorney, so we had to hold that seat with Dan LaRocque, Pat's assistant. Herb Lambert, the county coroner, had died and had been succeeded by Bill O'Connor of Mosinee. That meant that every single candidate except Ben Riehle and me would be new to the ballot. Where would we find strong candidates to take advantage of the national trend?

People tend to think that everything in politics is planned, but sometimes things just happen. Right after the April referendum, Norm Zietlow, the Wausau police chief, asked to see me. I went over to his office in city hall, and he said to me, "Dave, let me cut right to it, I think 1964 is going to be a good year for Democrats. I want to retire from this job and run for clerk of court on the Democratic ticket. Will you help me?" "Manna from heaven!" I thought. Norm was well liked in the community, but I had no idea he was ever intending to run for office. "I'm at retirement time in this job, but I can do good work as court clerk. I know the job, and I think I can win," he said. "I think you can, too, Norm. If you are in it, I'm for you," I told him. I was delighted. By accident we had a great candidate.

The key to the county courthouse, however, was the county clerk's job, which had been occupied for years by Lucille Zuelsdorf, a Republican. Pat Crooks had been working on Ray Ott, a well-known leader in the National Guard, to run for the job. One phone call and one nose-to-nose meeting with Ray, and we had the key candidate. That same day we got word that Howie Gernetzke had been at the courthouse taking out nomination papers. Howie had been the weatherman at Channel 7 for years. We had no idea what office Howie was running for or what ticket he was running on. Then we found out that it wasn't Howie but his brother, Bob, who had taken out papers for county clerk. "Great," I thought, "for twenty years we couldn't get a winning candidate for that job, and now we are going to be divided by a primary."

I knew Bob. He had been president of the student body at the technical school the same year I was student body president at the UW Center. He was a terrific guy with a great name because of his brother's TV presence, but the Democratic Party was not so prosperous it could afford to waste good candidates in a primary when we had other spots on the ticket to fill. Bob ran a well-respected neighborhood tavern on North Sixth Street, so Jerry Madison, Pat Crooks, Dan LaRocque, and I paid a visit to see if we could persuade him to change his target to the office of register of deeds. We told Bobby we wanted him on the ticket, but we were committed to Ott because we recruited him to run and we had no idea Bob was interested.

Bobby didn't like the message. "You guys are trying to push me around," he said. "We're not trying to push you around, we want you on the ticket," we said, "but we owe it to you to let you know about some things you may not have known when you started out." In the end Bob decided to readjust his sights. That decision gave us an imposing slate of candidates and led to a twenty-year stint in both the register of deeds and clerk's offices for Bob and Ray.

The only slot still open was for sheriff—and that was huge. Hank "Heinie" Gatesman had been chief of the county highway patrol, and Louie Gianoli had been the sheriff. A year earlier the county board had merged the patrol with the sheriff's department with the understanding that Heinie would be designated the chief deputy to whoever was sheriff. Hank did not like the idea at all, so he decided to run for the top job of sheriff on the Democratic ticket, and we had ourselves a powerful slate. Sheriffs were limited to two terms in those days, so Louie Gianoli, the incumbent, was going to be out of a job. (The practice in those days was for a sheriff to serve four years, be succeeded by his deputy or his wife, and then after four years rotate again into the office.)

Bud Wolf, Gianoli's chief deputy, was the GOP candidate to succeed Louie. Throughout the year we had assumed that Gianoli would rotate back to become chief deputy with Bud running for sheriff. But the sheriff/traffic patrol merger blocked him from doing that, so Louie surprised us by announcing he was running against me for the state assembly. When I saw the announcement I was worried. Louie and I were friends—in fact, we were both inducted into the Wausau Optimist Club the same day (both recruited by Pat Crooks), and he was the best vote-getter in the history of the county. I knew I would have to work hard.

I campaigned by hitting a plant gate at 6:15 a.m. to greet workers on the way to work. Afterwards I went home, drafted whatever press releases I needed to get out, or handled other campaign chores. After ten o'clock, I went door-to-door or appeared at neighborhood coffee hours. After seven o'clock, I went to the Labor Temple and talked to whatever local union meetings were occurring that night. Usually two or three unions met every night, Monday through Thursday, and in a month I could hit more than forty locals.

The Democratic Party would also hold rallies all around the county in late September and October—usually two or three times a week. We alternated between meeting in Wausau and meeting in the rural part of the county. Bill O'Connor, the coroner, always passed the hat to collect enough to pay for beer, sandwiches, and wildcat (raw hamburger, to the uninitiated). Each of the county candidates would speak for about five minutes. Gernetzke was low key and shy. He would simply say, "Hi folks, I'm Bob Gernetzke, the other Gernetzke (referring to his better known brother Howie, the TV weatherman). I don't have much to say. You don't have to give many speeches in the register of deeds office. Hope you will help me. Thank you." End of speech.

Marv Nellis, who later became coroner himself when Bill O'Connor died, was then news director of WRIG radio. He faithfully attended party meetings and reported them on the radio the next day. I remember the first speech Dan LaRocque gave at Ringle. I was worried whether Dan could hold Pat's DA spot with an unfamiliar, hard-to-pronounce French name running in a heavily German county. At the end of the meeting, Dan stood up and said to the crowd, "I have something I have to get off my chest. I know a lot of people think I can't win—a tough French name in a German county. Pat Crooks has been a household word, and I'm a nobody with a funny name that nobody can pronounce. Well," he said, "I'm going to surprise you. I'm a good lawyer, and I've done a whole lot of studying. You know we've got a law library in the DA's office, and it's got a lot of books." Marv Nellis was taking copious notes and running his tape recorder as he always did. "Well," said Dan, "I've been digging into those books, and I've discovered there's rampant discrimination in Marathon County." Marv kept writing. "I've discovered," Dan said, "that the dog tax for males in this county is $1, but the dog tax for females is $1.50, and if I were you women I would be up on my hind legs raising hell on this one," Dan thundered. Marv kept writing. "I want you to know I will make this a huge issue in the campaign, and I will never give up, never give up, until I have righted this grievous wrong," Dan said, pounding the table for emphasis. Marv's jaw dropped as he looked up in awakening disbelief. He stopped writing as he slowly realized that he had been had by Dan's droll sense of humor. An amused chuckle rippled through the room as the gathered farmers realized that Dan was pulling their legs. "I just thought this shindig needed livening up," Dan said. That was the first time I really thought Dan just might win.

In 1964 Ben Riehle, who represented the rural assembly district in Marathon County, was opposed by Loddie Loskot—another farmer from the western end of the county. The last week before the election we organized a literature drop throughout Wausau and the bigger communities in Riehle's district. A large crew of volunteers came over to my house, and we sent them on their way with maps and packets of literature. In those days national newscasts took fifteen minutes and the local station followed with fifteen minutes of news, weather, and sports. The week before the election, Channel 7 contacted me, Ben, and our two opponents to say that they would give each of us a block of five minutes to make an on-camera live presentation of our cases during the last week of the campaign.

We had just sent the volunteers on their rounds as the local news was ending at 6:25. Ben and I watched as my opponent, Louie Gianoli, the term-limited sheriff, began to make his pitch. Louie was a great raconteur with small groups of people, but as he sat before the camera in the TV studio, it was obvious that he was scared stiff. Sweating profusely, he gripped his script with both hands and read it, occasionally looking up into the camera and wiping his brow. Whoever had written his script had filled it with four-dollar words that Louie had just recently become acquainted with, and it showed. I felt sorry for Louie, but I was happy he was not making a good impression. But Ben's reaction was very different. His populist soul was getting angry. "That's outrageous," Ben kept muttering, "he's saying stuff that somebody else wrote. He should say what he thinks, not what somebody else writes."

The next evening it was Ben's turn. At 6:25 he came onto the screen. On cue, Ben looked into the camera and talked about the problems of farmers, education, and the dangers of DDT (he was way ahead of his time in warning about the effects of pesticides on wildlife and on the food supply). He chastised farmers for using "that junk," as he called DDT. In closing, he leaned forward, looked the camera right in the eye, and said, "And I want you folks to know I wrote this myself. I didn't have some slicker write it for me." He then stuck out his chin, grinned from ear to ear, showing his missing teeth, and he was done. It was a wonderful, straight from the gut performance. It was also the first time Ben had ever been on TV. At the party meeting in the town of Stettin that night at Gesicki's tavern, I congratulated Ben on his performance and told him I thought he had been terribly relaxed for someone who was on TV for the first time. "Why shouldn't I be relaxed," he replied, "I was just telling them the truth."

Election night was wonderful. LBJ headed the 1964 ticket, and he won in a landslide. Up and down the ticket, Democrats won. We even took control of the assembly 53 to 47. Everybody won except John Reynolds, the governor, who went down to defeat. John had run a powerful five-minute TV spot that brought a lot of voters back to his corner in the closing days of the campaign, but his flip-flop on the sales tax veto was too much for him to overcome. Warren Knowles, the silver-haired former state senator and lieutenant governor, eked out a 19,000-vote victory out of the 1,700,000 votes that were cast. Poor John became the only sitting Democratic governor in the nation to lose in the 1964 Democratic landslide. For me, it was another lesson learned. For two solid years the Republican leadership had pounded Reynolds at every turn. They had obstructed every initiative they could get away with. They promoted constant turmoil and tore John down in every possible way. They gambled that because the governor was the focus of attention, he would get the blame for the chaos they engineered—and they had guessed right.

The election was a big deal for Wisconsin Democrats: for only the second time since the early 1930s, Democrats had won control of the state assembly. In 1949 the state senate makeup had been twenty-seven Republicans to three Democrats (with three vacancies), and the assembly had been seventy-four Republicans to twenty-six Democrats. From those depths we had come a long way in sixteen years. At last Wisconsin was a true two-party state. After almost twenty years of GOP reign, we had held the governorship from 1958 to 1964, had won both U.S. Senate seats (in 1957 and 1962), and had finally broken through in the assembly. We knew it would be tough to hang on in 1966, but we were, at last, a two-party state in both gubernatorial and legislative elections.

༈

CHAPTER 4

Learning State Government

1964 was also a big deal for me. Bob Huber had promised me that if we took control, I would chair the Education Committee, but when I called Bob to revel in our good fortune, he threw a monkey wrench in my plans. I had been thinking about changes I would like to see in education, but Bob had other ideas.

"Davey," he said, "I don't think I can give you Education. I need you to be vice chairman of Joint Finance." The Joint Finance Committee was a joint assembly–senate committee with sweeping jurisdiction over all revenue and all spending. No spending that had been initially authorized by the legislature could actually take place until it was appropriated by the committee. Huber explained that George Molinaro—as the senior Democrat in the caucus and past Democratic leader—had to be the assembly cochairman of Finance. "But George is past his prime; he will focus more on local aspects of the budget as they affect his district," Bob said. "I need you to be my organizer, my planner, my staffer, and my strategist on the committee. I need you to look over George's shoulder and let me know every time he's missing an opportunity to make our case, and I need you to keep our team focused on the big picture. You won't have the chairmanship, but you will be the person I use to guide the committee where it needs to go. George will be happy to let you do the Jimmy Higgins work. He doesn't want to work that hard anymore."

I protested that I knew education but was no expert on taxes or the budget, but Bob cut me off and said, "You're young, you will grow. By the time you bring the budget to the floor you will know it better than anybody else except Pommerening, and that's good enough for me." Bob was referring to Glen Pommerening, a Republican from the Milwaukee suburbs who was recognized by both parties as the man who knew Wisconsin's tax code backwards

and forwards—much as Wilbur Mills was recognized for his mastery of federal tax matters. Bob didn't have to convince me; he had the authority. The
Speaker controlled all committee assignments, so I accepted his decision and
never regretted it for a moment. I threw myself into the work and learned an
immense amount about state and local government—and about every other
subject under the sun.

The only staff available to the legislature was provided by legislative support
agencies. The Legislative Reference Service supplied bipartisan bill-drafting
help to all members. It was headed by H. Rupert Theobold, who had immi-
grated to the United States after his years as a conscript in the German army
during World War II. Rupert was the classic civil servant. He was totally
trusted to keep confidences and to stay out of politics. In addition to drafting
bills, the agency often prepared research papers on various issues before the
legislature, and these papers were invaluable to members who took the time
to read them.

The other legislative service agency was the Legislative Council. The legislature often created interim study committees composed of legislators and
outside experts who, during legislative recesses, would do long-term analyses
of subjects that were expected to be considered in future legislative sessions.
In my first years in the assembly, the council was headed by Earl Sachse, a
scholarly figure who was never seen wearing anything but a three-piece suit
with a Phi Beta Kappa key prominently displayed on the pocket watch chain
that crossed his vest.

I quickly learned to rely on his deputy, Bonnie Reese. On countless occasions, when I had questions about various issues before the legislature, she
would put me in contact with people buried in agencies who could tell me
what I needed to know. I came to depend upon her more than anyone else
in the capitol, and we developed a long friendship that lasted far beyond my
years in the assembly until she died, far too young, of cancer.

The other key person I consulted on an almost daily basis was Dale Catte-
nach. Under the influence of Bob Knowles, who was an active leader of the
National Conference of State Legislative Leaders—an organization chaired
in those days by California assembly speaker Jesse Unruh—the legislature was
just beginning to avail itself of more professional help. The Legislative Fiscal
Bureau was created to give the legislature the capacity to develop budget information independent of the executive branch—as would the Congressional
Budget Office, which, years later, was created to do the same thing for the
U.S. Congress. In my work on Joint Finance, I learned quickly that no one had
better budget and policy information than Dale did. With the help of Bonnie

and Dale and the people they knew, I learned more things more quickly, and I began to think that, with their help, I might occasionally even know what I was talking about.

I enjoyed that 1965 session more than any period in my career—before or since. Divided government can produce gridlock, but in this case it didn't. We experienced plenty of disagreements, and we worked overtime to define our differences with the Republicans on taxes, education, transportation, and conservation; but after we had done that we also found ways to reconcile those differences in order to do some great things. And sometimes we discovered we really didn't disagree at all.

Our biggest accomplishment was transforming Wisconsin's Vocational Education system. Prior to 1965 Wisconsin had a series of old-fashioned, financially starved vocational schools scattered around the state, and they were housed in outmoded buildings equipped with outdated technology and supported by inadequate financing. A coalition of Republicans and Democrats in the assembly working with Wayne McGown, the governor's budget chief, began to put together a plan to upgrade the system.

George Molinaro, Frank Nikolay, and I were concerned that the blueprint for the new system being developed could wind up duplicating the University of Wisconsin's network of two-year liberal arts branch campus institutions, which were focused primarily on college-level academic courses rather than job-oriented training. The three of us went to Ray Heinzen, an open-minded Republican moderate from Marshfield, and told him of our concerns. We also talked to Bill Steiger and to Dave Martin (a GOP conservative from Neenah), both of whom were sponsors of the original bill. We finally agreed on a modified plan that would establish a series of geographical districts for each school, with guaranteed financing by 1.5 mills on the property tax, a statewide Voc Ed board, and a local board for each institution, with representatives from both employers and labor to keep a job market focus on course offerings.

At the time we knew that there were more students enrolled in job-oriented courses in the Wausau Vocational School alone than in the entire community college system in Illinois. Illinois and many other states were focused on making their system a feeder system for colleges, and we did not want to go that way. If students were determined to go on to a four-year college degree, that was fine, but we wanted the focus at the technical schools to be on job training for real jobs that existed in local job markets. We did not want the result of our efforts to be a system of watered down liberal arts programs. The six of us—Steiger, Martin, and Heinzen on the GOP side, and Molinaro, Nikolay, and me on the Democratic side—rounded up the votes and pushed the reform through. When Knowles signed the bill, we all felt we had been part of an effort that would be big and lasting. We had really accomplished something, and we made friendships across the aisle that would last a lifetime.

We also collaborated on restructuring the university system; we passed legislation that created a Coordinating Committee on Higher Education bringing greater coordination between the University of Wisconsin (which then consisted of the UW–Madison campus and its numerous two-year branch campuses around the state) and the separate system of four-year state colleges in communities like Platteville, Superior, Stevens Point, River Falls, Eau Claire, and so on—institutions that had grown out of the old teacher's colleges established two generations earlier. And we had many a battle outside the education arena.

That '65 session was amazingly productive. In addition to the sweeping education changes, we also passed an expansion of the state land acquisition program, which continued the pioneering legislation Gaylord Nelson had originated in 1960. But the state budget fight was as contentious as ever.

After months of debate, we finally put together a compromise. The way we finally reached agreement was a textbook illustration of legislative give-and-take, but it wouldn't look good in a political science textbook. We were supposed to have the budget passed by the end of June, but the hot days of summer came without any progress. At least one night a week, Huber, Tobias, Sweda, and I had dinner at Burke's (now Mariner's Inn). After dinner, we would have coffee and a B&B, and then go back to Capitol Square to see what the rumbles were in other political hangouts.

One hot evening, budget talks were not going well, and we four went to Burke's to map out some strategy for the coming week. As we were finishing dinner, Dottie Effinger, a lobbyist for the banking industry, came over to our table and told Bob she had a message from Bob Haase, the Republican leader. What she brought was an outline of a budget compromise that Haase wanted us to explore. We turned over our placemats and began sketching out some possible changes, with Ray Tobias using a slide rule to help calculate the cost of different actions. After about thirty minutes, Bob took a fresh placemat and laid out the outline of our counteroffer, and Dottie took it back to Haase. An hour later Haase called and suggested that with two or three changes we could put together a deal. By morning we had an agreement. The question then became how to manage it publicly.

We agreed that at the meeting of the budget conference committee the next day, Frank Nikolay would first offer a plan reflecting our first preferences, which the Republicans would reject. Next, Glen Pommerening or Gerry

Leonard would put the GOP's preferred counteroffer on the table, which we would reject. Then, with both parties on record with their preferred solutions, Nikolay would offer the deal that we had worked out with Haase the night before. Before the meeting, Huber, Nikolay, and I had a quick caucus with other Democratic conferees and filled them in on the deal. Frank followed the script by making the first offer, which the GOP rejected as planned—but then a hitch developed.

Bill Hanson was a new state senator from Stevens Point. Before coming to the senate, he had been president of the Stevens Point College, as it was then called. He was also Bob Dean's father-in-law. When Pommerening made his counteroffer and the roll was called, Bill got his signals crossed and voted "Aye." A startled and confused Pommerening blurted out loudly, "No, Bill," which instantly tipped off the press that the fix was in. I whispered to Bill, and with great chagrin, he changed his vote. Back on track, the deal was tied down, and we finally went home with a budget.

PROJECT '66 REVISITED

One other issue also dominated the legislative session. In the previous session the Republicans had torpedoed John Reynolds's Project '66 highway construction plan. But a year later, Warren Knowles, now seated in Reynolds's chair in the East Wing, resurrected the idea. He proposed that the state issue bonds to build many of the same highways up to four-lane standards but with a critical and irresponsible difference. Unlike Reynolds's plan, it did not raise the revenue needed to pay off the bonds. That meant Knowles wanted to get credit for the new roads but stick his successor with the necessity to raise taxes to pay for them. I had told Knowles that I was willing to sponsor a bill that didn't put the cost of construction plans on the cuff, but when Knowles decided to eliminate the financing and delay construction of several northern routes, I balked. To me it was irresponsible to be *for* the roads but *against* paying for them, and I announced that I would oppose them all until they were paid for.

When the legislature reconvened in October, the GOP leadership presented to Joint Finance a scaled-back bill that would run out of dollars before the northern roads like Highways 51, 29, or 53 were built—effectively accelerating construction of only the interstate routes in the southern part of the state. When the dollars ran out, I didn't believe the metropolitan areas would vote to raise a gasoline tax just to build roads up north because roads in the south would already have been upgraded, so I worked with Huber to scuttle the governor's plan, and we killed it in committee, 9 to 3. The plan would later be resurrected, but before that happened we faced other challenges.

A year earlier, on August 7, 1964, Lyndon Johnson had asked Congress to pass the Gulf of Tonkin resolution endorsing whatever action the president deemed necessary in response to an alleged North Vietnamese attack on American naval forces. Two days later Congress whooped it through unanimously in the House with only two dissenting votes—those of Ernest Gruening of Alaska and Wayne Morse of Oregon—in the Senate. When Johnson sent the resolution to Capitol Hill, Gaylord Nelson told William Fulbright—the distinguished, thoughtful chairman of the Foreign Relations Committee—that he was going to offer an amendment making clear that the resolution could not be used as a justification for introducing ground troops into Vietnam. Fulbright came back to Nelson and told him there would be no need for the amendment because Johnson had given Fulbright his "personal assurances" that the resolution would not be used for that purpose. Gaylord was dubious, but Fulbright convinced him that he was satisfied with Johnson's assurances and would not want to see Gaylord offer it: if defeated, the failed amendment would have the opposite of its intended effect, by putting the Congress on record against any such limitation. Gaylord withheld the amendment. In a few weeks, however, it became apparent that Johnson was using the resolution exactly as Gaylord had feared and within months he had voted against the first appropriation for the war.

Against that background, Nelson came to Wausau in October 1965 for a fundraiser on my behalf. Before the dinner, he and I went to Channel 7 in Wausau for an interview. When the newsman asked Gaylord about Vietnam, he looked into the camera and said that America was on the threshold of a terrible mistake and that if it did not change course, "we will end up with 500,000 troops in Vietnam." The interviewer raised his hand and said "stop the camera." He then said to Gaylord, "Senator, pardon me but I think you misspoke. You said we would have 500,000 troops in Vietnam." Gaylord replied, "That's right." The announcer raised his eyebrow and said, "Well, okay, it's your funeral," and resumed the interview. When we walked out of the studio Gaylord said to me, "Well, I may have just beat myself, but that's what I honestly believe."

In 1965 the Congress had also dealt with landmark Medicare legislation at the federal level, and the state had to take action implementing some of its provisions in Wisconsin. In January of 1966 I was appointed by the governor to a bipartisan commission to draft the necessary implementing legislation. Under the guidance of Wilbur Schmitt, the head of the Social Service Department, we put together a package that defined levels of state support for low income people who could receive health coverage under Medicaid and SSI. It was my first heavy involvement in the issue of financing health care coverage for people who couldn't afford it.

SCANDAL

In early 1966 I traveled to River Falls State University to appear on a panel with the Republican whip, Dave Martin, to discuss education funding. During dinner a teacher came up to Martin and me and asked, "What's this in Madison today about a grand jury investigation into illegal lobbying?" I had no idea what he was talking about, but as I was driving home to Wausau after our panel a radio news broadcast said that Bronson La Follette, the Democratic attorney general, had announced that a grand jury had been impaneled to investigate rumors of illegal lobbying. I was flabbergasted. As I would see many times in later life, once investigations started they seemed never to end.

For the next few weeks, all anyone was talking about in Madison was the lobbying probe. Wisconsin had extremely strict lobbying laws. No legislator could receive anything except a duly reported and disclosed campaign contribution from a lobbyist or a client of a lobbyist—not even a cup of coffee. Rumors were flying all over town. Some leaks began to appear in the press suggesting that the investigation was focusing on the passage of branch banking legislation and the highway legislation that Alfonsi and I had fought over the year before. Rumors quickened when it became known that Dottie Effinger, who had lobbied for Howard Meister, a Milwaukee banker interested in branch banking, had been called by the panel. Then several subpoenas for state legislators were issued.

On Friday, April 2, I had just come home from Madison when the phone rang. It was Bronson La Follette, grandson of old Bob and son of young Bob. "Dave, I have to tell you something you won't like. Leroy Dalton wants you to appear before the grand jury next week." Dalton was the deputy attorney general handling the lobbying investigation. "He'll be calling you within the hour," Bronson said. "Why?" I asked. "We know you received a check from Tony Wise last year," La Follette said. "Do you also know I sent it back," I said. "Yes, I do", he replied. "You are not a target in any way, but we need to understand the circumstances, and how it ties into a check Alfonsi got. We'll be talking to you."

La Follette was referring to a call I had received the previous fall when I had been blocking Knowles's highway bill. When I answered the phone, the voice on the other end said, "Obey, this is Tony Wise." A veteran of an army alpine unit and a skiing enthusiast, he had built a resort at Mount Telemark, near Cable in northwest Wisconsin. I had never met him, but I certainly knew of his reputation as a hard-driving promoter of tourism in that area of the state.

"Obey, I know you've been opposing Knowles's highway bill, but we really want it up here," he said. "I'd like you to come up to a meeting of the Highway 53 association. We want to have a chance to convince you to change your mind. Maybe you and Alfonsi could debate. I've already put a fifty dollar check in the mail for you to cover your expenses." "Look," I replied, "it would be a waste of my time and yours for me to do that. You can't change my mind, and I'm sure I can't change yours. I don't need to go all the way to Hayward to tell you that. I'm not going to take your money. I'll send the check back."

Wise continued to press, but I held fast and ended the conversation. When Wise's check arrived I sent it back with a note that said, "Thank you, but I don't think this would be wise for you or me." I heard nothing more from Wise and had forgotten about it until La Follette's call.

A few minutes after the call from La Follette, the phone rang again and assistant attorney general Leroy Dalton was on the line. He told me he was calling me and several other legislators to testify about lobbying on the highway bill. I told him about the call from Wise and asked if he understood that I had sent the check back. "I know you did, but Alfonsi and Hutnik didn't, and we want to know what *you* know about why they didn't," Dalton said.

"Look," I said, "I don't know anything about what they did on the highway bill. You already know that. If I testify, you will know nothing more than you do now. You won't be affected one way or another, but I will. You know, and I know, that the way the press covers this issue they will make it look like anybody who testifies is guilty of something. I don't see why I should have to go through that just to tell you I know nothing about what you're looking into." "Well," Dalton said, "we need you to testify, and we have to call you."

I asked Dalton who else knew I would be testifying and when the press would know. I told him I didn't want my relatives to read about it before I could tell them what it was all about. "Absolutely no one will know until you walk into the grand jury room on Monday," he said. And then he added, "But you can't tell anyone about it either. You can't discuss your testimony with anyone before or after you are in with the jury. It's secret." "You mean I can't tell my family so they won't worry?" I asked. "No, you can't," Dalton said.

The response angered me because I knew all kinds of stories were being written about what was happening in the grand jury. About an hour after

Dalton's call, I got a call from someone in the family telling me that they just heard on the radio that I would be subpoenaed to testify. I was angry and shocked. Dalton had just told me that no one would know until I walked into the grand jury room. I told Joan, "If the blasted prosecutor is going to lie to me and hang me out with lousy publicity an hour after he tells me that I have to keep this thing to myself and that he would, too—to hell with him."

I phoned Frank Nikolay and told him I was being called. He told me he was, too. "Look," I said, "you're a lawyer and I'm not. I've never had anything to do with a grand jury. I understand you can't have a lawyer in the room. Is there any advice you have about how I should deal with it?" "Just tell the truth. Answer only the questions that are asked, don't volunteer anything, and accept the fact that the press will drag you through the mud and you won't be able to answer back," he said.

Next, I called Huber to let him know Frank and I would be called. Then I called everyone in Joan's family and my own. "I can't tell you what it's about, but don't worry—I'm being called as a witness, and I'm not in anyway under investigation myself," I told them. "What are they calling you about?" they asked. "I can't tell you," I responded. "All I can say is they want to know what I know about some other people in the legislature." From the five o'clock evening news on Friday through Saturday and Sunday, radio newscasts blared that I would be called. The *Capital Times* in Madison and the *Milwaukee Journal,* then edited by Perry Hill, usually carried a line in their grand jury stories noting that most people called were not necessarily guilty of wrong-doing but were called as witnesses. Few others in the press demonstrated that same sense of fairness.

Monday, April 25, the front-page banner headline in my hometown news-paper screamed, OBEY, NIKOLAY CALLED BY LOBBY GRAND JURY. No sentence explaining that people called were just witnesses appeared in the AP story, just the sensational headline and story. I had never, ever before in my three and one-half years in office been lucky enough to have that paper put my name in their banner headline, but this time they made sure that nobody would miss the story.

On Monday morning, I walked, fuming, into the courthouse. After telling me what was expected of me, Dalton asked, "Have you discussed your testimony with anyone?" "With everyone I could get my hands on," I replied. "What do you mean?" he asked, "I told you that you couldn't discuss it with anyone." "You also told me that I didn't have to worry, that no one would know I was testifying until I walked in, and then you leaked it to the press. My name has been all over the news all weekend. People don't know I'm just being called as a witness, you SOB. Ninety percent of them will think I've done something wrong."

"I could have you found in contempt of court," he said. "I have no contempt for the court, but I sure as hell have absolute contempt for you," I responded. I told him he had an obligation to get at the facts but also had one to innocent people to protect their reputations. And I told the grand jury that it was not Dalton's jury, it was theirs, that they had the right to control the way the proceedings were handled, and that they needed to know that the way it was being handled was hurting innocent people. With that off my chest, I then answered Dalton's questions. When I was asked about what I knew about the circumstances surrounding the one hundred dollar check Alfonsi had received, I told the jury that I had no idea whether his conversation had been similar to mine and that I didn't even know for sure if Alfonsi had received one until the AG told me.

The next two weeks were nasty. Many rabid, partisan Republicans in my district sent me letters making clear they knew I was going to be indicted. So much for being considered innocent until proven guilty. It especially frustrated me that I could not talk about the case publicly, and therefore could not point out that the only reason I was being called by the grand jury was to testify if I knew why their *own* Republican leader had kept the same check that I had sent back. I was so angry about the unfairness of it all that I seriously considered chucking it all and not running for reelection. When I talked with Bob Huber about my thoughts he simply said, "Davey, you're in politics. Don't expect to be treated fairly; just outlive the bastards!"

Several weeks after Frank and I testified, Alfonsi was indicted. The trial took place the first week in July with Judge Bill Sachtjen of Madison presiding, and I was called as a witness. My role in the case was still unknown to the press and the general public. I had had many differences with Alfonsi, but I did not believe it was fair to conclude that just because I had returned Wise's check that Alfonsi was required to do the same thing. Conditions or understandings could have been different.

When the prosecution called me to the stand, the judge heard my testimony with the jury out of the room and then decided the prosecution could not put my testimony to the jury because, just as I had told Dalton earlier, I had no relevant knowledge of Alfonsi's behavior. He also required that the press not report it. I agreed with the judge's decision not to allow the jury to hear my testimony because it might prejudice Alfonsi's case, but the *Capital Times* ignored the judge's admonition not to publish and ran the story. Several days later, without hearing my testimony, the jury convicted Alfonsi, and

Paul was stripped of his leadership post and his assembly seat. Months later, the Wisconsin Supreme Court overturned Alfonsi's conviction, but that was of little comfort to him.

About a month before the trial, the highway bill was resurrected, with my support this time, because Knowles finally agreed that the bill should be paid for with a one-cent gas tax rather than borrowing up front and leaving some poor sucker of a successor to be stuck with the bill. With that crisis behind me, I turned my attention to reelection. I was opposed by Curly Schultz, the mayor of Schofield, and Ben Riehle was opposed by Ben Powell, a young teacher at Wausau Tech. Powell's slogan was "Give Marathon County the influence it deserves." Riehle took offense at that and let off some steam about it one night at a rally at Poniatowski. John Gesicki, an old Democratic warhorse, ran a tavern at Poniatowski, a tiny spot on the map in the western end of the county. Poniatowski's claim to fame was that it was located exactly at the center of the Northwest Hemisphere—45 degrees longitude, 45 degrees latitude. Gesicki was a big, big man whose firmly held opinions were as numerous as the inches on his waistline, and his tavern was in Ben Riehle's home territory.

Ben's hair was white and spare, his forehead large and broad. He had fought in World War I and was "damn proud of it." We both served on the Joint Finance Committee. When Ben's turn came to speak to the gathered crowd, he was especially outraged because his opponent had dared to say that he would be more influential in the assembly than Ben. Ben leaned on his cane with one hand and wagged his finger. "Why, he says he will give Marathon County a stronger voice in Madison. Why, there's only one county in the state outside of Milwaukee that has two people on the Joint Finance Committee and that's Marathon with me and Obey. Why, if they elect Powell you know where they will put him? They will put him on the Printing Committee, and he will never be heard from again," he thundered, flashing a grin. After the meeting, Dan LaRocque said to Ben in a confidential tone, "Ben, I thought you were chairman of the Printing Committee?" "Ya, I am," responded Ben. "But I didn't think this was the place to mention that."

I campaigned by promoting the bills I had sponsored and cosponsored, including the Voc Ed Act, the revamping of higher education, expanded scholarships for college and technical school students, the 1965 Civil Rights Act, the highway bill, Wisconsin's implementing legislation for Medicare and Medicaid, and the expansion of the system of property tax relief for senior citizens. My opponent ran a heavily financed race with a lot of newspaper ads and got quite a bit of free help designing literature and newspaper ads from the advertising department of Wausau Insurance. The local GOP leaders simply asked the company to put one of their public relations people to work designing a newspaper ad campaign for Schultz. The costs never showed up as a contribution to his campaign. I could not afford to hire a PR firm, so I designed my own ads. Curly Schultz pounded me in a coordinated media campaign, claiming that I was a big taxer because of my insistence that the roads the state was building should be paid for.

The best night of the campaign came when Ben Riehle and I debated our opponents in a four-cornered joint debate before the Wausau Teacher's Association at John Muir Junior High School on Wausau's west side. Each of us made an opening statement and then threw it open to questions. The teacher's union had not been happy with Riehle because he had not voted for an education budget that was as generous as they wanted, but he had supported more education spending than the Republican majority. Powell, eager to exploit an easy issue against Riehle with an audience of teachers, bounded to the microphone and told the crowd that he was for higher teacher's salaries, for greater state aids to school districts, for more state support for the university, and for a bigger building program for the university. But he also earnestly declared himself to be against higher taxes. To much applause, Powell sat down.

Riehle slowly pulled himself up and out of the chair, limped up to the microphone, leaned on his ever-present cane, rubbed his jaw with fingers, glanced from face to face, slowly began to shake his head, and finally said, "You are all teachers and educated people. You are supposed to be smart. If you are, you know some of the things you have just heard just don't add up. A couple of points for you to think about: It's true, I didn't vote for every dime you ever wanted, but I did vote for every dime you ever got! And there's a lesson there for you, if you think about it! But I didn't do it right after I promised to cut your taxes like my opponent just did." Then Ben went on.

If you are going to be for all of the things he says he's for, then you have to vote for the taxes to pay for them. If you aren't willing to do that, you aren't real, you really aren't for all the things you think you're for and that goes for anybody in this audience. If you are not willing to pay the taxes I voted for—and my opponent is against them—then you can't be for the spending that he says he favors. Where do you think the money comes from—out of the air? He will tell you that it comes out of somebody else's britches. But I say to you, I'm man enough to tell you that for every dollar I have put in your hands, I'm going to have to take a dollar out of your britches. There isn't any other way because we can't print money. It's that simple. He may have given you prettier words and made you feel better tonight—told you you could have it all, the easy way—but I have given you the truth and that's that!

As he shuffled back to his seat the crowd slowly began to clap and, one by one, stood to applaud. It was a good night for truth on the campaign trail.

The 1965 session had been one of those landmark sessions when everything got done. A strong budget was moving the state into the modern era. We had made sweeping reforms of higher education, passed landmark vocational education reform, strengthened the state school aid program, and expanded conservation programs. Instead of producing gridlock, divided government had produced landmark legislation, and everybody felt good.

It happened for three reasons. First, it was in Knowles's interest to work with the leadership of both parties to build an atmosphere of cooperation after the bitterness the Republicans had used to wound John Reynolds. Second, Bob Huber believed that the best politics was to get good things done. He recognized that Knowles was a moderate at heart and that we would get creamed unless we responded in a moderate way. And finally, a number of us from both parties were tired of the bitterness. We were personal friends across the aisle who took pride in those friendships, and we wanted to do some of the same things rather than make war on each other.

On election night I won comfortably, getting 8,624 votes to Schultz's 6,771, but Riehle had a squeaker and finally pulled it out by three hundred votes. But after that, the news was all bad. Many of the Democrats swept into Congress by LBJ's landslide were swept out again in 1966. In the state senate district from Marathon County, Walter John Chilsen, the news anchor of Channel 7 and the son of the publisher of the *Merrill Daily Herald,* was elected to succeed Charlie Smith by a margin of 18,000 to 11,000. And we lost control of the assembly by a 54 to 46 margin. We had lost fewer state legislature seats than almost any state in the Union, but our margin was so small to begin with that we could afford no losses. And worst of all, Frank Nikolay had lost.

I felt terrible about Frank's loss and called him. He said the year was just too tough to hold southern Clark County, and the grand jury publicity had hurt, even though, like me, he had not been a target but had merely been called to testify about what, as a party leader, he knew about the conduct of Alfonsi. And too, Frank had thought the process had largely been a fishing expedition. "It hurts like hell," Frank said, "but you will do a good job down there."

INTO THE LEADERSHIP

The day after the election, Huber called me. He told me, "Davey, you have to run for deputy leader. The way the session will go, I need to be a conciliator, and I need you to shake the trees once in a while. Besides," he went on, "we can't have a party leadership coming just from Milwaukee and Madison. If we're to have a chance at regaining the majority, we need somebody from the north in the leadership, and with Frank being bounced, you're it."

"How do you think I should approach it," I asked him. "I should play it soft," he said, "but Toby [Ray Tobias] will call some of the Milwaukee guys and sound them out. You need to call the northern troops and don't wait." "I hate to run against Norm Anderson; he's such a good friend," I told Bob, but I agreed we needed the north in the leadership. In early December the caucus met and I won a three-man race with Anderson and Fred Kessler of Milwaukee. The AP story on the election noted that Nikolay "besides being the number-two man among assembly Democrats was considered the voice of the north on many issues." "Obey," the article said, "now stands in the position of also becoming the champion of northern interests."

On the Republican side of the aisle, Harold Froehlich, a strong conservative much to the right of the previous Republican leadership, was elected Speaker by one vote. Capitol political reporters like John Patrick Hunter were writing that Glen Pommerening, who had retired and now worked as Knowles's legislative liaison, was privately predicting that the increasingly conservative GOP leadership would "play hob" with Knowles's program. Froehlich and I were miles apart politically, but he was honest and I liked him. Often after dinner, in the 1965 session, I had returned to the assembly chamber to read the bills coming up the next week and found Froehlich and Ed Nager, from Madison, doing the same thing.

The GOP was back in the driver's seat—although not by much. Budget negotiations were tough on both parties. The Republicans wanted to pass their own partisan budget without having to give much recognition to our priorities. But they had a tough time lining up enough of their troops to provide the necessary fifty-one votes. While they kept resisting our priorities, they kept asking for our votes. We wanted stronger support for education and more funding for consumer protection programs. We certainly did not want to support the way their budget transferred costs to local governments, putting more burden on the property tax, the least fair and most burdensome of all taxes for people on fixed incomes.

The Republicans wanted to keep the governor out of negotiations so that he would not be identified with any of the painfully unpopular choices that had to be made, but Huber and I insisted that we would not ask our rank and file to cast tough votes if the governor himself was ducking them. Finally, Knowles came to the table, but he took no positions on any options before us. He just lay in the weeds, committing himself to nothing. In our budget conference, I sat across the table from him and watched him duck, bob, and weave for hours. I had quit smoking the night I proposed to Joan when she issued her tobacco-abstinence ultimatum. But the longer I sat next to Taylor Benson (a Milwaukee state senator who always had a cigarette lit), and the more frustrated I became with Knowles's refusal to take a position on anything, the more I craved a smoke. About the third day of negotiations I reached over and grabbed one of Benson's cigarettes. By the end of the week the tension was so high I finally realized I had one cigarette in my hand and another alive in the ashtray. After two draining weeks, we finally reached agreement on a budget, and I went back to not smoking. Trying to get Knowles to take a position had been like trying to nail Jell-O to the wall. He just kept sliding and jiggling away, but he finally landed in one place, and we jumped off the budget cliff together.

In the closing days of the session, Jerris Leonard, the Republican assistant senate leader, and I worked out an agreement on a bill to take the first step to create a statewide educational TV network. Walter John Chilsen also played a role in the development of the legislation. I was pleased when the bill passed because of what it would mean for the north. At the time only two public TV stations served Wisconsin—in Milwaukee and Madison. The legislation meant that eventually every area of the state would have access to public television. That action, like many of the achievements of the 1967 session, demonstrated that, even if I was in the minority, it was possible to get things done if I was in the right places and worked with the right people. I also built a number of new friendships with conservative Republicans that would continue long after I had left the legislature.

While 1967 had brought satisfaction to my legislative life, the year brought pain to Joan and me in our personal life. Joan was pregnant again. We were excitedly anticipating the new baby, but when we went to the hospital in the early hours of August 14, our excitement turned to sorrow. While Joan was in the delivery room, I paced nervously in the waiting room (this was in the era before husbands were allowed in the delivery room). But when the doctor came out, he told me that the baby had acute respiratory problems and was not expected to live. Within a half an hour, Robert—we had decided to name him after Huber—had died. We buried him in St. Joseph's cemetery. The year had been a bad one for us, and 1968 was not looking much better.

Another downer came with the death of Ben Riehle. After his initial suspicion about my wetness behind the ears, we had, through the years, developed a fond relationship. Many mornings he would drop by the leadership
office, which Bob Huber and I shared, for a cup of coffee. He never failed to
greet me in the morning with "Hi, young buck," and I would reply, "Hi, old
goat." Ben cared about "the little people" as he called them. And he *really*
cared about small farmers. A case in point was his crusade against oleomarga-
rine. For years, Wisconsin had a law that prohibited colored oleo from being
sold in the state. When the bill to repeal the ban was debated in the assembly,
Jerry Flannigan from Milwaukee described opponents of the bill as "dumb
hay shakers." Ben shot to his feet as fast as his bad hip would allow, grabbed
the microphone on his desk, pointed it at Flannigan like a pistol, and growled,
"You will find a lot of dumb hay shakers here this afternoon when the votes
are counted." He was right; he won the vote. Ben had only an eighth-grade
education, but he knew his people at home and knew his stuff in Madison.
He spoke the truth as he saw it, and no one ever doubted his integrity.

THE CHAOS OF 1968

Throughout 1968, even a blind man could see things disintegrating for the
Democratic Party and the whole country. One evening in early 1968 I helped
my mother move into a new apartment in Kenosha. As I drove a U-Haul
trailer back to Wausau I had the car radio on because Lyndon Johnson was
speaking to the nation. Just as I passed Mosinee, I heard Johnson's voice saying, "I will not seek nor will I accept the nomination of my party for another
term as your president." I was stunned. I almost lost control of the car. In the
weeks ahead came the clash between Bobby Kennedy and Eugene McCarthy
for leadership of the antiwar forces, and Hubert Humphrey's entry into the
race. A few weeks later Martin Luther King was assassinated.

I still believed Humphrey was a great man, but after watching Bobby
Kennedy give his victory speech at a Los Angeles hotel, the night of the California primary, I switched off the TV to go to bed, turned to Joan, and said,
"Honey, I love Hubert, but Bobby has to be the man. He is probably the only
one who can keep the party from blowing apart." About five o'clock in the
morning the phone rang. It was a reporter asking my reaction to Bobby's
shooting. I was shocked and sickened. I could not believe it was happening
again. That morning I was scheduled to be at the dedication of a new senior
citizen housing project on Grand Avenue—Wausau's first federal senior housing project. I drove to the project, spinning the radio dial as I tried to glean

every bit of news I could about Bobby Kennedy. Just as the ceremony ended, we got word that he had indeed died. Once again it felt like the light had gone out of our world.

The ensuing Democratic convention in Chicago was a scene of political carnage: the street war between the Chicago police and antiwar demonstrators spilled over onto the convention floor where chaos reigned as Mayor Daley's enforcers manhandled Dan Rather of CBS News in full view of the national audience. When I thought of Hubert's chances under those circumstances, I despaired. I could not bear the thought that someone as paranoid and cynical as Richard Nixon could be elected to head our country.

On election day, I won by a vote of 10,640 to 7,690, and Laurence Day won by about the same margin in Ben Riehle's old seat. And happily for me, my friend Frank Nikolay won back his Clark County assembly seat. It pained me to watch Humphrey go down. I loved him and believe to this day that he would have made a wonderfully decent president. In the closing days of the campaign, after trailing Nixon badly, Hubert had enjoyed a last-minute surge nationally. But in small market TV areas like ours, the Humphrey campaign simply ran out of money and dropped most of their TV buys. When I heard that Hubert's campaign had run out of money for those ads, I was so distressed that ten days before the election I went down to Channel 7, cut my own media buy in half, substituted Humphrey's spots, and paid for them myself. I needed to know I had done everything I possibly could to help Hubert. I had no idea that Hubert's defeat would soon change my life forever.

CHAPTER 5

ᐧᐧ

"You're Going to Congress"

The first week in December, the National Conference of State Legislators held their annual conference in Hawaii, and the legislative leadership of both parties attended. On December 7 we were scheduled to participate in a wreath-laying ceremony on the USS *Arizona* memorial commemorating the twenty-seventh anniversary of Pearl Harbor. The conference ended the night before with a dinner. Scoop Jackson, the widely respected Democratic senator from Washington, was to be the main speaker. All of the stories out of Washington indicated that he was going to be named Nixon's secretary of defense, but the speech Jackson gave that night made it obvious that there would be no such appointment. As Jackson was laying down a number of challenges to Nixon on military and domestic policy, Huber looked at me and said, "Davey, ain't no way a man giving a speech like that is planning to work for Nixon."

The next morning we took a launch out to the USS *Arizona* memorial. As we approached the memorial I was moved by its grace, beauty, and poignancy. The bright white, open-sided structure straddled the sunken hull of the *Arizona*. Each end of the monument was slightly elevated so it appeared to be a set of wings rising above the old ship. The *Arizona*'s rusted gun turret was visible just above the water's surface. Inside the monument, at one end, the names of those who had died that infamous day were chiseled into the marble, listed not by rank but alphabetically—all equal in death. No one did much talking as we left after the ceremony. It was a sobering and moving experience.

A few of us had decided to extend our stay for three or four days. Two days after Jackson's speech, state senator Fred Risser came running up to Joan and me waving a newspaper and shouting, "Dave, you're going to Congress . . . you're going to Congress!" "What on earth are you talking about?" I asked him. "Here, look," he said as he handed me a copy of the *Honolulu Advertiser*.

On the front page above the masthead in huge pink letters it read: LAIRD: SECRETARY OF DEFENSE! I was stunned. Rather than Scoop Jackson, my own congressman, Mel Laird, had been nominated by Nixon to be secretary of defense. That meant there would be a special election to fill Laird's congressional seat. I was ready to swim home, but Joan said, "Hey, you only get to Hawaii once in your life. Let's enjoy the three days we have left." She was right. So, for three days we enjoyed the beauty of the place, but the moment I boarded the plane for the flight home I began to put together an outline of what I would have to do to run.

I was ambivalent about the whole idea. Since the seventh grade the one job I had dreamed about was being a member of Congress—not a senator, but a member of Congress. But in my heart, I really doubted I could run, for two reasons. First, I had no idea how I would raise the money. I had never spent more than $5,500 in any campaign. Laird's campaign had routinely spent about $40,000, plus money spent by the party, but Democrats had rarely reached above the $5,000 mark against him. Second, I doubted that I could get the nomination. I knew Bert Grover, the two-time assemblyman in heavily Republican Shawano County, would want to run. I also expected that Frank Nikolay, having spent his life in politics building the Democratic Party, would not pass up a free shot. And I knew in my heart I couldn't run against him because I had so much respect for him.

When our plane landed at O'Hare in Chicago, Joan and I had a two-hour wait for the connecting flight to Wausau. I thought I might as well use the time.

My first call was to Frank. I reached him at his law office in Colby. "Well, Frank, Laird sure changed the landscape; how do you see it?" I asked. Frank's immediate response was, "Dave, you ought to run. If you do I will back you. I would love to run, but when you look at it hard, you are from the media center of the district. You have had the coverage and have the name identification that nobody else has. It probably can't be won, but you have the best chance. The question is, How do you clear the field so you don't waste money on a primary? Your problem will be Bert. Tell me how I can help you to get him out." "Frank, I appreciate your offer more than I can say. Do you really think I have a shot or do you think I will just make a damn fool out of myself?" I asked. "Like I said, Dave, I think the odds are that Chilsen will beat you, but in a special election you'll get help that otherwise wouldn't come your way again. You could pull another Lester Johnson," he said, referring to the upset special election that Johnson had won in a western Wisconsin district in 1953, months after Eisenhower's election.

I was stunned by Frank's selflessness and by how far things had moved in a one-minute conversation. I had expected it would take a few days for Frank and others to think through their responses, but Frank had accelerated the timetable. Up to that point I had not asked myself the big question: Would I take the shot if I had a chance? Frank's comment made it instantly clear—it was time to take the shot. So without being able to fill Joan in on the conversation, with Frank still on the line, I made the decision in an O'Hare phone booth and told Frank that it was a "go." "How do you think I should start," I asked. "Well, you should call Wimmer," he said, "and ask him to set up a powwow between you, Grover, Dahl, and me." Jim Wimmer had just become state chairman; Larry Dahl was a Waupaca County farmer active in the National Farmers Organization leadership circles, who had run against Laird in the previous November election. I called Wimmer, and he agreed to call the meeting at the Edgewater Hotel in Madison.

We met a few days later. Wimmer opened the meeting by saying, "Look, we have a wonderful opportunity to win this seat, but the party can't raise the money needed to pay for a primary as well as a general election, and I don't think the three of you can either. As party chair, I don't care which of you runs," Wimmer said, "but I do know that if there is a primary, there will not be enough time for you to mount an effective campaign afterwards, so my message is that when you walk out of here, there had better be just one candidate because I won't put my reputation on the line for a hopeless cause."

I don't remember who talked next, but I remember most of what each of us said. Grover said, "Well, if you want one candidate then the others had better get out because I'm running. I'm the only one who can win, I'm the only one who can carry Shawano County, and that will break the Republicans' back. I have a more conservative record than you, Dave, and I will pound doors from dawn to dusk in a Proxmire way, and Proxmire will help me." Several years earlier, Bert had interned in Prox's office. "Well, Bert," I said, "if I were to defer to anyone in the room it would be to Larry because he ran last time and earned some credits. But I am in the race to stay." I then laid out the reasons that Frank had given for my candidacy and said that Frank had authorized me to say he was prepared to endorse me.

Larry Dahl then kicked in with his comments. I had not talked directly to Dahl. I didn't know him well, but several days earlier I had called Helen Sigmund from Stevens Point, who had been Larry's campaign manager in the previous November election. I told her I intended to run and asked her if she would talk to Larry on my behalf. She told me that "Larry is a good guy and a realist; he'll recognize you have the only chance." Larry's comments showed that her judgment was right on target. "Bert, if anybody in this room has a right to make an 'I'm going to run come hell or high water' statement, it's me," Larry said. "I was the only one who was willing to run last year when it was Laird we were up against. None of you guys would do it then when it was tough, so, by rights, I could say I'm going around the track again. None of us is likely to be drawing a federal paycheck when this election is over, but I didn't run against Laird in November to piss away our chances of actually winning the seat when we had a chance, so I will get out if everybody else will. Obey ought to be the guy."

We went round and round for another hour and the meeting broke up. As we broke up I said to Grover:

> Look, Bert, I know you want to run, Frank does, too. But he pulled his hat out of the ring without my ever asking him to. I ask you to please consider doing the same thing. Even if you run, you can't beat me in a primary, not because I am better than you but because Marathon and Portage counties will cast the overwhelming number of Democratic primary votes. The Republicans will overwhelmingly dominate the primary in Shawano and Waupaca, and only a tiny percentage of the vote in those counties will be in the Democratic primary. That means the areas of the district where you are strong in a general election will cast very few votes in a Democratic primary. But even if I beat you under those circumstances, it would be an empty victory because I would be out of money. Even if I win the primary, I know I can't win the general without you. If you get behind me I will never forget who made it happen.

A day later Bert called and said, "Look, if I get behind you, I want to win. I don't want to back a loser. I'll endorse you and I'll campaign for you, but you have to get over here and campaign hard and personal." And that was it—we were off to the races.

THE '69 CAMPAIGN

The first thing I did after announcing my candidacy was to fly to Washington with Jim Wimmer to talk to the House Democratic Campaign Committee, the DNC, and every pro-Democratic labor, reform, and environmental group we could find. Warren Sawall, Gaylord's senior political advisor, organized our schedule with help from Kaz Oshiki, Bob Kastenmeier's top man. I knew Washington Democrats would be skeptical because the seat had not been held by a Democrat in the twentieth century, so I had to break through the doubt by getting Wisconsin people who were respected in Washington to break down the conventional wisdom that I couldn't win.

At a labor luncheon organized by Sawall, Evie Dubrow, the legendary and much loved political rep of the International Ladies Garment Workers, was the first in with her pledge of help, and a few others followed. Most explained that they had to check with their Wisconsin people to get a formal endorsement. One union was conspicuous by its absence. The Wisconsin Teamsters were run by Frank Ranney, and he was more comfortable with Republicans. He had endorsed Chilsen out of the box. That made the local Teamsters unhappy as all get-out, because we had worked closely with each other. Ray Yessa and Dick Chamberlain, who led the Wausau local, told me, "Don't worry about Ranney. He may give Chilsen our money, but he can't give him our votes. We are with you!" And they stuck. A number of national unions were reluctant to support me because they didn't believe a Democrat could win. But one key man knew a lot more about Wisconsin politics than they did— Andy Biemiller, the chief legislative representative for the AFL-CIO.

Biemiller, originally from Milwaukee, had been elected to the Wisconsin assembly in the 1930s and then to the Congress in 1948. He had been a legislative sponsor of Harry Truman's national health insurance bill, and he knew the territory. He had written the civil rights resolution that made Hubert Humphrey famous at the 1948 Democratic National Convention. "I believe Obey can resurrect the farm labor coalition that elected Lester Johnson in 1953 in the old ninth district," he told anyone who would listen, and that's exactly what we did. Gil Rohde, the president of the Wisconsin Farmers Union, sold his national leadership on the idea that I could win, and Larry Dahl did the same with the National Farmers Organization, which put two of the three major farm organizations in my corner. Several of the national dairy coops hedged their bets.

Wimmer and I also huddled with Fred Harris, who had succeeded Larry O'Brien as the national chairman of the DNC. Harris promised his help, and he and his deputy, Mark Shields, delivered on their promises. Kastenmeier had organized a small contributor fundraiser of Wisconsin natives working in Washington. Bob Lewis, another old Wisconsin Farmers Union hand, and his wife, Martha, played a lead role, as did Pat Putzi, my old college buddy who was now working for the Bureau of Indian Affairs. We also met with Ken Harding, the staff director for the Congressional Campaign Committee. After the meetings were over, we were held hostage in D.C. for two days more than we had bargained for because a huge winter fog blanketed the Midwest and shut down the Milwaukee and Madison airports. When we finally boarded a

Northwest flight for the trip back, I looked out the window, saw the Capitol dome in the distance, shining against the night sky, and whispered a silent prayer, "Please, God, let me be part of that!"

I flew back to Wisconsin believing for the first time that, just maybe, there was a chance that prayer would be answered. On the organizational front, in need of a campaign headquarters, I rented an empty building on Third Street, right next to Joe Lepinski's Fur Store. By a nice coincidence, today that building houses Evolutions in Design, a highly successful floral and antique business run by our niece Lisa Macco and her business partner, Randy Verhasselt. I needed to put together a staff in a hurry, but the road was bumpy. Jerry Madison asked the local school board for a two-month leave of absence so he could be full-time campaign manager, but the board turned him down. Jerry could help part-time, but we needed one full-time person to put a face on the campaign. Jerry, Pat Crooks, City Attorney Tony Earl, and Lyle Stitt, the news director of the second TV station in town, WAOW-TV, Channel 9, huddled at our home to figure out who would fill the bill.

Lyle and his wife, Kathy, and Joan and I had become good friends. He was a South Dakotan who understood what the prairie progressive movement was all about. I asked Lyle if he would consider taking a leave of absence from the station to serve as a spokesman for the campaign, with Jerry available for the political backup he would need. "No," he said, "because it would be a conflict of interest for me to go back to the station after the election. It would bring into question Channel 9's objectivity, and I wouldn't want to do that. But I believe in you and I'm willing to gamble. I'll resign from Channel 9. That's the only way." I told Lyle I could not ask that. It would be asking too much of him, especially when I had such doubts about winning. "I can't do that to your family," I said. "Well, Kathy and I want to do it, so I think you're stuck with it," he replied. I was struck at that moment by one pattern that had run through the campaign so far, the extent to which other people had been willing to sacrifice for me—first Frank, then Larry, then Bert, and now Lyle. With huge guilt feelings about the risk Lyle was taking, I accepted his offer, and Lyle publicly announced his resignation the next day. It was the second most important day in the campaign, and it was the talk of the community.

The *most* important day in the campaign was the day that Warren Knowles revealed his 1969 biennial budget. In November, Knowles and the Republican Party leadership had campaigned on the fact that they had been able to pass a budget the year before without a tax increase. We had responded by saying that that happy circumstance was due to a number of one-time gimmicks that could not be repeated, including cost shifting to local governments and that the budget guaranteed there would be major tax increases *after* the election. They had denied it, but by January the budget gap had become too big to hide. We all knew the governor would have to propose an unpleasant tax increase. The only question was which taxpayers would get stuck with the biggest bill? The governor's budget speech gave us the answer.

Knowles proposed to raise state income tax rates on every tax bracket except the top one for the wealthiest. Immediately after the governor's address, a reporter said to me, "Assemblyman Obey, Senator Chilsen just said that the governor's tax plan was a 'reasonable plan.' How would you describe it?" "I think it's a rich man's tax plan," I responded. "It flies in the teeth of the La Follette tradition that those with the most ability to pay should bear the greatest sacrifice." The next day the papers carried both statements. We had our defining issue. Now the question was: Could we get the difference across to the public?

Shortly afterwards, Louie Hanson came down to scout out the campaign. He had been state chairman before Wimmer and had quit so that he could be Gaylord Nelson's top staff person in Wisconsin. Louie was convinced I could win and had arranged for Nelson to come back to Wisconsin to help me. Louie had come to Wausau to gauge how well the campaign was organized and focused. As he said after the election, "I took one look around and decided I had better stick around for a while." Louie became the de facto nuts-and-bolts campaign manager. He showed our volunteer core how to organize a schedule, set targets for my appearances in each county, helped plan press releases a week at a time to shape our message, and organized our mailings. He set up a "Farmers for Obey" advisory committee with Larry Dahl and Gil Rohde as cochairs—a minor miracle because the NFO and Farmers Union were normally at each other's throats. And as he settled in, the rest of the campaign settled down, including the candidate. Amateur hour had passed. Wasted motion was slashed, and a sense of hopeful, organized urgency took hold.

January and February were miserable months to campaign, and on more than one occasion, they almost killed me. The days were grueling. Wausau was three hours from Madison by car, and the district was huge. Each weekday morning, I would get up around four thirty or five, hit a plant gate in some part of the district—primarily Wausau, Stevens Point, Marshfield, and Wisconsin Rapids—then drive to Madison for a nine o'clock session. Because little important legislation would move in committee during the early days of the session, I headed back to the district as soon as the session ended at noon.

But that winter we were hit with a protracted period of warm temperatures with melting snow and ground fog. Drive times doubled because the fog was so thick you could not see thirty feet in front of your car. When I finally made it to wherever I was going, I would hit more plant gates, shake hands on Main Street, visit local press, attend public receptions or coffees in private houses, appear at service clubs, professional clubs, union meetings, and farm rallies until the little hand was on ten, and then head home the next day to do it all over again. I was so tired that twice in the same week I fell asleep on the interstate and woke up to find myself in the grassy median strip. That was enough to get the old adrenaline moving again.

Shortly after one of those near misses, Louie Hanson was sitting in the campaign office when three college students walked in. "We're from Antioch College. We just read about Mr. Obey's race in the *New York Times*. We took a month off for a class project. What can we do to help?" "For God's sake, one of you drive him. He's going to kill himself," Louie replied. And that's how Chet Atkins from Massachusetts became my driver for the last weeks of the campaign.

One of the first nights he drove, we were headed to a union meeting in Nekoosa. I was exhausted and on the ropes. My brain felt like solid stone. When I was introduced, I walked up to the mike in front of the room . . . and went totally blank! I could not remember where I was or who these people were. I stammered into the mike, "Please excuse me, but I forgot to do something that I won't be able to do afterwards." With that I went back down the aisle, pulled Chet aside, grabbed his shoulder, and whispered, "Chet, where the hell are we and who are these people?" Thank God he knew. I went back into the room, my brain in "drive" again, and got out of there without crashing. Years later, Chet and I would laugh about that evening after he had himself been elected to the House and had joined me on the Appropriations Committee. He was a fine, dedicated, honorable public servant in the years he so bravely served the people of Massachusetts, and I am still proud of the tiny part I played in his career.

In the primary, I had two token, absolutely unknown Democratic opponents, Bob Hack, a UW student, and Will Sandstrom, a self-professed biochemist. His main campaign issue in the landlocked Seventh Congressional District was the preservation of the great blue whale, a worthy cause but not one at the top of many priority lists in an area of Wisconsin where the biggest fish to be found was the musky or an occasional sturgeon.

On the Republican side, Chilsen was the clear favorite but faced a spirited challenge from Hyde Murray and modest additional opposition from Carl Dretzke, a retired businessman from Waupaca County, and Atlee Dodge, a Menominee Indian tribal leader. Dennis Morgan, the old '40s and '50s movie actor, had also explored running but eventually did not file. Hyde Murray was interesting. He was the son of Reid Murray, who had defeated Progressive Jerry Boileau in 1938 and served that district in Congress until 1952. Mel Laird had succeeded him, and his son wanted the seat back. He served as the Republican staff chief on the Agriculture Committee and later as a top staffer for the Republican caucus when Bob Michel was minority leader. We developed a friendly relationship in later years, but on that night, Murray was, to me, just another competing candidate.

When the votes were counted, Chilsen led all comers in both parties with over 28,000 votes, pulling more than twice as many votes as Murray's almost 14,000. Next was Dretzke at just over 3,000, and Dodge with nearly 1,700. On the Democratic side, I pulled over 18,000, Sandstrom less than 2,000, and Hack about 750. Republicans had out-polled Democrats roughly 46,000 to 20,000. Most of the press coverage added up the votes and assumed that the Republican who won the primary would win big in the general. But John Wyngaard, the veteran capitol political reporter, widely respected for his shrewdness and fairness, dissented from conventional wisdom. "Taking everything into account," he wrote, "no careful observer is likely to make a wager of substantial size on either aspirant." Immediately after the primary results, Chilsen raced to Washington and I raced to Manawa. I had better results.

Chilsen went to D.C. to raise dollars, to powwow with Laird and national Republicans, and to have a media visit with Richard Nixon. Newspaper articles described the highlight of Chilsen's three-day visit to Washington. The *Wausau Record Herald* reported it this way: "Chilsen said he told the president that his campaign theme is 'Complete the Team in Washington—Nixon, Laird, and Chilsen' and Mr. Nixon replied, 'Good.'"

I had driven to Manawa, a strongly Republican town in Waupaca County, because I had been getting word that Dretzke, who was from Manawa, was telling people that he thought I would make a better congressman than Chilsen. Chilsen kept telling people he would fight for dairy farmers, but Dretzke didn't believe him. Dretzke wanted to endorse me. Gaylord Nelson and I appeared at a farm dinner in Manawa and talked about the need to raise dairy price supports. Afterwards I met with Dretzke, and he volunteered his endorsement. I was delighted. Chilsen was in Washington, hanging as tightly as he could on Nixon's coattails, but I suspected Carl Dretzke could move more undecided voters than Nixon could.

Dretzke's endorsement was short lived, but it threw the GOP campaign into chaos. The day after Dretzke offered to say nice things about me, he called and said, "Dave, I just can't stick with it. The Republicans are all over me."

But he was mad at the GOP for pushing him around. And his press conference announcing his intention to stick with the Republicans by endorsing Chilsen did me more good than it did Chilsen—he told the press he was doing it simply because if he did anything else, it would make the Republicans too angry. And then he added that he still thought Obey was a fine young man who would be a reliable friend of the farmer. Not a bad week.

We had a second game of chess going on with Walter John. The concessioner for billboards in the area was Sig Goldberg, out of Wausau. Wimmer called Sig and asked him what a one-month saturation buy around the district would cost. Sig told him it would run about $10,000. Jim asked him if he would prepare a proposed contract for us to look at. Seeing an opportunity to double his business, Goldberg then called Chilsen's campaign and told them we were asking for a one-month saturation buy estimate and asked if they wanted to do the same thing. They responded that if Obey was doing a saturation buy for one month, they would do it for two. So the month before the primary, Chilsen's billboards went up all over the district. As February turned to March, Chilsen's camp kept waiting for mine to go up. They never did, because Wimmer had run a trap play on them.

From the beginning of the campaign, we had worked up a bad case of the cold sweats knowing that Chilsen would outspend me. We were trying to figure out ways to neutralize his advantage. When Chilsen's billboards went up, Goldberg called Wimmer back to let him know that he had a specific package ready if we wanted it and also dropped the news that Chilsen had bought twice as much as we were contemplating. Jim said to me, "Look Dave, we aren't going to have enough money to do everything well. You are already known in more than half the district and TV will boost that so you don't need name ID as much as you need to get out your base vote and do persuasion advertising. You do that with organization and you do that with TV. Billboards don't persuade anybody. Billboards just hike your name ID and you won't really need it that badly." Then he said, "Look, by doing a heavy billboard buy Chilsen is wasting his money because, as the Walter Cronkite of Central Wisconsin, he already has maximum name ID. He just wasted $20,000. If you don't make a buy, you can put that money into TV and radio where it will do you more good, and you will have eliminated $20,000 of his financial advantage."

And that is exactly how it worked out. Campaign reports after the election showed Chilsen's campaign had spent $64,200; we had spent $45,456. The entire difference was due to the $20,000 that Chilsen had spent on billboards to buy the name ID he already had. Without our billboard feint, I'm convinced we would not have won.

I also would not have won without the all-out support of Gaylord Nelson. I knew I would not get any headlines in Republican newspapers by coming to their communities, but Nelson could help change that, and he did. With Louie Hanson's guiding hand, Gaylord committed seven weekends of his time to me. Bill Proxmire came in twice. I campaigned on my own Monday through Friday, but Saturdays and Sundays Gaylord helped me in Antigo, Wausau, Manawa, Clintonville, Stevens Point, Marshfield, Wisconsin Rapids, and all over Clark County. Our main focus was tax equity, but Gaylord also salted in comments about farming, the environment, and the anti-ballistic missile (ABM) treaty. Farmers knew that Nelson's roots were in Polk County, dairy country, and that he genuinely cared about, and fought for, family farmers. Chilsen could talk all he wanted about the Nixon-Laird-Chilsen team. We talked about the Nelson-Obey team, and on farming Gaylord had more credibility than anybody.

We also campaigned at every stop for a strong set of national standards for water pollution. The paper industry that dominated the Wisconsin River Valley was the backbone of the economy, and we were worried that mill management would scare off workers by threats of job losses any time the subject of clean water came up. But I described to the crowds those huge pipes pouring junk into the Wisconsin River that I had seen when I worked at Wausau Paper Mills. I described the raw sewage that floated on Lake Wausau. I asked them if they really wanted to be represented by somebody who wouldn't do his damndest to clean it up, and I explained that without national standards, Wisconsin mills would be at a disadvantage competing with southern mills. Because Alabama, Mississippi, and Louisiana could always be counted on to impose weaker standards (and thus lower costs) on their mills than the Wisconsin DNR would impose on Wisconsin mills, we needed tough federal standards to level the playing field.

Gaylord and I also talked about the need for the ABM treaty. In those days, as is the case today, right-wing forces were pushing to build a defensive shield against offensive nuclear weapons before there was any likelihood it would work. No one in his right mind could oppose something like that in theory, but in real life the technology did not exist that could come close to making it work. The system could be overcome just by building a larger number of offensive missiles to overwhelm a rudimentary defensive system. Net result? A big hole in the taxpayers' wallets, with no additional protection, because it was a lot cheaper to build an extra thousand offensive missiles than it was to build an elaborate technological defense.

That issue was the centerpiece of Hubert Humphrey's speech when he came to the district ten days before the election to rev up the troops for one last effort to put me over the top. We expected about 800 people to come to the Newman High School gym for the event. Instead, 1,200 showed up. We had to use another room downstairs for the overflow crowd and pipe in the sound. Before the speeches, I took Hubert down to the overflow room so he could say hello and shake hands to ease their disappointment at not being able to get into the gym.

Hubert was wonderful. His speech was passionate, his message uplifting, and as always, comprehensive. He was at his eloquent best in describing the need for arms control. "Security does not come with more weapons," he told the crowd. "For every new defensive weapon an offensive weapon is devised. For every new offensive weapon there is a new defensive weapon." He said the time was now for bold moral decisions, for bold political decisions. "It is time to open negotiations with the Russians and to tell them it is time for mankind to be sane. It is time to halt the arms race and hopefully to cut back. There can be security only when the arms level is lowered." When Humphrey finished, the tears were streaming down his face, and the crowd rose in thunderous aching applause.

After Hubert left for the airport at dinner's end, I shook hands around the room and came upon four or five of the strongest anti-Vietnam War activists in the county. "He was wonderful, he was wonderful," they repeated. "If only we had known in November." Their comments were like arrows in my heart. I gritted my teeth and thought silently, "I tried to tell you, but you were so angry you wouldn't listen." That night they had seen Hubert as I had known him, freed from the vise into which Johnson and history had placed him. There had never been any doubt in my mind that if Hubert had been elected he would have moved immediately to negotiate an end to that war, and thousands of Americans would have been spared. Hubert's performance that evening drove that home to everyone in that hall. That's what made the evening so uplifting . . . and so poignant.

The main battle that defined the election was the difference between Chilsen and me on taxes, but another key fight was waged over an ugly outgrowth of the nation's agony on Vietnam—explosive campus violence. On that score the debate turned vicious. At the beginning of the year, antiwar students at the UW–Oshkosh stormed the office of campus president Roger Giles and trashed it. Their assault was stupid and generated a response in kind. Giles responded by summarily expelling or suspending almost every student found in his office when the police broke up the group. Giles's response was hailed by the governor and others, and a resolution was thrown together and introduced in the assembly by the Republicans, praising his action. But now there was a problem. Information began to come out that several students arrested in the president's reception area had been there on legitimate business, but Giles's response had caught all of them in the same net. The innocent, if there were any, were not separated from the guilty because no hearing had been afforded the students.

I hated violent student demonstrations. They stood in stark contrast to the thoughtful exchange of ideas that was supposed to mark academic life, and on a practical level they were as dumb as flag burning. I knew there was no way the Republican leadership would allow their resolution to be modified to take into account the need for due process, because their purpose was not to praise Giles; it was to nail me. They knew I would not vote for the resolution unless it was changed to reflect the need for due process, and they thought that could be used to cripple my campaign for Congress because of the public's general disdain for violence in the wake of the Chicago Democratic convention. It was an old McCarthy-like trick that the Wisconsin Republican Party leadership couldn't resist using every chance it got.

A number of friends in our caucus came up to me and urged me to "Just vote for the damn thing and forget about it!" but I couldn't do that. I had learned a long time ago that the things that weigh you down most in life are the things that you do *against* instinct, the things you do that your heart tells you are wrong. Throughout my career, every time I have faced a tough decision like that, I would think of Art Henderson and ask myself, "Would I be comfortable looking him in the eye and explaining my vote?"

I knew I could not vote for the resolution as it stood. I also knew that if I just voted against it no one would understand why. I decided that the only way I could minimize the damage was to lead the fight against it. In that way, I thought that the press would report at least some of my arguments. When the debate came, I offered a substitute resolution condemning the violence but asking for a due process hearing for every student who was being expelled. After the Republicans shot down my amendment, I voted "No" on final passage, and the Republicans rammed it through. That vote cost me a lot in the last two weeks of the campaign. It became clear it was the one thing that could cause my defeat.

In the closing days of the campaign, Chilsen began running a very effective TV ad. It started with a close-up of an angry dark face. As the camera slowly moved back it revealed an upraised arm about to come crashing down on whatever was in its way. The ad punched home the accusation that I was "soft" on campus violence and afraid to "stand up" to campus radicals. It was as effective as it was unfair. I knew it was having its desired effect: within hours of its first appearance, people stopped asking me about education and taxes and started asking, "Is it true you sided with the students at Oshkosh?" I knew the issue was too complicated to win the argument, but I at least had to limit its corrosive affect. First, I asked Dick Fallow, a skilled wordsmith who worked with COPE (organized labors' political action arm) to draft a pamphlet attacking the ad's big lie. Dick had the ability to get the pamphlets right to the workers on the shop floor where they worked and talked. Second, I bought a series of thirty-minute TV programs during which panelists would ask me a series of tough questions in a format that would give me a chance to get my point across and let people see what kind of person I was. And third, I decided to try to change the subject.

The only issue that had almost as much emotional content as campus violence was taxes, and the lion's share of the voters whose support I had a chance to get agreed with my position—not Chilsen's—on the subject. My TV ads and most of the pictures in my pamphlets were done by Fritz Albert, a dedicated, kind, and thoughtful agricultural journalism professor at UW–Madison. Drafted into the German army at the age of sixteen in the closing days of World War II, he had served as an aerial photographer. After the war he came to the UW on the forerunner of the Fulbright program, and he eventually became a professor there. He had done all of Gaylord Nelson's campaign films in 1968, and Gaylord had asked him to do my spots. He agreed on one condition—he would take no money except expenses. When I asked him why, his poignant response was, "When someday my children ask me what did I do about it, as I asked my father in Germany in the last war, I don't want to have to say 'Nothing.'" Frtiz, Lyle, Louie, and I put together a simple black-and-white spot describing the unfairness of the governor's tax plan that Chilsen had endorsed. Focusing on my opposition to it, our spot closed with this line: "A fighter for fair taxes in Madison will be a fighter for fair taxes in Washington." The ad hit hard, but it was clean. That was virtually the only spot we ran the last ten days, except for the half-hour *Ask Dave* programs.

The morning before election day, we got an unexpected break. Clifford Hardin, Nixon's new secretary of agriculture, had decided against an increase in the support price for dairy products. Nelson's Washington office called Louie Hanson at 7 a.m. Wisconsin time to tell him the news. I immediately raced down to WRIG radio and cut a radio spot. Louie then had drivers take the spot to Marshfield, Shawano, Waupaca, Clintonville, Neillsville, Medford, Merrill, Stevens Point, and Wausau with instructions to drop all previously scheduled spots and run the new one. In the ad we simply described the disappointing action of the secretary of agriculture and told farmers that if they wanted to send a message to the Nixon administration about its refusal to help dairy farmers, the quickest and most effective way to do it was to send me to Washington, so I could deliver the message loud and clear.

On election night we gathered at Pat and Rita Crooks's house on Grant Street to await the verdict. On the afternoon of election day, Fred Harris, the National Party chairman, slipped into town, along with his staff chief, Mark Shields. If this turned out to be an upset in the making, Harris wanted to be there to trumpet it; but if I lost, we wanted them to quietly slip out of town unnoticed. My race was one of four House special elections scheduled that spring. Ed Jones had just won the Tennessee special for the Democrats the week before. If I won, it would be a second big gain for the Democrats, and that could quickly be followed by two other special election pickups—Mike Harrington in Massachusetts and John Melcher in Montana. Those four elections could give the Democrats heart, coming so soon after Hubert's loss. On that April Fool's night we were hoping to be part of the ride. As the polls closed at 8 p.m., I asked Jerry Madison, Pat Crooks, and Louie Hanson to each write down on a piece of paper what they predicted our final percentage would be. I wrote down 48 percent. Louie wrote 52. Jerry wrote 51.5. At about 8:30 p.m. a handful of returns came in, and I moved ahead by about two hundred votes. Then for almost an hour nothing more came in. I felt like my whole life was hanging by a thread.

Then the extra phones we had installed began to ring. Returns began to come in from randomly scattered precincts, but they told us that we were just about matching the numbers we needed in those precincts in order to win. WSAU TV kept a running total on the screen, but it wasn't running; it was crawling. For almost two hours only a few thousand votes were showing on the screen. Then an unspecified block of votes were tallied, and the station reported that Chilsen had moved into an 800-vote lead. At that point I thought, "Well, here it comes; from now on we slowly sink." But we didn't. I wanted to win so badly that I had built into my head an expectation of defeat in order to keep the disappointment of a loss to manageable proportions. About twenty minutes later, large numbers from Marathon County checked in, and I slipped back into a 1,200-vote lead. That grew to 2,000, but I still would not allow myself to hope.

Our problem was that the AP was not reporting where many of the votes were coming from. So much depended upon which precincts were still out. If Portage and Marathon were mostly in, it would be bad news. If Shawano, Waupaca, and Waushara were largely in, it would be great news because that was the toughest territory for us. Then we got a call from Dan LaRoque at the courthouse—Waupaca was largely in. We had expected to lose it by close to 4,000, but we were running only about 2,200 votes behind.

I could not believe it. Maybe we did have a shot! Several of Portage County's heaviest Democratic precincts—Stockton, Hull, and others—came in, and our margin expanded to about 2,500 votes. When Harris saw those precincts ring up more than 80 percent in the Democratic column, he asked, "My God, what is the ethnic makeup of those areas?" Jerry replied, "Polish, just like Dave's wife." "God bless those beautiful Poles," Harris whispered back. Then reports dropped to a trickle. About 130 precincts were still out, but we didn't know which ones remained to be counted. If they were scattered around the district, we could be home free. But if there were a large block of Republican precincts not yet reported, we could still lose.

Jerry talked with LaRocque and Marv Nellis at the courthouse and asked about Shawano. We had been trying to raise the Shawano county clerk's office for more than an hour and had gotten no answer. Then we heard the strangest news: Shawano had stopped counting for the night. It was getting too late, we were told, so the clerk had told the counters to come back in the morning. Alarm bells went off. "The bastards are going to steal the election," Dick Fallow, our AFL-CIO coordinator shouted. "They are going to stall until they know how many votes they need, and then they'll stuff the damn ballot box. Mark Shields nodded in half agreement. I doubted that, but I really didn't know. "What can we do about it?" I asked. Louie Hanson said, "Call Kenny Traeger." Traeger was a Democrat who had been appointed Shawano county judge by John Reynolds. "Traeger can issue a court order to resume the count," Louie said. We woke Traeger, who couldn't believe the clerk's office had been arrogant enough to stop counting with all that was at stake. He issued a court order in Olympic time and told the Sheriff's office to deliver the order to the clerk to get the counting going again.

Before long it didn't matter. Returns kept building my lead. A little after midnight Jerry Madison leaned over to Joan and whispered, "He won't admit it yet, but your husband is the new congressman." Shortly thereafter the wire services officially declared me the winner. And Shawano was a shocker. While we had expected to lose it by 1,900 to 2,000 votes, Chilsen's actual margin was fewer than four hundred votes. Grover had been true to his word. Joan and I drove down to campaign headquarters for a victory statement. The place was packed with supporters, workers, and the press. Joan, Fred Harris, and I spoke to the crowd, then headed over to the backroom at the Gaslight to celebrate with a few drinks and snacks with our closest workers. The final margin was about 4,080 votes—51.2 percent—Jerry had called it right on the button.

We never went to bed that night. Joan and I went to the Wausau Paper Mill plant gate to thank the workers there. We finally climbed into bed around 7:30 a.m., but before we could fall asleep, the phone started ringing, and we finally gave up. I decided I was going to revel in it, so while Joan tried to bring some order to the house, I decided to just take a walk down Third Street, the main drag in Wausau, to see how people would react. I walked into the Mint Cafe and was amazed to find so many friends there who had been nowhere to be seen the day before. I had no plan for what to do next. I just wanted to taste the delicious moment.

About three o'clock in the afternoon, Henry Reuss called headquarters and said, "Look, Carl Albert, the Democratic floor leader, wants Dave here in Washington at noon tomorrow to be sworn in before we break for the Easter recess. Dave's margin is wide enough that they have waived any recount and the secretary of state is certifying him as we speak." So still without sleep, Joan and I packed two suitcases. The only way we could get to D.C. in time was to get up at three the next morning, drive to Minneapolis, and catch a seven o'clock flight to Washington. We were grateful to get four hours sleep, and the adrenaline surge kept us awake for the drive to Minneapolis until we took our seats on the airplane.

We had been told that the Wisconsin Democratic Congressional Delegation and the state press would meet us at the gate at Washington National airport. They would then drive us across the river to the Capitol, where I would be sworn in at noon. As the plane pulled up to the gate, a voice over the loudspeaker said, "Would Congressman Obey please step off the plane first. The vice president is waiting for you." I thought, "Good grief, what on earth is Spiro Agnew here for?"

When Joan and I descended the stairs, I saw immediately it wasn't Agnew—it was Hubert. Humphrey's limousine had pulled onto the tarmac right next to the plane, and he stood wearing a grin that was wide, even by Humphrey's standards. "Hop in," he said, "I'm driving you to the Capitol." I thought, "Gee, this is a nice change of plans." As we drove to the Capitol, Hubert told me that immediately after I was sworn in, he, Fred Harris, and I were scheduled for a press conference to introduce me to the national press and to talk about the national implications of my win. "Then," he said, "the two of you are coming with me to your first Washington power lunch—or out of power, as it is for some of us." Hubert's limo pulled onto the Capitol grounds and around and under the House-side Capitol steps. We walked in the door under the House steps and took the elevator to the Speaker's ceremonial office, just off the House floor. As we were ushered in, a member of the Speaker's staff said, "The Wisconsin delegation is trying to find you, Mr. Obey. They are still at the airport."

At that moment I realized there had been no change of plans at all. Hubert had simply been freelancing on impulse and had not told the delegation he was picking me up. When the Speaker's office told Reuss about the problem, they all hotfooted it back to the Capitol, but only Clem Zablocki made it to my swearing in on time because he had never gone to the airport in the first place. He had planned to simply see me in the Speaker's office before I took the oath. So instead of the usual ritual of being presented to the House by my home-state delegation, only Clem was there when I took the oath. The others came in just as I was finishing. The episode illustrated Will Rogers's old dictum: "I don't belong to any organized political party; I am a Democrat."

Immediately after the oath, Joan and I were swept out of the chamber to another room for my first Washington press conference. No planning, no prepared opening statement, just winging it with Hubert in enthusiastic high gear. In about twenty minutes it was over. Before Hubert could take me anywhere else, Fishbait Miller, the legendary doorkeeper of the House, said, "Mr. Obey, I have to put your mail somewhere. We've had over two thousand letters piling up for you in two days. We have to dump them somewhere and we can't until you pick an office. We've only got two, and I have to know which one you want." I quickly looked them over—they weren't what you would call choice real estate on Capitol Hill, but they looked pretty special to me. I picked 1417 Longworth, a fourth-floor suite, because it had a nice view of the floral garden that covered the Longworth parking garage. Then Fishbait said, "I sort of figured you would take this one, so I already had your mail delivered" and he waived his arm toward the desk behind the reception door. It was buried in a chaotic mound of envelopes—a perfect match for the gloriously jumbled day we were having.

After a quick "Welcome aboard!" meeting with the Wisconsin Democrats, it was off to the Madison Hotel with Hubert. We walked into the lobby, climbed the elegant circular stairs to the second floor, and went down the hall to a spacious room with a large circular table. "Dave and Joan, I would like you to meet some of my friends, and they will be your friends," Hubert said. He then introduced me to Eiler Ravenholt, from his staff; Tom Eagleton, the wonderful Missouri senator; Pat O'Connor, the treasurer of the DNC; Max Kampleman, who later would be Reagan's arms control director; Nelson Cruikshank, from the National Council on Senior Citizens; Al Barkin, the head of COPE for the AFL-CIO; and several others. If I had gotten enough sleep to be at least semiconscious, I would have been blown away by the speed and the chaos of the day, and by the never-flagging energy of our Minnesota friend. But all I could think was, "My God, I need to sit down and have a drink and get some sleep." By 7 p.m., we were back on Northwest heading home.

As the airplane was taxiing for takeoff, as the Capitol came into view, I reached for Joan's hand and thought of the same sight just a few months earlier when I had said a silent prayer asking God to let me be a part of it all. Less than ninety days later I was on my way home, the youngest congressman in the country. If I wasn't living the American dream, who on earth was?

SAYING GOODBYE

When Joan and I landed in Minneapolis, we drove to Jerry and Nelda's cottage on Pulaski Lake and relaxed for three glorious, restful, happy days. The following Wednesday was a bittersweet day. I drove to Madison to say goodbye to my friends in the legislature and clean out my desk with the help of my secretary, Jean King, and Bob Huber's secretary, Maxine Hesse. Harold Froehlich gaveled the assembly to order and then invited me to address the assembly from the Speaker's dais, a generous gesture from a friend. It was hard for me to say goodbye and it showed. Emotions welled up in me a number of times. Both sides gave me a standing ovation when I was finished, not in response to anything I had said but out of a common bond of friendship. And then it was done. A precious chapter in my life closed.

John Wyngaard, who had been one of the few political analysts who thought the race would be too close to call, wrote that day:

> The whole country has been told that the election was an upset. Perhaps it was to many persons, but those whose business it was to watch such matters knew . . . the vote margin was likely to be a narrow one and had concluded during the last few weeks . . . that the Democratic nominee might very well win. . . . [One] sign came when the young assemblyman shrewdly keyed his campaign on statehouse issues, including the state fiscal dilemma in a district where the otherwise victorious Republican governor Knowles had lost to his Democratic rival as recently as last fall. Obey got a bonus of a sort when he managed to get his opponent . . . on the defensive, something the experienced politician avoids like the plague. . . . Everything considered, the Obey defeat was a brilliant one for a young man who was marked as a politician with a future soon after he turned up in Madison as a boyish assemblyman seven years ago.

Putting ideology aside, there is a good deal of similarity between Obey and Laird. . . . Both came to the legislature as youngsters. Both came with a determination to build a career in politics. Both worked hard. Both were bright and personable. Both rose rapidly to leadership positions in state offices. . . . Now Obey has made the same kind of start that Laird made and coincidently also at the enviable age of 30 years. . . . There is a maxim in Washington that, all other things being equal, a congressman must be a dunce or a sloth or both to lose his seat once he has occupied it. . . . Obey will learn the ropes quickly enough. The Republicans have taken a hard punch on the nose!

I did have one additional pleasure on that day of many goodbyes. I said goodbye to the Democratic caucus and watched as they elected Frank Nikolay to succeed me as deputy leader, by a single vote—the same margin by which Frank had won over Bill Ward on my first day in the assembly after the 1962 elections. That night, as I walked out of the state capitol and into a new chapter in my life, I smiled as I realized that the caucus was once again in the hands of the same two men who had led it the first day I walked in—Bob Huber and Frank Nikolay. The more things changed, the more they remained the same.

PART 3

✦

ONE OF 435

Years of Learning

❧

CHAPTER 6

New Kid on the Block

At thirty, I was the nation's youngest member of Congress, starting from scratch. I started building a staff by hiring Lyle Stitt as my Washington staff director and Jerry Madison as my district staff director. Jerry's first act was to hire Win Spencer, our neighbor, as office manager. For our district office we chose the postmaster's office in the old post office building, which had become a federal office building when the postal service moved to new quarters. That meant that the building in which I, as a college student, had spent hours studying at a table in the lobby was now to be my office building. I liked that.

The Stitts and the Obeys flew to Washington to get organized and find a place to live. Joan and I stayed at a hotel near the Capitol while we carved out two days to find a house to rent. Kaz Oshiki had lined up a realtor to show us places. The day we started, Kaz was talking on the phone to Jack Kole, the Washington bureau chief for the *Milwaukee Journal*. When Kaz mentioned that he was helping us to find a place to rent, Kole told him that the house across the street from his in Arlington had just become vacant. We looked at it the next day and took it on the spot. No time! We just needed to keep moving.

Lyle and I moved slowly to hire staff. First, we hired an experienced case-worker, Bea Larson, who hailed from northern Minnesota, and a personal secretary, Kathy O'Hara, a twenty-two-year-old FBI-trained Kenosha native who had been working for Rep. Roman Pucinski of Chicago. My main concern was to hire a good legislative assistant. I wanted Linda Reivitz, who had worked for me in the legislature. Three years earlier, Huber had put me in charge of hiring a small leadership staff, and I had hired Linda. She was a smart, shrewd, tough-minded woman from Chicago, who knew me and my district. Linda had left the previous year to become special assistant to the New York City superintendent of schools, John Doar, a highly respected lawyer, from New Richmond, Wisconsin, who had been a law partner of Warren Knowles. When I first broached the subject with her, she turned me down, but within two weeks changed her mind. She made all the difference in those early years. She was a pro who learned, as I did, to negotiate the twists and turns of Washington. We developed a strong friendship that survives to this day.

SETTLING IN

For the first year, I thought I had made a mistake by running. In the legislature, as part of the leadership, I had been at the center of everything that happened. In the House, as the 435th person on the totem pole, I was included in nothing. It was "learn, learn, learn, wait, wait, wait, listen, listen, listen."

When I was sworn in, there was only one Democratic committee vacancy, Public Works, and that was where I was assigned. Committee assignments were made by the Ways and Means Committee acting in its capacity as the Democratic Committee on Committees. The chairman of the committee was Arkansas Democrat Wilbur Mills. Mills had gone through the ritual of asking what my committee interests were, but we both knew it was a pro forma act. "Where do you want to serve in the long run?" he had asked. I discussed my experience on the Joint Finance Committee and told him my long-term goal was Appropriations. "Well," he said, "go to Public Works, work hard, learn the subject matter, people will size you up, and we'll see." Message? "Don't call us, we'll call you."

Two weeks later Mills did just that. The week after the Easter recess I was working in my office about 9:30 a.m. when my secretary buzzed me and said excitedly, "Chairman Mills is on the phone." The staff reacted as if God were on the line. I picked up the phone and heard Mills say, "Dave, who the hell is this *Sandstorm* fella?" At first I had no idea what he was talking about, but it soon became clear. Mills told me that on Easter Sunday morning the phone had rung at his home in Little Rock. Mills answered it, and the voice on the other end said, "Mr. Mills, my name is Will A. Sandstrom and I want you to know that if you don't have a tax reform bill out of your committee in eight days I'm going to move to Little Rock and run against you. I won't beat you, but I got a lot of experience running against Dave Obey up here in Wisconsin, and I will give you fits." "Who the hell is this guy?" Mills asked. I filled him in. I didn't know it then, but Sandstrom's call was to have a major impact on my life just a few months later.

I knew that, as a freshman, I would have little impact on legislation and that I should spend my time learning how to operate in the House focusing on strengthening my position back home. I went back nearly every weekend those first two years. As I settled in, I soon discovered that coming to Congress alone in a special election was both an advantage and a disadvantage. Winning a midterm election, especially taking a seat that had been occupied by a cabinet member from the other party, meant that virtually everybody in the House and Senate knew who I was.

There were also disadvantages. By the time I came in April, the previous freshmen class had already begun to settle in. Friendships and buddy arrangements had already congealed, and other members were focused on their own problems. I needed a mentor who could explain the byzantine ways of the institution to me and help guide me until I had my sea legs. In the early days, I relied heavily on Bob Kastenmeier and Henry Reuss. Without them and their staffs I would have screwed up dozens of times. They helped me with the day-to-day tasks of getting organized, dealing with staff and mail, and building my strength back home. But I also needed to spend time understanding how the institution worked and how the House leadership worked.

MENTORS

The first person to help me do that was Dick Bolling of Missouri. Bolling had been a legendary figure to me since my college course on the legislative process with Ralph Huitt. A brilliant protégé of Harry Truman and Sam Rayburn, Bolling was a key figure on the Rules Committee, the least understood but perhaps the most important committee in Congress for either political party. It serves as the institution's traffic cop. After other committees hammer out legislation and vote it out, the Rules Committee decides whether that legislation will ever be voted upon on the floor, and it sets the terms and conditions of the debate—how long it will be debated, what amendments may or may not be offered, and the like.

Bolling represented Kansas City, Missouri. He had worked under General Douglas MacArthur at the end of World War II, and was one of the key people in deciding who came home first. Bolling ran for Congress in 1948 and won, and within two short years became a trusted lieutenant of Speaker Sam Rayburn. Through the years, Bolling helped the Democratic leadership overcome the autocratic obstruction of the notorious southern racist, Howard (Judge) Smith, who chaired the Rules Committee and had been blocking both John Kennedy's and Lyndon Johnson's efforts to pass progressive legislation, especially in the area of civil rights. After Rayburn died, Bolling became frustrated by the weak House leadership of Speaker John McCormack, who allowed the old bulls in the House to run their committees almost as independent fiefdoms. In frustration he had written two landmark books on the House, *Power in the House* and *House Out of Order*. Both books laid out a reform agenda, much of which would be refined, expanded, and adopted in future years.

Shortly after I was elected, Bolling introduced himself to me and said, "We have something in common; my mother was from Wisconsin. She battled my father's conservative instincts in the struggle for my political soul and won. When you have the time I would like to hear more about you, how you won, and how you are going to make sure you stay here." "When I have the time?" I thought. "He's the one up to his eyeballs in things." Over the next few weeks when he did have the time, he would sit in an end seat in the House chamber next to the doors to the Speakers lobby and take me to school. He gave me the lowdown on members who were on the floor, and explained process and parliamentary techniques far more intricate than I had experienced in the state legislature. Over the years I became a Bolling protégé. He taught me more about the House as an institution than anyone else.

Close behind Bolling as mentors were Phil Burton, a sometimes maniacally driven congressman from California, and Dick Conlon, the staff director of the Democratic Study Group. The Democratic Study Group was an organization of progressive Democrats in the House. It had first been put together by people like Chet Hollifield of California, Gene McCarthy of Minnesota, Frank Thompson of New Jersey, and John Blatnik of Minnesota to create a progressive power center in the House to counter the southern Democrat–GOP Conservative Coalition that had blocked JFK's agenda and strongly dominated the institution for almost three decades.

Phil Burton was, at once, the most brilliant and the most flawed young Turk in the House. First elected in 1964, he had been and remained a power in the California political landscape. He probably knew more about Social Security, Medicare, Medicaid, and welfare policy than anyone in the House and was passionate in his desire to weave them into a safety net that guaranteed health care and dignity to every American. In later years he also became passionate about preserving America's pristine and beautiful outdoor places for future generations, and he brilliantly maneuvered expansion after expansion of the national park system. But next to power itself, he was most passionate about the stupidity of the Vietnam War and the political leadership who had gotten us into it. He regarded himself as first among equals in reform circles.

He had a lot of competition. Mo Udall, a lanky, rugged, and extraordinarily gifted Arizonan with a sweet disposition, was as courageous as he was charming. He succeeded his brother Stewart Udall in the House after JFK had named him secretary of interior. Mo had staked out his claim as the leading advocate of change in the House by running what he knew to be a futile campaign against McCormack for Speaker in 1968. At one time McCormack had been a fierce, tough figure in the party, but in the late 1960s he was operating on fumes. Even so, he defeated Mo by a large margin.

John Moss of California was the premier member of the House when it came to running investigations. He was a fierce, gutsy crusader for economic justice and the public interest. Moss used his position on the Energy and Commerce Committee to fight special interests at every turn. He specialized in consumer protection and was a driving force behind the passage of the Freedom of Information Act. From the day he arrived in Congress until the day he left, he never lost his sense of rage at injustice and battled every waking moment to do something about it.

John Dingell was another giant who learned investigative skills from Moss and would put fear in the heart of any bureaucrat who departed from John's view of the public interest. He, Moss, and Paul Rogers, all with fiercely assertive personalities, dominated the Energy and Commerce Committee.

Ben Rosenthal was a New York liberal who also focused on consumer rights at home and human rights abroad. He used his sardonic wit to ridicule the old guard chairmen who in his view stood between the Democratic Party and its Progressive traditions.

Jack Bingham, a cerebral New Yorker who deeply understood the workings of the institution, worked hard to raise the level of political support for reform in the House. He told me that he had fond memories of Wausau because, as a very young man riding the rails during the Depression, he was allowed to sleep in the Marathon County jail one night when he had no money for a roof over his head. The next morning he was sent on his way after a good breakfast, courtesy of the taxpayers.

Jim O'Hara was a solid, thoughtful legislative craftsman from Michigan. One of the most frustrating characteristics of so many liberals or progressives in Congress throughout the years was that they were simply not operational. While they could give eloquent speeches that would stir souls, many could not strategize their way through a phone book. Jim was a spectacular exception. His specialties were education and attention to detail. In my mind, he was the engineer on the Education and Labor Committee who organized the tactically challenged education specialists on that committee into an effective fighting force. He not only knew the details of whatever legislation he was fighting for but also knew the rules better than anyone else except Bolling, and he—as did Bolling—knew how to put together winning coalitions. And, like Bolling and Udall, he was a truly decent man.

Frank "Thompy" Thompson from New Jersey was a slim, lanky irreverent iconoclast who had a nickname for everybody; he was totally committed to the need to give workers the ability to organize to defend their interests.

Billy Ford of Michigan was a shorter version of Thompy and passionately cared about strengthening education and workers' rights—he spent thirty plus years in the House fighting for both. The son of a truck driver, he never for one moment forgot his roots and was a passionate advocate of equal educational opportunity.

Lloyd Meeds of Washington was a quieter version of Ford, but just as effective. He had an outsized ability—lacking in many politicians—to step back, draw a deep breath, think things through, and figure out a way to bring everybody together by giving them just enough of what they needed to keep them at the table. He was a key person on Education and Labor because he was much closer to Bolling than to Burton and was an important bridge between the two groups in the caucus.

Don Frazer was a cerebral Minnesotan on the Foreign Affairs Committee, whose twin passions were human rights and ending the Vietnam War. He was a strong-minded and highly principled person whose style was so restrained that it often hid his passion.

Ab Mikva was a thoughtful and principled political reformer from Chicago who had often given Mayor Daley fits at home. He was one of the few liberals on the Ways and Means Committee who was operational and was one of the kindest and yet toughest people in the Congress.

John Culver of Iowa was an absolutely fearless advocate for peace and social justice. He was a man of incredible intelligence, whose force of will matched his awesome physical strength.

Bob Kastenmeier and Henry Reuss were also deep into reform efforts in the House. Henry focused mostly on tax reform and urban development; Kastenmeier on Vietnam, civil liberties, and copyright law. In later years Bob became the unquestioned and unrivaled congressional expert on intellectual property issues. He was ahead of his time in understanding the economic importance of copyright law in the high-tech age. In the 1990s it amazed me that, just when the Madison economy and the University of Wisconsin were moving into an era when technology often defined opportunity, they turned out of Congress the one person who could have given them a leg up in riding that economic revolution and creating thousands of jobs in the process— an incredible loss to Wisconsin's entire economy. But Bob's main focus was on Vietnam. There, too, he was ahead of his time—for instance, in holding the first teach-ins in the nation on Vietnam. Burton respected his reformist peers, but the only one he felt at all intimidated by was Kastenmeier—I think because Burton recognized in Kastenmeier a purity of purpose that gave him added moral weight.

As soon as I was elected, Burton asked Kastenmeier to schedule a drink with me. We went to The Rotunda, a watering hole two blocks from the Capitol on Ivy Street (later bought by the Democratic Party and converted to the Democratic Club, a downscale version of the Republican Club two blocks away). Phil was planning for the day he would run for majority leader, but I didn't know that then. For an hour Phil talked about the House, Nixon, and how I could get reelected. His focus was: "Go home, go home, go home." "The more people know you, the more they will ignore the lies the Republicans tell about you," he said. He then said something I thought was preposterous: "If you do your homework, you come from the kind of district and kind of state that will respond. I'll predict right now your election won't even be close. I know you think it will be, but Uncle Phil guarantees it. It won't even be close." I thought he was smoking something that wasn't legal, but I liked the thought.

The person I probably saw the most of that first term was Dick Conlon. Dick had been a Duluth reporter before he went to work for Gene McCarthy. By the time I was elected, he was running the Democratic Study Group. The DSG had become operationally skillful during the Johnson years. Its focus was threefold: Vietnam, economic policy, and House reform. DSG held weekly meetings to discuss short-range issues on the House calendar and long-term issues relating to Vietnam and internal House reform. Those weekly DSG meetings gave me insight into all of the major players and their relationships with each other. I learned a great deal more in those sessions about the people I was working with.

On July 16 Joan and I flew with a large number of members of Congress to Cape Canaveral, which had been renamed Cape Kennedy, to witness the launching of the spacecraft that would take Neil Armstrong and his crew to mankind's first landing on the moon. As we sat in the bleachers watching the powerful rocket rise slowly from the NASA gantry, I was surprised by the sound. I had expected the rocket to produce a low roar as it strained skyward, but it didn't roar—it crackled like a huge firecracker. The crowd applauded and cheered as the ground shook. Four days later, deep in the night back in Washington, we watched television with the rest of the nation as Armstrong took "one small step for man, one giant leap for mankind." As I watched that scene, I recalled the day just a few years earlier when Henry Ahrnsbrak and I had talked in the stairway at the UW–Wausau Center, the day the Russians had first put Sputnik into orbit around the earth. Armstrong's mission had indeed been a long leap for America since that profoundly unsettling day.

VIETNAM

During my first year in the House, the issue that most troubled me was Vietnam. Influenced by Gaylord Nelson, I had long since concluded that the war was futile but was unsure about what Congress could do about it. It was even more complicated for me because the secretary of defense was the man I had just replaced in Congress. I was also troubled by the fact that even if I didn't trust what Nixon was saying or doing, the administration had just come to power and could reasonably argue that since Johnson hadn't ended it in four years, they deserved some time to try it their way.

I decided to give Nixon one year before I took a position in support of congressional efforts to end the war. I hated to do it because the year would produce more American dead and wounded and more American POWs, but I felt it was the only fair approach I could take. I attended countless DSG meetings on the war and listened to countless formulations proposed by Burton, Fraser, Don Riegle—a Republican from Michigan who later switched parties—and many others. The problem faced by those opposed to continuing the war was that they had no mechanism that could be used to get a floor vote for a sensible amendment. The majority of Congress was still supporting the war, as were most members of the Foreign Affairs and Armed Services Committees. That meant opponents were blocked from bringing anything they thought made sense to the floor to force a vote. The only way members had been able to express their opposition to continuing the war had been to vote "No" on the entire DoD appropriations bill—and not many members wanted to do that.

Most DSG members wanted to produce a plan that called for a timetable, and they attached conditions for triggering that timetable, but House rules clearly blocked that. In those days, votes on amendments were not even recorded votes. When bills were considered for amendment, in order to eliminate the need for a full quorum of 218 members, they were considered in what was called the Committee of the Whole, to reduce the required quorum to one hundred. There were no roll calls on amendments voted on in the Committee of the Whole. The only way a member's position could be known on an issue decided in the Committee of the Whole was if a reporter in the gallery reported *which* line a member walked through when votes were counted in

"Teller Votes." Again, they were not recorded by name. Only if an amendment was adopted in the Committee of the Whole could a roll-call vote be obtained just before final passage of the bill immediately after the bill was reported back to the full House. Because an insufficient number of members supported any restraints on administration policy in Vietnam, no rational amendments on the subject could pass in the Committee of the Whole, and the House therefore could avoid a publicly recorded roll-call vote on the subject.

Another first-termer, Jim Symington, and I had countless conversations about our dilemma. Jim was the son of Stuart Symington, who had previously served as secretary of the Air Force under President Truman and had himself been a candidate for president in 1952 and 1956. We both believed the war was futile but did not want to be forced by House rules to vote for an unworkable or ineffective cutoff plan that did not accurately represent the kind of limitation we favored. As my self-imposed one-year grace period expired, both Jim and I began to support a variety of cutoff amendments, even if they were inartfully drafted and even if they did not fully reflect our position. It was not until several years later that the House was able to vote for the amendment that did finally end the war.

A Phone Call Changes Everything

In early November I received a phone call that changed my life in Congress. About 10:30 a.m. I was at my desk in my Longworth office when a call came from Martha Griffith. Martha represented Wisconsin and Michigan when the Ways and Means Committee, acting in its capacity as the Committee on Committees, filled committee vacancies. "Dave," she asked, "you still want to be on the Appropriations Committee?" "Of course I do, why do you ask?" I replied. "Well," she said, "Chuck Jolson [a senior New Jersey member] has just been nominated for a federal judgeship, and we also have a vacancy on Commerce. I had the Appropriations slot tied down for Billy Ford, but he decided he had too much seniority on Education and Labor, and wants to stay there, so it is still vacant and I think I can get it for you if you still want it." I was flabbergasted. "Who do I have to call or kill to get it?" I asked. "Only Wilbur," she said. "Danny [Rostenkowski] may raise it with you if he sees you because he's slated to get the Commerce seat for his region, but you should call the chairman and tell him I told you to call and kiss his ring."

Still not quite believing what was happening, I hung up, dialed Wilbur Mills's number, and asked for him. When he came on the phone, I said, "Mr. Chairman, this is Will Sandstorm" and then quickly added, "Just kidding, it's

Dave Obey from Wisconsin." Mills chuckled and said, "Martha told me I might get a call from you. She tells me you would do a good job, and I have no reason to disagree except for one thing. I don't quite know if I should be helping someone who dumps his primary opponents on the chairman of the Ways and Means Committee." Then he said, "Look, Dave, I can't promise anything because the committee has to meet and there could be some surprises, but Martha will make a good case for you." "When will the committee deal with this?" I asked. "Today," he replied. I thanked him for his consideration, hung up, and went to the floor for a quick stop, and ran into another Ways and Means member, Jim Corman of California, who teased me about being Martha's fair-haired boy. I met Lyle at the House Recording Studio, where I taped a five-minute constituent radio report. As I was leaving, the studio technician said, "Mr. Obey, phone call for you." Martha Griffith was on the other end saying, "You got it." The same words John Armstrong used years earlier to tell me that I had gotten the NDEA Russian Studies Fellowship. "Is it done, is it official, can I tell people?" I asked. "Yes," she said. "It's done. Our leadership will announce it to the House today. Now you hotfoot it up to Wilbur's office, just off the floor. I'll call Dev O'Neill [the House photographer] and meet you there. Wilbur and I will have your picture taken with us, and you can let your district press know. This is quite a coup for you. Laird educated your district about how important Appropriations is, and they will understand it." I practically flew to Mills's office with Lyle, and the next day the district papers ran the story.

Within the hour Bob Kastenmeier called and said, "Dave, Phil Burton wants to talk to you right away about Appropriations. Has George Mahon [the committee chairman] called you yet?" "No," I said. "Good, Phil wants me to tell you right away about your subcommittee assignments. Let's meet at the Rotunda." Bob, Phil, and I met about 5 p.m. Kastenmeier ordered a martini and I asked for a dry Manhattan on the rocks. Burton came in a few minutes later and ordered a vodka on the rocks. Before Phil had even sat down at the table, he said, "David, the first thing that you have to do is talk to Jeff." Jeff was Jeff Cohelan of California, Phil's brother-in-law and a member of Appropriations, soon to be defeated in the 1970 election by Ron Dellums (a California African American who would later rise to become chairman of the House Armed Services Committee). "Jeff will give you an idea of the culture of the committee and how it works and all that, but it's all important that you get the right subcommittee assignment," Burton said.

Burton then pulled out a sheet of paper showing the full committee roster and the membership of each of the thirteen Appropriations subcommittees.

He then explained to me that, unlike any other committee in the House, on Appropriations, seniority accrued by subcommittee rather than full committee. That meant that members did not rise to subcommittee chairmanships based on their length of service on the full committee, but rather based on their length of service on subcommittee. "That means," Phil said, "that if you want to become a Cardinal [the thirteen subcommittee chairs were known as the "College of Cardinals" and Mahon, the chairman, was known as the "Pope"], you need to get a subcommittee where people above you will be gone before too long." Burton then proceeded to give me a subcommittee by subcommittee rundown of all of the Democratic members, their philosophies, their districts, their legislative styles, and their career plans. He knew it all.

"Now, notice," he said, "the conservative old bulls have blocked access to every major subcommittee chairmanship." Phil explained that Mahon, who had the sole authority to appoint people to subcommittees, had used that authority to make certain that conservatives (mostly southern Democrats) not only held the key subcommittee chairmanships but also the first and second slots behind those chairmanships. What few liberals and progressives there were on the committee were largely confined to the smaller, less important subcommittees. "There are only two exceptions," Burton said. "Eddie Boland is HUD chairman and Julia Butler Hansen is the acting chairman of Interior because Mike Kirwin, the chairman, is sick. If you want a quick route to a Cardinal's chair try to get on Interior," Phil advised. "Kirwin is number one there, but he won't be back. Julia is next, but she has an elderly husband and wants to spend time with him. She won't be here longer than six years. Jack Marsh is number three but is more interested in other issues and doesn't intend to be around here long. Sid Yates is number four, but he is the senior Jew on Appropriations and will probably take the chairmanship of Foreign Operations because of his interest in Israel, rather than taking Interior. That means that with a couple of breaks you could be chair of Interior within six or eight years. If you like that stuff, that's what you should try to do. But don't let Mahon know that's your first choice or he won't give it to you. Jeff will explain it all to you."

The next morning Cohelen came up to me on the floor and handed me a copy of a large book by Richard Fenno, a nationally known political scientist from Cornell University who focused on the appropriations process. "Read the last chapter of this book on the socialization process of the committee. It will give you an understanding of the culture of the committee, the atmosphere; it's a very insulated committee with lots of taboos," he said. Then he asked if Mahon had talked to me yet. "Not yet," I replied. "He's probably still in shock," Cohelen said. "Your appointment came out of the blue. The chair usually has a hand in these things, but nobody saw this one coming," he said. Jeff also advised me to be coy about my subcommittee preferences. "Mahon doesn't want people on subcommittees who could be advocates for spending for specific programs, so if you want more dollars for education, don't tell him that. He will never appoint you to Labor-H. If you have a preference, tell him it's your third or fourth preference. Whatever subcommittee you appear to be trying for you won't get."

About a half hour later my secretary phoned me on the floor and told me that Mahon wanted to see me right away. I walked over to the committee office, just off the House floor, and told the committee receptionist who I was, and she ushered me into Mahon's office. I expected Mahon to welcome me to the committee, ask a little about me before he got down to business. Instead, Mahon got up out of his chair, came around his desk, and as he was shaking my hand said, "Young man, how on earth did you get on this committee?" I wasn't sure whether he was asking out of surprise, displeasure, or both. I recited the chain of events, told him of my experience on the Joint Finance Committee, and mentioned that Mel Laird's service on the committee had educated my district about the importance of the committee. Then he asked about my subcommittee preferences.

I had decided to take Phil Burton's advice and try to maneuver my way onto Interior, but I had to do it by indirection. "What subcommittees would you like?" Mahon asked. Remembering Cohelen's advice to mask my choices by describing them as third- or fourth-tier preferences, I decided to tell Mahon the absolute truth about my long-term preferences and be silent about my short-term goals. I told him that my first choice would be Labor-Health, Education, and Welfare and my second choice Defense. I indicated that because I knew there was no chance of getting them, that I didn't have strong feelings after that. "I do know what I don't want," I told him. "I recognize new members have to do duty on minor subcommittees like the District of Columbia, but I wouldn't want to be on both D.C. and something like Trea- sury Post Office." "We wouldn't do that to you," he said.

"I suppose if we put you on Agriculture you would be compelled to push for more money for rural development and other farm programs," he said. "Yes, I would," I responded honestly. "Do you have any mines or forests?" he asked me. "Forests, yes, but no mines," I answered. "We used to but they're gone now." "How would you feel about Interior?" he asked me. "Well," I answered, "I really don't know much about those issues, but I would be willing to learn," I said. "Of course, long-term I would still like to serve on Labor-H,"

I told him. "Well, why don't we put you on Interior and D.C. for the time being and see how it goes."

I walked out of Mahon's office delighted. Two weeks later when we sat down for Thanksgiving dinner, I had a lot to be thankful for. I had a wonderful wife and son, the job I had always wanted, and a new committee assignment that fit my interests and was understood back home. I couldn't have been more fortunate.

I spent most of the next year learning how the appropriations process worked while the Congress was focused on the war and the sagging economy. As a congressional rookie I had little to say about either, so I concentrated on more narrowly focused health and environmental issues.

When Medicare had first passed, the cost of prescription drugs was a small part of overall health care costs for seniors. But with ever-increasing attention to medical research, it was clear that they would become a bigger part of future costs. Gerry Sturges, my new legislative assistant (a former reporter who had been nominated for a Pulitzer Prize and had lost out to the reporter who did the exposé of Billy Sol Estes), suggested that while there was no chance for passing anything anytime soon, we could open a debate on the subject if the nation's youngest member of Congress introduced legislation to do something about this hole in the safety net for the nation's oldest citizens. I introduced the bill and began the process of trying to round up cosponsors. We pushed hard and got over eighty sponsors but could not get Wilbur Mills to even hold a hearing on the subject. Not being a member of the committee, it was hard for me to create the pressure on the committee that we needed in order to make it happen.

The other area I focused on was the environment. I joined Gaylord Nelson in sponsoring legislation to ban DDT, put more material in the congressional record on the dangers of mercury, joined John Saylor, a Pennsylvania Republican, in introducing a bill to prevent the hunting of wildlife from airplanes, and supported higher funding for water pollution abatement.

I spent most of my time in the first term learning the ropes on Appropriations, learning about the House in DSG sessions, and going home to the district. With rare exceptions, I would climb on a 7 p.m. Northwest plane to Madison, catch connecting North Central flights to Wausau, work the district on Saturday and Sunday, and catch the Sunday night plane back to Washington. Often Bill Steiger would catch the same return flight from Milwaukee to D.C., and we would talk as we enjoyed our small steaks—these were the days when most airlines served something besides peanuts and wretched sandwiches.

TYING DOWN THE DISTRICT

Back home, I knew the Republican Party regarded me as a one-term wonder, and I was determined to prove them wrong. While they scoured the landscape for a candidate to beat me, I blanketed the district. Jerry Madison, Louie Hanson, and I worked out a plan to spend a huge share of my time early in the year in the most Republican parts in the district. The more I could let Republican voters see I didn't have horns, the harder it would be for the Republican Party to distort my record. And the more Republicans saw me in their backyard, the more they would understand that no one was going to outwork me. That would make it harder for them to find a candidate. In March of 1970 they finally found one.

For several weeks I had been hearing through the grapevine that the Republican Party had recruited Andre LeTendre, the national chairman of the Jaycees, to run. Finally, a small story appeared about the possibility, and it was off to the races. LeTendre was thirty-three years old, originally from Chippewa Falls, and lived in Wausau when he was elected national Jaycees president. He had been a radio engineer in Chippewa Falls and the manager of a Wausau radio station. The press described him as "energetic, youthful, and articulate," and they were right on all counts. His wife, Mary Jean, was a thoughtful teacher with a warm personality.

I expected a tough, energetic campaign from LeTendre, and that's what he provided. He tried to resurrect the old canard that I was soft on student violence, but basically he ran a clean, issue-oriented campaign. Nixon cut a TV spot for him while visiting Green Bay but did him no favors by mispronouncing his last name (pronouncing it Andy LeTandy, rather than Andre LeTahnd). When the campaign began in April I expected a tough, tight race, but by August I felt a growing confidence that the campaign was going far better than I had expected. Wherever I went people were receptive and encouraging. I could tell that my work had paid off. The sagging national economy had also taken some of the sheen off Nixon, and by October I was confident of victory.

On Election Day I was stunned by the margin. I remembered Burton's prediction that I would win by a large margin. How right he had been. The next day the Wausau paper reported that with 319 out of 330 precincts reporting, I had received over 85,000 votes to about 40,000 for LeTendre. The paper reported that, "The lopsided victory left Obey's campaign workers speechless. The victor would probably admit he was surprised." The story then went on to say, "In his sixteen-year reign Laird was considered unbeatable, not only by his own party but by Democrats. However, he never piled up the majority Obey did Tuesday. While Obey won by 45,620 votes over his opponent, the best margins of Laird in recent off-year elections were 33,704 votes in 1966, 33,267 in 1962, 20,484 in 1958, and 17,753 in 1954."

The newspaper was right; I had been surprised. The election I was expecting to be tight was a rout. Pat Lucey had recaptured the governorship for the Democrats and had swept in a state assembly majority with him. I was delighted on all fronts. I was going back to Congress with a strong endorsement from my fellow citizens and with a Democratic governor and state assembly. That would mean I was guaranteed a fair shake in the reapportionment battle that lay ahead.

But before the next session began, our family underwent two huge changes. In early January my father died suddenly. Even though Joan was eight months pregnant, she flew home with me to the funeral. When we landed at Central Wisconsin Airport, I realized the plane wasn't slowing down enough to make its usual turn off the runway. The reverse thrusters had malfunctioned, and the pilot wound up taking the plane off the end of the runway into a snow bank. Fortunately, the plane had just enough runway to avoid a catastrophe. The week after we returned to Washington, Joan went into labor early, and our son Douglas David was born on January 23. We brought him home from the hospital on January 27, Joan's and Craig's birthday. Given our experience in losing Robert four years earlier, Joan and I were thrilled that Craig would finally have a brother. I was now surrounded by Aquarians. Doug's birth was welcome in another way as well, because it helped dull the pain of the loss of my father.

༄

CHAPTER 7

Digging in for the Long Haul

The first order of business in the new term was the election of a new majority leader to replace Carl Albert, who had moved up to the Speakership with the retirement of Speaker McCormack. I supported Mo Udall in a multifaceted race with Hale Boggs, Jim O'Hara, Wayne Hays, and John McFall. The race gave me my first opportunity to see how a caucus leadership race was organized. To me, Mo would have been a welcome breath of fresh air in a stale caucus, but progressives were split between O'Hara and Udall. As the only southerner in the race, Boggs had a much more playable hand. People knew that as the only southern candidate he would be one of the two finalists, which gave him an advantage in pressuring rank-and-file members who wanted to be with a winner.

Sam Gibbons of Florida, one of the members of Congress who had participated in the D-Day Invasion at Normandy, was Udall's campaign manager. His vote count had Mo within striking distance of victory, but when the actual votes were tallied, Boggs was a comfortable winner. That taught me a valuable lesson. In a secret ballot race, there was no way to tell which members did and which members didn't live up to their promises. In a multiballot race, members could keep their commitment to a candidate on one ballot and desert him on the others. If you wanted a hard count of your vote, the question you had to ask was not "How are you on the majority leader's race?" or "Can we count on your vote for Mo?" The only right question was "Can we count on you to vote for Mo on every ballot?" And even then, some of your colleagues would look you in the eye and lie through their teeth.

When the votes were counted, Mo's total fell well short of his commitments. When the votes were announced Mo asked the press, "Do you know how to tell the difference between a cactus and a caucus? With a cactus the pricks are on the outside." I would remember that experience years later in my own caucus races.

At the start of the next session, I was involved in my first fight to reform the moss-backed procedures that governed Congress in those days. Since my election to the Appropriations Committee I had done what every freshman was told to do in those days: I kept my mouth shut and got educated. I focused on my subcommittee work, learning about our national parks and forests, about our underground natural resources and the agencies that oversaw them. And I learned more about the House. I had been invited by Bob Kastenmeier to attend a weekly 8 a.m. meeting of progressive reformers called simply "the group." During those sessions Kastenmeier, Patsy Mink, Bob Eckhardt, Brock Adams, Lloyd Meeds, and others talked about everything from House procedures to the Vietnam War. The group was especially frustrated by McCormack, who seemed to have few policies of his own except to follow the lead of independent committee chairmen. When younger House members had a problem or an idea, they usually sought out the majority leader, Carl Albert, who was much more open-minded than was McCormack. The Kastenmeier group was universally pleased when McCormack retired and was replaced by the more vigorous Albert.

OPENING UP THE COMMITTEE

In February, right after the caucus leadership elections, the Appropriations Committee met to adopt its rules for the year. When Mahon presented the committee's rules for adoption, Sid Yates moved to amend the rules to require Appropriations public hearings to be public. Up until that time, even the committee's public hearings were held behind closed doors. That meant the public couldn't get in and neither could the staff except that of the chairman. After Sid explained his motion, I expected others to speak, but nobody did, so finally I stood up to support him. It was the first time I had risen to speak in full committee since I had been appointed to Appropriations.

As I rose, before I could utter a word, John Rooney, the crusty octogenarian from Brooklyn who chaired the subcommittee that oversaw the State and Justice Departments and the FBI muttered, "Sit down you smart-ass young punk. What do you know?" These were the first words that John Rooney had ever spoken to me. Surprised and angered by Rooney's words, I turned to him and said to him, "Kiss my fanny, you senile old goat. What do you know?" The committee let out a collective gasp. I thought senior members like Dan Flood, Otto Passman, Bob Sikes, and George Andrews were going to go into cardiac arrest. They were clearly shocked that one so new as I should utter a word of anything but the most profound respect for the sainted senior members. But Rooney slapped the table, he burst out laughing, and at that moment took an instant liking to me—even though the rest of the old bulls on the committee acted like I was a heretic who should be burned at the stake. Sid's motion finally passed, and the committee adjourned without blood on the floor.

Taking on the Chairman—The D.C. Subway Fight

The first significant fight I waged was on the question of whether the Congress would move ahead to pay for its share of the cost of building Washington's new subway system.

Shortly before I was elected to Congress, a dispute had broken out between the District of Columbia, the State of Virginia, and the Congress about whether or not a new bridge should be built across the scenic Potomac River between Arlington and Georgetown. Georgetown was already strangling in traffic, and the District government was resisting the construction of the new bridge. The D.C. Appropriations Subcommittee was chaired by Bill Natcher, a respected, courtly, tough-minded Kentuckian. The Congress had recently authorized the construction of a new subway system for the District, and Natcher had for the previous year held up the appropriation for it until the District dropped its opposition to the bridge.

As the most junior member of the subcommittee, I reluctantly acquiesced in Natcher's decision because I felt there was no way I could change the outcome. But when the dispute spilled over into another year, it became apparent that further delay would raise construction costs due to inflation. It was also obvious to me that obliterating the beauty of Spout Run by adding more lanes to the traffic and dumping even more cars into Georgetown's clogged streets was the wrong thing to do. When Natcher made clear that he intended to continue denying funds for the desperately needed subway system, I decided that, win or lose, I was going to start a fight by offering an amendment to the D.C. Appropriations bill restoring the needed funds.

I knew the second-ranking Democrat on the subcommittee, Bob Giaimo of Connecticut, disagreed with Natcher but had given no indication he would be willing to argue with him. I called Giaimo and told him that I could not continue to allow Natcher to go unchallenged on the issue. "I intend to offer an amendment unleashing the subway if I have to, Bob," I told him, "but the amendment should really come from you. People will listen to you who don't even know who I am," I told him.

"God, I agree with you," Bob said, "but taking on Natcher is damn near death defying in this place. You don't know him like I do. He never forgets who crosses him, and we will pay a hell of a price if we take him on—especially if we lose—and the odds of our overturning him are damn slim." "I know that," I told Bob, "but a few years from now if Spout Run is destroyed and Georgetown is a mess, I will wish to hell I had done something." We talked a few minutes more and Bob finally said, "You're right. We will probably lose our heads, but we ought to do it, and we ought to move fast." He then laid out a strategy for action. "I have to go to Connecticut today, but why don't you organize a meeting for next Monday. Call the other subcommittee members to ask if they would come. You should also call the mayor's office and the Subway Authority and ask them to send somebody so we can plan. We should also let the White House know, because the Nixon administration wants the subway built."

When I made my calls, I found little interest from other subcommittee members. When I called the office of deputy mayor Graham Watt to ask them to send someone to a strategy meeting, they reacted like I had leprosy. "Oh no, we can't send anybody," they said. "We can't risk antagonizing the chairman." "You have to be kidding," I said. "You want the money; the Subway Authority wants the money; you expect us to antagonize Natcher, but you don't have the guts to do the same thing?" I asked. Then I told them, "Look, the meeting is going to be held whether you come or not. We're sticking our necks out whether you do or not, but if you don't come, I will tell a press conference that the mayor's office is an Uncle Tom operation." The next week they showed up at the meeting.

Bob and I knew we could not beat Natcher without major league help. We believed the key was the White House. They wanted the money too but were also concerned about taking on Natcher. In the end they agreed to send Egil Krogh to work the Hill with us. They also convinced Carl Albert, the Speaker, to support the amendment, and he was able to persuade Mahon. We worked the phones and the floor around the clock, and when the vote came we won.

I felt ecstatic after the vote, but Giaimo was glum. "Don't count your chickens. Natcher can still win this," Bob said. "All he has to do is stall on going to conference with the Senate until the end of the fiscal year. If he slow dances and doesn't go to conference with the Senate, the bill will die and D.C. will be funded in a continuing resolution. That resolution will be at last year's spending levels with last year's terms and conditions. Since last year's bill contained no subway dollars, the continuing resolution won't either. The only way we can win this is if we can force Natcher to a conference."

All summer, Natcher did exactly as Giaimo had predicted—he refused to go to conference. But late in the year the White House prevailed on Albert and Mahon to insist that Natcher conference the bill. When the conference committee finally met, Natcher was determined that he would still not be beaten. The ranking Republican on our subcommittee was Glen Davis of Wisconsin. He and Natcher again slow danced us, working for a stalemate.

The Senate subcommittee was chaired by Dan Inouye of Hawaii. He knew his brief as well as Natcher. Together we kept the pressure on, and in the closing days of the session finally pushed the conference to a vote. We finally succeeded, and both the House and Senate passed the conference report. Natcher's hold on the subway had been broken. The day we won, I was holding a "Tom and Jerry" pre-Christmas party in my office in the Cannon building. Few members of Congress even knew what a Tom and Jerry was, but Tip O'Neill did. No self-respecting Irishman was ignorant of the blessings of Tom and Jerrys, a Christmas drink of hot water, an egg-based batter spiced with cinnamon, nutmeg, cream of tartar, and allspice, laced with rum and brandy. The party began at 5 p.m. and Giaimo arrived right on time—half to celebrate and half to bemoan our fate in Natcher's doghouse. As he sat on my office couch and sipped his drink, he became more and more melancholy. "Dave, it was a helluva job we did. Never thought we could do it until the end. It was the right thing to do, but nobody will ever thank us, and Natcher will never forget," he said. Giaimo proved to be right on both counts. When the subway was dedicated, I did not even receive an invitation. Jackson Graham, the head of the Subway Authority, never called to express appreciation. And Natcher didn't speak to Bob or me for two years. Today the subway has continued to expand. Without it, city roads would be even more congested than they are today.

Today there is virtually no one left in D.C. city hall or in the office of the Metro Authority who remembers how the impasse was finally broken. Mark Plotkin, a local media institution, may be the only member of the D.C. press corps who remembers. But I do, and I'm proud of the role I played in jumpstarting the fight that pried it loose.

A New District

My second term was dominated by the war, the presidential campaign, and the mother of all congressional crises—reapportionment. In a series of decisions, the federal court system had strengthened and intensified the constitutional requirement of "one man, one vote" in drawing congressional and state legislative districts. Before the *Baker vs. Carr* decision and *Reynolds vs. Sims,* the Constitution's requirement for redistricting congressional, state legislative, and municipal district lines every ten years to assure that each American's vote was equal in influence was widely ignored. Many state legislatures had gone several decades without redrawing district lines, and the population of those districts varied widely. The Wisconsin State Constitution required that in drawing congressional districts, county lines not be broken. But the new decisions required that congressional districts be virtually equal in population; that requirement meant that county lines would have to be broken to achieve that degree of equality. The existing district lines had largely been drawn by Mel Laird in 1964.

In February, the Wisconsin congressional delegation decided to ask Bill Steiger and me to try to put together a congressional redistricting plan that could be supported on a bipartisan basis. That was a tough thing to do because, under the new census, Wisconsin was entitled to one *less* House seat than it had before the census. That meant that unless somebody retired, at least two of us would end up running against one another, so it would be harder to reach political agreement. That increased the likelihood that the courts rather than the legislature would wind up redrawing the lines. Steiger and I were asked to do the job because we had the greatest familiarity with the state legislature and had both participated in the previous redistricting in 1964 when we were in the state assembly.

Bill suggested that the two of us get together and try to draft an initial map for discussion purposes, but I suggested a different approach. I proposed that he and I each draft a plan that we thought would be fair to both parties and then meet to discuss the differences. Today, computer technology can produce hundreds of variations in a matter of days, but in 1973 we did it by hand, using pocket calculators. We agreed that several principles would guide us. First, neither party would seek to use the redistricting process to win at the map-making table what they had not been able to win at the ballot box. Second, redistricting would not be used to artificially increase or decrease anyone's strength. The guiding principle was that redistricting would simply reflect changes in population; it would not be used to artificially create political changes that were not the natural outcome of population shifts. As much as possible we wanted it to be a demographic, not a political, event.

About a month after the first discussion, Steiger and I met in his Longworth Building office to compare maps. He had his map lying face down on the table. I laid mine on the table the same way. When we turned them over we were amazed to see that with the exception of minor differences in the southern part of the state and two counties in the northwest, our maps were virtually identical. My district was essentially dismembered, with pieces of it being moved to each of the surrounding districts. Most of it was combined with Alvin O'Konski's northern district. About 54 percent of the population in the new district was from my district, and 46 percent was from Alvin's. I didn't like the idea of having to run against another incumbent, but someone's district had to be eliminated and mine, being surrounded, was the logical one. When we ran it by other members, no one raised an objection. I had expected O'Konski to object to being placed in a district with me, but he didn't. He stayed out of it and told us he really didn't mind and would probably retire. Next, we had to thread the legislative needle. Bob Knowles was helpful in getting the package through the state senate, but we were almost torpedoed in the assembly. The source of the problem was ironic.

Eight years earlier when legislative reapportionment was before the assembly, we had almost reached a compromise agreement. But at the last minute, Harold Froehlich had engineered a change in Outagamie County that purposely torpedoed Bill Rogers, a Democrat from Froehlich's neighborhood. When that happened, I explained the choices facing us to the assembly Democratic caucus and urged them not to walk away from Rogers, even if it meant we were stalemated. With that history, I was dismayed eight years later when Rogers, of all people, led an assault on our congressional plan. Rogers was a free spirit who had grown increasingly flaky over the years. Increasingly resentful of his waning influence, he seemed to enjoy tweaking anybody and everybody when he had the chance. Rogers gave a hilarious speech on the plan, humor aimed at me and Steiger, and almost won the day. He offered an amendment to move Manitowoc County back into the eighth district, which would have killed the plan. It failed by one vote. After our bill squeaked through the legislature, Pat Lucey signed it and we avoided an expensive court fight.

Just as the legislature was considering the bill, O'Konski suddenly attacked the plan and suggested he might run after all. I knew it would be months before Alvin actually committed, but there was no point in trying to guess about it. I was determined to do two things: first, line up as many groups that had supported him in the past as I could, in order to convince him he couldn't win; second, proceed on the assumption he would run and simply outwork him. My goal was to work his part of the district hard enough to break even. If I did that, he couldn't win because I knew I could lick him in my district. In the 1972 presidential primary, Ed Muskie and Hubert Humphrey were left in the dust by the antiwar blitz of George McGovern. That meant 1972 was going to be a very tough year.

CHAPTER 8

∾

Alvin

Alvin O'Konski was a charming major-league charlatan. He was first elected
to the House in 1942 from the tenth congressional district in Wisconsin's far
northwest, defeating Barney Gehrmann, the last of the Wisconsin Progressives
in the House of Representatives. The colorful accounts of his career are the stuff
of legend. Stories abounded about him. Just one will give the flavor of the man.

Earlier in life, O'Konski coached high school debate. One weekend,
O'Konski's team hosted a debate with another high school; three teachers
from other cities did the judging. At the conclusion of the debate, as the host
coach, O'Konski announced the judge's decision. O'Konski's team had won
by a 2 to 1 vote. A few days afterwards, when the three judges happened to
meet, one said, "I don't know how on earth you could have voted for that
Pulaski team. They were terrible!" "I didn't vote for them," responded the second judge. "Neither did I," the third judge responded. They then realized that
O'Konski had simply announced the results he had wanted, figuring that the
judges would never know the difference.

To say that O'Konski was erratic would be an Olympian understatement.
Early in his career he developed the ability to fall off both sides of the same
horse. In 1944, at the height of World War II, he called for the consideration
of withdrawing U.S. troops from Europe. But later, in the 1970s, he suggested
the United States consider nuking China. He was clever and cagey. On domestic issues, he would throw just enough votes to organized labor so they would
have difficulty opposing him at campaign time. On several occasions, when
no election opponent surfaced, he would send a friend or one of his staffers
home to the district to file against him in the election in order to box out
other candidates. That way he had an excuse to raise campaign funds with no
real risk of being unseated.

Early in his career, Alvin gained a financial interest in a Wisconsin radio station, which he parlayed into obtaining a license for a TV station in Rhinelander when licenses were first handed out by the FCC. After the TV station was built, Alvin had his congressional staff do double duty at the station. When constituents called the district office, the phone would often be answered, "Channel 12!"

Leading up to the '72 election, Alvin played cat and mouse with me. After giving broad hints that he did not intend to run for reelection, he suggested that he probably would, then switched back and announced he had decided not to. But when the filing date came Alvin announced that because "volunteers" had filed nomination papers on his behalf without his knowledge, he would leave his name on the ballot after all. His earlier maneuvering had fooled at least one Republican—David Connor, Gordon and Mary's son— into thinking Alvin was on the level and was not running, so Connor had also filed nomination papers. In the September primary Alvin beat him, and the battle between us was joined.

That summer had been a tense time for me. I had been confident that I could beat O'Konski in any normal year, but 1972 was turning out to be a horrible year for Democrats. After a chaotic series of primaries and an even more chaotic party convention, South Dakota senator George McGovern was nominated for the presidency. He had chosen Missouri senator Tom Eagleton to be his vice presidential running mate, but when it was revealed shortly after the convention that Eagleton had been treated in a mental hospital for depression, he withdrew and McGovern replaced him with Sargent Shriver, the original director of the Peace Corps and Jack Kennedy's brother-in-law. By that time, the mood of most Democratic candidates around the country, myself included, had gone from apprehension to despair. Events were out of control.

No incident more readily exemplified the chaotic jumble of that political year than a Sunday afternoon summer campaign day, two weeks after the convention, in the Village of Glidden in Ashland County, in the far northern reaches of my new district. Ernie Korpela, the incumbent Democratic state representative, was running for state senate in the Douglas, Bayfield, Ashland, Iron, and Sawyer county district. Dave Kedrowski, a young teacher from Washburn, was running to fill Ernie's assembly seat. I had agreed to campaign with Dave at the Glidden fair. On a Sunday afternoon right after the National Democratic Convention, when we walked into the fair grounds, campaign literature in hand, we had no idea of what awaited us.

We first came upon a group of five men. We introduced ourselves and handed them our campaign cards. As we began to shake more hands, I heard a voice behind me say, "You for KorPEla?" accenting the second syllable of Ernie's name rather than the first. It was the voice of one of the men we had met just a second ago. "You mean Ernie KORpela? Sure!" I said. "Shame on you," came the reply. "He's a Communist! You for McGovern?" he continued. "Against Nixon, you bet," I said. "Shame on you," he thundered. "You're for amnesty, you're for acid, you're for abortion," he brayed. "That's silly," I said. "You're a pinko Jane Fonda Democrat," he shouted.

"Look," I said, "why don't you just vote against me, and we'll both feel good about it." Turning to Kedrowski I said, "Let's get away from this guy. Let's go over to the beer stand." We did and started to shake hands there when I felt two hands on my back. The guy who had been screaming at us had taken a sheet of paper and had written on it: "Acid, Amnesty, Abortion." He had put some tape on the sign and was trying to tape it to the back of my shirt.

"Buddy, lay off. Enough is enough," I said, trying to brush him away. I turned back to the crowd at the beer stand and again felt his hands trying to tape the sign to my back. "He's for McGovern, he's for acid, he's for amnesty," he said. Whirling around I grabbed him by his shirt and said, "Mister, if you touch me once more your fanny is going to kiss the ground. Get the hell away from me and grow up." Turning to Kedrowski, I said, "Dave, let's go to the other side of the grounds and start over." Poor Dave, new to the campaign trail, was not yet accustomed to the chaos that can sometimes befall a candidate, and he was desperate to escape the commotion.

We loped to the other side of the grounds and began all over again. A well-dressed woman approached us and said, "Congressman, I want to meet you. I met your opponent yesterday, and I'm certainly going to vote for you." "Do you know," she went on, "yesterday I complained to your opponent about this new low-income housing they are bringing in to this county. I told him I knew that the government was going to bring in a bunch of niggers from Chicago to live in those houses, and I asked him what he was going to do to stop it. He told me that I was wrong, that the housing would be for local people, but I know it's all a scheme by the Chicago Jews to get the niggers out of Chicago and repopulate them up here."

As I stood there listening to her, the absurdity of the afternoon washed over my mind, and I started to laugh. "Lady," I said, "you're nuts. Alvin is right. Where do you get that garbage?" By that time I could see Kedrowski had given up all hope of salvaging the afternoon. So had I. "Let's get the hell out of here and have a drink," I said. "I'll drink to that," Dave said. We put the day behind us, but I have never forgotten it. Often when I think I'm having a bad day, I think of that Sunday in 1972, and suddenly things take on a whole new perspective.

Alvin was a wily adversary. In late summer, my constituents opened their mailbox and found a thirty-two-page booklet extolling the virtues of Alvin O'Konski. Alvin had written and inserted article after article in the *Congressional Record* recounting his own accomplishments as he saw them. He had compiled them in a book and mailed them under the congressional frank. Today, that would be patently illegal under House rules, but Alvin didn't miss a beat.

Throughout his career Alvin had been legendary for exaggerating his experience on the world stage. In his early campaigns for Congress, he was famous for giving speeches denouncing the horrors he had seen while visiting the Soviet Union. "Do you know whose picture is on the joker on a deck of Russian cards?" Alvin would ask his audience. "Jesus Christ, that's who!" Alvin would answer. Unfortunately for Alvin, the *Capitol Times,* one of the very few truly progressive papers left in Wisconsin, had done an investigation of his travel claims. "Mr. O'Konski," their reporter said, "we've checked the record. There is no record of you ever going to the Soviet Union. You've never even been given a visa for the Soviet Union." "Whose name did you check under?" Alvin asked. "Well, yours, of course," the reporter responded. "Well there's the problem," Alvin said. "I went on a group passport." Of course, there was no such thing, but only a handful of people in the district knew that. Alvin had invented his way out of a box, and enough people believed him for him to survive.

O'Konski's TV ads in the '72 campaign were in a class by themselves. He fancied himself a communicator in the Carl Sandburg tradition. Alvin liked five-minute and half-hour spots—live in the early evening news slot. One October evening after the 5:30 network and local news shows, Alvin's visage materialized on the screen. Sitting in a hardback chair, leaning forward, elbows on his knees, looking up into the camera, Alvin said, "Kiddies, I want you to go into the kitchen or into the yard and find your mommy and your daddy, and you tell them that Alvin E. O'Konski wants to talk to them. Now, you go find them and I will give you a minute." He then leaned back, sucked on his pipe until the smoke was billowing around him, glanced at his watch, then looked up at the camera and said, "Thank you, kiddies, and now I want to have a word with your parents." For the next four minutes he made his pitch. Even I enjoyed it.

But there was one day I didn't enjoy. Alvin drummed home the theme that I was too young to know the ropes and that only he could get government agencies to do things for the folks back home. Well, I knew that as a member of the Appropriations Committee I could get agencies to do a lot of things that they weren't going to do for Alvin. The Apostle Islands project would be a good example of that. I knew that local leaders wanted to make sure that the Congress and the Park Service were going to put money into the new Apostle Islands Lakeshore in Lake Superior. At Martin Hanson's suggestion— Martin was Louie's brother and had been the driving force behind the designation of the Apostle Island National Lakeshore—I asked Julia Butler Hansen (no relation), the chair of the Interior Appropriations subcommittee, to come out and tour the Apostles. We had two purposes in mind. First, we wanted her to be favorably disposed to my future funding requests for the Lakeshore. Second, we wanted to make clear to local officials that Alvin wasn't the only candidate who could get things done for the area. We also arranged for the Park Service to bring their large launch, *Ranger III,* from Michigan to Bayfield so the locals could tour the boat and join us at a reception to meet Julia.

On the day of the event, the weather was absolutely miserable, temperatures in the forties with heavy rain and high winds. Julia braved the elements and toured the Apostles with me in an open Park Service boat. We were both soaked to our skins and close to being frozen stiff. We returned to the mainland about three o'clock, showered and changed, and got ready for the public reception on *Ranger III.* The event was simple, just cookies and coffee, but those steaming cups of hot coffee felt good. To my surprise, a TV camera appeared on board and briefly filmed the gathering. "Frosting on the cake," I thought to myself. "We've had a good day for the local folks, Julia will be helpful when I hit her up for money for the Apostles next year, and we're going to get good TV coverage as a bonus."

But I hadn't counted on Alvin. The TV crew had not been a regular station crew; they had been hired by Alvin. That night when I watched the Duluth TV station I didn't see a story about our event. Instead, the announcer said they had "guest footage" of Congressman O'Konski. The camera showed Alvin standing in the rain announcing that he had just won an agreement to return an ancient Native American burial grounds cite on Madeline Island to the local tribe. "We had wanted to take a ceremonial trip to the island to celebrate this sacred occasion," Alvin said into the camera, "but on a day like this it's too dangerous to go out in an open boat, and Obey has the big one tied up for his booze party."

We had been set up. Alvin had used his own camera crew to manufacture a story. If he had wanted to go to Madeline Island, there were ferries every one-half hour. We had used a small open Park Service boat for showing Julia the islands, and the only "booze" at our reception was Folgers. But Alvin had funneled his phony story to a buddy at the TV station, and he had clobbered us with it. I was frustrated at the unfairness of it all, but I couldn't help but chuckle that night as I went to bed. The old fox was a master of the half truth, and on that day, at least, he got the best of us.

BURGLARY ON THE CAMPAIGN TRAIL

When Congress adjourned, we had less than ten days to campaign. It had been a campaign with a beginning unique in American history. On June 17, 1972, the *Washington Post* had reported that a gang of men had been caught red-handed and had been arrested for breaking into Democratic Party Headquarters at the Watergate Apartment complex in D.C. As much as I disdained Richard Nixon, not even I could believe that his campaign was responsible. But several weeks later, the *Post* reported that the burglars did indeed have links to the White House. I heard the news on the car radio early one evening just as I was pulling into Fenwood, a tiny village in southwestern Marathon County for a local campaign rally. I walked into the meeting hall where a small group of Democrats had gathered, told them the news, and wrote out a press release saying that if the White House linkage proved true, Nixon should resign.

I do not believe I have ever been more angry in my political life than I was that night. The idea that the leader of the free world could be corrupt enough to condone the kind of thuggery represented by Watergate blew my mind. But what made me even angrier was my conviction that Nixon would get away with it. I was convinced that the incident would not be taken seriously by most of the media during the election; the dangers to our system of government would not even register with many Americans because of the public relations hatchet job that had already largely marginalized George McGovern.

McGovern was one of the most decent, conscience-driven men I had ever known in politics. He was a genuine war hero, a World War II bomber pilot in the European theater, but almost no one knew it. I knew that, in November, the country would be more willing to bestow its trust on that paranoid in the White House than they would on the soft-spoken war hero who had sense enough to know the difference between a war worth fighting and a misguided adventure that we were sucked into by our leader's own lies. The futility and outrage of it gnawed at my gut, but I knew there was nothing I could do about it. I hated the thought of four more years with such a political savage in the White House. McGovern was going down the tubes. The question was: Would he take people like me down with him?

On the campaign trail, O'Konski had taken to calling me "McObey." He would say, "By George, how is McObey today?" After pursuing Alvin for weeks, we finally got him to agree to one debate. Mel Laird had traditionally agreed to one debate at the UW–Stevens Point. Chilsen and I had continued that tradition in 1969, and after I beat him I continued it in the 1970 election with LeTendre.

When the day of the debate finally came, in his opening statement, Alvin told the crowd, "Now, my opponent will fool you. He will try to come across as a reasonable young fellow, but if you really examine him he's a radical. In fact, he's twice as liberal as George McGovern," and proceeded to pound me on all fronts, making up stuff as he went along. I decided as I listened that the only way to deal with his hyperbole was to laugh about it.

When my turn came, I took the podium, turned to Alvin and said, "Alvin, how dare you! You have told these good people I am twice as liberal as George McGovern. That is calumny." "Why," I said, "I'm at least three times as liberal as George McGovern. I've worked hard to establish that record. Don't minimize it. I plead fully guilty to the fact that I want to do more for education, more for a clean environment, more for health care, more for dairy farmers than even George McGovern." Then I said, "Now that we've disposed of George McGovern, do you think that we can have an honest debate about the real differences between Alvin O'Konski and Dave Obey?" Alvin was not amused, but the audience was. For the rest of the debate Alvin went through the motions. He seemed to sense that his line of attack was falling flat. I could see the steam was out of him, and I could sense that he knew he was beat.

On election night Portage County returns came in first, and I shot to a 2 to 1 lead. When the votes were in I had carried my part of the district by almost 70 percent. In Alvin's part of the district, I got exactly what I had been aiming for—51 percent. District-wide I had expected to get 55 or 56 percent, but we got 62 percent. I was thrilled. I had a great district, a great organization, and after four years of almost continuous campaigning I had, at last, a chance to spend more time legislating.

Alvin was a real gentleman about it. He called me and suggested we have lunch, and we met at the Claridge Inn in Rhinelander on a Saturday. As we glanced at the menu, Alvin said, "Thank you for what you said about Bonnie." Bonnie was his wife, a sharp, dynamic, and lovely woman. She had served as his staff chief in Washington (this was in the days before Neil Smith of Iowa had pushed through the House a new rule disallowing the practice of putting relatives on the payroll.). Although Alvin was not specific about his reference to his wife, I knew what he was talking about. A few months earlier I had been campaigning in Tripoli, a tiny unincorporated village of less than a hundred people near the Price, Oneida, and Lincoln county lines. Only a few people had showed up for the announced Q&A session at the local school. One eager Democrat had said to me, "You ought to hit Alvin for having his wife on the payroll. They are getting two salaries from the taxpayer." "Well," I told him, "I don't think so. I have a lot of bones to pick with Alvin, but Bonnie isn't one of them. She is a good worker; she runs a first-rate office operation. Whatever the taxpayers are paying her, they are getting their money's worth, so I think I'll focus my arguments on Alvin and keep her out of it."

I asked Alvin how he had known what I had said. "From the Phillips newspaper editor," Alvin responded. I remembered that at the Tripoli meeting a man had come up to me afterwards and said, "This is the first time I have ever seen a politician pull his punches on an opponent. I appreciate it," he said. That man was Bob Kempkes, the editor of the *Phillips Bee,* whom I had never met. He had later written of the incident in his newspaper, but in the hurry-up of the campaign, I had missed the story.

As we ate lunch, Alvin relived old times and told me stories about his poker games with Harry Truman, about this or that favor he had done for a church or for a Boy Scout troop in the district. He confided that he still had an uncashed check from Truman from one of those poker evenings. When the luncheon check came, Alvin insisted on paying. As we were standing to leave, a woman came up to me and said hello. I could not place her. Later I realized she was from the Register of Deeds office in Marathon County, but because she was out of context, I didn't make the connection. When she left, Alvin said, "Oh, Dave, you don't know what a favor you've done me. My God, how often that has happened to me. Why just this week," he continued, "I was in Merrill walking down Main Street when a fellow across the street hollered, 'Congressman, Congressman!' He bounded across the street, grabbed my hand, and said, 'I'll bet you don't remember my name.' I looked into his eyes and told him, 'I know I should. Give me a hint.' He looked at me and said, 'What's the first thing you want when you get up in the morning?' I looked him in the eyes and said, 'Your name couldn't be Mr. Piss, could it?' . . . His name was Coffee. You liberated me. Now I can say, 'No I don't remember your name and what's more I don't give a damn.'"

I saw Alvin four or five times after that, usually at his TV station when I stopped for an interview. Alvin and Bonnie are both gone now, and with them a little bit of color has gone out of Wisconsin politics.

෴

CHAPTER 9

Pushing for Change

As I went back to Washington, my immediate goal was to push the Democratic caucus to open up the Appropriations Committee to more progressive influences by changing the way committee members were assigned to subcommittees. By this time, I had become more and more focused on finding ways to break the stranglehold that southern conservatives had on the Appropriations Committee.

Appropriations was different from any other House committee in the way that members rose to subcommittee chairmanships. On Appropriations, members rose to subcommittee chairmanships on the basis of their seniority on *that* subcommittee, not the full committee. That meant that Mahon could determine who would be in line for subcommittee chairmanships by appointing to subcommittees anyone he chose. With that power Mahon had the ability, not just to determine to what subcommittee members were initially assigned but, in essence, to determine who would chair those subcommittees for a decade or more into the future. Using that power, Mahon had stacked the major subcommittees like Defense and Labor-H with senior southern conservatives and, with the exception of Eddie Boland (Tip O'Neill's roommate), had isolated northern progressives on smaller, less influential subcommittees.

Breaking the Southern Monopoly

Working with DSG staff director, Dick Conlon, I drafted a rules change that would break up the southern monopoly on those powerful subcommittees. It would be a compromise between Mahon selecting all committee assignments and giving the power to every member to select all of their own subcommittees on the basis of full committee seniority. It would have allowed senior members to grandfather up to two subcommittees, but then would have allowed any members who did not do so to choose one subcommittee of their choice. That would mean that over time each member (not just those who were already sitting pretty) would have a chance to get a good subcommittee assignment, and northern progressives would have a chance to chair key subcommittees.

Prior to the Democratic organizing caucus, I went to Carl Albert and explained my view that the Appropriations Committee would never be truly responsive to the majority progressive sentiment in the caucus—or to the leadership—unless the subcommittees were roughly reflective of caucus philosophy. I explained—subcommittee by subcommittee—how Mahon's absolute control over who went on which subcommittee had sidetracked northern progressives into minor subcommittees. I explained that I did not want to eliminate Mahon's ability to balance each subcommittee. I just wanted to prevent him from stacking them with the most reactionary members in the southern power structure. By giving each member the right to select one—but not all—subcommittee slots, and by allowing Mahon the power to fill the rest of the slots, we could bring a whiff of democracy and fairness to the committee while still leaving Mahon with significant leverage over every member.

I had not expected Albert's endorsement; I just wanted him to fully understand what I was doing, hoping that he would not be persuaded by the old bulls to fight it. To my surprise and delight, Carl told me he would speak for it in the caucus. Carl and I had a good relationship. Dick Bolling, despite having been defeated by Albert for majority leader, had also told me that Carl's instincts were good. Albert, who knew that I had been born in Oklahoma, had told several people that he trusted me to take a balanced approach to problems and thought that I was "operational."

But other factors also influenced his support of my reform plan. He saw it as a chance to send a signal to the junior members of the House that he would be more responsive to them than McCormack had been. And it came at little cost to most southern conservatives because my amendment applied to only one committee, Appropriations. It was designed only for those committees that used seniority on subcommittees, rather than on full committees, to determine subcommittee chairmanships. It would, over time, have a major effect on policy because Appropriations was such a far-reaching committee, but in personal terms, within the caucus, only a few members would be negatively affected. In the organizing caucus in December, after a tough battle and many rearguard actions by Mahon and his allies, my amendment finally passed.

Now, I had a choice to make. If I stayed on the Interior Subcommittee I was pretty sure I could be chairman in two years because Julia was talking about retiring. But I wasn't sure. And even with the chairmanship as a possibility, I was thinking strongly about moving to Labor-H. Interior was a wonderful subcommittee. It had jurisdiction over National Parks, the Forest Service, and a number of energy conservation programs. But my first love was education and my second was health care.

Several days after the caucus passed my amendment, Andy Biemiller, chief of the legislative shop for the AFL-CIO, called. "I understand you are trying to decide whether to stay on Interior or move to Labor-H," he said. I told Andy it was true and explained what was going through my head. "I love education and health," I told him, "but if Julia retires, I would be chair of Interior. That would not just give me a gavel; it would get me in the room every time the Cardinals meet, and it would make me a conferee almost every time we had a supplemental appropriations bill going through."

"That's true," Biemiller said. "No question that in the short term, in terms of power, you would be better to stay put. But in the long-term, Labor-H will give you far more reach on key issues. And as young as you are, if you move now, you could be chair of Labor-H some day, and that would make you a powerhouse." He then made his key argument: "Dave, I beg you to make this move, but not for reasons of personal power. Everybody in America who looks to Labor-H to get decent funding levels for education, for health, for antipoverty programs, for worker protection programs needs you on that committee. Right now," he went on, "you know how we are boxed out by the three-day code of silence." He was referring to each Appropriations subcommittee's marking up (putting its bill together) behind closed doors. After the subcommittees made their decisions, the bills would be polished by the staff, but until they were circulated to the full committee, the subcommittees kept their recommendations secret. "You know the problem," Andy said, "if the subcommittee screws us on education or worker protection, and it usually does, we don't even know about it. We have no time to organize an effort to change it and never will have until we get a friend on the inside who will forewarn us."

"Besides," he said, "Edith Green is trying to get on that subcommittee. If she makes it and you are not there, she will block everything you and I stand for." Then he said, "Once in a while we have to be the blocking back instead of the running back for the good of the team. Besides, I know you. I know where your heart is. Follow your heart!" About an hour later Phil Burton called. "You're not thinking of giving up Interior to go to Labor-H, are you?"

he asked. "Julia has told me this is her last term. My God, you will have gone from nothing to chairman in five years. That's almost unprecedented." He explained to me that Andy Biemiller had called him and asked him to persuade me to switch. Ordinarily, Andy and Phil saw the world as one, but Andy was focused on the needs of the outside, and Phil was focused on inside power. I began to walk through my thinking with Phil. "Phil, in the short run I would give up a lot, but if I stay here any length of time, the issues I most care about are on Labor-H. I simply think I would be happiest there. But even if we look at it only in terms of strategy, power, and influence, I think Labor-H wins," I told him. "If I don't jump now, someone else will get ahead of me on Labor-H. If I move now I maximize my chance of being the senior Democrat on Labor-H some day, and over the long haul I can do more there than I can at Interior." "I can't argue with that," Phil responded.

One other consideration tipped the scales. Energy issues were becoming more important, and Interior handled a number of them—issues such as oil drilling on federal lands and some energy research programs. But Mahon was talking about making some jurisdiction changes down the line. If Julia Hanson retired and I moved to Labor-H, Sid Yates would become chairman of Interior. Sid was very senior. I thought that if I were Interior chair, Mahon could probably move many of the energy programs to Tom Bevill's Public Works Subcommittee because I was very junior on the committee. But if Sid were chair, that would be difficult for Mahon because Sid had a lot more clout than I did, so I decided to make the switch.

I called Sid Yates to tell him what I had decided. "But Little David" (Sid always called me Little David; years earlier, after I had won the fight against Bill Natcher on the D.C. subway, Sid came up to me and said, "From now on I will call you Little David because you slew Goliath.) "But Little David, you are giving up a sure chairmanship. I don't want to look a gift horse in the mouth, but you would be giving up a sure thing," he said. I explained to Sid that I thought in the long run it would more than even out and that he would have a better chance to keep the major energy programs from being moved out of the subcommittee than I would. So when Mahon called, I made the jump. I suppose I felt a twinge of regret two years later when Julia left and Sid eased into her chair, but other than that fleeting moment, I have been comfortable with the choice.

Under my amendment, Mahon was supposed to call all committee Democrats into a meeting and allow the subcommittee selection process to take place with everybody in the same room—that way everybody knew what everyone else was doing. Instead, Mahon called members one by one on the phone, told them what vacancies existed, and asked them for their preferences. The problem with that procedure was that only George knew which vacancies actually existed. For example: Two vacancies existed on the Labor-H Subcommittee. If they were selected in accordance with my new reform, I would get the first vacancy and Lou Stokes, a classy black member from Cleveland could get the second. It would have been a first for the black community.

I had called almost every member to make sure I knew who was doing what in the bidding process, so when Mahon called I told him I knew there were two Labor-H vacancies and I would take the first slot. He said, "Okay," and that was it. But when Mahon called Stokes, either Lou had been talked out of taking the Labor-H slot by Mahon in order to accommodate Green, or he had not run a check to make sure he knew what his choices were and hadn't been given the full story by Mahon.

Edith Green was a new member of Appropriations. She had been a senior leader on the Education and Labor Committee, the authorizing committee that designed the programs for which we appropriated the money and had become increasingly alienated from the liberal and progressive Democratic members of that committee. Constantly outvoted by them, she switched to Appropriations because she wanted to use her Appropriations assignment to block funding for a number of programs she could not stop on her old committee. To do that, she needed to be assigned to Labor-H, and Mahon was anxious to oblige. But when my amendment was unexpectedly adopted by the Democratic caucus, it upset their game plan.

When Mahon announced the new subcommittee lineups, to my amazement and consternation Lou Stokes was not on Labor-H, but Edith was. I asked Stokes what had happened. He said that when Mahon had called, he told Stokes that there were no vacancies left on Labor-H, so Lou took a different slot. That infuriated me. It became obvious that the old bulls would only play by the rules they liked. It meant that to level the playing field we would have to go through the fight again in the next Congress. But before Congress could do that, we would deal with a host of other issues. The most fateful were Vietnam and Watergate.

Vietnam Comes to a Head

According to *Congressional Quarterly,* there were ninety-four recorded votes on Vietnam from 1966 to 1972. The major efforts in both Houses to cut or eliminate funding for the war began in both the House and Senate in 1971. Because of the House rules, it had been virtually impossible to get a meaningful vote

on cutting off funds. Nonetheless, the number of votes on both sides of the
Capitol grew from five votes in 1969 to thirty-five in 1972. Until 1973, everything that every president wanted from Congress on Vietnam, he got. Just in
time for the election, in October 1972, Henry Kissinger, Nixon's legendary
national security advisor, declared that "Peace was at hand," but the agreement that so many Americans thought was just around the corner did not
materialize, and the war continued. On January 27, after the election, the
Vietnam Peace Accord between the United States and Vietnam was signed,
defining a process to end the direct participation of the United States in the
ongoing war. In two months POWs had been exchanged and the last U.S.
troops were pulled out of Vietnam. But U.S. aid to South Vietnam and Laos
continued for several more years.

Since the first day I walked into Congress, Vietnam had been the all-
consuming issue that had dominated congressional work days. Every possible
formulation for an amendment had been explored in hope that the tide
would turn, and we would be able to bring that agonizing chapter in American history to an end. Finally, Joe Addabbo, a New Yorker on the Defense
Appropriations Subcommittee, won adoption of his amendment by deleting
language in a Defense Supplemental Appropriation that approved further
transfer of Defense funds to activities in Vietnam and Cambodia. The administration claimed the power to ignore the amendment under the president's
authority as commander in chief, but the die was cast. Opposition to the war
had reached critical mass in the House of Representatives.

For two more years, the war dragged on with the United States providing military aid but no combat ground troops. In 1975 Congress finally voted
to bring U.S. involvement in Vietnam to an end. The night of the final
Senate vote, Gaylord Nelson called me and suggested I come over to Stan
Kimmet's office where an eclectic group of senators often gathered for a drink
and conversation in the evening hours. Kimmet, a retired military officer,
had been appointed secretary of the senate by majority leader Mike Mans-
field. In Kimmet's office I found Gaylord with James Eastland of Mississippi,
the notorious segregationist southerner senator, Fritz Hollings, the always
colorful and outspoken senator for South Carolina, and Tom Eagleton, the
thoughtful, irreverent senator from Missouri. We had a drink while we waited
for the final vote to begin. Eastland turned to Gaylord and said, "Gaylord, I
do believe this is the first time in memory that you and I have voted on the
same side of a major issue." Gaylord grinned and said, "Yes, Mr. Chairman,
I do believe that is right and, outside this room, for the sake of both of our
careers, neither one of us had best talk of it again."

When it finally did end, the war had cost us more than 56,000 dead and over 300,000 wounded. Congress had appropriated more than $140 billion. *Congressional Quarterly* reported that University of Utah's James Clayton had concluded that we had spent "more money on Vietnam in ten years than the United States had spent during the nation's entire history for public higher education or for public protection." As *CQ* said, "The war cost ten times more than support for all funds for education and fifty times more than what was spent for housing and community development during that same period."

Drip, Drip, Drip

As the war simultaneously wore on and wore down, the country was being put through the daily grind of hearing more and more outrageous truths about Watergate. On March 23, L. Patrick Grey, the FBI director, revealed that the Nixon White House had tried to use the FBI to cover up White House actions. On May 17, White House lawyer John Dean testified that he had warned Nixon that a "cancer was growing on the presidency." By the summer of 1973, the possibility that the president could be directly snarled in the affair was beginning to dawn on everyone.

Joan and the boys had gone back to Wisconsin for the summer, and I was stuck in Washington alone. One summer evening, I invited a few friends—Bob Kastenmeier, Bob Drinan, Don Edwards, Dave Broder, and several others—over for some backyard barbecued chicken. While we were eating on the back patio, Drinan, a Jesuit priest from Boston, announced that he would introduce a resolution of impeachment. We were all alarmed. Revelations seemed slowly to be painting Nixon into a corner, but there was still a long way to go to tie down the facts. At that point, not enough information had become public to make the public comfortable even talking about impeachment.

Under House rules, Drinan's resolution would be considered privileged, which meant that any member could demand immediate House action on the proposition. We were concerned that minority leader Jerry Ford would immediately call up the resolution for a vote. The result would be a huge majority against action. Such a vote would surely end the pressure for further investigations before they even got off the ground. But the next day Drinan went ahead and introduced the resolution anyway. We held our breath, fearing that Ford would call it up for a vote and kill the impeachment idea before it had a chance to take wing, but he never did, and the process continued to unfold. Meanwhile, I settled in to the routine of dealing with my new responsibilities on Labor-H.

LABOR-HEALTH, EDUCATION, AND WELFARE

I loved the challenge of my new subcommittee, but I did not exactly fit into the culture of the panel. The chairman was Dan Flood, a self-styled Shakespearean actor from Wilkes-Barre, Pennsylvania. Flood had slicked-back black hair streaked with gray, sported an enormous pencil-thin waxed mustache, and occasionally wore a cape. Thin as Ichabod Crane, with a stentorian voice and speaking style, he had survived a bout with stomach cancer. In both appearance and manner he reminded me of John Carradine, the old movie actor with the almost sepulchral voice.

The subcommittee's senior Republican was Bob Michel, a solidly conservative, midwestern Main Street, Rotary Club, Republican from Peoria, who would later become minority leader. Once a year, at Christmas time, he would take the well of the House and, in his warm baritone voice, sing Christmas carols. Broad shouldered and affable, Michel was a first-rate human being. He always made it clear he was a skeptic about Great Society programs and would just as soon reassert Bob Taft–Republican values on all matters congressional.

The second-ranking Democrat after Flood was Bill Natcher, proper, well groomed, well dressed (plenty of starch, please, and dark 41 long suits!). He was old school and proud of it. Our relations were civil but cool—a leftover from our clash on the D.C. subway issue. Next was Neal Smith, a moderate from Iowa. Neal personified the workmanlike, bland, "Know your subject, but no fancy stuff, please!" approach to legislating. He was the House expert on food health and safety issues, and he also focused on education.

Eddie Patten was fourth in seniority on the Democratic side. As flamboyant as Natcher was straitlaced, Patten was a bulky hulk of a man with a perpetual cigar in his hand and an almost childlike happy smile continually on his face. He represented Perth Amboy, New Jersey. He brought the kind of heart-stopping, head-slapping "My God, what will he do now?" color to Congress that we don't see anymore. In a committee hearing a few months earlier on the run-down, rat-infested conditions of some urban public housing, Patten blurted out, "Hey, I didn't come here to kill rats; I came here to build battleships."

At the first White House Christmas party Joan and I attended in 1969, we found Eddie and his wife just ahead of us in the receiving line to shake hands with Nixon. As we reached the president, one of the Marine guards attempted to take Eddie's tall glass of scotch from him. But Eddie insisted on hanging on tightly to the glass as he shook hands with the president. As we neared Nixon, Joan and I both noticed that he was sweating profusely. He was clearly uncomfortable making small talk. When Eddie seized the president's hand, he threw his head back, glanced from side to side around the room, and said, "Hey Dick, nice shack you've got here" and laughed. Nixon knew it was supposed to be funny, but he was so uptight he just could not bring himself to do anything but look mortified. It was the only time in my life, until the agony of impeachment, that I felt sorry for him.

Eddie did not just mortify presidents. He did it to heads of foreign governments as well. One year he had been part of a congressional delegation sent to a British Crown Colony to witness the ceremony celebrating that country's new independence from Great Britain. Thousands were gathered on a great open field. Men in military garb were resplendent in the bright sun, and in front of them stood a long line of horses. As the ceremony was about to begin, a silence descended on the crowd. At that instant, Eddie shouted out, "They're off!" Funny now; eye-rollingly embarrassing then.

A few years later Patten was on a trip to Yugoslavia. Marshall Tito had been able, through sheer force of will and skill, to hold the country together despite the centrifugal forces that threatened to put Croatians, Serbians, Slovenians, Bosnians, and other ethnic groups at each others throats. That skill was important to the West because Tito had been able to maintain an arm's-length relationship with the Soviet Union on many issues even though he occasionally provided a modicum of cooperation with the Russians. American presidents and Congress had been on the lookout for ways to strengthen U.S.–Yugoslavia relations even as the aging Tito's grip began to slip and political successors maneuvered for position. As the visiting House delegation sat with a group of high-ranking Yugoslav officials discussing how to get more American aid, Eddie suddenly blurted out, "But you know you've got a problem. Yugoslavia, Yugoslavia, that's such a bad name! Now if you could just change your country's name to something with more sex appeal we'd have a lot better chance." The delegation froze in horror, and their Yugoslav hosts sat in stunned disbelief as Eddie continued, "But other than that, I'm with you all the way."

Eddie also used his diplomatic skills to equal effect back home in New Jersey. Before coming to Congress, Eddie had been New Jersey secretary of state. During the governor's inaugural ceremony, he was supposed to present the official New Jersey state seal to the new governor, symbolizing the official transfer of power from the previous governor to the new one. Eddie caused quite a commotion when he presented the incoming governor with the seal with the statement "Governor, I present to you the great STEAL of the state of New Jersey!" Given the sometimes impure political traditions of that state, some political observers thought Eddie had purposely caught the true essence of the moment, but six to five, it was simply Eddie being Eddie. With colorful characters like Eddie, the other two Democrats on the panel, Edith Green and I, paled by comparison.

One other person on the subcommittee achieved almost legendary status during his years in the Congress. Second in line behind Bob Michel on the Republican side was Silvio Conte. Sil was a flamboyant son of Massachusetts, a life-loving showman with a progressive spirit and a long-standing friendship with Tip O'Neill. On many issues Sil was probably the most progressive member of the subcommittee, until I came.

The culture of the subcommittee was indistinguishable from the committee as a whole. Its highest value was consensus. When the committee put its recommendations together, actually having a vote on an issue was regarded with horror. The practice was to "work it out." That meant in practice that the chairman of the subcommittee would present his recommendations to the subcommittee—recommendations usually worked out beforehand in consultation with the ranking minority member. Other members would have brought their requests to the table through subcommittee staff. The chair and the staff would usually decide which requests could be accommodated, and the members were expected to accept the recommended mark as a realistic determination of what the chairman and the ranking minority member believed was possible.

If members wanted more money for a particular proposal, they would haggle with the chair until consensus was reached. To request a vote was frowned upon and usually futile. When the chair and ranking member agreed on a matter, they usually had the votes, and it was either "Better luck next year!" or—in cases of a big issue—"Try your luck on the floor." But before markup time had come the hearings. Multiple hearings were held by Appropriations subcommittees virtually every day Congress was in session. Many of them were routine and dull, but over a decade a tremendous amount of knowledge could be picked up by subcommittee members. That knowledge is what made the Congress, at its best, a formidable force.

The breadth of human problems dealt with by the Labor-H Subcommittee is truly breathtaking. It covers a broader range of problems than does any other congressional subcommittee. It oversees the Department of Health and Human Services, including the agencies that administer Medicare, Medicaid, Health Resources, Medical Training, Medical Research at the National Institutes of Health, and many others. It deals with almost all of the health and social services that government provides to our people. It covers all the education activities in which the federal government is engaged—education research, education for disadvantaged children, children with special handicaps requiring special services, teacher training, student assistance, and the like. It oversees the agencies in the Department of Labor that have the responsibility to provide a healthy and safe workplace and a fair deal at the collective bargaining table. More than any other subcommittee, it deals with the problems and needs of children during their learning years, of workers during their working years, and of seniors during their retirement years. Virtually every family in the country, from the most privileged to the most desperate and destitute, is touched by the actions of that subcommittee in some way. The stewardship responsibilities of that subcommittee are immense.

I have always felt that, with the exception of the Ways and Means Committee, which writes the nation's tax laws, the three best places for a member to serve in the House if he or she wants to maximize the opportunity to influence what America does at home and abroad are on the Labor-Health, Education and Social Services Appropriations Subcommittee, the Defense Appropriations Subcommittee, and the Foreign Operations Appropriation Subcommittee. Although I did not know it then, I would, over my career, have the incredible opportunity and privilege of serving on all three: Labor-H as ranking member and chair, Foreign Ops as chair, and Defense as ranking member and chair of the full committee—which entitled me to serve on Defense and all of the other twelve subcommittees. By virtue of the latter two positions I would also receive crucial intelligence briefings on the most important and sensitive intelligence matters our government faces.

One of the most interesting aspects of serving in Congress is the way we develop the knowledge that guides us through our duties. The first Labor-H hearing I ever attended set me on a thirty-year path of involvement in worker health and safety issues. Shortly after joining the panel, I walked into the subcommittee hearing room late one morning just as Dr. David Rall was testifying. Rall, the director of the National Institute of Environmental Health Sciences at NIH, was an impressively focused and innovative scientist who cared deeply about the effect of medical research on human beings. As I took my seat I heard him tell the committee that 40 percent of British shipyard workers who had worked with asbestos in World War II had died of mesothelioma—a cancer of the lining of the lung. That got my attention because in my father's floor-covering business I had worked with asbestos. Rall explained the pioneering epidemiological studies done on asbestos by Dr. Irving Selikoff, of Mount Sinai Hospital, and others. I took a quick interest in the issue and struck up a friendship with Rall that lasted until his death in an automobile accident in Europe in 1999. As a result of that hearing, I asked Peggy Taylor, who was serving an internship in my office under the American Political Science Association, to staff me on the subject. Peggy worked on the issue during her stay on my staff, and when she left, she turned the file over to my new legislative assistant, Scott Lilly.

A NEW PARTNER

Until that time I had two legislative assistants, Linda Reivitz and Gerry Sturges. But when our staff allowance was increased, I interviewed a number of people for a third legislative assistant spot on the staff. Over lunch, Linda, Gerry, Lyle Stitt, and I talked about which of three candidates I should hire. Linda and Gerry each preferred a different candidate, and Lyle was not sure which one he preferred. But all three agreed that their third choice was a fellow by the name of R. Scott Lilly. Lilly had occupied a key position at the DNC during the McGovern campaign. Before that, he had worked in the Missouri legislature and started law school but had not finished. I had a hunch about him and was surprised when the staff unanimously ranked him as their last choice. I said, "Look, Abe Lincoln once overruled his cabinet by saying 'The vote is five to one against. I vote yes. The ayes have it,' or something to that effect. I just have a hunch about Lilly," I said, "and I want to go with him." That decision began what was to be a thirty-two-year partnership.

The first job I gave Scott was to get up to speed on the worker health and safety cluster of issues—especially asbestos. For the first two months I thought I had made a wrong choice. Congressional offices have a limited number of people to cover all the issues in the universe. Staffers have to be able to dig into issues, but they also have to be quick studies. Scott seemed to be digging and digging and digging into workers health but producing very little—and he certainly wasn't giving any indication of being able to take up other issues besides worker health. Within three months, however, Scott gave me a series of memos that analyzed the worker health issue with subtlety and depth. It was a terrific piece of substantive scholarship and a solid political analysis of the problems, the players, the opportunities for defining those problems, and some of the actions we could demand of the agencies to move the subject to the front burner.

Having gotten the ball rolling on worker health oversight, Scott then quickly stretched to cover a number of other issues, and I knew I had someone with real talent on my hands. In later years he would rise to be my legislative director, then my associate staffer on Appropriations after a rules change that I offered creating that position, then chief of staff when I chaired the Joint Economic Committee. He would succeed Dick Conlon as staff director of the DSG when Conlon died in a tragic sailing accident on the Chesapeake. Finally, he became staff director for me when I served as chair of Appropriations. He held that position until he retired in February of 2004. He is truly my best friend in Washington and the best legislative staffer I have ever worked with. In so many ways my alter ego, Scott has enriched my legislative service and has done the same with my personal life.

Music, Music, Music

A few months after Scott came to work with me, he came into the office and said, "Look, I know you play the harmonica; I play in a bluegrass band with some buddies. We're getting together with some other people at Jim Aboureszk's house to do some picking, and I thought you might like to join us." I played the harmonica all right but just for my own enjoyment, never with other people. And besides, I knew little about bluegrass. I listened to it on several D.C. radio stations and knew of only one or two bluegrass bands back home in Wisconsin, but I had never played it. "I don't know that kind of music; I don't think I would fit in," I said. But Scott retorted, "It's easy, I guarantee it." So that Friday night Joan and I went out to Aboureszk's. We met John Holum, a banjo player from South Dakota, who had been George McGovern's chief of legislation and had played a key role in his presidential campaign. Harlan Severson was another fugitive from South Dakota, who worked with the Rural Electrification Administration by day and played bass fiddle.

I also met two unforgettable people that night. Libba Cotton was a self-taught, guitar-playing, tiny speck of a woman. She had taught herself to play guitar left-handed and had written a number of songs that everybody in America knew—"Freight Train," "Shake Sugaree," and others. The second person was Floyd Westerman, a good-looking, rawboned Sioux Indian, who had recorded several albums and written scores of songs speaking to the experience of Native Americans as their culture had been undermined by unknowing and uncaring white Americans. Years later Westerman would give a memorable performance as the old tribal chief in the movie *Dancing with Wolves*.

"My God, am I out of my league," I thought. "I could kill Scott." But by the evening's end I was enjoying myself. That night opened up a whole new

musical experience for me. Until that time, I had played two kinds of
music—popular, which I had learned from my dad, and some classical, which
I had picked up by playing along with classical records. After that night, I
began to play regularly with Scott's group. We began calling ourselves the
Capitol Offenses. Other friends like Randy Ihara, Sam Morgan, and others
joined through the years as did my two sons—first Craig on the guitar, then
Doug, first on piano, then guitar and bass under Harlan's tutelage. Today we
have three albums to our credit. On the last one we were joined by our two
daughters-in-law, Kirstin and Kate. How good are we? My response to that
question has always been, "We're good enough to play in public but not good
enough to get paid for it."

So much in my legislative and personal life has flowed from that decision,
made over lunch at the Democratic Club, to hire Scott. It was, perhaps, the
key decision in my congressional life. Without Scott, I would not have had
the personal joy that music has brought me, and my legislative and political
accomplishments would be much thinner indeed. Scott's staff work directly
led to my work with grain elevator workers in Superior who were having terrible health problems because of grain dust. We were able to work with local
unions to bring in Dr. Irving Selikoff to do epidemiological studies. It led to
a six-year effort to get NIH and the National Cancer Institute to focus more
research on the role of environmental exposures in triggering cancer in people
who were genetically disposed to one form of the disease or another. His work
enabled me to climb all over OSHA's back during the '80s through the years
when they were betraying working people. Without Scott I would not have
emerged as a leading voice in education. I would never have been able to put
together the progressive budget and tax alternatives that defined our party's
fiscal and budget priority differences with Reagan in the 1980s, nor would I
have published the Joint Economic Committee studies on the growth of the
income gap in the country from 1973 to the 1990s, and I would certainly not
have been in a position to become chairman of the Appropriations.

All that was ahead of me when I brought Scott on board in 1973. But at the
time, while I was doing my everyday work, I, like everyone else in the country, was caught up in the maelstrom of Richard Nixon's impeachment.

☙

CHAPTER 10

Nixon Goes

Throughout 1973 and the winter and spring of 1974, Nixon descended into political hell, and the rest of us felt sucked down with him. Today, many people assume that because I was a Democrat and because Democrats benefited politically in 1974 from Nixon's disgrace, that it must have been an enjoyable experience. Far from it! Politically I appreciated the opportunity that Nixon's unraveling presented to my party as events began to roll across the nation like shock waves from a tsunami, but as the country became more cynical about Nixon, that cynicism spilled over all of us in public life. Judge Sirica's hardball tactics forced the Watergate burglars to talk. Then came news of their links to the White House through Gordon Liddy and the other henchmen, followed by the stories of money laundering and the resignation of H. R. Haldeman and John Ehrlichman, the staff director and domestic policy director for Nixon's White House.

The political tension increased as the nation witnessed televised hearings by the Watergate Committee under the colorful chairmanship of Sam Ervin of South Carolina. On May 17, 1973, it heard the "cancer on the presidency" testimony of White House Chief Counsel John Dean. Then the stunner—Alexander Butterfield's testimony that the White House had a taping system that had recorded Nixon's conversations in the Oval Office. That gave the whole country an opportunity to answer Howard Baker's question: "What did he know and when did he know it?"

By then, the House Judiciary Committee had begun the laborious task of assembling the unfolding evidence. Cards—each representing a known fact—were organized, by subject, first under the volunteered services of Dick Cates, a former Madison law partner of Gaylord Nelson, and later under committee counsel John Doar, who also had Wisconsin roots. Next came congressional

subpoenas for the White House tape recordings of Nixon's Oval Office conversations, Nixon's resistance, and a 9 to 0 rebuff to the White House by the
Supreme Court in response to Nixon's stonewalling of Congress's requests for
the tapes.

One night stands out in my memory as the moment when my revulsion at
Nixon's tortured song-and-dance routine finally boiled over. The Chamber of
Commerce used to sponsor a Washington fly-in for chamber leaders from
throughout the country at the Washington Hilton's International Ballroom.
A large contingent of Wisconsin chamber members came to Washington and
expected the Wisconsin congressional delegation and their staffs to attend the
evening dinner. The night of the dinner, at the peak of the controversy surrounding his refusal to turn over those tapes, Nixon was scheduled to speak
to the nation. As an alternative to complete disclosure, Nixon had sought to
turn over transcripts of many—but not all—tapes, citing national security and
other reasons.

As dinner began, Joan and I were seated at a large, round table near the edge
of the room with a group of seventh district chamber leaders from Wausau,
Wisconsin Rapids, and Stevens Point. To ensure that members of Congress
did not desert the dinner for Nixon's TV performance, the chamber had
arranged for large television screens to carry the Nixon address in the hall. At
the appointed hour Nixon peered into the camera, transcripts stacked behind
him for effect, and tried to assure the nation of his cooperation and innocence. But it was too much. When Nixon's presentation was over and his face
disappeared from the TV screens, several chamber members—Nixon supporters all—turned to me with eyebrows raised hopefully. "Well, what did you
think?" one asked. I shook my head slowly and said the first thing that came
into my head, "Does anybody have a barf bag?" I asked. After that night, it
was all down hill—for Nixon and the country.

When the tapes were released under court order, the headlines screamed:
EIGHTEEN-AND-A-HALF-MINUTE GAP IN TAPE. When Nixon's secretary Rose-
mary Woods tried to demonstrate how she could have accidentally erased
eighteen minutes of a key tape, the picture of her stretched ridiculously from
foot peddle to telephone convulsed the nation, and America plunged into a
cynicism that I had never seen.

~

I had always enjoyed visiting high schools and speaking with students. They
usually seemed much more tuned in, so much more focused on the larger
needs of the nation than so many of their parents. But Vietnam had taken its

toll on their trust, and Watergate had done it in. Students who, in previous years, would have asked challenging questions and engaged in sharp give-and-take exchanges with me, now would respond to my appearance with sullen suspicion. Many of them, by their questions and comments, conveyed their deep suspicion of anyone who was a public official. It was clear they believed that if the president did it, everyone did it.

I searched for ways to cut through that suspicion and cynicism and found that if in an answer to a question I replied, "I agree with you," I would see knowing smirks from the audience and could sense they were thinking, "Oh sure, he agrees. He's just trying to butter us up and soft-soap us." Often the only way I could cut through that cynicism was to go out of my way to empha-size my disagreement with them. For example, if someone asked me a three-part question and I agreed with them on two out of three points, I would say, "Well, I probably agree with you on parts one and two, but let me tell you why I don't agree with you on the third." Then I would emphasize that disagree-ment. By doing that I was able to neutralize, to some extent, their cynicism and felt that some of them were thinking, "Well, I sure don't agree with him, but at least he's honest." To this day I make it a practice to use that approach, and I know that goes back to my Watergate experience. It took a long time for that student cynicism to subside. To me, that was the most distressing thing about Watergate. It took from an entire generation of young people their capacity to believe in their leaders.

Before the saga ended, Spiro Agnew bit the dust. Dogged by leftover scan-dals from his Maryland governorship, Agnew finally copped a plea and re-signed the vice presidency. Then House Republican leader Gerald Ford was named by Nixon to be the new vice president. The flashpoint came in Octo-ber with Nixon's firing of special prosecutor Archibald Cox. The "Saturday night massacre," as it was called, came when both attorney general Elliott Richardson and assistant attorney general Bill Ruckleshaus resigned rather than comply with Nixon's demand to fire Cox. Nixon had to reach down the Justice Department ladder to Robert Bork, the solicitor general, before he could find someone who would carry out the order. The backlash Nixon en-countered forced him to hire Leon Jaworski to take Cox's place, and the rest is history. When the House Judiciary Committee reported the first article of impeachment sponsored by Paul Sarbanes of Maryland, the jig was up. On August 8, 1974, Nixon resigned. At noon Gerry Ford was sworn in as presi-dent. An accidental president, he performed with a humble, steady sense of duty that brought the country together.

I didn't think much of the economic program that Ford pursued during his time in office, but I liked the way he governed. He was a tough adversary if you disagreed with him, but he "played well with others." He was respectful of other people with other responsibilities. He was earnest, honest, unspectacular but solid, a healer, and a uniter. Unfortunately for him, that was not what a lot of ideologues in his party wanted. They mounted a campaign to force Ford to move the Republican Party to the right. Their chief spear-carrier was Ronald Reagan, who contested Ford's reelection bid. Their drive culminated in forcing Ford to replace vice president Nelson Rockefeller (who had been selected by Ford and ratified by the Senate to fill the vacancy caused by Ford's elevation to the presidency) with the former chairman of the National Republican Party, Kansas senator Bob Dole, a fierce, slashing partisan who had not yet mellowed, as he would in the 1980s and 1990s. Republican division, Ford's courageous pardoning of Richard Nixon, and uncertain economic times combined to sink him in the general election.

House Reform

Nixon's resignation and the maelstrom out of which it emerged scuttled the Republicans in 1974. The Democrats picked up fifty-one seats. The huge new Watergate crop meant that we finally had enough votes to push through the reforms and the changes in committee chairmanships that DSG and Dick Bolling had wanted for a decade. Two years earlier, we had changed the manner in which Democrats had been appointed to committees. Until then, the Ways and Means Committee had determined committee assignments for Democrats. That had been the key to Wilbur Mills's power. Our reforms had shifted that power to the Steering and Policy Committee chaired by the Speaker, but in that Congress we made no effort to dump any chairmen. Two years later, however, the stage was set to put into motion the procedures we had designed two years earlier.

Two items were at the top of my agenda. The first was to tie down the Appropriations subcommittee selection process change I had won two years earlier. The second was to require that the Appropriations subcommittee chairs be ratified by the caucus in order to make them more responsive to the progressive majority in that caucus. I tried again to get Mahon to agree to pull Democrats together in the same room for a caucus so that the subcommittee selection process could take place in view of everyone, the way it was supposed to work, but he wouldn't budge.

I realized that with all the new freshmen in caucus, I would not be able to get their votes for something that was limited to getting junior members the right to bid for only one subcommittee assignment. They would only support reform that gave members the right to choose all subcommittees. I didn't want to go that far, but Mahon had given me no choice if we were to break the hold that southern conservatives had on key Appropriations subcommittees. I offered the rules amendment that way, and after some rearguard resistance from Mahon and, of all people, Phil Burton, it passed and Mahon had to play ball.

When I offered the motion in caucus, Phil Burton, who had his own ideas for committee reforms, had stood up and raised a point of order against my proposal. Phil announced to the chair, "I make a point of order against the amendment of the gentleman from Wisconsin." "On what grounds?" the chair asked. Burton, who was a master at power politics but had never learned the most rudimentary procedural floor rules became flustered and sputtered, "On the grounds that it will . . . ah . . . screw up an understanding between me and the Hanson committee." The Hanson committee, chaired by Julia Hanson, had been established to review proposed changes to caucus rules. Bob Eckart, the courtly Texas liberal, took the floor and said, "Mr. Chairman, I have heard many a point of order lodged in my time, but I have never heard of one being upheld on the grounds that it would screw up a deal of the gentleman of California." The caucus laughed, the chair ruled against Burton, and the subcommittee selection rules passed.

My second amendment required that Appropriations subcommittee chairmen be subject to ratification by the caucus. The theory behind my amendment was that Appropriations subcommittee chairs were equal in power to full committee chairs on authorizing committees. For example, the chairs of the Interior Subcommittee or the Labor-H Subcommittee certainly equaled the power of the chairs of the Interior authorizing committee or the Education and Labor authorizing committees. After the amendment passed, the Appropriations "Cardinals" knew that their stewardship could now be judged by the caucus. It gave me great pleasure to see Otto Passman, the reactionary and dictatorial chair of Foreign Operations, in his quest for support, sidle up to John Seiberling, a relatively junior member from Ohio, and assure him that he had "always used Seiberling tires." "That's nice," Seiberling replied, "but I worked for Firestone before I came here."

We pushed through a series of wide ranging reforms and dumped three committee chairmen. Eddie Hebert, the chair of Armed Services, was the worst. He had succeeded Mendel Rivers as chair and ruled with a cynical hand. When two liberals, Pat Schroeder ("Horror of horrors, a woman!") and Ron Dellums ("Good grief, an antiwar black!"), were elected to his committee,

Hebert demonstrated his contempt for them by arranging for the two of them to have only one chair to share on the committee dais. That news had gotten around. Two years later the world had changed, but Hebert didn't know it.

Dick Conlon at DSG had secretly prepared a report analyzing the manner in which every chairman governed his committee. The focus of the report was not on the philosophy of the chair but whether he had used his powers in a fair or arbitrary manner. Conlon then slipped the report to Common Cause with the understanding that they would publish it as their own. The report catalogued the arbitrariness of Hebert, Hays, and several other chairmen, and it got a lot of press. That report helped immensely in convincing caucus members that the attack on the chairs was based on the question of fairness, not ideology. The freshmen invited committee chairmen to come before their group and outline their plans for the coming year. Hebert sealed his fate when he opened his comments by saying, "Well, boys and girls." He was toast. So was Bob Poague, the Texas curmudgeon who chaired the Agriculture Committee. Another Texan, Wright Patman, lost his Banking Committee chairmanship to Henry Reuss. Wayne Hays, the bullying chairman of House Administration, was also voted down by the Steering Committee but regrettably the caucus overturned that action.

The purpose of the reforms was to rein in what had been the unaccountable power centers (the chairmen) and thus strengthen the power of the elected leadership. Dick Bolling, in his two insightful books on the House, had provided guidelines for many of the reforms that the DSG brought to fruition in 1975. Chairmen like Eddie Hebert had routinely stiffed the progressive majority in the Democratic caucus, made alliances with the GOP, sandbagged the Democratic policy positions in defense and military affairs, and treated young liberals and progressives on his committee like pond scum.

In his writings, Dick Bolling had driven home the point that our seats in Congress were licenses from our constituents, and the caucus could not, therefore, tell us how to vote in the House. On the other hand, our committee chairmanship posts were licenses from the caucus, and so we had an obligation not to use them to block the party's position in committee without giving leadership an opportunity to talk about it—even if we later voted against whatever it was on the floor. The idea of moving the committee assignment power from Ways and Means to the Steering Committee was meant to give the party leadership more muscle, thus making members more aware of their obligations to the caucus and the leadership. The idea of selectively removing chairmen was to drive home the message that they could not repeatedly and systematically block the caucus's will on key issues or treat other members unfairly without reaping the consequences.

Phil Burton added to the action by taking the subcommittee selection process I had fashioned for the Appropriations Committee and making it applicable to every standing committee. Burton's change applied to *all* committees other than Appropriations and provided no opportunity at all for senior members to grandfather subcommittee assignments. In my heart of hearts, I felt Burton's changes went too far in taking away the ability of the chair to balance subcommittee memberships. I felt mine did too, but Mahon and the Old Guard had given me no choice. They would not settle for a middle ground and had forced us to up the ante all the way in order to win.

~

CHAPTER II

New Job, New Rules,
New Enemies

The new rule meant that I would also be able to serve on the Foreign Operations Appropriations Subcommitte. That opportunity began a chapter in my life that would lead me to focus daily on America's role in the world, to think about the human condition in the far corners of the globe, and to study and visit more than forty countries. It began a three-decade-long challenge that enabled me to meet and get to know a wide range of leaders around the world and to work with—and sometimes against—four presidents in promoting American values and interests.

I brought into the office through the American Political Science Association fellowship program a savvy, thoughtful, and gutsy Foreign Service officer by the name of Jim Cheek. Cheek was a Latin American expert, but he also had a keen knowledge of the Middle East. I also hired a young international affairs graduate named Mike Marek because, under the terms of the APSA fellowship program, Cheek would be with me for a limited time only and I needed someone who could staff me long term. The first thing that Jim did for me was write a memo cautioning me to never allow the State Department to get its hooks into me and analyzing the department's relationship with subcommittee chairman Otto Passman of Louisiana. "The State Department and the White House always look for pressure points on members of Congress," Cheek said. "When they find that there is something you really want, they will have leverage on you. Almost every member of Congress sooner or later will want something so strongly that they will wind up being an easy mark for the executive. Your job is to be a responsible, but independent, analyst of every one of their policies. The best way to have a constructive relationship with them is never want something so badly that you will sacrifice your ability to raise hell with them in order to get it."

Long before I got to Congress, the name of Passman had been synonymous with reaction and ignorance. His hearings were often monuments to irrationality. He would regularly denounce foreign aid from every legislative mountain top within his reach and then, after he had extracted his price, allow it to pass. He was as high strung as any Kentucky thoroughbred. Frank Thompson nicknamed him "Native Dancer"—when Passman stood at the mike in the well of the House, he would grasp the sides of the rostrum in each hand and excitedly shift his feet back and forth so rapidly he resembled a nervous horse in a starting gate. Thompy said that Passman was the only man he had ever known who was so nervous that he wore out his suits from the inside.

"Your chairman is nuts," Jim said, "and the State Department and the White House will be looking for ways to get around him. But in the end, they'll cut a deal with him, so let them know you'll be helpful when Passman is out of line. But remember: in foreign policy it is very hard for Congress to push *any* administration where it doesn't want to go. The most effective power you'll have is a negative one—the power to deny all the money it wants unless its policy measures up to your standards. Don't be afraid to use that power. The negative power of the purse is the strongest weapon you'll have to accomplish something positive."

FIRST MIDDLE EAST TRIP

I took my first trip to the Middle East in the summer of 1975 and led a three-man delegation (with Ed Koch of New York and Joe Early of Massachusetts). On the way, we stopped in Portugal. Portugal had just experienced a political revolution. Events were still in flux, and our government really had no idea who would wind up on top. Henry Kissinger had already told the Nixon White House that chances for a democratic outcome were slim to none, but our ambassador, Frank Carlucci, strongly disagreed. A military junta had taken over, but Carlucci was convinced that there was a chance that democracy would win out in the end.

Koch and I greatly admired what Carlucci was trying to do. When we arrived in Lisbon, we had a frank discussion with him, but then the meeting went downhill. Koch and I had sent word ahead of time that we wanted an opportunity to talk to the democratic political opposition to the ruling junta. The opposition leader was Mario Soares, a Socialist. But when we asked Carlucci about meeting with Soares he told us that was impossible because Soares was "in hiding in the countryside" to avoid a possible arrest by the government. We pressed the embassy to arrange some meetings with other opposition figures, and they grudgingly reported that we could see a low-level official at Socialist party headquarters.

We arrived for the meeting in the early afternoon and had a forty-minute conversation with the party spokesman. When we got up to leave, he looked surprised and said to me, "I don't understand. Don't you want to see Mario?" "Certainly," I said, "but our embassy told us it was impossible because he was hiding out in the countryside to avoid possible arrest by the government." "Nonsense," he replied, "Mario is upstairs holding a press briefing right now. You can see him next if you wish." "Of course, we do!" I said. Fifteen minutes later we were escorted upstairs. "You will please excuse Mario, but he is being examined by his physician. He is not feeling well lately, but he will see you while the doctor is examining him," we were told. For the next hour, while Soares sat with his shirt off answering questions from the doctor, he also fielded questions from us. He was open, affable, cheerful, and flatly predicted that the junta would respect election results and that he would be the winner. And four months later he was. Soares led his country for ten years and was the key person in restoring democracy to Portugal. Carlucci was also key. He may have been out to lunch concerning our ability to meet Soares, but he was on the button in refusing to accept Kissinger's pessimistic conclusion about Portugal's chances to join the list of the world's democracies.

Our visit to the Middle East was much less pleasant but just as informative. Our trip came on the heels of Kissinger's efforts to negotiate a second round of Israeli mini-withdrawals from the Sinai after the 1973 war. Kissinger was shuttling from one party to another, patching together an agreement, and we were following him around trying to figure out what it would cost us and where, if anywhere, it might lead.

The trip to Egypt was an eye-opener—not for what we learned about the Egyptians but for what we heard from the ambassador about our own chairman. Before we met with Egyptian president Anwar Sadat, our ambassador pulled me aside and said, "Mr. Congressman, is there anything you can do about your chairman?"—he was referring to Passman. He explained to me that Passman was in town but had refused to see Sadat until the Egyptian government signed some rice contracts (Passman's Louisiana produced rice in significant quantities). "Sadat wanted to hear from Passman about whether Congress will follow through on Kissinger's promises, and Passman won't meet with him until those contracts are signed." The ambassador's comments confirmed everything I had ever thought about Passman. I told the ambassador there was nothing I could do about Passman while I was in Egypt, but as soon as I returned to Washington I would tell the Speaker what he had said, and I urged the ambassador to follow up with the Speaker and the White House.

Our delegation met with Sadat at his residence in Alexandria. I was fascinated by Ed Koch's response to him. Eddie was a strong sympathizer with Israel and highly suspicious of any Arab leader—Sadat included. He was not prepared to be impressed by Sadat, but I could tell he was. As our conversation with Sadat began, Eddie sat stiff and erect in his chair. His questions and comments to Sadat were polite but clipped and reserved. Ten minutes into the conversation Koch became more relaxed, and he began to lean slightly forward in his chair. By the end of our meeting he was leaning forward intently, elbows resting on his knees in animated give-and-take with Sadat.

During our talk I asked Sadat if he felt he could negotiate with Yitzhak Rabin, who was then in his first tour as Israeli prime minister. "Oh, no!" Sadat replied. "Why," I asked. "Weak," was his reply. As we started to leave, I asked, "Mr. President, is there any Israeli leader you could negotiate with?" Sadat paused, smiled, looked at me and said, "Oh, yes, the old lady!" (meaning Golda Meir). "Why is that?" I asked. "She has balls!" he said. That night at the Hilton Hotel, Koch, Early, and I were discussing the days' events, and Eddie was getting more and more snippy with me. I finally realized Eddie wasn't mad at me. "Eddie," I said, "you aren't really angry with me; you're angry with yourself. You didn't want to like Sadat, but you came away liking him, and now you're upset with yourself for feeling that way." Eddie demurred, but it clearly was the truth.

When we stepped off the plane in Damascus into the hot August sun, it felt as if we had walked into a blast furnace—temperatures were well above 110 degrees. We got a briefing on the Damascus water project that the United States was being asked to help underwrite. We also met with Syrian businessmen who, in spite of their anti-Israeli rhetoric, were clearly chomping at the bit to do business with Israelis. The next day we met with President Hafiz Assad for about an hour and a half. He impressed me as sly, stealthy, stubborn, ruthless, and bright—the kind of man you don't want to play poker with even when you have a really strong hand. He played the role of inscrutable enigma, giving us no useful indication of how he would respond to any possible U.S. or Israeli initiative in the region.

After that meeting, we flew to Jordan for an 8 p.m. meeting with King Hussein. Vital, vigorous, and thoughtful, Hussein made it quite clear that he had been pushed by the Arabs into a war he did not like and was determined to do everything he could to make sure it never happened again. He expressed some dubiousness about the intentions of Assad but urged us to keep all channels open to him.

In Israel we met with a variety of Israeli leaders, journalists, and our own diplomats. Our most interesting meetings were with Defense Minister Shimon Peres and Prime Minister Yitzhak Rabin—two men who were to play a central role in that country's events for a generation. In the 1980s and '90s Peres would acquire a reputation as the more dovish of the two, but in 1975 it seemed to be the reverse. In his position as defense minister and, with us, he seemed to take a significantly harder line than Rabin, although Rabin was certainly no dove. Rabin defended Israel's creation of settlements on the West Bank and in Jerusalem by saying, "We are tired of being attacked. We are creating new facts on the ground. Sooner or later the Arabs will have to negotiate or be overwhelmed by those facts." Joe Early's hackles were raised at the meeting in Rabin's office. When Joe asked a question about the long-term costs of Kissinger's negotiations for the United States, Rabin responded by saying something like, "I'm sure your taxpayers will feel privileged to make a key financial contribution to the advancement of peace in this region." Joe leaned over, put his elbow on Rabin's desk, and said, "Mr. Prime Minister, where I come from they call that a crock."

We also visited the West Bank and toured the Golan Heights with General Mordecai Gur. Near the end of the tour I asked him, "General, some people say retaining these settlements is militarily necessary to serve as a trip wire in the event of Arab attack. Is that your military judgment, too?" He replied, "Mr. Congressman, if you want my frank opinion, they're a pain in the ass. Militarily, they complicate my job of defending territory." I was as surprised by his frankness as I was by the substance of his response.

I was sobered by what I had seen in the Middle East. I doubted Assad would ever cut a final deal with Israel, and I was disquieted by the prospect of more and more Israeli settlements on the West Bank becoming a long-term stumbling block to peace. I was also concerned by the high level of corruption in Egypt. That country obviously needed economic help and was key to our influence in the Arab world, but I doubted much progress could be made on the economic front as long as corruption was so rampant. After minimal congressional review of the administration's appropriation request, Kissinger got what he wanted in the way of added financial aid to Israel and Egypt.

Mo

When I returned to the states, my attention turned to the upcoming presidential election. The economy was in trouble, and my hopes were high that Democrats could finally nominate a winner for president. But the field looked as dull as dry toast. One afternoon on the House floor, Henry Reuss and I began to talk about our choices. Both of us were admirers of Mo Udall, but the conventional wisdom was that presidential races were the province of senators and governors. I was also a fan of Fritz Mondale, my neighbor from Minnesota.

Henry and I talked with Mo and told him that we knew it was a long shot, but if he were really interested, we would like to help him. A few days later, Mo's chief of staff Terry Bracy called and asked me to come over and talk. We knew that it would be hard to get House members to make a hard commitment at that stage, but we reasoned that a sense of institutional pride might get some names on a letter suggesting that a number of House members were qualified to be president, singling Mo out as one example and expressing our willingness to encourage him to make the race. We got the signatures of twenty-four members, which produced a series of modest stories about the effort. I still felt somewhat divided between Mo and Mondale, but Fritz took himself out of it at an early stage, saying that he just did not want to spend two years of his life sleeping in motels in order to run a successful campaign. Mo joked that Fritz's statement was conclusive evidence that Fritz was the only man who was mentally balanced enough for the job.

I began spending more and more time helping Mo—making pitches for him at a variety of forums in Maine, Maryland, Pennsylvania, Massachusetts, Michigan, Wisconsin, Iowa, Illinois, Florida, New Jersey, and several other states. Early in the cycle, prior to caucuses at which delegates to the national convention were selected, Iowa held a series of district level forums. I went to one of them in Rep. Ed Mezvinski's district and appeared as a stand-in speaker for Mo. Birch Bayh and Sargent Shriver were both there. Also participating was a little-known southern governor. Before the forum, I had been neutral on Jimmy Carter. Based on what little I knew of him, I thought that he might be my third or fourth choice. But when I returned from the forum, I told my staff that Carter would be my last choice. "He pandered to every antigovernment sentiment in the audience," I told them. And something else bothered me. Carter conveyed the sense that he did not really enjoy politics or governance, that he found it a hard-to-bear struggle—a drudgery. He kept talking about being an engineer and seemed to approach government as though it was a problem to be managed rather than a set of challenges to be confronted. I thought he would do well with primary activists because of his antipolitics message, but I didn't think he had the instinct or the enthusiasm needed to energize the country and make it follow him. Several years later I nodded in agreement when I read a comment by the columnist I. F. Stone when he wrote of Carter: "He is a well-meaning man who often tries to do the right thing, but has the soul of a tinkering fussbudget engineer."

Fussbudget or no, he won the nomination. Mo Udall did far better than I had expected when we started. He battled Carter until the end and finished second in four major primaries—losing each, including Wisconsin, by less than 2 percent. Mo should have been a natural for Wisconsin, but it took time to get his campaign going. I remember the maddening frustration I felt trying to convince a number of Dane County Democratic friends that Mo really was liberal enough to warrant their support as long as Oklahoma's Fred Harris was in the race.

We had hoped Wisconsin would be Mo's breakthrough state, but after Carter's Peanut Brigades did so well in Iowa's caucuses, Carter took a lead in the state's polls. Mo fought back, and we had modest hopes for an upset. On election night, for the first three hours it looked like Udall lightning had struck. He took a slim early lead and held it for close to two hours. The lead kept narrowing as the rural vote trailed in, but most people thought he would hold it. One network—I think it was CBS—declared Mo the winner.

Mo's political brain trust wanted him to make a victory statement based on that declaration—the late evening news would cast him as the winner and give him a badly needed boost. I didn't like the numbers that were coming in from the rural western part of the state and thought Carter still had a fifty-fifty chance to win. Sitting in our Milwaukee hotel room, I urged a slightly different approach. I urged Mo to go before the cameras and say, "No one thought we could win tonight. It looks like we may have pulled a great upset. Even if we haven't, we have come so close that we have essentially fought Carter to a draw. His bandwagon has been slowed to a crawl, it's now a two-man race, and now that we've slowed him down, we will pass him up in the next primary." I told them that we had exceeded expectations and ought to say so, warning that if Carter eventually pulled it out, a flat-out victory state-ment would be thrown at them the way the *Chicago Tribune* was thrown at Dewey in 1948. I was overruled. They gambled their lead would hold. It didn't. With that disappointment, it was a miracle Mo's campaign did as well as it did in Michigan and other states that followed. That it did was testimony to the quality of the man and the hunger of the party for someone with a pos-itive progressive message. I truly believed that if Mo had won, he would have won in November and would have been a far stronger candidate running for reelection in 1980. But it was not to be.

One event during the Wisconsin primary foreshadowed Mo's sad end, but no one knew it at the time. Some time after the election, Mo lost his balance and fell from a ladder at his home in McLean, Virginia, and broke both wrists. Mo quipped, "When you lose the ability to use both hands, you really find out who your friends are." Over the next few years, Mo began to have more physical problems and was finally diagnosed with Parkinson's. He said to me, "Dave, do you remember that day in Milwaukee during the primary when I shot baskets with Wayne Embry and kept missing?" (For a short time in his youth Mo had been a professional basketball player, despite having one glass eye because of botched eye surgery when he was a young boy). I did remember that as a campaign media event Mo had arranged to shoot baskets with Embry, who played with the Milwaukee Bucks. With the press in full attendance in a Milwaukee gym, Mo took a series of shots and missed one after another after another. He was clearly agitated and embarrassed that he hadn't done better. "That day," Mo said, "I knew something was wrong. I never missed that many shots in my life. I really believe that even back then it was already starting to bite me."

That summer I attended the Democratic National Convention, watched Mo give a generous and gracious speech, heard Fritz Mondale, Carter's selection for vice president, rally the troops, and listened to Carter's call to the nation for a government of goodness. Election night was a happy one. Carter won Wisconsin and the nation.

Pushing Reform and Making Enemies

After the election, I returned to Congress and immersed myself in an effort that was soon to make me some powerful lifelong enemies.

In 1975 the House had been hit with a mini-scandal surrounding Rep. Wayne Hays of Ohio. Hays was the chairman of the House Administration Committee, which set the rules for office expenditures for committees and individual members, and he was a bully. My first encounter with him came in my first year in Congress. My staff and I were located in 1417 Longworth, a two-room suite with an annex far down the hall. I was looking for a way to move the staff in that annex closer to the main office. I noticed that a room right across the hall never seemed to be used. I asked Carl Albert if he could tell me who had it. He checked and told me it was Wayne Hays. I had no idea who Hays was, but I called him, explained my situation, and asked him if there was any way he would consider swapping rooms so I could consolidate my staff. "I'll be right over," he said. Five minutes later he walked into my office and said, "Come here, kid; I want to show you something." He pulled a key out of his pocket and opened the door to the room I was asking about.

Inside was a roomful of crated French furniture. "Now look, kid, I belong to the North Atlantic Assembly and several times a year I fly to Europe on an air force plane. When I come back I bring this furniture. I'm going to furnish my house in Steubenville with it. Now you wouldn't want me to risk scratching it just to do a favor for some chickenshit freshman, would you?" he asked. I got the picture.

For one hundred years, House administrative matters had been handled almost as an afterthought by the House leadership through patronage-filled House offices—the clerk, sergeant at arms, doorkeeper—under the day-to-day supervision of the Committee on House Administration, which Hays chaired. Hays was as feared as he was arrogant until newspapers carried the story that he had hired a woman whose services were definitely not secretarial. The press started asking all kinds of questions about the use of member's office accounts. At the urging of John Brademas, the party deputy whip, Carl Albert appointed me chairman of a task force to recommend reforms in the way members of Congress could use those office accounts. Also appointed to the task force were Lloyd Meeds of Washington, and Norm D'Amours of New Hampshire. We recommended a series of reforms, including the public disclosure of every expenditure out of those accounts. Until that time, those transactions had never been made public. Our recommendations were adopted, but they focused only on how office money could be spent.

We had not had time to develop a more far-reaching set of reforms on how the House itself was administered. To do that, we recommended the establishment of a Commission on Administrative Review to analyze the financial administration of the House and make in-depth recommendations about administrative changes. The commission was to be composed of members of Congress, plus a selection of public members with expertise on the Congress and on financial and management systems. Speaker Albert appointed me to chair the commission and also appointed from the Democratic side Mel Price of Illinois, Lee Hamilton of Indiana, and Meeds and D'Amours. As public members he appointed Lucy Benson, national chair of the League of Women Voters, and my old advisor Ralph Huitt, who had served LBJ as assistant secretary for legislation for the Department of Health, Education, and Welfare. He also named Chuck Daly, who had served Jack Kennedy as deputy lobbyist for the White House on Capitol Hill and would later run the Kennedy Presidential Library, Bill Hamilton, a well-known survey researcher, and Bill DuChessi of the United Steelworkers. Minority leader John Rhodes selected Roscoe Eggar, a vice president for the Price Waterhouse accounting firm, later to become IRS commissioner, and Bob Galvin, president of Motorola, as public members. From the GOP caucus he appointed Bill Frenzel of Minnesota, a moderate, and two fierce partisans, Bill Armstrong of Colorado and Bob Bauman of Maryland.

I hired Dr. Joseph Cooper, a nationally known congressional scholar from Rice University, as chief of staff, and Alan Katz, a first-rate lawyer who had been my legislative director, to ride shotgun as legal counsel to the commission. The staff organized into a number of task forces and began to develop scores of recommendations. But before we could finalize them, another event intervened.

With the 1976 election concluded, Tip O'Neill was elected Speaker and wanted his tenure to begin with a signal that Congress was getting a fresh start. He asked my commission to go beyond administrative reforms and produce a new code of ethics for the House. I knew he was very close to Dan Rostenkowski, and that made me wonder how much reform Tip really wanted. I mentioned to him, "Tip, there are a lot of ways to handle this issue. The farther we go the more people we will tick off. Do you expect us to do a once-over-lightly patch job or do you want us to go all the way?" "Go all the way, Dave," was his response. "I want a fresh start for this Congress." That was all I needed to hear. I asked Lee Hamilton to chair the task force to develop the new code. We worked together as partners in developing the recommendations, but he would present them to the commission when they were done. My commission had no authority to get into campaign finance legislation, so we focused on the other obvious conflicts before us.

Hamilton and I were planning to focus on two proposals: first, to limit severely the amount of money that could be earned from speaking fees, and second, to apply those same limits to outside earned income from any source—law practice, service on corporate boards, and so forth. Before we could finalize our recommendations, a monkey wrench was thrown into the gears by some terribly well-meaning people.

In 1968, the year before my election to Congress, a proposal had been passed under which Congress delegated to the president the authority to establish a commission that would recommend appropriate adjustments, every four years, in salary for the president, his cabinet officers, members of Congress, the federal judiciary, and other high-ranking government officials. Unless Congress overturned those recommendations within a specified period of time, they became law. The sponsor of that reform had been Mo Udall.

One evening, I got a phone call from Mo. "Dave, I hate to spoil your evening, but you need to know something that will complicate your life." He told me that Pete Peterson, the former secretary of commerce who was serving as the commission chairman, had just phoned him at home to tell him that his commission intended to recommend a significant pay raise for all government officials, including members of Congress, but planned to tie it to the passage of a government-wide code of ethics. They did not intend to produce that code but wanted to make the congressional pay raise effective only after such a code had been passed. Mo told him it was a bad idea. "Look," Mo said, "Dave Obey is working on a new code of ethics for Congress right now and will have a hell of a time passing it. If you tie the two together, people in Congress who want no code will demagogue the pay raise and use it to kill the ethics code. You'll be better off if you just set the pay at whatever level you think it should be at and let us pass this code of ethics separately." But Peterson was not persuaded. By the time the commission recommendations were approved by the president, they had called for a $12,000 pay raise for Congress. The problem was this: with our recommendations to limit outside income and law practice income, we were taking away many times that amount from key members.

Our first recommendation was to limit all outside earned income to 15 percent of salary. We wanted to establish the principle that Congress was a full-time job and that members of Congress had only one master, as it were: the taxpayers who paid their salaries. The idea of imposing a limit rather than an outright ban eliminated the likelihood of significant conflict of interest while allowing some de minimis outside activity. We also doubted we could pass an outright ban. We applied the same principle to outside speaking fees. Those recommendations cost Tip a substantial amount of lost income from his insurance business. They did the same to Rostenkowski. Their reactions couldn't have been more different. "It's the right thing to do, Davy," Tip said, when I gave him advance warning of what we were planning. "You're a crazy son of a bitch!" Danny told me, when he found out about it, and I had made an enemy for life. Payback time would come four years later when I ran for Budget Committee chairman. Danny managed Jim Jones's successful campaign against me, beating me on the third ballot after two tie votes.

With some justification, people who were going to lose big money because of the limit on outside *earned* income objected that conflicts from outside *unearned* income were just as bad. They sometimes were, but under the Constitution it would have been an illegal taking to confiscate someone's inherited income or their passive income from investments. For investment income, disclosure was the only constitutional avenue open to us, and that's what we were recommending—disclosure of all investment income.

Our third recommendation was especially controversial. We decided to place an absolute ban on outside income from law practices. We had heard too many horror stories to do otherwise. One lawyer member from New York came up to me and said, "Dave, you don't understand. My law practice doesn't take any time away from my job. It's just that as I rise in seniority, the lobbyists toss more business our way, and I get a piece of the action." "I know, I know," I replied. I could see bafflement in his face. He truly thought that we were acting out of a big misunderstanding. In fact, we understood all too well. He never did quite realize that we *meant* to do what we were doing— different worlds, different understandings. We made some other recommendations that were truly important, but these three were the toughest.

The House, with much consternation, accepted our recommendations. Many Republicans fought a rearguard action against us and they had some allies on the Democratic side, but in the end we won by a vote of 402 to 22. We had gotten the code through the legislative hot box. Over the next decade, before it was updated, more than a dozen members of the House were disciplined under our new rules, including one House Speaker, Jim Wright. But after the ethics package passed, a backlash set in. Our second set of recommendations, on administrative reform, was brought to the House on October 12, 1977. Frank Thompson, my old friend who, with the departure of Wayne Hays, now chaired the House Administration Committee, had been leading an underground resistance movement against our reforms on the Democratic side of the aisle because he felt that the creation of a House administrator would undermine his authority. He had other eager allies on the Democratic side, including Rostenkowski and Pennsylvania Rep. Jack Murtha, who made no secret of his view that in most cases "reform" was a four-letter word.

But the bulk of the opposition came from the Republicans. They didn't like the idea of a professional administrator, and many of their more political types simply did not want to see the Democrats get credit for reforming the institution. When the rule that set the terms for debate on the package was brought to a vote, it went down by a vote of 160 to 252, effectively killing the package. Democrats voted for the package, 160 to 113, but the GOP brought it down by voting unanimously against it, 139 to zero. At the time it pained me to see so much work go down the tubes, but over the next ten years, one by one, the vast majority of our recommendations, including the appointment of a professional administrator, was implemented.

❧

CHAPTER 12

Life with Jimmy

Jimmy Carter's presidency was a new experience for me. Until his election, I had only served with Republican presidents. I had been elected to the Budget Committee at the same time that Jimmy Carter was moving into the White House. Serving on that committee exposed me to budgeting from a whole different perspective, as did serving with a Democratic president. On Appropriations, we focused on program details, the micro level of government spending. On Budget, we focused on the broad, macro picture, including the economic conditions in which that government spending took place.

My first exposure to the new Carter administration team was a meeting at Blair House, the building across the street from the White House often used by visiting foreign dignitaries. Carter called Congress down in small groups, gave an earnest appeal for cooperation, and answered questions. It was a sincere performance, and members gave him high marks.

His staff was something else again. A number of senior Carter staff, such as press secretary Jody Powell, were highly regarded. I particularly liked Carter's new budget director, Bert Lance, a good old boy from Georgia with a banking background, who was direct, pragmatic, and did not seem to have a need to impress anyone. But Carter's congressional relations team was weakly led and some, like staff chief Hamilton Jordan in particular, seemed to have come to town with king-sized chips on their shoulders.

Carter got off to a bad start with the congressional leadership on both a personal and professional level. His staff seemed to have little regard for Tip O'Neill, and the feeling was reciprocated. Carter's budget choices, too, often seemed clumsy. I saw that the key to understanding the Carter administration's legislative strategy was to recognize that, in reality, it often had none. Effective presidents understand that they must rely on their political base, in

Congress and out, and need to govern by adding different groups to that base as they move from issue to issue. It became apparent to me, however, that Carter felt no need to build from that base. His idea of governing seemed to be to put together one coalition on education, another on energy, another on taxes, and yet another on other issues that came up, without regard to whether his political base was with him or not. He seemed to think nothing of producing a proposal that would be opposed by a large number of Democrats one week, defeating them with the help of Republican votes, and then going to those same Democrats the next week for support on something else.

Carter seemed to think that one coalition was just as good as another. He didn't understand that when the going got tough, Republicans would leave him in a flash, and he would need to have his own party fully behind him. Until late in the game, he took no real steps to build a relationship with his own party, and this hurt him badly. The man who would succeed him, Ronald Reagan, never made that mistake. He would understand that to survive in national politics a president had to have a strong cadre supporting him through thick and thin, and that meant he worked out differences with his base first—and then looked for other allies.

Through the months I could see Carter drifting into a gray zone, no one strongly for him, no one strongly against him, no one feeling any particular bond with him, personally or philosophically. I knew presidents like that didn't last. When the White House set up a system under which any member of Congress could talk to the president for fifteen minutes on a time-available basis, I called Bill Cable and told him I wanted to see the president. "What do you want from him," he asked. "Nothing, I want to do something for him," I said.

One early afternoon I was asked into the Oval Office. Carter came around his desk, yellow pad in hand, motioned me to a chair, and sat down next to me. "What can I do for you, Dave?" he asked. "Nothing, Mr. President, I just want to talk to you about your presidency," I replied. "What do you mean?" he asked. I told him that I very much wanted him to succeed but I thought he had one problem that was going to make that success difficult to come by.

"Mr. President," I said, "What worries me most is that when the going gets really tough on the big issues in Congress, you won't get from the Congress what most other presidents have gotten—the benefit of the doubt. Most other presidents have been personally well known when they get here," I said. "But not many people on the Hill know you as a person. On so many issues, if the question is close and members have no strong feelings, they will give the president the benefit of the doubt and *that* can make all the difference. But you aren't getting those votes, and you won't until people feel that they have a personal relationship with you, have some feel for what makes you tick. Right now, when members come down here for briefings, they are impressed by how smart you are, how well intentioned you are, and how much you know. But they still feel they don't know you."

Carter was taking notes. I continued, "Mr. President, I know what I am about to suggest may sound trivial, but nothing in politics that effects human chemistry is trivial." I urged him to bring members of Congress down to the White House in small groups—not just for policy discussions, but for social get-togethers. "Ask them down, ten or fifteen at a time, for an hour at the end of the day. Offer them a drink. Ask about their families and their districts. When that hour is over, they will go back to the Hill, they will go back to their districts, and they will tell their local Rotary club, 'When I was with the president last week, I told him blah, blah, blah, blah!' They will feel they know you, and when close questions come, they will be more inclined to give you a vote. It's not as intellectually stimulating as a policy briefing, but in the end government is run by people, not policy."

I saw Carter had laid his writing pad down. I could see his eyes drift. I could see he was tuning out. I stood up, thanked him for his time, and left the Oval Office with a resigned feeling. I knew he would never personally connect with people on the Hill, and I knew if he couldn't connect with people he worked with every day, he could never relate to people throughout the country who would never meet him. I knew it was going to be a long four years. A good deal later Carter did have several small gatherings at the White House, but by then it was too late. Not that he didn't try. He was an honorable, thoughtful, highly intelligent and highly motivated person—next to Clinton, probably the smartest president I ever knew. He had guts, and he knew how to analyze and dissect a problem. He was fiercely honest, and I would have trusted him with the last dollar I had in the world. He just didn't seem to know how to communicate a sense of being up to handling everything that history could throw at him.

That wasn't true at first. The first time he truly needed to communicate with the American people, when he gave his famous energy speech outlining the challenges America faced from the Arab oil boycott and the steps that needed to be taken to build a long-term energy policy, he did a first-rate job. He was effective in winning the support to nearly double the key energy research programs (which later were largely wiped out during the Reagan-Bush years). But after that, when he spoke to the nation, he often came across as perplexed, worried, and weighed down. On several occasions, even when the administration did try to take on a problem, it was slow to grasp political realities and wound up playing defense when it didn't need to. When that happened, I learned it was sometimes easier to work around the White House and deal directly with agencies.

One example of that approach involved the Middle Income Student Assistance Act. During the 1970s, Congress had passed the Basic Opportunity Grant program (since renamed the Pell Grant program) to make it easier for working-class families to send their kids to college. That program initially covered close to 70 percent of the cost of college for very-low-income students, but it was vulnerable to political attack because eligibility was so limited and so targeted to low-income families that most middle-income families, even those with modest means, had incomes too high to qualify. The Republicans tried to take advantage by talking about a tuition tax program that would have heavily benefited high-income families. Billy Ford, John Brademas, Frank Thompson, and I wanted to counter that by expanding eligibility for the basic grant program to middle-income families. The White House Office of Management and Budget (OMB) dragged its feet in facing up to the problem. Joe Califano, the HEW secretary, and his congressional liaison, Ken Levine, understood the need for speed and tried to work behind the scenes with us to squeeze OMB. Fritz Mondale also understood the problem, and we were finally able to get a letter from him expressing support for making room in the Budget Resolution for an expansion of the Basic Opportunity Program, which we named the Middle Income Student Assistance (MISA) Act.

We were finally able to get Bob Giaimo and Ed Muskie, the House and Senate Budget Committee chairs, to finesse the problem. They put a number in the Budget Resolution for student aid expansion but left unclear whether it would be used as we wanted, for the MISA Act, or as the Senate GOP wanted. Then, working with Califano, we were able to designate funding for the MISA Act in the Labor-H appropriations bill, even before an authorization bill was passed. It had been twice as difficult as it should have been because OMB was so slow in coming to a realization that they needed to get the administration out front on the issue. In spite of these difficulties, Carter was still able to produce good outcomes in several arenas.

Jimmy Carter was the best president for farmers in the last half of the twentieth century. A farmer himself, he genuinely understood the problems, and he was comfortable in rural culture. Dairy farmers did better under his administration than they have ever since. Rep. Al Baldus and I enjoyed working with his agriculture secretary, Bob Berglund, in support of dairy legislation that put a healthy safety net under farmers who were at the mercy of markets over which they had absolutely no control.

Because I had also been elected chairman of the DSG in a race against Dick Ottinger of New York, I also spent a lot of time on a wide range of issues not related to appropriationsor the budget. One subject that took a huge amount of our time was labor law reform.

Organized labor was losing membership because of changes in the economy and because deficiencies in the law made it too easy for recalcitrant employers to throw up formidable road blocks to workers' efforts to unionize. To change that situation, organized labor and the Carter administration tried to push labor law reform through the Congress. As DSG chairman, I worked with Vice President Mondale's office and the congressional leadership to try to persuade southern Democrats to vote for the package. Many were reluctant to do so because labor was so weak in their districts. Dick Conlon, Phil Burton, Jim O'Hara, Billy Ford, Frank Thompson, and I argued that it was in their interest for workers to be given added bargaining power. We argued that unless labor was strengthened, members of Congress from the South would be increasingly vulnerable politically because a weak labor movement meant a weak Democratic Party. We finally won the vote on a watered-down bill in the House, but the administration came up a handful of votes shy in the Senate, and the bill died. Today, I am absolutely convinced that the defeat of that bill was a key event in putting progressive forces in this society on the defensive. I'm also convinced that until a major political event occurs in this country to galvanize Congress into giving workers more protection against intimidating anti-union practices from companies like Wal-Mart, justice at the bargaining table will be unattainable, the gap between rich and poor will continue to grow, and progressives in the political system will continue to operate with one hand tied behind their backs.

Out with Otto, In with Doc

Notwithstanding my work with the administration on domestic issues, my greatest day-to-day contact with the administration occurred in dealing with them on foreign affairs. With the defeat of Otto Passman for reelection in 1976, the subcommittee chairmanship of the Foreign Operations Appropriations subcommittee passed to Clarence "Doc" Long, an erratic former college professor from Maryland. Even with all of his idiosyncrasies, in many ways Doc Long was a breath of fresh air after Otto Passman. He was a supporter of human rights, whereas Passman wouldn't have known what they were. Doc was dubious about the value of much of our military aid, especially when it shored up repressive regimes in Africa and Central America. On the other hand, Doc couldn't put together a two-car funeral.

In 1977 Doc had handled his first bill on the floor. It was a fiasco. The administration did a poor job of lobbying Congress, and the GOP was able to pass a number of crippling amendments and force deep cuts in the administration's requests—all in all a serious setback for the new administration. The next year, to avoid a repeat of the fiasco, Don Ritchbourg, the subcommittee clerk, told Fred Mohrman, the Appropriations Committee staff director, that if the central committee office didn't find a way to work around Doc, the subcommittee would be unlikely to produce a bill. Ritchbourg sat down with me and Ed Powers of the central committee staff to find a way to produce a bill satisfactory to the administration. I worked with Don, Bob Bechel, the administration's congressional lobbyist for international affairs, Mike Marek, my own foreign policy advisor, and Genta Hawkins, a career foreign service officer who worked temporarily in my office under the American Political Science Association fellowship program. With the help of Matt McHugh, Texas Charlie Wilson, and Silvio Conte, moving with much delicacy, we put together an alliance that effectively fenced in Doc and produced a legislative product that we and the administration could live with.

PANAMA

The region that began to occupy more of the subcommittee's and the administration's attention was Central America. My first involvement in Panama occurred several years before Carter was elected. In my first months on the subcommittee in 1975, during the Ford administration, Lee Hamilton called and asked if I would accompany him on a trip there. The Nixon and Ford administrations had been doing some planning about transferring sovereignty over the Panama Canal from the United States to Panama, but I was not aware of the contemplated transfer until I received Hamilton's call. Lee obtained a small Jetstar from DoD, and we and his staff chief Mike Van Dusen flew to Panama for a weekend of meetings.

The Panama Canal had been built by Teddy Roosevelt after he engineered Panamanian secession from Colombia at the turn of the century. Under a treaty with the fledgling Panamanian government, the United States had been given sovereignty rights over the canal and a narrow strip of land on each side of it, known as the Panama Canal Zone. The canal had been an example of America's "Can do!" approach and of American imperialistic tendencies in the Western Hemisphere. But by the 1970s, rising nationalistic fervor in Panama was making it evident that in a world where Britain and other Western imperial powers were relinquishing their empires, the United States would be in an untenable position in the court of world opinion and throughout Latin America if we insisted on hanging on to the most vivid symbol of American imperialism in the region.

In the context of the Cold War, at a time when the Soviet Union and Fidel Castro were doing their best to find issues that could expand anti-American sentiment in the region, it seemed wise to try to eliminate a focal point of anti-American fervor by recognizing the inevitable. If we didn't, we might lose the use of the canal anyway because of sabotage or political turmoil. The canal itself was becoming obsolete, and without a new positive relationship with the region to facilitate modernization, it might be rendered useless within a brief period of years.

At that time, the Panamanian government was run by a military dictator, General Omar Torrillos. Lee and I expected to meet with him, but when we landed in Panama we were told that he had unexpectedly taken a quickly scheduled trip to Spain. After a series of meetings with Panamanian officials and U.S. embassy and military officials, and an inspection of the canal itself, Lee and I were invited to dinner by Torrillos's stand-in, President Dimitrio Lakas. He was a hulk of a man with a ten-gallon Texas accent. Educated at Texas Tech, he looked and sounded like LBJ. Over dinner Lee and I asked him questions about the canal and Panamanian politics. After dinner we continued with our earnest questions. Finally, he draped his arm around my shoulder and said, "Look boys! I don't think you get the big picture. Things are unraveling down here. It's very simple. You know what politics is, it's nothing but bullshit, bullshit, bullshit, and the truth of the matter is: if we don't get a new treaty, we done run out of bullshit! Without it the string runs out, yours and ours." Nothing like a little Texas bluntness to drive home a point.

When Carter became president, he faced the problem squarely and agreed to a new canal treaty, which set in motion the transfer of sovereignty of the canal to Panama. On our subcommittee we fended off a number of efforts to hold some administration policies hostage to the canal issue. The issue generated so much emotion that in the next election, many of us saw our election margins go down significantly.

EL SALVADOR AND NICARAGUA

The second Central American country that began to consume us was El Salvador. El Salvador had been wracked with violence for years. The country was grotesquely dominated by a small land-owning elite, and a huge percentage of the population was landless, penniless, and hopeless. Those conditions created a fertile breeding ground for revolution, and that's exactly what the country was experiencing.

There were essentially three factions in El Salvador: (1) the ruling elite led by Roberto D'Aubuisson; (2) the revolutionaries—a coalition of factions of varying degrees of militancy who were dedicated to changing the old order; and (3) a more moderate group in the middle led by Napoleon Duarte. Duarte's mildly reformist faction had been caught in a bitter struggle between the committed revolutionaries on the left and the reactionary elites on the right, and the country was awash in killing. Right-wing death squads associated with the military made war against both the revolutionaries and the Duarte government—and they didn't mind chewing up any poor peasants who got in their way. The right-wing oligarchy pushed for U.S. military aid to quell the revolution, but they resisted Carter's insistence that in return they support political and land reform, which would give the average Salvadoran a stake in putting down the revolutionaries.

Catholic Archbishop Romero, a theological conservative who had nonetheless spoken out for political reform, had been gunned down at the altar by death squad henchmen while saying Mass. Several American Maryknoll nuns working in El Salvador had also been brutally killed by the same groups. It was obvious that both incidents were caused by the death squads, but the proof was hard to come by in a country dominated by terror. D'Aubuisson was widely regarded as the leader of the death squads. He would often publicly finger the next target for assassination by denouncing them on television as "enemies of the state." At one point he outrageously described Jim Cheek (who had returned to the State Department as the deputy assistant secretary for Central America) the same way. Cheek had been in Salvador to deliver a message to the military dictatorship that if they staged a coup against Duarte (who had been democratically elected), the United States would unilaterally shut off all aid to the government in its fight against the left-wing revolutionaries. That is what triggered D'Aubuisson's attack on Jim.

When I visited Salvador to get a firsthand look at the situation, a young Salvadoran businessman, who ran the only brewery in the country, said to me, "Sir, you have to understand how different things are here. I'm a capitalist; I have a lot to lose if the rebels win. But to appreciate the difficulty of saving this country, you must understand how things run down here. In the States, when you sit down at a Rotary club lunch you see a friend across the table. But when I sit down at the Rotary club, I look across the table into the eyes

of another businessman who has put out a contract on my life. Why? Because
I have been trying to help President Duarte communicate with the business
community, but many of them think Duarte is a Communist. That is how
sick this country is," he said.

The third Central American country that occupied our attention was Nicaragua. The country had been ruled for years by Anastasio Somoza, a military
dictator who had been kept in power by the United States. Like other Latin
dictators, he had bled his country dry and was finally overthrown by the
Sandinista rebels led by Daniel and Humberto Ortega in 1979. American
policy makers did not quite know how to deal with the Sandinistas. Lawrence
Pezzulo, our ambassador, tried mightily to establish a working relationship
with the new regime. Congress itself was badly split about whether we should
try to work with them and provide aid. A running debate ensued among members of the former ruling class there about whether they should try to carve
out a relationship with the new government or simply take their money out of
the bank, leave the country, and try to finance a long-distance military counterrevolution from the United States. That debate would not be resolved until
much later during Ronald Reagan's presidency.

MIDDLE EAST AND CAMP DAVID

The single most admirable feature of Carter's presidency was the sense of
duty that drove him to put his popularity on the line to attack tough problems. Unlike so many politicians I have known, he really did prefer to deal
with problems rather than to play with them. I especially admired his efforts
to bring peace to the Middle East.

In July of 1977, six months into Carter's presidency, I traveled again to the
Middle East, this time with Lee Hamilton, Abner Mikva, and Ben Rosenthal.
After a thirty-year string of Labor governments in Israel, the right-wing Likud
coalition under Menachem Begin had come to power. We wanted to get a firsthand feel for how his election changed the equation in the region. Our meeting with Begin was most unsatisfactory. In nose-to-nose discussions, Begin
flatly promised me that Israel was not confiscating any private Arab-owned
land on the West Bank. But that promise was misleading because, to Begin,
the lands being confiscated were not Arab. They were, in his eyes, permanent
parts of Greater Israel, which had just been temporarily occupied by Arabs.

Our meeting with Arafat was just as unsatisfactory. In those days, only
a handful of members of Congress would meet with Arafat. I felt—as did
Hamilton—that we could not get a true feel for the situation without getting

a firsthand feel for Arafat himself. Before we left the States, we contacted Arafat's lieutenants to ask for an appointment. We told them the questions we would be asking Arafat and the order in which the questions would be asked; we were assured that Arafat would be forthcoming in his replies. We had originally arranged to meet Arafat in Beirut, but the day before our scheduled meeting a PLO faction hijacked an airplane, and Arafat was busy trying to negotiate the release of the hostages. His people asked us to meet him a week later in Cairo.

The night of the meeting, at about 11:30 p.m., we were picked up at our hotel by two men in a Mercedes. Rosenthal and Mikva had originally planned to join us but decided they would take too much heat from the Jewish community if they did; they asked us to brief them after we returned to the hotel. American State Department personnel were forbidden to meet directly with the PLO, so our State Department escort officer, Bob Flaten, could not accompany us. The driver gave Flaten a phone number he could call if he needed to reach us. He would in turn be given a second phone number to call that would complete the connection. We expected to be driven to some out-of-the-way, back-alley place in the Cairo neighborhoods, but instead, to our surprise, we were driven to the Meridian Hotel in downtown Cairo.

The meeting started with Arafat reciting a long list of Palestinian grievances. When we finally got to ask him questions, he played verbal "loop de loop" with us. In an answer to our fifth or sixth question, we might eventually get a partial answer to our first or second question, and so forth. Finally, at about 3 a.m., Arafat asked, "Would anyone here like a refreshment, a drink?" Without thinking, Hamilton responded, "I would really like a Coke." At that time, the Arab world was engaging in a boycott of products produced by companies that did business in Israel, so Coke was officially on the Arab boycott list. When Hamilton asked for a Coke, Arafat broke into a grin and said, "Ah, ordinarily that would be impossible, but this is Sabri's room so you can have anything you want." They opened the minibar in the room, and it was loaded with Coke. From our evening's conversation we got the impression that Arafat was looking for ways to begin negotiations but was extremely reluctant to take anything but the smallest steps to bring them about. We did not get much out of Arafat that night, but the Coca-Cola incident showed that on many things in the Middle East there was a large gulf between professed policy and actual practice. And while Arafat may have been unwilling to take anything but baby steps to change the region, others were just as determined to take big ones.

Months later, after years of futile standoffs between Israel and Egypt, Anwar Sadat cut through the stalemate by flying to Jerusalem in a grand gesture that electrified the world. When Sadat got off the plane, Golda Meir, the "old lady" Sadat had referred to in his comments to me four years earlier, gently asked him, "What took you so long?"

Sadat's Israeli counterpart was Prime Minister Begin. After the recognition of the State of Israel in 1948, the Labor party dominated Israeli politics for the next three decades, and Begin was the leader of the opposition coalition, the Likud. After the 1956 Suez War with the Arabs, Labor governments returned the land they had captured but received nothing for it. But after the '67 war, they decided, "No more!" They intended to hang on to the territory they had won on the battlefield until they could get something from the Arab world for returning it. That "something" was peace, official recognition, and normalized relations. But Begin had gone farther. His position was "No!" to returning what he referred to as Judea and Samaria to the Arab world. No negotiations, period! To Begin, Judea and Samaria on the West Bank of the Jordon River were to be part of Greater Israel for all time.

U.S. policy was reflected in UN resolutions 242 and 338, which called for Israel to withdraw from occupied territories in return for full, normalized relations and the recognition of Israel's right to exist behind permanent and secure borders. The Carter administration had continued the Nixon and Ford administration's policy of strong support for Israel, but it was more insistent that the settlements, which Israel had been building on the West Bank, were illegal and should be stopped. For that he took a lot of heat from groups like the American Israel Public Affairs Committee (AIPAC). I shared Carter's view. So did many knowledgeable Israelis, especially those in the military with whom I talked. When Sadat went to Jerusalem, I was thrilled with the prospect of breaking the Middle East logjam. When Sadat spoke to the Israeli Knesset and said, "Let us make war no more," it looked as if a miracle had happened. But the parties still needed outside help to come to an agreement on how they would proceed to write a new chapter in Middle Eastern history. And Carter was determined to provide that help.

In September of 1978 Carter invited both Begin and Sadat to Camp David in an attempt to agree on the details. Several times the Camp David discussions almost broke down, but, pressed by Carter, both men finally signed an agreement. Israel would withdraw from Egyptian territory in the Sinai, and Egypt would recognize Israel's right to exist. In March of 1979, when the Israeli-Egyptian treaty was finally agreed to, Joan and I attended the signing ceremony and celebration dinner on the White House lawn. During dinner I talked with Herman Eilts, our ambassador to Egypt. "Do you think this will be a separate peace between Israel and Egypt or do you think it will lead to a more comprehensive peace for the region?" I asked him. "That's up to the Arabs," he replied. The next week officials from the Syrian embassy were in my office to discuss the status of the Damascus water project. "What do you think will happen now?" I asked. "Will you be able to move toward a follow-on agreement with Israel or not?" "Oh, no," came the reply. "We don't think Israel meant it. We don't believe they will follow through," they said. "Besides, the timetable is too long. The step-by-step withdrawal by Israel from Egyptian territory will take three years. That's too long to wait to get back the Golan." So now it has been twenty-eight years and because the Syrians have steadfastly refused to deal, they still don't have it back.

Several months later, I was again in Egypt and met with Sadat in Alexandria. I asked him the same question I had asked Ambassador Eilts. "Mr. President," I asked, "do you think this agreement will turn out to be a separate peace between Israel and Egypt, or do you think there will be a follow-up on comprehensive agreement with the Palestinians?" "I do not know, but for sure I can tell you one thing," he answered. "If it is not the latter, I will be dead within five years." And he was.

In the Middle East, radical Muslim groups were beginning to establish themselves. Back home in my district, homegrown radicals of a quite different sort were emerging as well. In the 1970s, in the wake of Vietnam, the cultural revolution of the sixties, and the Watergate scandal, radical anti-government sentiment began to rise. In Wisconsin, and especially in my district, that sentiment was exemplified by the emergence of a number of right-wing, anti-government vigilante organizations. The most notorious and visible called itself Posse Comitatus. Another similar group called itself the Citizens Council for the Preservation of the White Seed.

Their wacky, anti-government extremism led to a wild chapter in Wisconsin political history. Its leaders, Thomas Stockheimer, a Marathon County farmer; Arnold Iwen, a Lincoln County chemist; along with James Lewis, a Republican state assemblyman, weaved a web of intrigue that led them from attempts to obtain a laser weapon to attack the control tower at Chicago's O'Hare airport to an effort to illegally sell laser weapons to the government of Guatemala. The activities of the Posse and associated right-wing neo-Nazi fringe organizations are skillfully chronicled in a recent book by Sharon Thatcher, *On the Laser's Edge*. As Thatcher accurately describes:

> The Posse Comitatus had started setting up camp in the eastern part of Marathon County, and the western part of the adjoining county of Shawano, in the early 1970s. Part of a small, loosely organized national organization, it was named

after an old law of posse comitatus that allowed for a posse of citizens to help establish law and order. The group's platform was a mongrel mix of religion and politics. On the religious side, they preached that the U.S. would have fewer problems if it had fewer Jews. Jews, too many of whom were manipulative bankers, held too much control, they said, and were conspiring with the United Nations to create a new world order. God's chosen people were of Aryan descent and they had the right to take the federal government back by force.

Potential members who didn't buy into that had a more popular political choice: they advocated no taxes, minimal federal control or licensing, and no authority higher than the local sheriff: it wasn't mainstream, but it had its appeal.

Thatcher described the Posse platform as being that, "There was a secret government operating at the federal level which was controlled exclusively by Jews. Revolution was necessary to break that power." Their public pronouncements included announcing their intention to burn a cross on the lawn of Wausau's Jewish rabbi.

My first encounters with the Posse came in the early 1970s when its founder, Thomas Stockheimer, and others began to disrupt constituent town meetings in Marathon, Wood, Clark, Taylor, and Lincoln counties. Stockheimer had a succession of brushes with the law, beginning with his physically beating Fred Chicken, an IRS agent. Throughout the decade their actions became more and more visible and belligerent.

One morning, in the mid-70s I was scheduled to hold a meeting with senior citizens in the basement of a small church in Clark County. When I walked into the basement room, I noticed five or six muscular young men leaning against the walls around the room. Larry Dahl, who was traveling with me, grabbed my arm and whispered, "Dave, these are Posse guys. I don't know if they mean to cause a ruckus or not, but my money says they will." He then said, "I'm going up to the car and try to find the sheriff, but let's have a plan." He suggested that I make sure to end the meeting just before eleven. "I will try to find some cops. If they give any sign of trouble, tell them I went to get the law. Tell them I'm going to blow the horn when the sheriff has the place surrounded. I'll blow it at 11 o'clock sharp."

I really thought Larry was being melodramatic, but I agreed to his plan. I wrapped up the meeting about ten minutes to eleven and started to work my way to the stairway. Two of the Posse boys stepped forward and said, "We want you to come with us." "No," I said. "I want you to come with me." I told them that I knew they were Posse and had sent Larry for the sheriff. I told them that when the sheriff had his men in position, he was going to sound his horn and if I wasn't out of the building immediately, they would all be arrested on sight. Within minutes, the horn sounded. The "boys" directed nervous glances at each other and backed away. I bounded up the stairs, climbed into Larry's car (he hadn't been able to find the sheriff), and we sped away, leaving the boys behind, thanks to the plan of a farmer from Tigerton who knew the territory. Over the next several years, Posse activists showed up and tried to disrupt numerous meetings with their anti-government tirades.

In the late 1970s Gaylord Nelson and I were both scheduled to speak at the National Farmers' Organization state convention in Marshfield. Days after news of our expected appearance became public, the Posse announced that Gaylord and I had committed treasonable and unconstitutional acts and declared that when we appeared at Marshfield high school they were planning on performing a citizen's arrest, trying us, and hanging us for treason. I chuckled at the outlandishness of the threat until the FBI came by and told us that it was no laughing matter, that the Posse nuts were serious. On the day of our appearance at the convention, Gaylord and I walked into the high school lobby with dozens of police surrounding us as they escorted us through the crowd. Dozens more law enforcement personnel were posted around the building to make sure we avoided our "hanging."

After a long series of legal battles, Stockheimer, Iwen, and State Representative Lewis all wound up in jail for charges ranging from giving false testimony to a federal grand jury to counterfeiting and assault. The Posse was known to be furious with President Carter because of his action in agreeing to turn over the Panama Canal to Panama. When Carter agreed to come to Wausau in late March of 1979 to celebrate the tenth anniversary of my election to Congress, rumors floated around of a possible Posse assassination attempt, but fortunately nothing came of them. With their ringleaders put out of commission by dedicated law enforcement and the undercover information provided by a citizen volunteer, Mike Muckerheide, a talented scientist and laser expert, the Posse gradually faded into the woodwork. But that did not bring an end to controversy and turmoil.

Abortion Kills My Grandfather

After Camp David, Carter enjoyed a temporary bump-up in popularity, but it was short lived. A few weeks later, Carter came to Wausau to help celebrate the tenth anniversary of my election to Congress. In 1969 Hubert Humphrey had spoken to 1,200 people at a dinner at Newman High School. For sentimental reasons we wanted to celebrate our anniversary at the same place. The celebration at Newman was terrific. The crowd was huge. Carter gave a fine speech, but the aftermath was bitter. Abortion had become a nasty, divisive issue, after the Supreme Court decided in *Roe v. Wade* that a woman's right to have an abortion was, within certain limitations, constitutionally protected.

For me, the issue had been more difficult than almost any other. I detested the very idea of abortion and was offended by some of the pro-choice enthusiasts who demanded agreement, not just about the constitutional right to have an abortion but about the desirability of having one. As a Catholic, I agreed with the teachings of the Church that abortion was basically wrong, but the issue was not simple for me, for two reasons. First, while I believed that abortions were usually morally wrong, in circumstances such as rape, incest, or serious threat to the health of the mother, reasonable people could, in a multireligious society, reach different conclusions about actions that the state could impose. Second, my deep suspicion of government power told me that granting government the authority to make that decision could be dangerous because a government that could today *forbid* abortion could tomorrow *require* one. Over the years, the policy of the Chinese communist government to require abortions after the first child was to me ample proof of the validity of that fear.

In governing any society, public officials must often make distinctions between what they *desire* and what they will attempt, through force of law, to *require* of others who do not share one's own religious beliefs. But that argument is subtle. It requires, in Eric Sevareid's words, a "willingness to maintain the courage of one's doubts in an age of dangerous certainties." And on some issues like abortion, the emotions surrounding the issue lead many decent people to be so angered by the subject that they do not want to look for common ground. Under those circumstances, when everybody is in a "send" mode, nobody hears what anyone else is really saying, and discussions are pointless. Jimmy Carter's visit to Wausau demonstrated how mean the issue could be, and how good people could get caught in the inevitable crossfire.

When we rented Newman High School auditorium for Carter's visit, I never dreamed that Carter's visit would be turned into a debate on abortion. Newman was one of the few Catholic high schools in my district. My sister, Diane, had graduated from Newman, and I had spoken to classes there on numerous occasions. Carter's visit had nothing to do with abortion. He had come to talk about the Middle East, human rights, and economic policy. But it was turned into a confrontation about abortion by a group of my political enemies, and two innocent people got hurt. The first victim was Father Langer, the Newman principal. The second was my grandfather.

When they heard that Father Langer had rented Newman hall to us, a group of local Republican Party activists—some of whom were Catholic—contacted Bishop Freking and demanded Langer's head. The bishop obliged, and Father Langer was fired. My grandfather Chuck was a devout Catholic. One afternoon, shortly after Carter's visit, he was sitting on the front lawn of his home in the town of Weston when the paperboy delivered the daily edition of the *Wausau Record Herald*. He opened the paper, read that Langer had been fired as principal because he had rented the hall to me, had a heart attack on the spot, and died. The stress of seeing a controversy between me and the Church to which he was devoted was too much for him.

As I saw it, the bishop, Father Langer, and my grandfather had all been caught in a squeeze because a small band of my political opponents created a controversy where there should have been none. They chose to turn Carter's visit into a debate on abortion when neither Carter nor I had brought the issue up. Some of those involved were genuinely concerned about abortion, but for many it was simply a political opportunity to get at Dave Obey and a president they despised. No other issue has pained me more deeply because of the many conflicting and deeply held values surrounding it, and never did the issue pain me as much as the day the rancor surrounding that issue literally drove my grandfather to his death.

BUDGET SQUEEZE

In 1980 Carter also faced a budget crisis brought on by oil price inflation and an economic slowdown. The second round of huge oil price increases generated by the oil sheiks sent a shock wave of higher prices throughout the economy. The Federal Reserve tried to combat that inflation by steadily and repeatedly raising short-term interest rates, which in turn slowed down the economy.

Paul Volcker, the head of the Federal Reserve, had told Carter that the deficit was going to reach at least $35 billion and that action was needed to reduce it. To scale it back Carter asked the congressional Democratic leadership to pull together key Democrats to produce a package of changes to his budget that would cut about $16 billion. We met in Bob Byrd's conference room with Carter's budget director, Jim Free, and his domestic policy advisor, Stuart Eisenstadt. We went around the table, budget function by budget function—education, housing, worker training, health, and so forth. OMB staff and others would lay out a series of options, and we would make our selection for cuts in each category.

The sessions had been triggered by Volcker's warning that the deficit would go up to $35 billion—we needed to cut between $13 and $16 billion to hold it down. That's what we cut, but the deficit still went up, but not to $35 billion. It ballooned to almost $65 billion—the second highest deficit in history at that time. That experience demonstrated once again the importance of understanding that budgeting is much more complicated than the country is led to believe. The entire episode was a reminder of what John Maynard Keynes tried to drive home in the 1930s—sometimes cutting spending is not a surefire way to cut the deficit. In fact, sometimes the deficit problem is not caused by spending as much as by weak economic growth that produces falling revenues. The strength of the economy is usually much more important in determining the size of the government deficit than is the level of spending. An economy that produces $100 billion extra in revenue because of healthy economic growth will invariably be far more important in determining the size of the budget deficit than will a sharp pencil.

More Carter Troubles

Carter's was a star-crossed presidency. My philosopher friend, Archy the Cockroach, whom I often quote in debate, seemed to have Carter in mind when he said, "Now and then a person is born who is so unlucky he runs into accidents that started out to happen to somebody else." What was worse, Carter seemed to know it. During his presidency he was hit with four crises over which he had little control: the return of the Panama Canal, the second energy crisis caused by the actions of the oil-producing Arab states, the Russian invasion of Afghanistan, and the seizing by Iranian militants of the American hostages from the U.S. embassy in Tehran. Carter handled all four issues with thoughtfulness and stoic courage, but his demeanor and language conveyed to the average American a sense of worry rather than a sense of determination. And the national press, especially the national news networks, made things worse for Carter and the country by the way they reported the hostage dilemma.

ABC's late-night news program *Nightline* is a familiar fixture today, but that program didn't exist before the hostages were taken. Originally intended as a special broadcast updating the nation on the hostage situation, it instead became a permanent late-night fixture. It examined every nuance of every word of every Iranian official who could be found, and helped to inflate the news value of the problem. Walter Cronkite, the respected and admired anchor of CBS news, would end his broadcast with the words, "And so it goes, on this the 79th [or 105th, or 109th] day of America's captivity." As they breathlessly repeated each of the latest developments, the networks intensified the world's focus on the event and thus raised the value of the hostages to the Iranian hostage takers.

I believed then, and still do, that the hostages could have been freed much earlier had it not been for the almost orgasmic urgency conveyed each night by the TV networks. Their coverage had the effect of personalizing the chess game between the Iranians and the Carter administration, and helped ensure that the hostages would not be released until Carter was out of the White House. Although Carter's people eventually negotiated their release, the timing was held up by Iran so that they would not actually be freed until Reagan's inauguration day—one last jab in Carter's eye by the Ayatollah Khomeini. Thanks to Carter's "cool" in the face of all the pressure and frustration he must have felt, in the end, every single hostage was safely returned home. But prudence and carefulness are not exciting virtues, and Carter never got the credit he deserved for steering the ship of state through those frustrating and explosive times.

Politically, Carter was barely holding his own by the time the 1980 campaign started. But after Ronald Reagan's affability came through in the debates, and he demonstrated he could complete a sentence without stepping on his tongue, Reagan surged ahead and won a sweeping victory.

Dave Obey (far right) with Stan Zuckerman, State Representative Lloyd Barbee, and Jackie Robinson at the University of Wisconsin student union, 1960.

Wedding day, June 9, 1962.

A 1965 conference on the state budget in the governor's conference room. Governor Warren Knowles on far right, Dave in center, Assembly Speaker Bob Huber on left, State Senator Jerris Leonard (back to camera). Looking on, from left to right, are State Representative Ray Tobias, State Senator Frank Panzer, and Paul Hasset, an aide to the governor.

Obey's first Washington press conference, April 3, 1969. From left to right, Senator Fred Harris, the Democratic National Committee chairman; Hubert Humphrey; and Dave.

Seventh District office staff, Federal Building, Wausau, Wisconsin, June 1969. Left to right, Win Spencer, Larry Dahl, and Jerry Madison.

Dave Obey and Senator Gaylord Nelson, Statuary Hall, U.S. Capitol, 1972. Robert LaFollette statue is in the background.

From left to right, Egyptian Vice President Hosni Mubarek, Dave Obey, Egyptian President Anwar Sadat, Representative Ed Koch, and Representative Joe Early, Alexandria, Egypt, 1975.

Israeli Prime Minister Yitzhak Rabin with Representative Joe Early, Representative Ed Koch, and Dave Obey, 1975.

Dave Obey (left) and Representative Henry Reuss (right) show Representative Mo Udall the Wisconsin Ice Age Trail, 1975.

From left to right, Senator Gaylord Nelson and Craig Obey with Interior Secretary Cecil Andres (face partially obscured), Apostle Islands tour, 1979.

Senator Robert Byrd (in dark suit seated at end of table) hosts an emergency budget cutting conference, 1979. Dave is in foreground at far right. At far left are Stuart Eisenstat, President Carter's domestic policy advisor; Jim Free, Carter's budget director; and Senator John Culver of Iowa.

Budget Committee meeting, 1979. Dave conferring with Representative Tim Wirth. Scott Lilly is between Dave and Wirth.

From left to right,
Representative Henry
Reuss, Joan Obey,
President Jimmy
Carter, and Dave
aboard Air Force One,
March 1979.

Douglas Obey
presses the button
that lights the U.S.
Capitol Christmas
tree from Fifield,
Wisconsin, 1983.

Dave at podium introducing Democratic presidential candidate Walter Mondale and vice presidential candidate Geraldine Ferraro, Merrill, Wisconsin, Labor Day, 1984. At the far left are Governor Tony Earl and Joan Obey.

Dave says goodbye to retiring House Speaker Tip O'Neill, 1986.

Dave, leaning forward in dark suit on right, chairing the Foreign Operations Subcommittee, 1990. The witness testifying at left is U.S. Secretary of State James Baker.

Dave converses with the former leader of the Soviet Union, Mikhail Gorbachev, 1992. Interpreter on far left and Representative Tom Downey look on.

Folk singer Pete Seeger gets a laugh out of Doug Obey, Dave, Craig Obey, and John Holum at Dave's fiftieth birthday party.

Dave with Northern Ireland political leader and Nobel Peace Prize recipient John Hume, 1994.

Dave talks with Vice President Al Gore at the White House, 1995. CIA Director George Tenet is over Gore's shoulder.

President Bill Clinton signs the appropriations bill for the Departments of Labor, Health and Education at the White House, 1997. Looking on from left to right are Secretary of Labor Alexis Herman, two unidentified guests, Vice President Gore, Representative John Spratt, Dave, Senator Jeff Bingaman, and Representative John Porter.

Former Seventh District congressman and Secretary of Defense Mel Laird talking with Dave in Stevens Point, Wisconsin, 2005.

~

PART 4

YEARS OF
RESPONSIBILITY

❧

CHAPTER 13

Fighting Reaganomics

Reagan's election had personal consequences for me and profound consequences for the country. The chairmanship of the Budget Committee was open, and I decided to run for it, facing competition from two quality candidates, Jim Jones, an Oklahoma conservative, and Paul Simon, an Illinois liberal.

ROSTY'S REVENGE

As a result of visits with a large number of my Democratic colleagues over the summer and fall of 1980, I was confident that I had a substantial lead in commitments. But on election night, we lost thirty-three seats and the large majority of members who had gone down were committed Obey supporters. The election not only wiped out a number of my supporters but it also made the caucus more timid and cautious. With Reagan's win, the Senate also fell under GOP control. A number of southern members who had been open to my candidacy in the summer were less sure about it after the election. For tactical reasons, several felt that perhaps a more cautious, conservative line was in order. The caucus met in November to make its decision, and going into the balloting I thought it was likely that I would lose by a handful of votes. Mo Udall's earlier experience in the majority leader's race had taught me not to believe every promise tossed my way by eager-to-please colleagues.

I was determined to run a tighter vote count than Mo. My counting system was simple. We assigned to every person in the caucus a number from one to five. One meant a rock-solid commitment; two, leaning right; three, undecided; four, leaning against; five, for the other guys. In a caucus election, members are often caught between several friends and will try to please both of them. They often say, "You bet, I think you will be a terrific chairman."

Only the naïve would count that as a vote. It is a get-off-the-hook statement designed to convey the impression of support without technically promising to do so. My rule was this: Don't count on anyone unless they said the magic words to me, "Yes, Dave, I will support you on every ballot," and that these words had been confirmed by two other people. I knew that Paul Simon was running third and many of his supporters were likely to swing to me after he dropped out on the first ballot. That would make it razor close, but the way I counted it I would be two or three votes short.

Dan Rostenkowski was managing Jones's campaign. He had two reasons to support Jones. First, Jones was a member of his committee and had often worked with Danny. Second, Danny detested my reform role in the House and hated any thought of my winning. When the votes came, Simon came in third in the balloting, as I had expected, and dropped out. The vote had been 100 for me and 100 for Jones—a tie—and 39 for Simon. It was then down to a face-off between Jones and me. The next ballot was excruciating—118 to 118, another tie vote! I had actually gotten two votes more than we were expecting, but I knew by then I was beat because Danny could promise more to fence-riding members than I could. He could also break someone's arm easier than I could because of his Ways and Means chairmanship. On the third ballot I lost 121 to 116. In analyzing the vote tally afterwards, it was clear that I had not lost because of any conservative or moderate defections. I had been done in by a handful of liberals.

I had not gotten a single Colorado vote. I found out afterwards that key people from the oil industry had leaned on the Colorado delegation to support Jones because Colorado, like Oklahoma, was an oil state. I never did get Tim Wirth to commit to me, and Pat Schroeder missed the vote. She told me later that she was in her office with the flu, too sick to come over to the caucus to vote. Walter Fauntroy, the nonvoting delegate from D.C., missed the vote because he went to the dentist. That was hugely disappointing to me, because without me D.C. would never have broken loose the money for its new subway. Under House rules, as a nonvoting delegate, Walter could speak but not vote on the House floor. I found it ironic that on one of the few occasions when he could have cast a meaningful vote, Walter managed to miss it.

Thirty seconds too late, after the voting had closed, Don Bonker of Washington rushed into the caucus to cast his vote. He had been giving a speech downtown. "I'm sorry, I'm sorry," he repeatedly said. I looked him in the eye and simply shook my head. A comment Dick Bolling had made to me flashed through my mind: "All other things being even, conservatives will usually beat

liberals because they have iron asses and liberals don't. Liberals may give the
best speeches, but the trouble is while they are off giving their damn speech
that they think will change the world, conservatives will simply show up, stay
in their seats, and vote . . . and voting beats talking every time." So like my
good friends and heroes, Bolling and Udall, I lost a close caucus election to
a southerner.

REAGANOMICS

Ronald Reagan's presidency was almost the reverse image of Carter's. Carter
had conveyed a sense of worry; Reagan exuded optimism. Carter was studi-
ous; Reagan was the farthest thing from it. Carter worked fourteen-hour days;
Reagan complained when he had to burn the midafternoon oil. Carter was unlucky; Reagan was the luckiest man to occupy the White House since Teddy
Roosevelt. He was also one of the most reckless and irresponsible. When
Ronald Reagan was sworn in as president, I had no idea that I would wind up
being the House of Representative's principal progressive dissenter to much
of his economic program. To this day I am more proud of the role I played in
rallying progressive opposition to that irresponsible program than of anything
I have ever done in the Congress.

Reagan embarked upon two courses that put the country on a long-term
path to social and fiscal irresponsibility. First, he planted the seeds for the
confidence-sapping corporate scandals that destroyed the investments and
pensions of hundreds of thousands of Americans by initiating a moratorium
on new government regulations. That was the first of many steps in a decade-
long deregulation binge that, twenty years later, left so many investors, workers, and responsible companies virtually defenseless in a sea of corporate
executive sharks. Second, he sent to Congress a budget that blew the lid off
the federal deficit, piled up mountains of debt, and destroyed for decades any
legitimate Republican Party claim to fiscal responsibility.

No economic issue has been more demagogued through the years than the
federal deficit. Since the days of FDR, Republican politicians have bemoaned
government spending at every rubber chicken political dinner they ever
attended and have blamed "tax and spend Democrats" for the problem. That
rhetoric has ignored three historical facts. The first is that the last president to
balance the budget over the length of his entire term was Harry Truman—a
Democrat. The second is that until Bill Clinton did it, the last president to
submit a balanced budget to Congress was LBJ—a Democrat. The third is that
from the end of World War II until Ronald Reagan came along in 1980, U.S.

debt as a percentage of total national income (and that's the only economically meaningful way to look at debt) steadily declined under Democratic and
Republican presidents alike.

During World War II, FDR and Congress didn't worry about government
debt. They fought and won the war first. If they hadn't, Nazi flags would still
be flying over many of the world's capitals. In 1946 publicly held debt was a
little over 126 percent of annual GDP (that's total national income). That is
the right way to measure debt. For instance, if you tell me you owe $100,000,
I have no way of knowing how significant that is until you tell me how it com-
pares to your income. If you earn $20,000 a year, $100,000 in debt is a heavy
load. If you earn $200,000 per year, your $100,000 of debt burden is effectively ten times lighter. The same is true for the federal debt.

By 1979 the federal debt as a percentage of total national income had declined from its World War II high of 126 percent to a little over 24 percent,
one-fifth of its prior level. Despite all the screaming about it by GOP politicians on the lookout for something to squawk about, the U.S. debt picture
had been getting better every year under presidents of both parties. Debt
became a lighter and lighter load when seen from the perspective of the government's ability to repay it. Ronald Reagan and the 1981 Congress did not just
halt that steady downward progress; they reversed it in spectacular fashion.
Beginning in 1981 with the Reagan budget and continuing through the last
budget of George H. W. Bush, the federal debt as a percentage of GDP steadily
rose to almost 50 percent, a profoundly irresponsible legacy—especially when
viewed in the light of today's controversy about the nation's ability to keep
Social Security solvent.

When Reagan sent his first budget to Congress, I shook my head in disbelief. It was understandable that FDR had piled up debt to win the war. But
Reagan was planning to pile it up at a record rate during *peacetime*. Of course,
Reagan denied he was planning to do deficit spending. He and his economic
team, led by whiz kid OMB director David Stockman, blithely told the country that through the magic elixir of supply-side economics, we could repeal the
rules of mathematics and double military spending, cut tax rates by 30 percent, and magically produce a surplus in four years time.

BUDGET BIDDING WAR

A classic dilemma in politics is: What to do when you think you are likely to
lose? Do you try to shave whatever little you can off your losses and try to salvage at least a sliver, or do you face the fact that you are going to lose, define

your differences with clarity, accept the short-term loss, and take the issue to the country in the next election so that you might reverse it over the long haul? When Reagan first produced his plan, congressional Democrats in the House were split on how to react to it. The split was not so much conservative versus liberal—although, as usual, that's the way the national press, led by the *Washington Post,* wrote it. The split was more accurately between optimists and skeptics.

Two groups in the caucus fought the tactical battle for Tip O'Neill's mind. Danny Rostenkowski and Jim Jones were the optimists. Jim did a solid job of pulling together an alternative to Reagan's budget that tried to minimize the long-term fiscal damage of the Reagan budget. On the Thursday before the House floor vote, Jim thought he had the votes to win, but Stockman played one of the games that the new budget process allows Congress and presidents to play. He put together an analysis that made Jones's budget look much less attractive in comparison to Reagan's. How? By simply using a different set of economic assumptions, different growth rate projections, and the like. The assumptions were wildly unrealistic—half fantasy, half sleight of hand—but Reagan had the only megaphone in town, and he used those phony estimates to make it appear that his budget would produce a smaller deficit than Jones's.

Unlike Rostenkowski and Jones, I never believed we had a chance to beat Reagan's budget. I felt we would keep losing the argument and the votes unless we defined our differences more clearly than the Jones budget did, so Scott Lilly and I put together a progressive alternative that spent less, borrowed less, and provided smaller deficits than either the Reagan or Jones plan. When the votes came, my amendment went down 119 to 303. Jones then lost 176 to 253, and the Reagan budget passed 270 to 154. My amendment had lost handily, but a majority of Democrats had voted for it. That was to prove useful in the national debate two years later.

After the budget resolution passed, the next battle focused on the implementation of that budget through passage of the Reagan tax bill that called for deep cuts in revenue—even as defense spending was scheduled to double. Rostenkowski desperately wanted to stop Reagan's tax bill for two good reasons. First, he thought it would blow the budget and run up huge deficits. Second, he just hated to lose.

Reagan's tax plan phased in large rate cuts over a three-year period. Rosty thought he could limit the fiscal damage by trying to prevent the third-year cuts in the Reagan plan. Both Reagan and Rosty were determined to win. They pulled out all the stops, and a huge bidding war ensued. They competed for interest group support by out-bidding each other for the size of the tax cut targeted for one group after another. I told the *Washington Post* in an interview, "It would probably be cheaper if we simply gave everyone in the country three wishes!" As I watched the spectacle unfold, I despaired, convinced that Rosty could not, in the end, outbid the White House, and the country would witness an emerging spectacle—both parties running an auction for special interests on the tax break front. I vehemently argued that the best course for us to follow was to put up a much smaller tax bill stripped of special-interest favors and redirect a much greater percentage of the cuts to low- and middle-income taxpayers.

Obey, Udall, Reuss

Mo Udall, Henry Reuss, and I worked to put together a more fiscally responsible progressive alternative, which people could vote for before voting on Rosty's alternative. To do so, we needed the technical help of the staff at the Joint Committee on Taxation, but that staff was under the control of Rostenkowski, and he was in no mood to cooperate. He thought we would undercut his alternative; we thought just the opposite. We thought that a large number of progressives were so offended by the size of the deals Rosty was offering in the bidding war that the only way they could vote for his substitute to the GOP package was if they first had a chance to vote for a less costly, more progressive alternative. Dick Gephardt gave us some key under-the-table help. He felt that as a member of the Ways and Means Committee he had to support Rosty, but he also believed we were right. He quietly used his access to the Joint Tax staff as a member of Ways and Means to help us obtain the technical help we needed to put together a decent and fair plan. When the votes came, as was the case with the budget resolution, our amendment lost 144 to 288, but a majority of Democrats again supported our progressive approach. We got five courageous Republican votes. Rostenkowski's alternative failed by a vote of 195 to 238, and Reagan won, going away with the support of fifty-nine Democrats. Even Dick Gephardt voted for Reagan's supply-side tax scheme on final passage—a vote he now describes as one of the two worst votes he ever cast. After passage, Don Regan, the secretary of the treasury, told the press, "Our program is now in place."

Jack Kole, *Milwaukee Journal* bureau chief, described the spectacle in an August 2, 1981, column. He reported that the wealthiest 5 percent of taxpayers would get more than 35 percent of the total tax breaks while the bottom 40 percent would receive a paltry 8.5 percent.

Not in their wildest dreams could conservatives have expected such largess for the privileged of America. In their frantic bid to win a victory, the Democrats on the House Ways and Means Committee threw in all sorts of special-interest bonanzas, hoping to sway conservatives to their version. But that was a dangerous game and Reagan and his cohorts eagerly upped the ante on just about everything. When they were through, they reduced revenues to the federal Treasury through fiscal 1986 by some $750 billion. For example, when the Democrats came in up with $10 billion in tax breaks for the oil industry, the White House was right there with a sweeter version, $15 billion in benefits.

Kole quoted a DSG report, which said: "Thus one after another, both Democrats and Republicans had loaded up their bills for special interests such as commodity traders, oil companies, savings and loans, and businessmen residing overseas."

When the bill passed, Kole quoted O'Neill as saying that "Wednesday was a great day for the aristocracy of the world, what with the royal wedding [Prince Charles and Princess Diana] in the morning and a royal tax cut in the afternoon." Kole went on to say that "the Democrats had indulged in the old game of playing to the special interests and they got burned in the process. Their bill did give less generous benefits to wealthy families, but that wasn't enough" to pull in enough votes to win. Stories like Kole's demonstrated why I had believed we needed to offer a tax bill that was sharply different from Reagan's, even if we lost. We would never snap back if we were seen as giving goodies to special interests almost as often as the GOP.

At this point, the country was overwhelmingly in Reagan's corner. Polls in my own district at the time showed that 67 percent of the public believed Reagan was right and that his plan would balance the budget. I knew full well it wouldn't, but few Americans could bring themselves to believe that an affable Republican conservative could possibly be fiscally irresponsible. But ever so slowly, perceptions changed. By the 1982 election, Democrat after Democrat would come to me and say, "Thank you for giving us that budget tax alternative to vote for. I ran my whole campaign on it." But at the time of the vote, we all felt that we might be committing political suicide because of Reagan's popularity.

STOCKMAN GOES TO CONFESSION

A few months after Reagan's package passed, David Stockman, Reagan's OMB director, confessed to Bill Greider in the *Atlantic Monthly* that it was all an analytical and mathematical fraud—a Trojan horse designed to bring down the tax rate for the most wealthy. At a Budget Committee hearing, I confronted him with his comments. And in a newsletter to my constituents, I quoted Stockman's comments extensively and described the whole sorry chain of events this way:

> The Reagan administration budget can be summed up three ways: (1) $180 billion in increased military spending over the next five years; (2) $140 billion in domestic spending cuts over that same period. Well, you might say, that doesn't seem too bad. It only adds $40 billion to the deficit. But then add the third number—(3) $750 billion in tax cuts. With those three numbers, how do you get anything other than record high deficits? How do you do it without changing the computer results, as Mr. Stockman said in the *Atlantic Monthly* article?
>
> Now we have the admission of the principal architect and spokesman for the administration's program that for six months he had been explaining to the West Wing guys that these numbers just didn't add. He explained that he got his budget deficit projections for the administration-backed Gramm-Latta budget *"down to $31 billion by hook or by crook, mostly the latter. We didn't think it all the way through. . . . We didn't add up all the numbers. We should have designed those pieces to be more compatible. But the pieces were moving on independent tracks. It didn't quite mesh. That's what happened. But, you see, for about a month and a half we got away with that because of the novelty of it all."* It took this country from 1776 to 1968 to run up a national debt of $370 billion—192 years. The Reagan administration plan will do it in four.

When I wrote that article, I didn't realize that I was underestimating the size of Reagan's future deficits. I reported in the same newsletter the *Atlantic Monthly*'s explanation of the atmosphere surrounding tax cut decisions: "The tax lobbyists of Washington, when they saw the outlines of the Reagan tax bill, mobilized the business community, the influential economic sectors from oil to real estate. In a matter of days, they created the political environment in which they flourish best—a bidding war between the two parties."

Since that time, whenever I am asked what I am the most proud of in my years in Congress, I answer that—on the basis of economics and on the basis of social justice—it is the fight that I waged and lost to prevent the Reagan 1981 budget tax scheme from passing. We didn't win, but we stood up to an immensely popular president, and we were right. And the way we fought the fight helped to define the issues for the future and made it easier for us to correct the problem down the line.

Move to JEC

After the 1982 election, my six-year term on the Budget Committee expired. My experience on Budget had reinforced my understanding that almost every budget decision was heavily influenced by assumptions that were made about the economy. Virtually every decision about spending and taxes takes place within the broader context of the economy and our expectations for it. I knew that, as a still relatively junior member of Appropriations, I needed an extra platform if I was to influence the economic debate. Henry Reuss suggested that I try to get a spot on the Joint Economic Committee.

The committee had been created in 1946. The same year Congress passed the La Follette congressional reform legislation, it also passed the Full Employment Act. The driving force behind it had been Leon Keyserling, a leading economist in the Truman administration. As part of that act the Congress created the Counsel on Economic Advisors to give the president long-term analytical advice about the economy. To provide Congress with a similar analytical capacity, the congressional Joint Economic Committee was created. Unusual by congressional standards, it was composed of members of both House and Senate, and operated under a chairmanship that rotated between the two bodies every two years. In the early years of its existence, the committee was highly respected for the quality of its membership and its effort to achieve consensus. The committee's ability to do that was eventually undermined in the 1980s as moderate Republicans of an intellectual bent were gradually replaced by less well-informed partisans.

After heart bypass surgery, Reuss decided to relinquish the chairmanship of the Banking Committee and took the chairmanship of the JEC instead. He used that committee to conduct a number of hearings that provided an intellectual critique of Reaganomics. Henry had asked me to go on the committee because he was planning to retire and wanted someone with progressive values to replace him. When I approached Tip about it, he was enthusiastic. "Davey," he said, "I owe you. I know I didn't do enough to help you win the Budget chairmanship, and I know you got hurt because of what you had to do on the ethics stuff. JEC would be a perfect fit for you." So Tip appointed me to the JEC pretty much as a belated consolation prize for losing the Budget chairmanship. I was able to use the committee to issue a number of studies on family income, which showed that average middle-class families were falling behind economically, and that the combined effect of market forces, labor bargaining weaknesses, and unfair government policy was creating the biggest gap between the wealthy and the poor since the 1920s. These issues were to be used effectively by Bill Clinton a decade later in his successful campaign for the presidency.

Over the next two years, Congress continued to be divided, with GOP control in the Senate and Democratic control in the House. A huge amount of energy was consumed by the question of how to deal with the deficits created by the Reagan budgets. Within two years the Congress passed a partial rollback of some of the excesses of the Reagan budget and tax actions, but the deficits continued to roll up, adding record amounts to the federal debt. Deficits, which had never been larger than $70 billion before Reagan took office, hit $128 billion in 1982, $208 billion in 1983, and $185 billion in 1984, $212 billion in 1985, and $221 billion in 1986.

At the same time the deficits were mounting, the administration was asking for large increases in the military and foreign aid budgets. I had a long record of support for humanitarian aid and efforts to strengthen the economy of our Third World trading partners, but I resisted increasing military aid and political support funds—much of it aimed at shoring up repressive military regimes in Africa and Central America. Those efforts by the administration led to a profoundly disturbing meeting with Reagan himself.

REAGAN GIBBERISH

After Memorial Day in 1982 or 1983—I don't remember which—in response to a White House request, a number of us went to the White House to talk with Reagan about his aid request. As we gathered around the huge table in the Cabinet Room, I was determined not to say anything. I had objected to so much of what Reagan was doing that I was determined to avoid further confrontation. I sat four chairs down the table to Reagan's right across the table from George Schultz, the secretary of state. Reagan came into the room from the Oval Office, a number of index cards in his hand. He sat down at the table and began to read to us from the notes on his cards. After about three or four minutes he stopped, put the cards down, turned to Jack Kemp, the ranking Republican on Foreign Operations, and said, "Jack, why don't you run the meeting." Jack then gave a pitch for supporting the president and proceeded to call on people, almost all of whom gave assurances that they would support his request. I just listened.

Finally, Jack turned to me and said, "Dave, you haven't said anything. Where are you on this one?" I sighed, looked at Reagan and said,

> Mr. President, I hadn't intended to say anything. I don't want to be the skunk at your garden party, but if you really want to know, I'm sorry, but I have no intention of supporting your aid request, for a number of reasons. Politically,

there is no reason for me to do it. You have been on TV telling the country that my party is tearing up the nation's credit card and establishing higher deficit limits, even though you know that is not the case. As George Will has noted, your budgets spend as much as ours do; you just spend it in different places. Substantively, I don't agree with you on two counts. First, you are trying to cut education and training and other domestic programs, but you ask for large increases in foreign military aid. Second, I don't agree with your Contra aid policy and your Central American policy, so there is really no reason for me to vote for your package, and I will be doing everything I can to change it.

Reagan's mouth opened. He slowly started waving both hands from side to side, glanced up and down the table for the longest moment, saying nothing. Finally he blurted out, "Well, I had to restore the defenses of the country because my predecessors decimated them." The comment was jarring because no one had raised the issue of defense spending. Reagan then went on, "And on the domestic front, we didn't mean to hurt the truly needy, but you see we did this study of welfare in Pennsylvania and discovered thirty-nine people in prison who were on welfare." He rambled on and on about welfare and prison reform in Pennsylvania. What he was saying was totally disconnected from anything I or anyone else had said. You could sense that the people in the room were embarrassed for him. Collectively, it seemed as if everyone was looking at their shoes. I know I was.

Finally, when Reagan finished, the meeting mercifully broke up. George Schultz walked around the table toward me and said, "Well, Mr. Congressman, I'm sorry you can't be with us, but I want to thank you for not following up." I left the room profoundly sobered by what I had seen and heard. I turned to someone and said, "My God, when the secretary of state has to thank a lowly member of Congress for not following up with the president of the United States, this country is in real trouble."

I was not sure what I had seen. Either the president had an off day or he was seriously slipping. I didn't know which it was, but after that, whenever a major issue came up, the first thing that crossed my mind was, "Who is running the show on this one?" Reagan, to me, always seemed to be a profoundly nice guy, but his "out of it" performance that day stunned me, and I have never forgotten it. How many other days had he put in performances just like it? I finally reached the conclusion that if the subject was something with which Reagan had had personal experience—for instance, his legendary resentment about having to pay income taxes at the 90 percent rate during his Hollywood days during World War II—then he could intellectually engage and he was fine. But if it involved something that did not plug into his personal experiences, his comments could often seem to be written by Daffy Duck.

Lebanon Fallout

A few months later, my misgivings about Reagan's policy in Lebanon put me in a confrontation with a key member of my own party. Located just to the north of Israel and to the west of Syria, Lebanon had once been a peaceful, beautiful country. Christians and Muslims had worked out power-sharing arrangements that had lasted for decades, but demographic changes and political events conspired to increase the percentage of the population that was non-Christian, and the formulas that determined how much power each group had not changed to reflect the new reality. Now, conflict had broken out between Christian and Muslim groups, and as many as seventeen different political factions were competing for power. Adding to the turmoil was the presence of the PLO in Lebanon and the decision of Syria to try to dominate its neighbor. The Reagan administration had thrown its support behind the governing Christian faction and, in August of 1982, had sent American troops in to act as peacekeepers. I thought that was a mistake because the leadership of the Christian faction was not agile enough to manage the situation and the non-Christian groups were so wildly different that we could become sitting ducks for violent attacks.

Doc Long and I had very different views about how to assure Israel's long-term security and how to deal with the Middle East in general, but we agreed that the administration's use of American troops in Lebanon as peacekeepers was flawed and could indeed make our troops magnets for terrorist attacks.

Tip O'Neill and Jim Wright had endorsed the administration's policy, but Doc and I wanted the Appropriations Committee to try to raise questions about what we felt was a mission plagued by internal contradictions. We succeeded in convincing the Appropriations Committee to declare its opposition to the use of U.S. troops in that way. At the Democratic whips meeting the morning after the committee vote, all hell broke lose.

The House Democratic leader, Jim Wright, began to speak in low, slow tones about the Appropriations vote that Long and I had engineered the day before. "Mr. Speaker," Jim intoned, "I note that yesterday several of our colleagues on the Appropriations Committee undertook to raise objections to U.S. policy in Lebanon. Evidently, they did not recognize that the leadership of our party has fully supported that policy. Perhaps they do not recognize that assignment to an exclusive committee, such as Appropriations, carries with it an obligation to stick with the leadership position. Perhaps they should consider resigning from the committee if they cannot find their way to support the leadership position."

Jim was mad, and the longer he talked, the more my temperature rose. When Jim finished, I asked for the floor. "Jim, I have great respect for you and the leadership," I began. "And I will match my loyalty to the leadership with anybody in the caucus and sure as hell with the Texas delegation. But let's get one thing clear. When I voted for you for majority leader I elected you to be my leader, I didn't elect you to be my damned conscience. And when it comes to the issue of American troops, pardon me, but I will vote my conscience. Anytime you think that my loyalty doesn't measure up, all you have to do is ask for my resignation from Appropriations and you've got it," I concluded. "Now, now, no one is asking for your resignation," Jim answered. "It's just that this is a damned important issue," he said. We both let it go at that.

Jim's comments had especially irritated me because I recalled that after Nixon had unilaterally invaded Cambodia during the Vietnam War, Jim had gratuitously introduced a resolution expressing support for Nixon's action, despite the fact that many Democrats, including Tip O'Neill, had expressed opposition to Nixon's war policies. But soon, Jim and I cooled down, and I went back to work. On October 23, 1983, our worst concerns became a vivid reality when a truck bomb exploded at the Marine barracks killing 241 people. It was then revealed that the rules of engagement *prevented* the Marines guarding the compound from chambering the ammunition in their rifles without an order from their superiors. That had made them sitting ducks. A short time later, the Reagan administration recognized that insertion of American troops in the snake pit that was Lebanon was a mistake, and they withdrew our troops. Shortly after that I took on two major responsibilities that threw me into a close working relationship with Jim Wright on two very different subjects: U.S.-Nicaragua policy and the growing gap between rich and poor under Reagan's economic policies.

❧

CHAPTER 14

Two New Jobs,
One Secret War

In the 1984 November election, Doc Long was beaten by Helen Bentley, a tough old Republican warhorse in Maryland politics. On election night, I did not even know Doc had lost until an official from the American Israel Public Affairs Committee called and said they were looking forward to working with me in the new Congress. At first I thought they were simply calling to extend general good wishes on my reelection. It didn't dawn on me that he was talking about working with me *as chairman,* until he sensed my confusion and said, "You do know that Doc Long lost tonight, don't you?" "No, I didn't," I told him. "Well, you will have your work cut out for you now," he said. Neither of us knew the half of it. With Doc's defeat, I was going to be in charge of Foreign Ops. What I didn't know was that I was also about to take the helm of JEC.

CHAIRING JEC

In the previous Congress the JEC chair had been held by Republican senator Roger Jepson of Iowa. It was scheduled to rotate to the House, to Gillis Long, a Louisiana Democrat. Gillis was a tough, shrewd southerner who had stood up to southern racists during the Civil Rights crisis. He and I had become fairly close because both of us were disciples of Dick Bolling, with whom Long had served on the Rules Committee. Gillis was a member of the famously infamous Long family of Louisiana. Gillis's cousin, Huey, had served as governor and U.S. senator and had been a populist tub-thumper during the New Deal. He had been seen by some as a potential rival to FDR until an assassin's bullet struck him down on the state capitol steps in 1935. Huey's brother, Uncle Earl Long, had also served as governor when he wasn't a patient in the state's mental institution.

Gillis was a great storyteller, especially with those regarding his family. During the Watergate turmoil, he returned from Louisiana one weekend and joined us in the weekly meeting of Dick Bolling's circle in Otis Pike's office. We were discussing Nixon's state of mind, and Gillis related a conversation he had had the previous weekend with a family friend, a physician who had once treated his Uncle Earl. "So help me," Gillis told us, "I'm wondering if Nixon is close to cracking up. I was talking to this doctor friend at a party and he said, 'Gillis, I'm concerned about the president. Every week he's leaving Washington and running off to San Clemente, to Camp David, to Key Biscayne. I tell you that psychologically, that's no different than the way your Uncle Earl used to put a pillow slip over his head and walk down Main Street to get away from people.'"

Several years earlier, Gillis had made a losing run for governor. After the election, he told us a story to illustrate the mixed feelings his family had about his candidacy. He said that his second cousin, Russell Long (Huey's son), at that time chairman of the immensely powerful Senate Finance Committee, had done his dead-level-best to avoid getting involved in the race for the governorship. But near the end of the primary campaign, he got so many questions that he worried he would look disloyal to his family if he didn't say something for Gillis, so he finally agreed to one campaign swing with him. As Gillis tells it, Russell introduced Gillis to one crowd by saying, "Folks, I want to tell you Gillis is the smartest of the Longs, he's the hardest working of the Longs, he's the most honest of the Longs; why he wouldn't tell you a lie . . . unless it was absolutely necessary!"

Gillis was a colorful, dedicated politician who was tired of seeing a once-Democratic South slowly falling, district by district, into Republican hands. He was fed up with some of the knee-jerk liberal Democrats who had come into the party with the McGovern campaign and who focused primarily on fringe issues, which he felt drove many working-class Democrats away from the party. Gillis wanted to move the Democratic Party closer to mainstream economic issues and saw the JEC as a vehicle to accomplish that goal. But life would not cooperate.

As the incoming chairman, Gillis had just replaced Jamie Galbraith, who had been the Democratic staff director for the committee, with Al From, who in most ways shared Gillis's outlook on the party. Shortly after the election, just as I was getting used to the idea that I would be running the Foreign Ops Subcommittee, Al phoned me at home. I knew Gillis had been sick, but I did not know how sick. "Dave, Gillis is dying," Al told me. "Get ready to take over JEC." I was shocked. Two days later Long was dead.

I had a tough choice. I agreed with Gillis that the party was sending out messages that its focus was too much on fringe issues, and I shared Al From's desire to correct that problem, but I thought that without Gillis around, From would try to steer the economic debate away from squarely raising the issue of economic equity and thus try to use the JEC to align the Democratic Party too closely with big business interests. I was willing to keep Al on the staff because he had obvious talents, but not as staff director, because I did not believe his emphasis and mine were fully compatible. We mutually agreed he would stay on for a transition period and then leave.

My next action was to call Scott Lilly and tell him I wanted him to be the JEC staff director. We got off to a rocky start. Because of the staff turmoil and the lack of time, we issued a not-very-good economic report, but then we got our sea legs and began work on a series of reports that focused on the family income squeeze and on the growing disparity of income and wealth in the United States. The chairmanship also gave me a platform to critique the budget and tax policies of the Reagan administration. We worked with Governor Cuomo of New York to block GOP efforts to eliminate taxpayers' ability to deduct on their federal returns the amount paid in state and local taxes.

Our first study pointed out that the economic recovery being touted by Reagan had been largely confined to the two coasts, with America's heartland states experiencing anemic growth. After issuing that study, our focus turned to what had *really* happened to the income of working families since 1973. The Reagan image machine had been pumping out a steady message that everything was coming up roses in the economy. Well, there was no question that for some families on the high end, real progress was the reality. But our study showed that wealth was not being shared.

Our most controversial study was a 1986 report on the growing concentration of wealth in America. The Reagan administration had been peddling the myth that their policies had spread the wealth throughout all income classes. JEC published an analysis of Census Department data that showed just the opposite. It demonstrated that the average financial assets for 90 percent of American families were just $40,000. In comparison, the most well off—one-half of 1 percent—averaged $9 million! The Reagan administration put together an attack squad to try to discredit our findings, but they could not refute the fact that the top 1 percent of all households now owned 66 percent of all assets in unincorporated businesses and 60 percent of all personally held stock. The top 10 percent of all families owned 94 percent of all unincorporated businesses and nearly 90 percent of all personally held stock. When equity in houses was eliminated from the equation, 90 percent of America's families owned only 6 percent of the nation's family-owned wealth!

Every time we raised the question of distributive justice, we would be accused by the GOP of focusing on a problem that wasn't there. But any objective analysis of income and wealth disparity would show that the concentration of wealth (and the power that flows from it) had grown exponentially—in one generation the United States had gone from being the one Western industrialized country with the smallest gap between the rich and the poor to the one with the largest. We did everything we could to inject those facts into the national debate on economic policy.

Another initiative during my chairmanship was to conduct a symposium celebrating the fiftieth anniversary of the passage of the Full Employment Act, which formed the president's Council on Economic Advisors in the executive branch and the Joint Economic Committee in Congress. The idea behind the act had been to create institutions in the government that would act upon the economic lessons that had been learned by the country's experience during and after the Great Depression. The purpose of our symposium was to generate a two-day dialogue between some of the best economic minds in the country and to include the presentation of the participants in a book for classroom use. I co-edited that book with Paul Sarbanes, the Senate vice chairman of the committee. After two years, the committee chairmanship rotated to the Senate and, since the Democrats had retaken the Senate, Sarbanes succeeded me in the chair in 1987.

CHAIRING FOREIGN OPS

As the JEC chairmanship passed out of my hands, for the rest of the decade my institutional responsibilities were largely focused on international affairs and foreign policy. After a decade of service on the Foreign Operations Subcommittee, most of which was spent trying to moderate the actions of an erratic chairman, I had finally taken the chair in January of 1985. The committee faced a whole range of difficult responsibilities.

The most important—and least understood by most members of Congress—was the question of how to strengthen our national security interests and economic interests by using international financial institutions, such as the World Bank and the regional Development Banks, to promote the kind of Third World economic growth that could lead to greater political and economic stability. The second issue was the question of how we were using U.S. foreign military assistance to achieve our policy goals in the world. The third

issue was the degree to which U.S. bilateral aid should seek to promote economic development in the Third World as a value in itself as opposed to being
a quid pro quo for political support of various U.S. foreign policy initiatives.
The fourth question was how best to use our aid program to promote our various regional interests around the world, especially in Central America and
the Middle East.

To me, the fifth and most neglected consideration was the question of how
our aid program could be used to address our responsibilities to our fellow
creatures on this planet, three billion of whom were forced to exist on less
than two dollars a day, and how to build a foreign policy consistent with our
professed values, especially on the human rights front. Later in the decade
we would be confronted with a totally unexpected question: How should we
respond to the death of the Soviet Empire and the rebirth of democracy in
Central and Eastern Europe?

As the committee dealt with those issues, I was fortunate to have the invaluable help of Mike Marek, who had handled foreign policy for me since
1975. Two brilliant Appropriation subcommittee staffers, Terry Peel and Bill
Schuerch, were also invaluable, as was Mark Murray, a bright and talented
man who joined the subcommittee two years later. Terry would serve ten years
as the subcommittee staff director.

GETTING CONTROL

When I took the Foreign Ops chair in 1985, the subcommittee was in sham-
bles. For eight years the committee had been led by Doc Long, a bright but
erratic former university professor who was arbitrary, paranoid, and almost
wholly without influence in the House. In five of the ten years prior to my
becoming chairman, the committee had not been able to pass its own bill.
Because of controversy, and because foreign aid was so politically unpopular,
the bill could not pass standing alone; at the end of the year it was usually
either wrapped into other bills or carried into a continuing resolution. When
I became chairman, Jim Cheek had advised me, "Remember, Dave, the first
thing you have to do is get control of the process. You can't win on issues
unless you have the process under control." With that in mind as I took the
chair, I decided to keep my policy goals modest until I could get people used
to passing bills again.

My immediate goal was to restrain the administration's use of military aid
to questionable regimes for questionable purposes. I could see no reason to
support lavish aid to a number of kleptocracies like the Mobuto regime in

Zaire, which had amassed a multibillion-dollar fortune by ripping off U.S. aid. I wanted to eventually move some of that aid to long-term development and humanitarian assistance in the region—especially programs that impacted on public health and the health needs of children. It was painful to remember that in some countries receiving our aid, one child in five died before the age of five. And in Central America, I did not want to expand military aid to the Salvadoran government so long as that government was being blocked by the right-wing oligarchy from instituting land reform—reform that was necessary to give someone besides the twenty or thirty richest landowning families a stake in Salvador's future.

Because the administration's principal policy goal appeared to raise spending for military aid—so much of which went to military dictators around the world—I figured that the only way I could make the administration work with me was to support an overall spending level for the bill that was *lower* than the White House request. I explained to Matt McHugh and Bill Lehman that while I would not have the votes on the House floor to push for higher levels of humanitarian assistance that we wanted, I could get the votes to deny the administration the increases they were seeking for military foreign aid, and then use those lower levels as leverage to push the GOP into more generous funding for humanitarian programs.

That first year, against all odds and assumptions, we passed the bill. We made modest changes in the percentage of the bill going to economic and humanitarian aid as opposed to military aid and political support funding. After people had voted for the bill once, it made it easier to get them to vote for it again the following year. And over time, each year that we passed the bill helped me to reshape it to reflect more and more progressive priorities. That first year the final bill contained about a billion dollars more for economic and humanitarian aid and about a billion dollars less in military aid than the Republicans had wanted. Over time the differences grew, and the more the GOP recognized the bill was likely to pass, the more leeway we had on a whole range of issues.

Only a handful of Republican House members wanted to support significant economic aid, and a large number of Democrats, especially from rural areas, would not support foreign aid at all if members of the president's own party were bugging out on it. Republicans had been in the minority for so long that they seemed accustomed to avoiding responsibility for any action that might be the least bit unpopular. The worst example of their irresponsibility in dealing with the aid bill was their lack of support for funding for the International Monetary Fund and the World Bank, especially the soft loan (low interest) window at the bank known as IDA, the International Development Association, which provided assistance to the poorest countries in the world.

Every president since World War II, regardless of party, had pleaded with Congress to support the IMF and other international financial institutions (IFIs) because of their critical role in fostering economic development in the poorest parts of the world. I agreed, even though I often objected to specific IMF policies that seemed more focused on the interests of Western banks than they did on promoting economic prosperity for Third World workers.

In 1983 the Reagan administration proposed an increase in funding for the IMF. House Republicans offered an amendment to preclude any of that funding from going to communist countries. The Reagan administration asked us to oppose the amendment because under its charter the IMF could not accept earmarked or limited funds, and the amendment would therefore eliminate our contribution. Imagine our surprise when, after we had given the administration our votes, the Republican Congressional Campaign Committee sent out press releases into our districts attacking us for "supporting foreign aid giveaways to the IMF and the World Bank." Of course, they didn't tell the whole story—that we had voted for the aid money at the request of the leader of their own party, Ronald Reagan!

After the election, in the next Congress, the administration sent James Baker, the secretary of the treasury, to our committee to testify on behalf of their request to pay off arrearages that had accumulated in our obligation to the World Bank and other IFIs. When the day came for the committee to mark up the bill (it was a supplemental appropriation, I believe), we held an open markup with the public and the press present. When the vote on the bank package came, the Republicans voted "No" except for Silvio Conte. At that point, I announced I was changing my vote to "No" and asked Democrats to do the same thing. Several of them didn't want to switch, but I explained that I would be damned if I would allow the GOP to beat us up again for doing our duty in providing bipartisan support for their own administration. "I will be happy to reconsider when the administration has gotten its own party members to support their request," I said. "But not before." I was indeed willing to do my duty, but I was not going to be sucker punched by an irresponsible Republican Party.

The administration was stunned by our action and complained they could not control their own party members, but I told them I would not play softball while their team was playing hardball. The GOP had thought that we cared about the IFIs so much that we would carry the administration's water alone. When the administration saw that we were serious, they turned their GOP members around and provided what we told them we had to have in the first instance: bipartisan support for their request. That episode demonstrated that no chairman can get very far if he doesn't have a lot of help from others on his committee. I was lucky in many respects.

First, I had a key partner on the committee in Matt McHugh, from upstate New York. I often kidded Matt that he was what every Catholic mother wanted her son to grow up to be. Matt was a profoundly decent, thoughtful legislator, a true social gospel Catholic who shared my views on almost every issue before the committee. He was emotionally and intellectually even more committed to the IFIs than I was, so it had been hard for him to pull the GOP up short, but he did it. He was as committed to support the state of Israel as was I, but he and I were also solidly in favor of trying to reach an understanding between Israel and the Arab world. He probably had some doubts about my hard-nosed negotiating with the administration, but he backed every play and without him I could not have succeeded. He was a great partner. I regarded him then, and still do, as being (along with Dick Gephardt, Bob Kastenmeier, and Martin Sabo) as close to a brother as anyone I ever served with.

Another key player was Charlie Wilson, the most conservative Democrat on the committee. He was a frank, able, informed, fun-loving, tough Texan. Charlie was no romantic in anything except his relationship with women. He was a hardheaded pragmatist I often used in order to pull my most liberal members back to tactical reality. His credibility with conservatives in the Democratic caucus was absolutely crucial in convincing them that the bills we produced were tough-minded enough for them to support.

Sid Yates was almost like a father to me. An elegant, classy, committed liberal of immense decency, he was also the smartest man in any room he ever entered. He played several key roles in Congress. As the chair of the Interior Appropriations Subcommittee, he was one of five or six key players on environmental issues in the House. He had been a leading antiwar Democrat during the Vietnam War and remained influential on questions involving the use of military power. A passionate advocate of human rights, he was also the senior Jewish member in the House; he cared deeply about Israel and was steadfast in his support of economic and military aid to that country. He did not always agree with my position on the Middle East, but he trusted me on the issue because deep down he knew how difficult it would be, given demographic realities, for Israel to remain a Jewish state over the long haul if some way were not found to separate the Israelis and Palestinians on the West Bank.

Bill Lehman of Florida was another key asset. A former car salesman—he had been known as "Alabama Bill" before he came to Congress—he was exactly the opposite of the stereotype associated with that profession. Bill was the sweetest man I ever knew in Congress. Like Sid Yates, he was Jewish and cared strongly about Israel, but his strongest concern was for people, especially the poor, the sick, and the vulnerable. He never stopped caring about refugees and children. Lehman was profoundly sympathetic with my desire to push the peace process forward, and he backed me up at every opportunity. He tried every day to measure up to the highest responsibilities of the Judeo-Christian "care for thy neighbor" tradition, but that never stopped him from displaying toughness when the situation called for it.

Bill Gray of Philadelphia was a savvy, street-smart, black Baptist preacher who focused on issues affecting Africa and later became Budget Committee chairman. Through the years, Democrats like Bob Mrazek, Julian Dixon, Ron Coleman, and Esteban Torrez, and especially Larry Smith, Nita Lowey, and Nancy Pelosi, provided valuable help along the way.

I was also blessed with three responsible ranking Republicans. Jack Kemp was largely distracted by his presidential plans, so he didn't spend a lot of time on committee matters. He and I had major disagreements on policy, but they were rooted in honest, substantive views, and we could usually work them out. Mickey Edwards, the head of the conservative caucus, and Bob Livingston, who in turn served as ranking members after Kemp, were both committed conservatives, but they had responsible worldviews and respected the committee requirement to stand up for congressional oversight responsibilities, all of which made it possible for us to do the jobs we needed to do.

Another crucial piece of good fortune was that Dante Fascell and Lee Hamilton were key foreign policy players on the Foreign Affairs Committee. Except for the IFIs, which were authorized by the Banking Committee, the International Affairs Committee authorized almost all the other foreign assistance programs that we funded.

Hamilton and I were in 90 percent agreement on almost every issue that came before us. His chief of staff, Mike VanDusen, and Mike Marek had a close working relationship, and through the years we would consult with each other on an almost weekly basis. We also worked together on the Joint Economic Committee—although there my views were somewhat more populist than his. Lee had first been elected from a southern Indiana district in 1964, the year of the Johnson landslide. He was a tall, ambling former Indiana All-Star basketball player, as sober and thoughtful on international affairs as any member I ever served with. He had the best foreign policy mind I ever encountered in the Congress. In the 1980s Lee became very much the "go-to guy" when our leadership was looking to draft policy resolutions on Central America. Lee and I also worked in tandem in later years on Middle East, Eastern Europe, and Russia.

VENDETTA AGAINST CHEEK

The Carter administration had conditionally supported a modest amount of nonlethal military aid to the Salvadoran government so long as it made efforts at economic and political reform. But during Carter's years, Jim Cheek, as deputy assistant secretary for Central America, had worked furiously to make the right-wing Salvadoran military (and the landowning elite that backed them) understand that if they blocked reform and continued their support for death squads, we could not sustain U.S. support for them. That had enraged the imperialistic right wing of the Republican Party in the United States. At that time, Reagan had an informal but very real group of kitchen cabinet advisors who had helped finance his political career, reactionaries such as Holmes Tuttle, Justin Dart Sr., Joseph Coors, Alfred Bloomingdale, and several others. Tuttle's son served as deputy director of personnel in the Reagan White House. They wanted the entire Central American bureau at State—people like Cheek and Robert White, our ambassador to El Salvador—blacklisted and driven from the Foreign Service.

Larry Eagleburger, a career foreign service officer from Wisconsin and a protégé of Mel Laird and Henry Kissinger, played a key role in the Reagan administration. It was pretty clear, after Reagan's victory, that there was going to be a wholesale bloodbath in the Central American bureau at State—much as Republican attacks had wiped out the old China hands in the State Department in the McCarthy heyday. I talked quietly to Eagleburger about it, especially about Cheek. "Jim's a good officer," Larry said. "I don't know what I can do, but I will do everything I can to save him," Larry told me, and he did. After a year spent on leave at Howard University and at Tufts, Jim was sent to Nepal—a post as far away from Washington as could be found. Jim kidded later that the reason Nepal was still a beautiful country, and the reason Nepal was safe from harm, was that neither the Soviet Union nor the United States had yet decided that Nepal was important enough to merit their attention. Jim would survive the next twelve years of Republican rule by serving in distant, remote missions like Nepal, Ethiopia, and Sudan. He finally decided to retire in 1992, but a fellow Razorback, Bill Clinton, resurrected him by making him ambassador to Argentina. So he ended a distinguished career as

"Mr. Ambassador" long after Justin Dart and the other primitives tried to ruin him.

Cheek's exile during the Reagan years is a disgraceful example of how U.S. policy toward Central America was being conducted in those days. And with what the Reaganites had in mind, they *had* to get rid of people like him. They didn't want any naysayers around when they began their secret war against the Sandinistas in Nicaragua.

THE UNDER-THE-TABLE WAR

Nicaragua had been ruled for years by Anastasio Somoza, a corrupt dictator much like Fulgenceo Batista, the Cuban dictator who was overthrown by Castro in 1959. Somoza and his cronies had bled the country dry, failed to alleviate the poverty of most of its citizens, and sown the seeds of their own destruction. The revolution in 1979, during Carter's presidency, was broad based with participation by progressive businessmen, religious leaders, and a well-organized group of leftist leaning nationalists—some of whom were Marxists. Two leaders of the governing junta were the Ortega brothers, Daniel and Humberto. When revolution hit, the United States had a choice of two policies: engagement or isolation. Carter had tried engagement by offering a $75 million aid package to try to build bridges to the new government.

In 1979 I went to Nicaragua with other key members in a delegation led by Dante Fascell, who was then the number two Democrat on the Foreign Affairs Committee, after Clem Zablocki of Wisconsin. Our purpose was to get a feel for whether the new regime was hell-bent on establishing a Marxist government or represented something more benign, to assess what kind of relationship we might develop with them, and, when calm and order had been restored, whether the junta would allow free elections and other manifestations of democracy. I recall meeting with Jaime Wheelock, the twenty-seven-year-old minister of agriculture. Fascell led the questioning and probed them about the junta's willingness to create some democratic space within the country and build a constructive relationship with the United States. "I'm going to support this aid request," Dante told them. "But remember, 'Fool me once, shame on you; fool me twice, shame on me.'"

In trying to determine whether it made sense to support the Carter administration policy of engagement, we were especially impressed by the arguments of a Nicaraguan businessman, Adolfo Callero, who had once been jailed by Somoza but who, as head of the Coca-Cola bottling works in Nicaragua, clearly was a capitalist and was most definitely not a Marxist. His argument was that there was only a fifty-fifty chance that the revolution would lead to a good outcome if we provided aid, but that there was no chance at all if America did not demonstrate its willingness to provide aid and help build a relationship. I found his argument persuasive. Within several years, Callero would become a key leader of the military opposition to depose the government (the Contras).

Carter's ambassador to Nicaragua, Larry Pezzulo, was a street-smart, career foreign service officer from Brooklyn who was skeptical of the Sandinistas but convinced that we ought to try to work with them until they demonstrated it was futile. When we asked Pezzulo what was the most effective thing we could do to help, he kiddingly said, "Send baseballs; this country is nuts about baseball." He said that the biggest hero in the country was Dennis Martinez, a Nicaraguan who pitched for the Baltimore Orioles. During the 1980 election, Reagan crucified Carter on his Nicaraguan policy. When Reagan won, he replaced CIA director Stansfield Turner with Bill Casey and thoughts turned from baseballs to guns. Over the objection of Ambassador Pezzulo, the new administration cut off aid, Pezzulo was removed, and Reagan moved to expand our involvement in El Salvador and engage in what became a secret and illegal war against Nicaragua.

The Reagan administration's war on Nicaragua began as a $19 million plan, which was described to the Congress as a limited operation to prevent Nicaraguan arms supplies from reaching the rebels in Salvador. But the reality of the operation extended far beyond that and was clearly aimed at overthrowing the Sandinista government.

In 1982, when the scope of the administration's plans became clear to us, the Congress passed an amendment sponsored by Eddie Boland, the Intelligence Committee chair, to prohibit the use of U.S. funds to overthrow the Nicaraguan government—and Reagan signed it. But under the table, the administration ignored the law by maintaining the fiction that the goal of the U.S. action was not to overthrow but simply to harass and contain the Sandinistas in order to prevent an effective alliance between them and the rebels in El Salvador.

For the next six years, the war raged between the Sandinistas and the Contras (operating from bases in Honduras). Most of us in Congress who opposed U.S. support for the Contras had little use for the Sandinistas. That was certainly true of Lee Hamilton, Matt McHugh, and myself. But given the sorry history of U.S. imperialism in that region—the overthrow of Arbenz in Guatemala in 1954, the Nixon-Kissinger–backed coup against Allende in Chile, and the U.S. support for Somoza and a host of other dictators—we did not believe the administration should be involved in a military attempt to return the old order to power. Nor did we believe another round of American gunboat diplomacy would enhance our long-term standing in the region. The CIA's involvement there was so blatantly out of control that even Barry Goldwater raised hell about it on the Senate floor.

In 1983 Jim Wright had asked a number of us to join him in sending a letter to Daniel Ortega urging him to follow through on the proposal Ortega had made to hold a "fully open and democratic election." Jim had drafted the letter at the suggestion of Alfonso Robello, a Nicaraguan businessman with long ties to the United States, who believed there was a chance that if the elections were procedurally fair, a well-known challenger might actually defeat the Sandinistas at the ballot box. The letter, which the Republicans ridiculed because it began with the salutation "Dear Commadante," closed by reminding Ortega that some of us who had signed the letter had opposed the Reagan policy against Nicaragua and believed that if free and fair elections were held it would "significantly improve the prospect of a better relationship between our two countries."

Our letter was aimed at putting pressure on Ortega to live up to his promise of free elections. Jim thought that because we had opposed the Contra war, our comments would put more pressure on Ortega than would a letter from those who were on record supporting U.S. action to remove him. To our surprise, instead of receiving expressions of appreciation from the administration for voicing our support for its insistence on free elections, we were instead attacked by a cadre of GOP right-wing House members, led by Newt Gingrich and political commentators like Pat Buchanan. In a series of late evening speeches on the floor, after the close of business, and with no notice and no one around to respond, they attacked our patriotism in a style that would have made McCarthy proud. Gingrich and his troops suggested that we were more comfortable with the KGB than the CIA. Bill Young implied that Wyche Fowler, a Democrat from Georgia, had a greater allegiance to other countries than he had to America. Bob Walker accused us of being prepared "to accept and accommodate communist successes" while being unprepared to accept successes by "pro-American freedom fighters." Gingrich accused us of voting to "unilaterally disarm." The administration and its Republican congressional allies were determined to politically punish anyone who questioned their actions. And they were often willing to lie.

The Congress continued to struggle with the administration to get at the truth about how the Contras were being financed. Witnesses like Elliott Abrams would stonewall or play word games during our congressional hearings. Finally, the depth of administration duplicity on the issue was revealed with the discovery that the administration had secretly traded arms for hostages with Iran and funneled some of the proceeds to the Contras. Oliver North, a gung-ho lieutenant colonel, was at the operational center of the madcap scheme. In effective violation of the law, a freelance, under-the-table, private war was being conducted by the administration *without* congressional approval or knowledge, while at the same time it was selling weapons to a terrorist nation, Iran, that was most likely involved in the murder of U.S. marines in Lebanon several years earlier. When the daffy operation was revealed, Reagan went on television to claim blissful ignorance of the deal. John Poindexter, the national security advisor, was removed from his job as was Ollie North. In the congressional investigation that ensued, the committee gave a number of administration witnesses immunity, which in the end allowed several of them, including Poindexter, to escape prosecution on a technicality. In the end, the committee investigating the affair pulled its punches and Reagan's successor, George H. W. Bush, pardoned a number of administration figures in the affair including defense secretary Caspar Weinberger and Elliot Abrams, a State Department figure.

The issue came to a head in Congress in 1987 and 1988. For six years, a congressional debate had raged about the Contra scheme. In 1988 the House voted to severely limit the administration's ability to fund any further military operation against Nicaragua. In the House, the fight over the fate of that effort took place on my Foreign Operations Appropriation bill, but in the Senate, language opening the way for broader aid was attached to the Defense Appropriations bill. Ted Stevens, the GOP ranking member on Defense who strongly supported the Contra operation, wanted the issue negotiated on the DoD bill in order to give him more leverage, but Wright, Foley, and I insisted it would be handled as it had been previously, in Foreign Ops. In conference, which took place on the Senate side of Capitol Hill in the new Hart Senate office building, I pressed for the House position. The issue was just one of many in a broad-ranging supplemental appropriations bill. Stevens wouldn't budge and raised unshirted hell, demanding I relinquish jurisdiction to the DoD Subcommittee, which he could much more easily influence.

Stevens was then, and remains today, one of my favorite people in Congress. He and I are poles apart in political philosophy, but I respected him because he was extremely able and liked him because his political style was so unadorned. He did not play games or sneak around. He said what he believed, straight, hard, and blunt—no sugar coating, no baloney. In that, he is refreshingly different from so many people I have dealt with through the years. It was common knowledge that at least once in any conference Stevens would theatrically slam the table, get up, and begin to walk out if he could not get what he wanted. His short fuse was real, but he was not above staging his walkout just to see how far he could push his case.

During one especially heated exchange between us, the bells rang indicating that a Senate floor vote had begun. At the very same time, the committee clerk came to me and said that a House floor vote had also begun. I left the room first to head down to the subway to catch the trolley over to the Capitol. I walked out of the committee room into the adjoining hallway where three or four TV cameras were lined up, along with a gaggle of reporters. As I walked toward the elevators, Stevens burst from the committee room behind me and, before seeing the cameras, shouted to me, "Obey, up yours!" Only then did he notice the gathered press. His action was so unexpected it surprised me as much as it did the press. Struck by the humor of it all, I began to laugh, both at the situation and at the expression on Ted's face as he realized we were surrounded by press. "Don't worry," I shouted to the press, "we really love each other," and then stepped into the elevator, leaving them to wonder what had happened in the conference to cause Ted's outburst.

Negotiations went on for days. Finally, in a meeting in Bob Dole's office presided over by Colin Powell, Foley, Bonior, and I agreed on a compromise with Stevens and the administration. The agreement established a timetable and a process, which would decide the issue. The agreement essentially provided money to feed and cloth the Contras in a stand-down mode, along with additional money to help finance a new election in Nicaragua. That was indeed ironic because the "Dear Commandante" letter that we had signed (and for which we were pilloried by the Reagan administration and the Republican right wing) had called for just such an election. We agreed that aid to the Contras would end by a specific date but defined a process by which the president could be guaranteed a congressional vote if he asked for an extension. I was confident that we could defeat any such vote. We approved $48 million in "nonlethal" aid to carry them in a stand-down position through the end of the fiscal year in September and $27 million more to tide them over until April 1, 1989.

STRIKING A SIDE DEAL

After the election, Jim Baker, the new secretary of state for the incoming Bush administration, wanted a further extension of nonmilitary aid to give him leverage in pushing the Sandinistas to follow through on holding elections.

With the November elections behind us, many Democrats were afraid that the new administration would try to resurrect military aid. They thought that the agreed-upon timetable would finally end the war; they did not want to accept Bush administration requests to provide an extension of economic aid, which they feared could be used as a bridge to keep the Contras together while the administration used that time to build support for resuming the war. Baker insisted the administration would not do that.

I would not have considered giving the Reagan administration any such leeway because I simply did not trust them, but I liked and trusted George H. W. Bush and Jim Baker. So I suggested that the administration's ability to continue humanitarian aid for the purpose of reintegrating the Contras into Nicaraguan society be made subject to the informal notification process that often lubricated financial agreements between the executive and the Congress. Under that informal agreement, the Foreign Operations Appropriations Sub-committees in the Senate and House and the Foreign Affairs Authorizing Committees would all have to approve an extension beyond eight months. That would create the possibility that the administration could extend aid beyond the eight month cut-off without a vote in the full House and Senate, an option that would be useful to the administration in their negotiations with the Sandinistas. The disadvantage for opponents of the war was that the agreement would be an informal one, and the administration's legal beagles could argue that use of the notification process amounted to an unconstitu-tional legislative veto, which they did not legally have to honor. But Jim Baker assured me privately that the administration would honor the agreement. He and I sealed that understanding with a handshake in Jim Wright's office, and the deed was done.

Baker and I and several others took heat for the agreement from opposite directions. Some liberal Democrats attacked me for being naïve enough to trust the administration. One group, CISPES (Committee in Solidarity with the People of El Salvador), confronted me on the Capitol steps and later staged a sit-in in my Capitol subcommittee room to protest my "selling out." Baker was attacked by several hard-line members of the GOP right wing and by conservative columnist Bob Novak. The President's legal counsel, C. Boyden Gray, also attacked the agreement on legal grounds, but the deal stuck; it gave me a good feeling, after eight years, to be dealing with an administration I could trust. Meanwhile on the ground, in the region, progress was being made in bringing the conflict to a conclusion.

Under an agreement negotiated under the leadership of Oscar Arias, the visionary leader of Costa Rica, Nicaraguan elections were set. Against all odds,

under close international supervision, the Sandinistas lost, and a democratically elected government peacefully came to power. Under heavy pressure from
Jimmy Carter, who headed up international inspections, the Sandinistas—
contrary to the expectations of many—accepted the outcome and went into
political opposition.

CHAPTER 15

Working with Bush I

Central America was not the only region of the world where I found it easier to work with the Bush administration than the Reagan administration. There was also a huge difference in their approach to the Middle East. In contrast to the Reagan administration, the Bush administration made a concerted effort to bring the Middle East closer to a settlement, and I worked closely with them on their efforts.

MIDDLE EAST PARTNERS

For almost two decades, the Soviet Union had refused to allow more than a handful of Jews to emigrate, but in 1989 the number of Jews allowed to leave exploded from 13,000 to 180,000, and many of them wanted to go to Israel. The United States provided $400 million in loan guarantees to help Israel finance the immigration with one stipulation: no settlement should occur outside of Israel's 1967 borders.

Since the 1967 war, Israel had followed a policy of creating "new realities" on the ground by allowing Israel to settle beyond the Green Line (the 1967 borders of Israel) in the newly occupied territories. In 1975, during my first visit to Israel, Rabin had told me that the creation of these settlements would force Palestinians to come to the table to negotiate before so many settlers populated the West Bank that Israeli withdrawal would become a political impossibility. But since 1967 it had been U.S. policy—especially since Camp David—that such settlements actually were illegal and were obstacles to peace. The Bush administration was trying to serve as an honest broker between Israel and the Palestinians, and didn't want its aid for Jewish refugees to be seen as underwriting settlement expansion. The Israeli Likud government under Yitzhak Shamir had assured the administration that no refugees would be settled in the occupied territories, but that pledge was never honored.

In the spring of 1991, Israel surfaced a request for an additional $10 billion in loan guarantees to help cope with the financial impact of resettling one million Soviet Jews in Israel. Because the administration was especially interested in moving the peace process forward, it was concerned that, without a guarantee from Israel that the refugees would not be resettled beyond the Green Line in the West Bank, the loan guarantees would be viewed in the Arab world as evidence that the United States was financing the Israeli occupation of disputed territory, which would blow away any chance to move the peace process forward. Requests by Bush and Jim Baker for Israel to halt expansion of settlements were flatly rebuffed by Shamir, and Israel's housing minister had displayed plans for over twenty thousand new houses in the occupied territories. Baker was frustrated and complained that every time he visited Israel, he was confronted with a new round of settlements and was tired of it.

Baker asked Shamir to delay the loan guarantees to give him a chance to get progress in the peace process, but Shamir was told by AIPAC, the lobbying arm of the Jewish community on Israeli related issues, that they could ram their request through Congress despite the opposition of the Bush White House. AIPAC was accustomed to having its way on Middle Eastern issues and some of its leaders had an easy habit of branding anyone who opposed their agenda as "anti-Israel." In fact, many American and Israeli Jews felt quite differently. They understood that the expansion of settlements in the West Bank was not only an impediment to peace but also a threat to the long-term vision of Israel as a Jewish state. They understood, because the Arab population on the West Bank and Gaza was growing so fast, that demographic trends meant that Jews would no longer be a majority of Israel's population. They reasoned that only by relinquishing the occupied territories could Israel secure the long-term vision of Israel as a Jewish refuge for the world's most historically abused people.

Because I strongly supported the administration's opposition to new settlement activity, AIPAC continued to try to get around me, lobbying my subcommittee members to outvote me on the Foreign Operations conference. In a tough, blunt conversation in a Capitol hallway outside the conference room, I made clear to AIPAC, and to a representative of the Israeli embassy, that I was not budging on the issue. "You may get members to outvote me," I said, "but I have one power you can't reach. As chairman I don't have the power to guarantee other people's votes, but as chairman I have the power to decide whether to take up the bill on the floor, and I guarantee that if you get people to outvote me, I will never bring the bill to the floor for a vote." I told the Israeli embassy representative, "You have no business trying to muscle the committee or the president." The White House raised the specter of a possible veto if the guarantees were not delayed, and I went on ABC's *Nightline* to defend their position. We both hung tight, and the guarantees were delayed.

I was furious at the Israeli embassy. I took pride in my role in helping Israel pay for resettling the first Jews from the Soviet Union. But now Shamir was letting his determination to expand Israeli settlements in the West Bank get in the way of the chance to amicably resettle Soviet Jews in Israel and was hurting U.S. interests in the process.

Discussions resumed in early 1992 on how to deal with the impasse. Israeli ambassador Zalmon Shoval had worked with a number of key House and Senate members to arrange a meeting in the Capitol. I arrived late, and as I listened to the comments around the room, it soon became apparent to me that the embassy was trying to arrange another congressional end run around the president. Every seat in the room was taken, so I stood next to the door, listening to the sales job. Finally I spoke up.

Mr. Ambassador, I want to help Israel settle Soviet Jewish refugees, everybody in this room probably does, but not at the expense of gutting the administration's ability to be seen as honest brokers in the peace process in the Middle East. Settlement expansion in the West Bank is contrary to U.S. policy in the Middle East. The administration has described them as impediments to peace. I have shepherded billions of dollars in aid to Israel through the House since I have been chairman. I may not have voted for every dollar that you wanted, but I voted for every dollar that you ever got. But I will not be party to day-in, day-out end runs around the president on this issue. He is not of my party, but he is our president. He is defending long-standing U.S. policy and I will not cooperate in any attempt to undermine that policy.

Then I left. The next day I got a call from President Bush. "Bob Dole told me that you stood up for me yesterday in that Hill meeting on the loan guarantees, and I just wanted to say thank you," he said. Bush, by his principled stand on settlements, had actually put in motion a series of events that jumpstarted the peace process. The open split between Bush and Shamir, as well as economic chaos in Israel, helped ensure the defeat of Shamir's Likud government in June of 1992. That brought to power the tough Labor Party pragmatist, Yitzhak Rabin.

Rabin was determined to dramatically scale back the Israeli subsidy incentives for settling on the West Bank (his views on Golan were different). In his memoirs, Jim Baker wrote that Rabin had told him, "For the sake of 3.9 million Israeli Jews and a million Israeli Arabs who should not have to mortgage their future because of the 100,000 settlers in the territories, I intend to persevere." The impasse was broken, Israel received the financial help that it sought, and the door was open to an expanded Israeli-Palestinian dialogue.

Within eighteen months, enough progress had been made for Bush's successor, Bill Clinton, to hold a ceremony on the White House lawn between Rabin and Arafat to politically endorse the next step in "land for peace," the Oslo Peace Agreement negotiated between the Israelis and the PLO. The day before the event I called Bush and told him, "Mr. President, if you hadn't stuck to U.S. policy on settlements this meeting would not be taking place. I hope you feel good about the role you played. You should." He told me he appreciated the call and that he did indeed "feel good" about what he had done. Several years later, Arafat was to throw away the best chance of his life to secure a deal in the West Bank. The violence that occurred after he gave the cold shoulder to a generous offer from the Israeli prime minister Ehud Barak would once again demonstrate that the Middle East is always in a race between progress and chaos.

EASTERN EUROPE

Another totally unexpected opportunity for me to work with the Bush administration came in Eastern Europe and the Soviet Union. But to explain what we did with the Soviet Union and Eastern Europe in the Bush years, we need to retrace events of the 1980s.

Poland and the Pope

Cracks in the Soviet empire had begun to show in the late 1970s. Over nearly two decades, human contact between those behind the Iron Curtain and those in the West, through business, trade, and other normal economic and social intercourse, planted the realization that things in the East should be better. Western television beamed its images of modernity, change, and prosperity to the East, despite the best efforts of communist governments to stop the process. Awareness grew until differences could not be denied. It was obvious that the East was falling farther and farther behind.

In 1980, months before Ronald Reagan came to power at home, Gdansk shipyard workers, led by Lech Walesa, sparked a society-wide protest against communist rule, under the banner of *Solidarnosz,* "Solidarity." The turmoil generated by Solidarity caused the Polish communist government to impose martial law in December of 1981, cracking down on dissidents and jailing Walesa and other leaders. In Washington, a fierce debate broke out about how to react to this turmoil. The Reagan administration took a number of steps to impose sanctions on the Polish government, but a number of critics were demanding a more punitive response. The question at hand was where to draw the line in establishing a tough enough policy to make the government pay a political price for their actions—without being so harsh that these policies would cause the Polish populace to blame Western-oriented reformers for the pain generated by those sanctions. My Republican friend on the subcommittee, Mickey Edwards, and I decided we should lead a delegation to Poland to evaluate the Polish situation for ourselves.

A rising debate had engulfed Washington about whether General Jaruzelski was a Soviet puppet who carried out their order to apply martial law in order to stop the uprising, or whether he was a Polish patriot who imposed martial law to prevent Russia from taking over and reacting with Soviet-style brutality. Because of martial law, we could not get to Walesa, but we met with Cardinal Glemp, Solidarity leaders, and a wide variety of journalists, academics, and Polish government officials. The most impressive of them all was Bronislaw Geremec, the principal intellectual strategist of the reform movement. We got the same message from most Solidarity officials—Jaruzelski was no social democrat, but he was a useful layer of insulation between Poland and the Soviet Union.

We had no idea how the Solidarity effort would fare, but we learned a lot just by going to church on Sunday morning in Warsaw. Normally, Catholic churches had been half full, but during the crisis, the church held Masses every hour on the hour, and the churches were overflowing. Why? The church had become the nation's tom-tom, the center of their communication system. Churches were overflowing because people were getting their news from the pulpit. They were getting information about what was happening and clues about what they should do from the church.

The most disturbing meeting we had was with several members of the Sejm, the communist-dominated national legislature. We peppered them with questions about what was happening on the economic, political, and human rights front. When we asked about the degree of freedom for Polish academics, one deputy responded by asserting that the only intellectuals who were giving anyone trouble were the "cosmopolitans"—their term for the Jews. He then went on to say, "Only a few of the cosmopolitans want to leave, but if they don't stop stirring up trouble they will not be allowed to leave."

On our last day in Poland I was hit by a miserable cold. I decided to skip an evening meeting to get some rest and asked Matt McHugh to stand in for me. We had been traveling by military plane, and the plane was parked at the Warsaw airport overnight. The next morning at about six o'clock, our military escort officer came to me with some shocking news. "Sir," he said, "someone broke into our plane last night. We don't know if it was Polish military or Russian KGB, but the door has definitely been tampered with." He told me that they could find no evidence that the on-board safe containing various communications codes had been violated, but as a precaution they had flown the plane to the U.S. base at Ramstein. There, they had security officials check over the plane and found no evidence that security had been breached. The plane had been refueled and was ready to go. I was feeling sick as a dog and totally exhausted, but the colonel's news had given me a major league dose of adrenaline.

I was not sure how to respond to the incident. My overriding reaction was one of anger that the Poles or Russians would do something that outrageous. But another thought lurked in the back of my mind. The Reagan administration was running our government. It was the administration of Bill Casey. The administration was deeply divided on how to respond to the martial law situation. Having lived through FBI dirty tricks, the phony Gulf of Tonkin resolution, and other examples of executive branch setups and lies, I asked myself, "Could it possibly be that some hard-liner apparatus within the administration had phonied-up the break-in in order to justify a harder line against Poland?" As I turned to that question over in my mind, my sense of anger welled up against all those who, in the past, had so abused their executive power that I had, even for a moment, harbored the thought that someone in my own government might use us as pawns to stage such a setup.

I mentally shook myself and thought that while some political apprentice of Casey might arrange a setup like that, I doubted that the military would have been part of it. I concluded that there was probably a 90 percent chance the Russians or Poles were responsible and decided to raise hell with our Polish hosts. When two cars full of Polish political and military people met our bus at the airport to see us off, I confronted the officer in charge, told him what had happened, and then told him in the bluest language I could conjure up, how outraged we were at the incident. After blistering him, I refused to shake his hand and boarded the plane.

From Poland we flew to Rome, because I had thought that it would be useful to discuss what we had seen and heard with the pope. The next morning, prior to our audience with him, we were ushered in to the Vatican for a briefing by Vatican secretary of state, Cardinal Casseroli. Casseroli was a thin-featured man with a thoughtful demeanor. We described to him briefly what we had seen and heard. He told me how the audience with the pope would proceed. "You will be taken into his chambers and be seated in chairs below his throne," he said. "When he enters, he will proceed to the throne and then read a prepared statement. He will then motion you to a microphone and invite you to respond. He may have a question or two."

We were ushered in and seated. The room had a high ceiling, gold-colored walls, and beautiful yellow, gold, tan, and brown marble flooring. At the front was a white marble throne with a high, golden back flanked by two marble statues. The throne was resting on a platform atop three carpeted marble steps. When the pope came in, he strode to his chair and sat down. But, instead of reading a statement as the secretary of state had told me to expect, he simply smiled and motioned me to the microphone. I had expected to take a few notes on his comments so I could respond in an organized way, but that was now out of the question. I rose from my chair, thanked him for seeing us, and gave him a rundown on our trip.

When I was finished, he thanked us for briefing him. Then, stepping down from his chair, he gave us each a rosary, shook hands, and then began to ask me questions. When I told him about the Polish senator's threat to prevent the "cosmopolitans" from leaving the country, he flared. Grasping with both hands the chain holding the cross on his chest, he responded, "That is outrageous, outrageous. Every person has a human right to travel, to enter and leave his own country, even me, even me!" he said, pointing to his own chest as he spoke. At that time, there had been stories suggesting that he was thinking of returning to his homeland to send a signal to the Russians to stay out, and there had been some discussion about whether the Polish government would allow his plane to land. When the pope exploded, I thought to myself, "No doubt in the world; he's going." But other events intervened, and he did not return to Poland until much later. I will never forget the aura of physical force he exuded on that day. More than two decades later it was painful to see how stooped and frail his body had become under the assault of Parkinson's disease. When I attended his funeral in April of 2005, my thoughts constantly drifted back to the memory of that discussion. When our delegation returned home, we reported to the National Security Council that we thought the administration's sanctions were just about right: it would probably be counterproductive to take some of the more harsh actions being urged by critics, because blame for those measures might fall on Solidarity and its allies.

One key issue being debated by the administration involved chicken feed—literally. Poland was desperately short of food. In protest to the imposition of martial law, the West had placed an embargo on exports to Poland. It was supplying food but only through private, nongovernment charities so the Polish government could not use food as a weapon against its own people. But there were gray areas. The Poles had no feed for their chickens. The administration was split between allowing chicken feed into the country in order to keep their chickens alive or shutting if off and allowing hundreds of thousands of baby chicks to die—thus losing a large source of protein for the country. The Solidarity leaders we had talked to urged us to tell the administration to allow the chicken feed into the country. They were worried that if the United States cut it off, the Polish government would blame Solidarity for the loss of the chicken flock, and that could hurt their cause. Edwards and I both counseled the administration to allow the feed to be shipped, and they eventually agreed to do so.

Revisiting Soviet Politics

Over the next several years events in Poland, and other issues that arose from the way the Soviet Union handled sweeping changes in Eastern Europe, required that I focus more of my time on the Soviet Union than I had ever imagined.

Through the years I had occasionally met with visiting Soviet figures. After Leonid Brezhnev died, Soviet leadership passed into the hands of two more old men. Two meetings with the Soviets just a few months apart illustrate how quickly that leadership changed. Brezhnev was succeeded by Yuri Andropov, a long-time KGBer who was regarded as having a keen mind, but by the time he took power he was in physical decline. In July of 1983 Tom Foley led a delegation to the Soviet Union and asked me to join him. Andropov was known to be ill, and talk of reform was in the air. We stopped first in Leningrad before going to Moscow in time to participate in a July 4 Independence Day celebration at our embassy there. After two days in Leningrad we moved on to Moscow.

After our first day in Moscow, we gathered in our control room in the old Hotel Moskva to relax. Our delegation had been concerned about the situation faced by Russian Jews (Refuseniks) who were not being allowed to leave the Soviet Union. We had agreed early in the trip that we would try to visit a number of Refuseniks, but only one or two of us at a time would step out of our meetings with the Russians so we would not show disrespect for the meetings in progress. As we were gathered in our hotel control room, one of the Russian escorts asked to talk to the U.S. embassy person in charge of our visit. The young foreign service officer who had been assigned to us by the embassy was in his first week on the job. In a confidential tone the Russian told the control officer, "Look, we know what your people are doing. They are visiting Jews. It is my duty to tell you that the neighborhoods your congressmen are going to in order to visit the Jews are dangerous, and if they persist, we cannot guarantee their safety." The young control officer leaned into the face of the Russian until his nose was about six inches from the Russian's and whispered, "Do you know what the word *bullshit* means? Consider that our reply in triplicate! Bullshit, bullshit, bullshit." Startled, the Russian stepped back with raised eyebrows. Our control officer then nodded politely to him, leaned over, and said, "Now I think I will have a beer." That was exactly the right reply. We heard no more threats from the Russians. They had needed to lodge an objection to our neighborhood visits, and we had needed to let them know we would not be deterred.

Our meetings with the Soviet officials were scheduled to focus on four issues—arms limitation, human rights, regional differences, and economics. Foley had assigned Tom Downey of New York to lead discussions on arms limitation, Henry Waxman of California on human rights, Tim Wirth of Colorado on economics, and I was assigned to discuss regional differences.

Our first business meeting with the Russians was a study in contrasts. The format of the meetings called for us to begin an opening plenary session in which our entire delegation would be seated on one side of a long table and our Russian counterparts seated on the other. After that first general session, we were scheduled to break down into smaller groups for individual topic discussions. The lead Russians were a high-ranking politburo member, Boris Ponomarev, and Marshal Sergei Akhrameyev, who was later to commit suicide after a failed coup. Russian reaction to that first meeting was revealing because it showed how much the Russians were intimidated by American technology.

Ponomarev opened the session with a long monologue, which he read stiffly, word for word, from a twelve-page written document. When he finished, Foley responded extemporaneously for about fifteen minutes. After an hour's discussion, the meeting ended. I was seated next to Foley on his right. I thought nothing of it at the time, but Foley had a small pocket calculator on the table next to his right hand, which he used to keep time during his remarks. As the meeting broke up, one of the Russians said to me, "Your Mr. Foley, he has a machine." "What do you mean?" I asked. "Well, he has no notes; he had a machine," he responded. Then I understood. The Russians were so intimidated by America's technology that they thought Foley's pocket calculator was a mini-teleprompter. Comprehending, I grinned and said, "No, no, that was just a pocket calculator with a clock because Foley wanted to keep track of how long he was talking." "But he had no notes," the Russian replied. "He doesn't need any," I replied. "Tom has photographic memory." The Russian expressed skepticism.

After a snack, we headed for our breakout discussion groups. Our experience in those meetings was very different from the plenary meeting. I was the American discussion leader, and Boris Stukhalin was the Russian's. Our conversations were much more free flowing and open. We discussed Russian–United States differences in Eastern Europe, especially Poland, the Middle East, Africa, Central America, and Afghanistan.

The Russians professed that they had lost interest in Central America and made comments indicating that they regarded Castro as more of a burden than an opportunity. On the Middle East they made a point of asking why we were so willing to give the Russians an opening with the Arabs by appearing to be so locked into Israel's positions. "We really don't want to be so heavily involved. Egypt cost us so much money before Sadat disengaged from us," Stukhalin said. "But you make it easy for the Syrians and others to ask for aid to balance your dollars for Israel," he said, "and we are in no position to turn them down even though it is expensive."

The most interesting issue was Afghanistan. They didn't want to talk about it. It was obvious that most of them saw it as their own Vietnam quagmire, and they simply didn't know what to do about it. For months, Charlie Wilson, my Texas colleague on the Foreign Ops Subcommittee, had been talking about the need to provide meaningful military help to Afghan resistance fighters who were giving the invading Russian troops a tough time. I agreed with Charlie but expressed my concerns about our inability to keep control of Stinger missiles once they were provided. In Moscow I was uncertain about how the Russians would react to talking about Afghanistan. Their comments convinced me that they regretted their involvement there as much as we had regretted ours in Vietnam. It was clear that the experience was sapping Russian morale, and in fact they had no idea how to extricate themselves from the mess.

The next day the Soviets gave us a tour of the Kremlin complex. We saw the bedrooms of the tsars and the rooms where so many of them were buried, and we toured the gleaming white cathedrals with gold onion domes that Americans have seen so many times on television. In the dark, bleak, sun-deprived chamber, with icons peering out from every wall, our Soviet guide pointed out where various royal figures had been buried. Jim Billington, a great American scholar of all things Russian and the new director of the Library of Congress, began to correct him. After Jim had corrected him three or four times about who was buried where, the guide turned to Billington in embarrassment and said, "Sir, you obviously know this better than I do; you take over."

Later, as we walked past the Ivan the Great Bell Tower, we came upon a huge, black, cast-iron bell resting on the ground. A large piece of the bell was broken off. The guide told us the story of the bell, where it was cast, when it was hung, the weight of the bell, the story of how the piece broke out of it, and even the weight of the broken-off piece. As we walked back to our buses, one of our guides, probably KGB, said, "Mr. Foley, we're told you have a photographic memory. What do you remember about the bell?" Without missing a beat, Foley repeated the whole story right down to the weight of the bell and the weight of the broken piece. The guide's jaw dropped, and the bus exploded in applause. At that point, the Russians recognized that Foley was a person to be reckoned with.

Shortly after we returned to the States, Andropov died and was replaced by another aging apparatchik, Konstantin Chernenko. Months later, a Soviet delegation came to Washington to repay our visit, led by Vladimir Scherbitsky, one of the old-line party leaders. We continued the discussions started in Moscow, but in the midst of an evening dinner at the Hay-Adams Hotel, we were informed that the Russians had to cut short their visit and return home. We thought a power shakeup was occurring in Moscow, and soon discovered that the reason was the death of Chernenko.

Gorbachev

Chernenko's demise brought to power a young, vigorous protégé of Andropov, Mikhail Gorbachev. The difference in leadership was stunning. Brezhnev, Andropov, and Chernenko were tired, gray, dull, bureaucratic, and traditional. Gorbachev, by contrast, was powerful, imaginative—and young. Gone were the baggy, badly tailored funeral suits. Gorbachev's wife, Raisa, was modern and stylish. Gorbachev brought fresh air into the Kremlin and into the Soviet Union's relationship with the United States He announced his intention to lead a renewal of Soviet society, its economy, and its political system through what he called *Perestroika* and *Glasnost*. Perestroika was to be a bold effort to reform the economy, to renew its strength and vitality through major reform— the death of Marxist orthodoxy. Glasnost was to be a new political openness that tolerated dissent.

Gorbachev's actions represented an implicit recognition of two facts. First, communist institutional rigidity and orthodoxy had produced a system that was incapable of allowing the Soviets to compete in the modern world. Second, modern technology and communications had created such a visible gap between Soviet stagnation and Western prosperity that there was no hope of hiding from Soviet citizens the overwhelming failure of their system.

Gorbachev's diplomatic representative to the West was Edward Sheverdnadze, a thoughtful, sad-eyed Georgian (with a strong resemblance to the actor who played Detective Morse in the British public television series), who expressed a strong belief in the necessity for immediate reform. The two men worked with Jim Baker to take the giant steps that brought the postwar period to an end. Together, they would preside over the retreat—and finally the collapse—of the Soviet empire and the end of the Cold War. My subcommittee played a key role in America's response to those events, and because of an earlier visit from former Iowa senator Dick Clark, I was able to deal with those world-shaking events in an informed way.

In 1985 Clark came into my office with what I thought was a naïve and outlandish request. He told me that he was working on a program at the Aspen Institute and wanted to know if I would give him an honest reaction about whether it would work. He wanted to work on a long-range project to build a significant cadre of congressional experts on the Soviet Union, and the first three people he was contacting were Tom Foley, Jim Leach, and me because all of us had been Soviet scholars in college. His idea was to bring together, on a recurring basis, a core group of members of Congress and European parliamentarians—both Eastern and Western European—with a broad range of academic experts on the Soviet Union. He asked if I thought he could get ten or fifteen congressmen and senators to agree to attend conferences twice a year for three years. My first reaction was negative. I told Dick I could not imagine getting members of Congress to agree to anything three years in advance because of the squeeze on their official schedules and on their family time.

Dick explained that the Aspen Institute recognized that difficulty and was willing to make it more inviting by scheduling the conferences during congressional recesses and by inviting spouses to attend—and participate—if they desired. The Institute had planned to hold the conferences in places that would be inviting for spouses and families, and yet remote enough so that members wouldn't constantly be on the phone with their offices. They scheduled the first meeting in Bermuda, which they thought would be attractive to Europeans, especially the Eastern Europeans, and the second conference in an Eastern European capital. The proposition was attractive on several fronts. Intellectually, it was a wonderful opportunity to spend a five-day block of time with America's and Europe's best experts on the Soviet Union. It would also give us a chance to explore ideas and concerns with key politicians in Europe in meetings that were off-limits to staff, lobbyists, and telephone calls. It would also be an opportunity for our spouses to learn the same things we were learning and get some relaxation at the same time.

The Bermuda conference in 1986 included senators Dan Quayle, Thad Cochran, Dan Evans, James McClure, Alan Simpson, John Warner, Joe Biden, Al Gore, Sam Nunn, Carl Levin, Paul Sarbanes, and Paul Simon. The House contingent included Dick Cheney, Jim Leach, Mickey Edwards, Lynn Martin, Doug Bereuter, Tom Foley, Les Aspin, Bill Gray, Steve Solarz, Lee Hamilton, and me. Participants from European parliaments included Gro Harlem Brundtland from Norway (who later became prime minister and then head of the World Health Organization), Joris Voorhoeve of the Netherlands, Dietrich Stobbe, the former mayor of Berlin, Jean Andre Francois-Poncet of France, and many others. Soviet scholars joining us were the Librarian of Congress Jim Billington, William Griffith, William Hyland, Seweryn Bialer, Arnold Horelick, David Hamburg, and Heinrich Vogel.

That conference began a fifteen-year series of conferences that helped us work through our changing relationship with the Soviet Union, and they continue to this day. Additional conferences were added by Aspen on issues such as South Africa, Cuba, China, global environmental challenge, education, and, after 9/11, the nature of Islam. These conferences provided some of the most intellectually enriching experiences of my life. They helped American legislators to come to know a broad range of Soviet and Eastern European officials, including people like Andrei Kozyrev, the former foreign minister of the Soviet Union and Russia; Andrei Kokoshin, deputy defense minister; Janusz Onyszkewicz, the future foreign minister and deputy defense minister of Poland; Dietrich Stobe, the former mayor of Berlin; and even Shevardnadze and Gorbachev. Those discussions put us in direct contact with a wide variety of first-rate scholars and experts with executive branch experience, people such as Robert Legvold, Gail Lapidus, Ted Warner, Robert Conquest, Alex Dallon, Stephen Sestanovich, ambassador Warren Zimmermann, Michael Mandelbaum, Charles and Toby Gati, ambassador Arthur Hartman, Madeleine Albright, and Warren Christopher—both later secretaries of state—Jeffrey Sachs, and William Perry (later secretary of defense). Most important, they were bipartisan and bicameral. They enabled us to get to know and understand on a much more personal basis people in the House and Senate with whom we worked every day, especially those across the political aisle, and form a better understanding of how they thought. Dick Cheney is one example. Dick Lugar is another.

I first met Cheney when he was a staffer for Bill Steiger. He had deep Wisconsin connections. A student at the University of Wisconsin in Madison, he had worked in Steiger's office and for former governor Warren Knowles. After leaving Steiger to become a special assistant at the Office of Economic Opportunity, he moved to the White House staff, eventually serving as staff chief. After returning to Wyoming, he was elected to Congress and later served as secretary of defense. Upon his departure from the House, where he served as the Republican whip, he was succeeded by Newt Gingrich.

I will never forget Cheney in those Aspen conferences. When Gorbachev first took power and was pursuing his policies of perestroika and glasnost, Cheney fervently argued that the United States could not trust Gorbachev, that he was not really a reformer, and would not fundamentally change Soviet policy. In Cheney's eyes Gorbachev was a KGB apparatchik at heart and was using reform simply to revitalize communism before mounting another effort to challenge the West. He said it was not in our interest to see Gorbachev's reforms succeed and we should do as much as we could to establish unquestioned U.S. primacy and drive the Soviet Union and Russia into the dust. I had a very different view, based on my view of history, my perception of political dynamics at the time, and my own personal knowledge of Soviet issues. I saw Gorbachev as a civilized man who, even within the context of his commitment to communism, wanted to change directions for his country. In my view he was a godsend to the United States and the world and deserved our support.

The American hard right had insisted that Gorbachev could not be believed. In the end, however, he and Shevardnadze, through negotiations with the United States and West Germany, allowed all of Eastern Europe to secede from the empire without firing a shot. As the process was unfolding, the West faced the question of how we could help ease the transition in countries that had formerly been held captive by the Russians.

The Wall Comes Tumbling Down

Lee Hamilton, Dante Fascell, and I were amazed that the administration was, at first, slow to respond with economic help to the former Soviet satellites. As the old Marxist economies in Eastern Europe transitioned to a market-oriented system, it was clear to us that the workforce in the region would experience tremendous economic hardship. At no time in world history had there been an attempt to devolve a rigid, centrally controlled Marxist economy into a capitalist one—and the potential for chaos was enormous. Without economic and technical help to ease them through the chaos and loss of income

associated with transformation, economically displaced workers might produce a backlash against Western-oriented reformers and thus resuscitate the
Marxist apparatchiks who had run the region for a generation.

Events occurring every day in Central and Eastern Europe were truly unprecedented and transformational. The challenges, the opportunities, and the
stakes were enormous. Eastern Europe had been without freedom, without
the rule of law, and without a functioning market economy for half a century;
Russia had *never* experienced them. What was at stake was whether events
would lead to the establishment of open, civic societies, or a slide back into
authoritarianism. It would be a race between opportunity and chaos.

It was clear that West Germany would provide whatever help was needed to
bring East Germany along, but the other former Soviet satellites would need
immediate help. The countries that seemed most ready to receive it were Poland
and Hungary, with Czechoslovakia next in line. Countries that had been operating through centralized governments and centrally run economies needed to
develop a system of real markets, real pricing, a real commercial code to govern
real transactions in a real, privatized capitalistic system, a real court system with
due process of law, and, at the least, a new set of public institutions to help make
all those things function. They also needed a large infusion of Western capital.

Hamilton and I wanted to develop a congressional aid package that was
more aggressive than that envisioned by the Bush administration. I talked
to Larry Eagleburger, Jim Baker's deputy secretary of state, and urged him to
ask for more funds for both political and economic reasons. Politically, we
thought that if America were stingy, it might weaken the hands of the most
pro-Western elements in Eastern Europe. Economically, we felt not only that
Eastern Europe would eventually provide good markets for American goods
and services but also it was not in America's economic interests to have the
West Germans, French, and British beat us into those markets.

While the administration did not want to ask for a larger package, they
would not block one, and they were unsure of how to proceed. Eagleburger
asked one thing of me. "Look," he admitted. "Frankly, right now we are not
sure what aid will do the most good and where we ought to focus it. We think
that opportunities will be very different in Poland, Czechoslovakia, and Hungary, for instance. Give us some elbow room. Trust us. For the first year, give
us as much flexibility as possible in where and how to spend whatever you
appropriate. After the first year, if we screw up, give us hell. But let us take
advantage of what opportunities come up."

When you have a reasonable degree of trust in someone, policy options are
much broader than when you don't. I trusted Eagleburger and thought that

he made sense, but we did not give them carte blanche. We made funds available subject to the notification process so before they made major decisions, we retained the capacity for significant input. But beyond that, they were given a significant degree of flexibility. Hamilton worked with the authorizing committee to shape the authorizing legislation, and together we pushed to expand the administration's package.

The Bush administration's initial response in 1989 was a modest package of assistance directed largely through the international banks. After much prodding from Dick Gephardt, Hamilton, Fascell, and me, the administration proposed a tiny $125 million bilateral aid package over three years for Poland and Hungary. Lech Walesa was urging a $10 billion Western aid effort. Dick Gephardt, the House majority leader, pulled together a task force to fashion a much more expansive proposal, and in November we pushed through a $650 million appropriations package.

The next year the administration asked for what was essentially a status quo budget for the region—a $300 million request—actually less than what we had appropriated the year before. They did, however, ask for an increase in military assistance to Third World countries. I pushed through the House an alternative that rejected the increase in military aid and contained a $490 million aid package for Eastern Europe. The Senate passed a $390 million plan, and in conference we produced a $440 million compromise, a 45 percent increase in Bush's request.

Matt McHugh and I also took the lead in pushing absolutely crucial debt relief for Poland. During the 1980s the Polish communist government had followed incredibly irresponsible fiscal policies, which had thoroughly disrupted the Polish economy. To cover their mistakes they had borrowed almost $40 billion from Western governments and commercial banks. That debt was largely uncollectible because Poland was broke. The banks knew that, but they continued to carry the debts with promises of repayment on their balance sheets to improve the appearance of their books. I was concerned that if a new source of capital became available through the creation of the new European Development Bank that the administration was recommending, the banks would then suddenly be able to insist that money extracted from America's taxpayers for the purpose of helping to build Poland's economy would instead be recycled to pay off Western European governments and banks. That would mean that American taxpayers' money would be used to repay those banks for loans they should never have made to the old communist government, because of its irresponsible economic policies in the 1980s.

To protect the taxpayers from that scam, I insisted that our committee would only support funding for the new bank *if* the administration led the charge to recognize that the official government-to-government debt was largely uncollectible, and if they pressured West European commercial banks to do the same. Poland's success was crucial to the stabilization of Eastern Europe and could serve as an example to reformers in Russia that transformation was possible. The issue threw me into partnership with—of all people—Danny Rostenkowski, who understood what was at stake for Poland, and despite our other differences, we worked together to win administration support.

At first, the administration opposed my demands but finally acquiesced. After we passed legislation conditioning U.S. membership in the bank on recognition of the uncollectibility of most of Poland's debt, David Mulford, Treasury Undersecretary for International Affairs, was able to convince other governments of the necessity to do that. Our efforts to persuade Western commercial banks to recognize the same reality and provide comparable treatment was more difficult and were not dealt with until the Clinton years, when the issue was handled by Clinton's Treasury undersecretary, Larry Summers. Leszek Balcerowicz, the Polish deputy prime minister and minister of finance, later told me that the action we had taken on the Polish debt overhang was the single most helpful action the West had taken in assisting Poland's transformation to a Western capitalist democracy.

Russian Aid

The most challenging and controversial issues surrounding the collapse of the Iron Curtain were those involving the collapse of the Soviet Union itself. The task of moving the Soviet economic system from an ossified, centrally planned Marxist economy to a more market-oriented economy was immense. The process had caused the collapse of the value of the ruble and the precipitous decline in the earning power of Soviet workers.

The backlash against reform was as immense as it was predictable. Soviet citizens may have been excited about the prospect of newfound political freedoms, but they were shattered and disillusioned by the collapse of their buying power. Many became suspicious that the economic pain and chaos associated with the transition was due to Western economic prescriptions rather than the inevitable side effects of the collapse of an archaic way of doing business.

Seventy years earlier, after World War I, the West had squeezed Germany dry by requiring large war reparations. When the German economy failed during the worldwide Great Depression in the 1920s and 1930s, Hitler blamed America and Europe for the economic hardships that ensued. German bitterness was exploited by Hitler in his rise to power, which resulted in the deaths of millions of people. After World War II, under the leadership of FDR and Harry Truman, America had learned a lesson. We built a network of financial, economic, and military institutions, and we produced the unprecedented Marshall Plan, which rebuilt Germany and much of Europe. While we did not have the capacity to rebuild Russia after its collapse in 1990, we tried to cushion their fall in order to minimize the chance for a very unhappy ending to the story. We also needed to be careful about the nature of U.S. involvement in Soviet economic changes lest we take ownership of Soviet policy failures in the eyes of the Russian people.

For three years the U.S. debate raged about how much help was justified and how it should be delivered. In August of 1991, Communist Party stalwarts staged a last-gasp counterrevolution against Gorbachev's government. That explosion took place the week before we were scheduled for another Aspen conference—in Budapest. Among those attending the conference from the Congress were Sam Nunn, Dick Lugar, and Carl Levin from the Senate, and Les Aspin, Lee Hamilton, and me from the House. Several key Russian officials, such as deputy defense minister Andrei Kokoshin and deputy foreign minister Andrei Kozyrev, had been scheduled to join us. As we flew to Budapest, however, the events we saw on CNN were bleak. It looked like the old-line communists had won the day. Then Boris Yeltsin mounted the tanks surrounding the Kremlin, rallied the nation, and the communist counterrevolution collapsed. By the time we got to Budapest it appeared that the counterrevolution had been put down, but we expected to be meeting without our Russian counterparts. To our delight and amazement, both Kokoshin and Kozyrev showed up. Kozyrev told us a revealing story.

At that time, Gorbachev was president of what was left of the Soviet Empire and Yeltsin was president of Russia proper. Gorbachev had been out of Moscow at his country dacha when the counterrevolutionaries struck. He and his wife had been held in virtual house arrest. When the uprising occurred, Yeltsin was barricaded in the Russian White House. The world watched as he dramatically mounted a tank and rallied the crowd in defense of the government.

Kozyrev told us that Yeltsin had seen George H. W. Bush interviewed on television and was highly disturbed by what he had conveyed: a sense that the counterrevolutionaries had won and that the United States would have to try to work with the new government. Yeltsin called Kozyrev and told him he had to get out of the country, get to the West, and let people know that the issue was still hanging in the balance. He recounted how he had stepped through the lines of tanks at the Russian White House, gone home to get his passport, and headed for the airport. Security forces, responding to orders from the counterrevolutionaries, had instructions to watch for Kozyrev and arrest him on sight, but they made a key mistake—they still thought like old-line Soviet bureaucrats. Since government officials always traveled with special arrangements of convenience, the security forces staked out the airport VIP exit rooms that were normally used by Soviet officialdom. But in this case Kozyrev left through the regular departure gates used by the general public and thus avoided their net. When he got to the West, he gave a number of media interviews urging Western leaders to recognize that the fight was not over. Their attitude noticeably stiffened, and within days Yeltsin was back in control.

The second day of our conference, Kokoshin and Kozyrev asked a few of us to gather for a private meeting. They described their worries to us in blunt terms. Kokoshin was worried that there might be a rebellion from Russian army officers who had been asked by Gorbachev to withdraw from East Germany. Army officers were accustomed to decent living quarters in East Germany, but in Russia they faced a housing crisis. There was no decent place for those withdrawing Russian army officers to be housed as they came home. "That made them more susceptible to suggestions that they were better off under old-line communism, and that they should help stifle Gorbachev's reform drive," Kokoshin said. He urged us to think about helping to establish a Russian officer housing fund to increase the officers' acceptance of Gorbachev's decision to peacefully leave Eastern Europe.

Kozyrev's concern was even more disturbing. He told us that the biggest threat to security in the old Soviet Union was the collapse of the Russian economy and Russia's inability to pay Soviet military and Soviet nuclear scientists a living wage. He said that there were hundreds of opportunities for out-of-work nuclear weapons scientists, military facility guards, and security forces to succumb to the bribes and blandishments of terrorists and agents of rogue governments, giving them access to nuclear material and tactical nuclear weapons. Both Kozyrev and Kokoshin urged us to establish an effort to defuse the situation by (1) providing funds that could be used to transition scientists into other lines of work and (2) helping assure that those guarding nuclear material did not think that the only way to feed their families was to sell access to the material.

When we returned home, McHugh, Hamilton, and I worked out an agreement to put some stopgap funding into the appropriations bill until Les Aspin, Sam Nunn, and Dick Lugar could establish a regular authorization for such a program. I sat down with Dick Gephardt and Jack Murtha, the Defense Subcommittee chairman, and we agreed to use a combination of defense and foreign aid funds to initiate assistance to the former Soviet Union. This supplemental aid initiated what is now referred to as Nunn-Lugar assistance. I was stunned by the resistance that confronted us within the Congress when we tried to push the idea. A surprising number of members still saw the world through Cold War glasses, did not want to help the Russians on anything, and refused to recognize that, in this instance, by helping the Russians we were helping ourselves. Fortunately, we were eventually able to overcome that resistance, and the initiative was established. The program remains in effect today and is now known as the Nunn-Lugar fund. I continue to be astounded that even in the wake of 9/11, some Republican conservatives have persisted in dragging their feet on the issue of adequate funding for this absolutely crucial initiative.

It is clear that without the Aspen Institute conferences, the Nunn-Luger program would not have come about until much later. Those Aspen conferences helped deepen the knowledge of key members about Eastern Europe, the Soviet Union, and Russia itself. They brought us together with dozens of U.S. experts and many Eastern European and Russian officials who would never have been as frank with us in official government meetings as they were over dinner and drinks. Besides adding to our knowledge of the many issues that defined our political relationship with each other, the conferences added a personal dimension. We came to know politicians from East Germany, Poland, Czechoslovakia, Hungary, the Ukraine, and Russia in a much more personal way, and that made a big difference in our ability to understand events as they unfolded. Viewed from today's vantage point, that period is truly breathtaking in the changes it produced. In the five years since Gorbachev had come to power, one change after another had cascaded across the face of Europe.

- In January 1986 Gorbachev addressed the communist central committee announcing his intention to proceed with his twin reforms *Glasnost* and *Perestroika*. That speech triggered a cascade of events that changed the world.
- In December 1988 Gorbachev made a dramatic speech at the UN that renounced the Brezhnev doctrine, which had been used by the Soviets to control Eastern Europe.
- In January 1989 peaceful protests began in Czechoslovakia. That same month, Shevardnadze announced that fifty thousand Soviet troops would be pulled out of Warsaw Pact countries along with their tactical nuclear weapons.
- In February 1989 Vaclav Havel was released from jail.
- At the end of March 1989 East and West German militaries met to begin discussions of disarmament.

- In April 1989 the Soviets announced a timetable for withdrawing troops from East Germany.
- In May 1989 an opposition newspaper was published in Poland, followed by elections for the Polish Sejm.
- In July 1989 Wojciech Jaruzelski was elected president and was forced to select a Solidarity leader as prime minister in Poland.
- In August 1989 Hungary announced it would allow East Germans who wanted to emigrate to the West to cross their territory. Later that same month, Finance Minister Balcerowicz announced Poland's decision to undertake a sweeping change to a market-based economic system, which our committee helped to facilitate.
- In October 1989 East German prime minister Eric Honicker resigned—the last of the old Soviet-style East German leaders. That was followed by the resignation of the East German Council of Ministers. Two days later East Germany opened its borders. The next day Bulgarian communist leaders were dumped, and the Berlin Wall came crashing down.
- Three weeks later the East German Communist Party collapsed.
- Over the next two weeks, the Czechoslovakian communist government dissolved. On December 25, 1989, Nikolai Ceausescu, Romania's primitive prime minister, was executed. Four days later, Vaclav Havel, who just a few months earlier had been a prisoner of state, was elected president of Czechoslovakia.

All of this happened without Soviet troops firing a shot. The wave of history rolled eastward.

- In Russia itself, Shevardnadze resigned as Soviet foreign minister and warned of an impending hard-liner coup. He was replaced by Andrei Kozyrev.
- By New Years Day 1990, Central Europe was transformed. The postwar imprisonment of Central Europe behind the Soviet Iron Curtain was over. The old order had crumbled; next to go would be the Soviet Union and Russia itself.
- In March 1990 Gorbachev announced that the Soviet Republics could leave the Soviet Union. Boris Yeltsin was elected president of the Russian Republic in June. August brought the countercoup by the old-line Soviet hard-liners.
- As we traveled to Budapest for our Aspen Institute conference, scheduled for August 24–30, the world changed before our eyes. Yeltsin mounted the tanks and rallied the Russian nation to defend its new revolution against the last gasp counterrevolution of the old guard communists. Gorbachev was released from house arrest by the coup makers who had been holding him and was reinstated as president of the Soviet Federation.

- On August 24, 1990, the Central Committee of the Communist Party of the Soviet Union itself was disbanded.
- Within months after we had returned home, the Ukraine voted to declare its independence from Russia.
- Four days before Christmas, December 20, 1990, the Soviet Union officially dissolved, replaced by a loose federation of former Soviet Republics. On Christmas Day Gorbachev resigned.
- Later in 1992, Shevardnadze would take over as head of state for Georgia. Kozyrev hung on as foreign minister until 1996 when he resigned under pressure for being too pro-Western. He was replaced by Evgeny Primakov, a former head of Soviet foreign intelligence.

The world had indeed changed. Thirty years earlier, back in college studying Russian politics, I had never considered it possible that the Soviet Union would collapse in my lifetime. Even farther from my mind was any expectation that I would play any role in dealing with such sweeping change. I had become chairman of the Foreign Operations Subcommittee at exactly the right time to be involved in the greatest foreign policy transformation in fifty years. Just two months before Gorbachev came to power in March 1985, I was fortunate to have accumulated ten years of valuable experience on the subcommittee, which better prepared me to deal with the challenges we would encounter. Through it all I was fortunate to have partners like Lee Hamilton, Matt McHugh, Mickey Edwards, Bill Lehman, Sid Yates, Charlie Wilson and Silvio Conte—especially McHugh and Hamilton—to help fashion a reasonably intelligent and responsible congressional response to the tumultuous changes the decade had produced, especially when the Bush administration's response to events in Eastern Europe were initially understated and slow footed.

IRELAND

Eastern Europe had not been the only place in Europe where the executive branch was slow to respond to change. During the 1980s, like many other Americans, I had grown accustomed seeing stories on the nightly news about bombings and other atrocities in Northern Ireland. Decades ago Eamon DeValera had succeeded in winning political independence from England for the Republic of Ireland. But independence had not come to the whole island. While Ireland as a whole was heavily Roman Catholic, the counties in the northeast were dominated by Protestants who wanted no part of independence under a Catholic majority. They insisted on remaining under British rule and the island was partitioned.

Over the decades, Catholic forces continued to agitate for reunification while Northern Ireland Protestants continued to resist their demands. The Irish Republican Army began a campaign of violence to force the British to withdraw. The island had been plunged into civil strife for years, with Irishmen killing Irishmen in a sacrilegious dispute heavily rooted in differences about how to worship God. Recurring efforts to end the dispute had met with failure. But in 1985 a new agreement was signed between the British and Irish governments. That agreement established a process for taking the first steps leading to eventual self government for Northern Ireland. As part of the agreement, the parties also agreed to establish the Ireland Fund, a fund to finance economic development in the border counties along the line that separated the two countries.

When the agreement was signed, John Hume, the great leader of peace forces in Northern Ireland, called Tip O'Neill and asked him if the United States would contribute to the fund in order to send a clear signal that America was behind the reconciliation and economic development effort. Tip worked Ronald Reagan on the proposition, and our committee was asked to provide a small $50 million contribution. Tip and Tom Foley contacted me to explain the situation, about which I knew very little, and asked my help in getting the money included in the budget. To get a better understanding of the issue, I called my old friend Chuck Daly. Daly, who had worked for John Kennedy in Larry O'Brien's congressional relations office years earlier, had been born in Dublin and still spent summers at Bantry Bay. He had served as president of the Joyce Foundation and was the person who had convinced Chicago mayor Richard Daley to try to shut off Irish-American contributions to the IRA. Chuck was enthusiastic and suggested that I talk to John Hume the next time Hume came to the States.

I met Hume shortly after Tip's call. He told me that the American support for the Ireland Fund was essential, not so much for the value of the dollars we provided but more for the moral force we would put behind efforts to help get Catholics and Protestants to work with one another in work projects financed by the fund. After the program got under way, I visited Derry and Belfast, and saw young Protestant and Catholic teenagers working side-by-side in community development projects, rebuilding neighborhoods that had been bombed by terrorists. I also saw the bombed-out buildings and scarred walls that defined both cities. Our committee provided only a small amount of money for the fund, but we had faced large obstacles in doing it. First, the very fact that Tip O'Neill supported the fund made it a target of the know-nothing Republican right. They viewed the program as just one Irish pol sending some money back to the "old sod." They ridiculed it as Tip's boondoggle. The IRA hated the idea too. It was not difficult for them to prod several Irish-American organizations with close ties to the IRA such as the Ancient Order of Hibernians to denounce the program as wasteful.

Despite harassment by the GOP O'Neill-haters and American IRA patsies, we kept the money in the bill. It made no earth-shattering contribution in Northern Ireland, but it did put the United States visibly on the side of promoting the peace process and has probably done more good than much of the aid we provided to countries around the world through the years. On a personal level, this process enhanced my life because it brought me to my friendship with John Hume. A visit to Ireland in the early 1990s allowed me to watch him work, as he, on a daily basis, engaged in acts of reconciliation. It also exposed me to one of the most stunning examples of venality that I have ever encountered.

In 1991, after the Aspen Institute Conference on the Soviet Union in Budapest, I joined Tom Foley in Ireland for a series of meetings there. After visiting with Hume we met with Ian Paisley, the leader of the Ulster Protestant Unionists. When Paisley greeted us, I was struck by his command of the English language. He was an erudite conversationalist and spoke with an almost Churchillian flair, but he was no Churchill! Within ten minutes of our arrival he was spewing forth a vicious anti-Catholic diatribe. Members like Foley and Richie Neal tried to lead him into constructive dialogue, but he would have none of it. Finally, several of us stood up to leave and informed him that insofar as we could determine, he was a person of absolutely no redeeming social value.

The difference between Paisley and Hume was stunning. Paisley was a fierce and vicious proponent of the status quo who sought victory by tenaciously appealing to the worst and most paranoid instincts of his fellow man. Hume was just the opposite, risking his life to try to bring about peaceful change by appealing to the very best in human nature. Seeing Paisley just once was enough to make me understand how difficult it is for more reasonable Protestant leaders like David Trimble to keep the lines of communication open between the two camps.

Since that trip, I have continued to see John and Pat when they come to this country for St. Patrick's Day celebrations. Today, a governing structure in Northern Ireland has been established that has led to a power-sharing arrangement between Catholic and Protestant leaders. Unfortunately, it has been suspended three times when the actions of extremists on both sides have outflanked the compromisers. Until recently, a core problem has been the insistence of the IRA on dragging its feet in decommissioning its stores of weapons and resolving to use only peaceful methods to settle grievances. When asked through the years by Irish Americans what could be done to help the situation, I have told them that the single most constructive step they can take is to refuse to send the IRA one dime until they publicly lay down their arms and—once and for all—renounce the use of violence. That would remove the strongest argument Paisley has used to resist reconciliation and would help move Ireland toward a new day. The IRA played too many games for too long on that issue and, in parliamentary elections in Great Britain, Trimble forces lost out to the seventy-nine-year-old Paisley, who is once again in the ascendancy in Protestant Ulster politics. One happy note is that, with a few isolated exceptions, the killing has stopped. The IRA belatedly agreed to the decommissioning of arms. Had they done so earlier, they would have had a more forthcoming adversary to deal with in Trimble than they do in Paisley.

Looking back at those events now, there is no question in my mind that in the ten years that I chaired the Foreign Operations Subcommittee, Congress played a key and constructive role in helping to manage the collapse of the Cold War and the bipolar world we had lived in since 1945.

For three years, the authorization committee had not been able to pass a foreign aid authorization, in large part because the Reagan and Bush administration wanted to stave off policy directions from the authorizing committee. That meant that most issues had been fought out on our appropriations bill. That was a much more difficult venue for us because congressional rules of procedure limited the policy actions Congress could take on appropriations bills. But we were able to have a major impact on policy because Hamilton and I worked well together and also we had such an effective House subcommittee team and a cooperative Senate counterpart in Pat Leahy.

In the eighties, working with Jim Wright, Dave Bonior, and so many others we created enough pressure to bring the Contra war to an end, give several administrations the backing they needed to move the Middle East peace process forward, raise human rights considerations to a higher level than would have otherwise been the case, buttress the clandestine efforts to harass the Russians in Afghanistan, and push the Bush administration into more aggressive assistance to Eastern Europe and Russia itself. We passed, in 1988, the first foreign assistance appropriation to deal with the emergence of a new disease that would wipe out millions of people around the globe—HIV/AIDS—a disease that had not even existed when I was first elected to Congress. We decided to specify in the Foreign Aid bill a defined amount of funding for HIV/AIDS programs run by the World Health Organization because the Reagan administration would not initiate a program on its own. At the urging of Nancy Pelosi and John Porter, I also held the first hearing on the international HIV/AIDS issue ever conducted by the Congress.

For part of that decade I also worked with Bob Kasten (who defeated Gaylord Nelson for his Senate seat in 1980 and who became Senate chair of Foreign Operations) to make the U.S. Agency for International Development and international financial institutions like the World Bank more sensitive to environmental impacts of their development projects. We were also successful in designating the first funding for child survival programs—programs like immunization and prevention of such childhood diseases as polio and measles—programs that led to saving the lives of millions of children from preventable diseases.

Most rewarding to me, in human terms, was the knowledge that we had been able to make a difference to hundreds of thousands of children around the world. Americans are not fond of foreign aid, but they would feel much better about that particular use of their tax money if they fully appreciated how many children's lives have been saved by the actions of international agencies, including private charities through whom their tax money was put to life-saving use. Of all the awards and citations I have ever received, the one that gave me the most satisfaction is the one I received from UNICEF. When presented with the award at a dinner in Washington, Abe Pollin said, "You have no idea the number of children's lives that have been saved because of your support for global children's programs." He was right; I didn't, but however many it has been, it has been a privilege!

A Transitional President

George H. W. Bush was one of the most pleasant men to deal with in politics. As a product of World War II, and as a combat veteran, he had experienced firsthand the consequences of war. He understood the international institutions that had been built by FDR, Harry Truman, and the other legendary "Wise Men" of that era. His experience as CIA director and as ambassador to China gave him a textured understanding of the complexities and subtleties of world affairs and stamped him as a committed internationalist. He was comfortable in international affairs and that was where he focused his attention, but he was not nearly as comfortable dealing with issues at home, and it showed.

Domestically the Bush years were marked by recession and an ever-burgeoning deficit. As the recession bit into the national psyche, the huge popularity Bush had garnered with his handling of Iraq disappeared. That was not what any of us expected. A decade earlier, during the 1980 presidential primary campaign, Bush characterized Ronald Reagan's assertion that the budget could be balanced while doubling military spending and cutting taxes as being "voodoo economics." But after two terms as Reagan's vice president, he was stuck. His "Read my lips; no new taxes!" pledge at the 1988 GOP convention had locked him into continuing the Reagan fiscal policies that piled deficit upon deficit.

In 1988, shortly after Bush defeated Michael Dukakis for the presidency, Rep. Sonny Montgomery, a conservative Mississippi Democrat and an old Bush friend, called me and said, "Dave, George Bush asked me if I would put together a small group of reasonable Democrats whom he could meet with. Would you be willing to come down to the vice president's residence and have a drink and some conversation with him?" "Sure," I said. Bush invited me into the sitting room, motioned me to the bar, and said, "Have a drink and grab a chair." My mind flashed back to the earlier time when I had asked Carter to have the same kind of meetings with House members.

Minutes later Nick Brady, Bush's new secretary of the treasury, walked in. Seated in a corner chair, Bush motioned Brady to the bar and said, "Nick, would you get me the usual with just a splash." I wondered what "the usual" was. I watched Brady pour vodka into a glass and then drip a thin layer of gin across the top of the drink and hand it to Bush. We sat around talking for about an hour. I was struck by how relaxed and practical Bush's comments were. He certainly came off like a Yale preppie, but a very nice one. I walked out thinking, "Here is a practical man who had gotten himself in a box with his 'no tax' speech." I was convinced that he would stick to that promise for a few months, but that the reality of the future deficit numbers would move him off his promise. I was off by a year.

For the first year of his presidency, Bush kept the country on the Reagan glide path, but by the second year the long-term deficit numbers were so serious he had to move. A budget summit conference was convened at Andrews Air Force Base. After several weeks of hard negotiations, a deal was struck calling for significant additional spending restraint and some increased "revenue enhancements" (as Bush people preferred to call tax increases). I wanted to vote for the package because we badly needed to cut the rising deficit, but the deal loaded deficit reduction on the backs of the middle class, the poor, and Medicare while not laying a glove on the richest. The package increased taxes on taxpayers in the $20,000 range by roughly twice the percentage that it did for those making $200,000 plus.

George Miller of California and I, in the House, and Byron Dorgan, in the Senate, raised our objections with our party leadership. My Wisconsin colleague, Jim Moody, called it "the Leona Helmsley budget" because it said that "only little people pay taxes." On the Republican side Newt Gingrich led a rebellion against the package; he wanted no tax increase whatsoever. So both of us, for opposite reasons, worked to bring the package down. Both of us were gambling that if the package went down it would come back in a form more favorable to us than the original. One of us had to be wrong, but we didn't know which. When the vote came, fifty-five House Democrats joined Miller and me in killing the package on a 254 to 179 vote. Tom Foley was furious with us. For three days we rode out a firestorm, but in the end, Danny Rostenkowski and the White House got the message that Democrats would swallow hard and cast politically painful votes for a tax increase, but *only* if it was fair to working people.

In the days before the first budget package went down, Byron Dorgan and I got together and began to work out a set of alternatives to provide a more progressive package that those of us who were voting against the original proposal could buy. More than fifty Democrats signed onto our package to put pressure on the Ways and Means Committee to move our way. Rosty had breakfast with the president and told him he was changing the revenue package to move a larger share of the tax hit up the income scale to the high rollers. The share of new taxes paid by middle- and lower-income taxpayers dropped significantly, while the tax hit on those making $200,000 or more increased from $2.3 billion to $9 billion.

The final package called for additional spending restraint and moderately raised taxes on a progressive, ability-to-pay basis. Number-crunchers estimated that future deficits would be about one-third larger without the package than they would be with it. Bush's support for the package would cost him the support of the Republican Right in 1990, but it was the right thing to do. It was the first necessary step in getting control of the deficit—a job that would not be finished until the election of Bill Clinton.

George H. W. Bush had been a transitional president. The world changed mightily on his watch. The 1990 budget deal began to put in place needed changes in U.S. fiscal policy. And close to home for me, change had swept the Congress as an institution, and not all of it was good.

CHAPTER 16

❧

Poison in the House,
Poison at Home

In some ways, over the decades, the House had become a better place to do business. Junior members were treated with more respect than had been the case a decade earlier, and the education level of members had risen markedly. But politics was also slowly changing in ways that made Washington a much nastier and more bitter place.

When Jim Wright succeeded Tip O'Neill as Speaker on January 6, 1987, I felt a sad ache in my heart. Six years earlier I had been greatly disappointed—but not surprised—that Tip had done so little to help me with the Budget Committee chairmanship. I knew that Tip had been under heavy pressure from Danny Rostenkowski, Jack Murtha, and his young staffer, Ari Weiss, to do as little as possible to help me. Danny and Jack each had their personal reasons, and Tip was concerned that, in the wake of Reagan's sweeping win, maybe a more conservative chairman like Jim Jones was the safer way to go. In the days after that Budget chairmanship election, I felt that Tip had let me down—especially because I believed I had been hurt with people like Danny and Murtha precisely because I had carried the load Tip had asked me to carry on the ethics package four years earlier. Tip pretty much said the same thing in his autobiography *Man of the House*.

Recounting the controversy over the ethics code that Lee Hamilton and I had written, Tip wrote, "The ethics bill was highly unpopular and on a secret ballot it would have been defeated overwhelmingly. Although Dave Obey did a terrific job, that bill made him so many enemies that a couple of years later he was narrowly defeated in the caucus for chairman of the Budget Committee, a vote he should have won easily. Obey is a great legislator, but my confidence in him may have inadvertently thwarted his rise to a position of elected leadership."

273

Bob Michel, the GOP minority leader, saw it the same way. "Dave cleaned the place up," he told the *Milwaukee Journal* in 1990. "He feels strongly about the institution. And as a result he was pretty soundly maligned by his own party." The *Milwaukee Journal* reported it this way: "Probably the most angry was Dan Rostenkowski (D-Ill.) the chairman of the powerful Ways and Means Committee. The often heard comment on Capitol Hill is that Dave Obey's limit on outside income cost Rostenkowski, and he spent the 1980s trying to get even. It's no secret that Rostenkowski directed the campaign against Obey for the prestigious budget chairmanship of the House in 1998. . . . His press secretary, Jim Jaffe, said Rostenkowski wanted Obey beaten for budget chairman but Jaffe wouldn't say revenge was the motivator." In the same story I told the *Journal,* "The ethics package earned me the long-term enmity of some senior members around this place. I was asked to do a job and I did it with enthusiasm. You pay a price for those things. I took the heat. The old bulls were mad because Tip didn't save them from the reformers. I was the guy out there carrying the spear." But my personal disappointment was minor in comparison to my admiration for the man.

When Reagan came to power, the White House and the GOP Campaign Committee tried to make Tip a national punching bag—a symbol of everything that was wrong with government. They pounded him unmercifully and personally, but he knew what he believed and never apologized for it. He rope-a-doped them until we could get our footing and fought back with the heart of a lion. And gradually, instead of seeing him as the caricature the GOP tried to make of him, the country began to see him as a fighter for fairness and justice for the little guy. I loved him as a person, I admired what he stood for, and I was sorry when he retired.

WRIGHT GOES DOWN

When Jim Wright succeeded Tip as Speaker in 1987, I expected to be disappointed in his leadership, but he quickly impressed me as a far more effective leader than I had anticipated. Out of the box, he focused on four issues: job creation, infrastructure modernization, the illegal Contra war, and the growing gap between rich and poor. He quickly made clear to me that our JEC reports on the concentration of wealth should be at the center of the Democratic Party message. He dug both deep and wide into whatever issue he tackled—a quality that I had not previously seen in him. When the White House asked him to get involved in Nicaragua, they must have expected him to be compliant with administration policy—as he had earlier been with the Nixon administration's undercover war in Cambodia. But the administration got more than they bargained for. Wright was one Texan who knew Central America. He spoke the language. Determined to preserve congressional war-making prerogatives from encroachment by the executive, he became a powerful force for ending that war.

Newt Gingrich was so infuriated by Jim's refusal to be a patsy that he mounted an attack on Jim's ethical vulnerabilities. After Wright's effectiveness on Nicaragua became clear, Dick Cheney joined in the attack. Within two and a half years, Jim was driven from office, a victim of minor ethical peccadilloes and Washington's increasing meanness. And he was not the only victim of Washington's changing culture; another was the House of Representatives itself. Increasingly the House was becoming a snake pit. One major cause of that development was the changing nature of politics and the altered human relationships that flowed from it; the other was the camera.

By 1989 the House had become a very different institution than it had been when I first entered it twenty years earlier. In 1969, except for a few issues like the Vietnam War, the House was a place of political controversy, not political war. Like the Wisconsin legislature, members would debate and clash during the day but then often have a friendly drink across the aisle in the evening. Members brought their families to Washington. They got to know each other's spouses and their kids. It was pretty difficult to cut somebody's heart out in a political debate on the floor when you would see their families socially the next evening. But by 1989 all that had changed. More and more members were leaving their families at home in their districts. That made it harder and harder to get work done on Mondays and Fridays because members were pushing for time at home with their families. Also, politics was changing. More polling and more consultants meant costlier campaigns, which meant more fundraising. And some of those consultants knew how to get down-and-dirty mean.

In the 1950s America's quintessential character assassin had been Murray Chotiner, Nixon's political hitman. High-powered hit-and-run consultants were then mostly confined to presidential campaigns and a few Senate campaigns that could afford to be professionalized. But by 1979 consultants and polling firms had multiplied and penetrated scores of House campaigns. Campaigns became more vicious. They had become "Atwaterized" (Lee Atwater was the ruthless "Go for the jugular, win at any cost!" consultant who dominated GOP politics in the 1980s until he died prematurely of a brain tumor). And the kind of people coming into the House was changing, too, as was the language they were willing to use to get and stay there.

Newt Gingrich arrived in the House in 1978. Disciples like Bob Walker came shortly afterwards. In his first try for public office, Newt had run against Georgia conservative Democrat John Flint as a Rockefeller Republican and as an environmental "New Ager," but it didn't take long for Gingrich to change. Attending a conservative Republican political conference arranged by Paul Weyrich, Gingrich experienced a "St. Paul on the Road to Damascus" conversion. He realized that the path to power within the Republican Party led through the right wing because that was the road paved with—and smoothed by—a highly developed network of big money and ideological think tanks. He learned a new political language, and after his election began to recruit like-minded souls to run for the House. Those candidates were relentlessly coached and given lists of loaded words they should use to cut up and tar their political opponents—words like "corrupt," "decayed," and "sick" that changed political opponents from being "wrong" to being "evil."

When Reagan came to office in 1980, he had been presented with comprehensive plans of action designed by that same network of right-wing think tanks—such as the Heritage Foundation—financed by the country's high rollers. Newt and his allies expanded that network. They became more and more aggressive and vicious in the rhetoric they used on the floor. In any previous time that would not have amounted to much, but one aspect of the House—the camera—allowed them to reach a far wider audience than in the past.

Under Tip O'Neill, the House agreed to allow TV coverage of the floor by C-Span, and the camera changed everything. BC—Before Camera—members delivered speeches during debate that were aimed at undecided members in order to win a floor vote. To be effective in debate, you had to be thoughtful, persuasive, and needed to appeal across the aisle. AC—After Camera—fewer and fewer speeches were aimed at changing the minds of undecided colleagues through reason and persuasion. Instead they were aimed at inflaming the viewing audience. The Gingrich forces began to use Special Orders (speeches given on the House floor at night, after the day's legislative business was completed and almost everyone had left) to spout inflammatory rhetoric aimed at undermining the Democratic majority. The attack that Bob Walker, Bob Livingston, and Gingrich leveled at Jim Wright and a number of others, including me, for writing our letter to Daniel Ortega urging free election in Nicaragua was but one example.

I was convinced that Newt's attacks on Jim Wright were rooted in the fact that Gingrich and Cheney were becoming more and more alarmed about Jim's effectiveness. Gingrich was quoted in the press saying that, with time,

Jim might prove to be the most effective Democratic House leader in a generation. Newt was looking for ways to cut Jim down before that could happen, and he finally found one. Wright had published a book that came under fire from Newt as violating the House limit on outside income.

Because we had not wanted to discourage members from adding to public knowledge about how government worked by writing about it, the new ethics rules that Lee Hamilton and I had written specifically provided an exception for book royalties to the outside-income limitation rule. Jim, however, had followed an unusual route in publishing and distributing his book, and some lobbyists had evidently made bulk purchases. Gingrich and his allies demanded an investigation by the House Ethics Committee, and the committee finally appointed a special counsel to dig into the situation. I could not speak to Jim's other business arrangements, but I felt that the code's royalty provision specifically exempted Jim's situation from review. In a memo I told the committee that if Jim's conduct had strayed from the rules, he should be charged under the code's "general duty" clause, which provides that every member has the general duty to conduct his or her financial affairs in a manner that does not bring discredit upon the House.

I asked to appear before the committee to explain what our intent had been when we drafted it, but Richard Phelan, who had been appointed special counsel, would not allow me to testify. I thought then, and still do, that his refusal was wrong. It meant that Wright was being judged by what Phelan *thought* the intent had been, after the fact. In the "if they're accused, they must be guilty" mood that permeated Washington in those days, Jim never had a chance, and within weeks he resigned. Ironically, years after Wright's scourging, Gingrich himself would announce that he was receiving a six-figure advance from a Rupert Murdoch publishing house to write his own book, an event that triggered his own downfall.

Changes in the House were also magnified by the way the institution was covered by the press. In the 1950s and '60s the press had much more of a mind to separate official life from private life when covering the actions of public officials. They were, in fact, more willing to give public officials the benefit of the doubt all across the board. Vietnam and Watergate changed all that. So by 1989 everything about Washington—the politics, the politicians, and the press—was becoming simultaneously meaner and more trivial. Politicians were being covered less as policy makers and more as political soap opera celebrities.

In that atmosphere, the Congress itself became a target of one cynical press attack after another. The frenzy was fed by several right-wing interest groups that used the controversies to try to discredit Congress in order to give their government deregulation agenda a greater chance to succeed. Their goal was to weaken the public's confidence in Congress as an institution so that they would vote out the Democratic majority, which stood in the way of corporate America's ability to do whatever they pleased. These special-interest groups fed the press countless so-called think pieces attacking the Congress, trying to build public resentment.

With Wright's downfall, Tom Foley became Speaker, but not before he, too, was dumped on by Gingrich's political garbage truck. Newt was ever busy spreading his poison around Capitol Hill. In the chaos of the Wright downfall, he wanted more than just Jim's blood, and one of Newt's staffers was anonymously quoted for spreading spurious rumors about him. That episode convinced me that Gingrich was totally without redeeming social value—a political sociopath whose venality matched that of Joe McCarthy's.

Tom Foley was an able, thoughtful, dignified, and decent human being. More than any other incident, the campaign of personal destruction waged against him demonstrated how much the House had come to resemble a poisonous snake pit. It was clear to me that, in the eyes of the GOP leadership and their political allies around Washington, there was only one rule: "Anything goes!" It was clear that some House Republicans had been out of power for so long and were so desperate to come in out of the wilderness that there was no limit to the damage they were willing to do in order to again seize power. V. O. Key, the noted political scientist, once defined a political party as an organized, legal conspiracy to seize and hold power. Never had I seen a more vicious and ruthless example of that definition than the path to power that Gingrich had chosen to pursue. He had become the ultimate practitioner of the politics of personal and institutional destruction. And that was the atmosphere in the Congress as the Bush administration was experiencing its last days.

POISON AT HOME

Throughout the 1980s and into the early 1990s, the House had been awash in political poison. During that same period, Wisconsin was immersed in its own toxic controversy. It began with a federal court decision in the State of Washington.

In 1974 I watched my friend Lloyd Meeds struggle with the public anger that engulfed the State of Washington when a federal court ruled, in the Boldt decision, that nineteenth-century Indian treaties, long assumed obsolete, were alive and well. United States district judge George Boldt ruled that treaties negotiated between the federal government and Native American tribes, which moved those tribes to reservations to make way for white settlers, had reserved to the tribes the right *in perpetuity* to take 50 percent of the salmon harvest in those states. When the court decision hit, it caused massive confusion and anger. Lloyd tried to push the state and the tribe to negotiate an end to the conflict by reimbursing the tribes for relinquishing the most sweeping rights they had won under the court decision. But negotiations take time, especially when blood runs hot. In the next election, Lloyd's electoral margin dropped dramatically, and personal attacks occurred on an almost daily basis.

Lloyd finally reached his limit; he decided that life was too short to take the kind of abuse directed at him because of a problem he had not caused and could do nothing to solve. He announced that he was leaving Congress. "People chose to make me a target and a scapegoat. They would not listen to a damn thing I said," Lloyd remarked. "I'm just fed up with being crucified for a problem I didn't cause. I've got better things to do with my life." Lloyd had taken a three-year pounding. My turn would come next.

In 1976, in the Voight decision, the same issue erupted in Wisconsin. Federal judge Jim Doyle ruled that the tribes had implicitly given up their treaty rights when they accepted reservations in 1854. The tribes immediately appealed, arguing that in treaties they had signed with the U.S. government in return for ceding their territory—which encompassed most of the northern half of the state—they had indeed retained the right in perpetuity to take as many fish from the streams and lakes as they wanted.

Like almost everyone else in Wisconsin, until the Voight decision, I had no idea that Wisconsin tribal treaty rights had not been extinguished long ago. As the debate raged, some people looked for a solution, while others looked for a fight. In January 1983 the Seventh Circuit Court of Appeals reversed Judge Doyle and ruled that the nineteenth-century treaties were still in effect and thus upheld treaty rights for Wisconsin's Chippewa tribes. In October 1983 the U.S. Supreme Court refused to hear the case, thereby confirming the appeals court ruling. The case was then remanded back to the district court for implementation.

In February 1987, in accordance with the higher court decision, Doyle ruled that the tribes could take as much fish as they needed—even up to 100 percent in some lakes—in order to sustain a modest standard of living. On March 3, 1989, Judge Barbara Crabb, who had taken over the case from Judge Doyle, issued a decision establishing court-drawn fishing regulations for the Chippewa. That decision was interpreted to give the tribes the right to take all the fish they wanted, and declared that absent a negotiated agreement between the state and the tribes, the Chippewa were not subject to state regulations.

Led by tribal leader Tom Maulson, the Lac du Flambeau tribe in Oneida and Vilas counties in northeast Wisconsin was the most aggressive in exercising its newly rediscovered treaty rights. Passions rose to fever pitch in the spring spawning season—a time that had traditionally been off-limits to fishing because walleye gathered in lake shallows to deposit their eggs and were extremely vulnerable. Sportsmen who had long sought the walleye with hook and line after the spawning season was over and the fish had returned to deep water were appalled as tribal members gathered at the boat landings and speared fish after fish as they fluttered in the shallow spawning grounds.

The news media, especially the television stations, hyped the story beyond all limits. Every night, the TV cameras showed up at the boat landings where tribal members were expected to be spearing. The presence of the cameras attracted hundreds of angry nontribal fishermen who wanted to protest what they regarded as "shooting fish in a barrel." Demonstrations turned violent, guns were in heavy supply on both sides, and hundreds of arrests were made. Meanwhile, George Meyer, a thoughtful key official in the Department of Natural Resources (DNR), worked mightily to keep the situation from exploding. I tried with only limited success to get church leadership to use their influence to calm the scene. A few religious leaders, especially those from Episcopal, Methodist, and Presbyterian churches, tried to help.

I held meeting after meeting with sportsmen who demanded that I get the Congress to abrogate the treaties. The congressional committees with jurisdiction in the matter made it quite clear that they would not under any circumstance do that. The Reagan Justice Department said the same thing. I tried to explain that the only way to achieve a resolution of the problem was through negotiation between the state and the tribes. The issue was so emotional that lifelong friends turned against me—even Harry Weinberger, who had been co-chairman of my state assembly campaign. Angry sportsmen set up an organization called Protect American Rights and Resources (PARR), led by Larry Peterson of Park Falls. In June 1989 Peterson announced that he would begin a petition drive, beginning in January 1990, seeking a recall election against me. That created an interesting situation, since the U.S. Constitution did not allow recall of a member of the House of Representatives. PARR ignored the fact that federal election law superseded state law. They proceeded under state law, which gave petitioners sixty days to collect forty-four thousand signatures that would trigger a recall election.

Although the House of Representatives would not recognize any such recall, the state elections board suggested that they would, in all probability, proceed to hold one anyway, unless someone sued to prevent them from doing so. I did not want to be a party to such a suit, so I decided I had no choice but to mount a campaign to educate people that the recall was just a protest publicity stunt that would waste taxpayers' money and, in the end, would be thrown out. We mounted a grassroots campaign of our own to counter the attack. When the deadline came for the petition drive, PARR fell short of the required number of signatures under state law. Not content to leave the matter there, they then turned their attention to Bob Jauch and Jim Holperin in the state legislature.

Jauch had been the leading voice of sanity in the state senate on the issue. Holperin, representing Oneida and Vilas counties, the very hotbed of the controversy, had played the same role in the state assembly. The recall effort against Jauch went nowhere, but it succeeded against Holperin. Petitioners got enough signatures to force him into a recall election, but Jim was so well regarded in the community that he survived the election. After the recall efforts, cooler heads began to prevail. Several leaders of the resort industry in Holperin's district— led by Evelyn Hartlep, executive director of the Minocqua Chamber of Commerce, and several others—realized that the constant headlines and perpetual turmoil were hurting tourism. I worked with them and others, and slowly the issue became manageable. After two more years of negotiations and several other declarations by the court, parties negotiated an agreement that scaled back the "take" by the tribes, and the state gradually settled down on the issue. But the controversy was not completely over. For more than seven years, it had made life a living hell for anyone in public office. Over that period, virtually every time I walked into a grocery store, gas station, hardware store, or restaurant I would encounter a cold shoulder or a sullen snarl from someone who was still angry about the issue. Not a week went by that did not deepen my understanding of why Lloyd Meeds had finally decided "to hell with it all." And Jauch's and Holperin's experiences demonstrated that I was not the only one with those encounters. With Jauch, the story took an especially ironic twist.

In his state senate district, the Lac Courte Ourielles tribal leader Gaishkibos had taken a more moderate line than had Tom Maulson from the Lac Du Flambeau district, but he wound up being just as tricky. Jauch had taken an enormous amount of guff in his district for saying forthrightly that while he did not like the impact of the treaties, he would not demagogue the issue of tribal sovereignty and would support negotiations, not fruitless efforts at abrogation. Imagine his surprise when the thanks Bob got for his defense of tribal sovereignty was an announcement by Gaishkibos that he was running against Bob. In the end, all I could think of to explain Gaishkibos's betrayal of Jauch, was the old adage: "No good deed goes unpunished."

Today the issue has largely subsided. It still generates significant, under-the-surface resentment, but people have at least learned to get along. In the end, reasonable people sat down with other reasonable people and, within the limits allowed by the court, worked out a series of accommodations. On occasion the issue still flares up briefly. It has been transformed from a near civil war to an irritant that conjures up unpleasant memories. In my district, the issue was by far the most tumultuous in my forty-two years of public life. The toxic atmosphere that it generated at home matched the equally poisonous changes that engulfed the Congress in Washington. And more change was on the way.

THE RISE OF CLINTON

By the early 1990s, with the loss of the Soviet Union, our major external enemy, the international consequences of domestic political decisions now began to take on a much less sober tone. That made it easier for the nation to take a flyer on the presidential candidacies of people like Ross Perot and Pat Buchanan. With no overarching need to worry about the international consequences, many Americans felt it was less dangerous to the country to cast a protest vote against the status quo by voting for a national crank. For months Buchanan, and, to a greater extent Perot, occupied the nation's attention. Millions of Republican voters were detached from George H. W. Bush by Perot's cranky outbursts, and millions more were pulled away by Pat Buchanan. When Perot then withdrew from the presidential race at the time of the 1992 Democratic convention, millions of people said, "Hell, I'm not going back to Bush!" and they were then open to an appeal for change from Bill Clinton.

All this had to happen in two stages. The public would not have been willing to leap two steps from Bush to Clinton in January, but they were willing to jump one step to Perot. Then, when Perot pulled out in July, and they had a choice of jumping back to the GOP or taking one more step to Clinton, they said, "Ah, why not!" and moved to Clinton. By the time Perot jumped *back* into the race later in the year, he had already marginalized himself. With a large assist from Buchanan, who bled off the Republican Right from Bush, Perot, in effect, elected Clinton. Eight years later Ralph Nader returned the favor for the GOP, but that is another story.

Clinton's election was a stunning example of just how spectacularly wrong conventional wisdom could be. After the 1991 Iraq War, Bush's popularity rating stood at 90 percent and virtually every political pundit (and most politicians) thought that he was unbeatable. My first choice for president was Dick

Gephardt, just as it had been four years earlier, but Dick and a number of other Democratic heavyweights took themselves out of the running early in the game.

In 1992 Clinton jumped in and began to line up support. As he began to build momentum, he was hit by gossip stories about his past relationship with women. At one point it appeared those stories would demolish his campaign in New Hampshire, but he battled back and finished second, a much stronger finish than the pre-election polls had predicted. Even though he had finished second, Clinton labeled himself the "Comeback Kid" and began to drive toward the nomination.

By the time of the Wisconsin primary, the race had been whittled down to a fight between Clinton and former governor Jerry Brown of California. I endorsed Clinton. The New York and Wisconsin primaries were held on the same day. The week before primary day, I met Clinton on a foggy, cold night at the Mosinee airport where he had just flown in from New York. All day the headlines had pounded him mercilessly. When he stepped out of the plane and climbed into the waiting car for the drive to the Legion Hall in Stevens Point for a rally, he was in a subdued mood.

That night, I saw a side of Clinton I was to see many times over the next eight years. As we pulled out of the airport, I asked him, "How are you doing? I know it's been a rough week." Without looking up at me he began to stare at the back of the driver's seat and slowly rub his hands together. "I'm all right," he said barely above a whisper. "I'm all right." Although he looked totally exhausted, he said, "But I'll get through this." He repeated again and again, "We'll get through this; we'll get through this." As we drove Clinton seemed to be mentally digging miles deep into himself. He breathed deeply four or five times, then seemed to climb emotionally back into the world around him. When we pulled up to the Legion hall he said quietly, "This is going to be a good night."

As we walked into the hall, Clinton paused, raised his head, glanced at the ceiling, drew a long deep breath, lowered his head again, and then plunged into the room. The crowd was overflowing. A rope line had been strung to give us a few feet of open space between the microphone and the crowd. From left to right Clinton worked the line. Slowly, one by one, he grasped each person's hand, holding onto it as he looked directly into their eyes, responding to each, in turn. With every person he met, he seemed to brighten as if an internal rheostat was slowly turning up the juice. I was struck by how much he seemed to be feeding on the energy and human warmth of every person with whom he talked.

With every handshake, the crowd was warming him up and energizing him. By the time he spoke, he had been transformed from a physically pallid, preoccupied, million-miles-away figure to a funny, charming master of the crowd. The energy of that crowd had flowed into his body and spirit every bit as much as if he had been given a blood transfusion. It was a remarkable thing to watch and feel. I remember thinking that I had never seen a human being who possessed such an ability to draw upon his own inner resources as he had shown in that car ride to Stevens Point. And I had never seen a politician with such an astonishing ability to soak up every bit of warmth and energy from a crowd and make it his own.

The week before the National Democratic Convention in New York, some polls showed Clinton running third behind Bush and Perot. But Perot withdrew just as the convention began. That convention made Clinton a star, and he was on his way. The week after the convention, Clinton and Al Gore, along with their wives, hit the campaign trail with an "America's Heartland" bus tour of the Midwest. When I introduced them at a barn rally on the Peck family farm in Chippewa County, I told the crowd that in my service in Congress, the only thing I every really wanted was to serve with one really great president for whom it would be worth taking giant risks. I had high hopes Clinton would be that man. He had a lot of work to do to clean up the mess left by his predecessors.

In terms of fiscal responsibility, the previous twelve years had been a disgrace. During Reagan's eight years in office he had never once sent to Congress a balanced budget. During his two terms as president, deficits totaled $1.3 trillion, and the total national debt exploded from less than $1 trillion to almost $3 trillion.

In the first year of his administration, George H. W. Bush had continued the Reagan fantasy that fiscal responsibility could be achieved with his "Read my lips; no new taxes!" approach to governing. In 1990 Bush had recognized belatedly the need to backtrack on that pledge, and the 1990 budget compromise had passed; but, as Bush left the White House in 1993, that package had only done about one-third of the job needed to get us back to balance. Clinton would have to do the rest.

~

CHAPTER 17

The Clinton
Clean-Up Brigade

When Clinton walked into the White House, the country was struggling to climb out of the 1991–92 recession, and the budget deficit was projected to rise to over $300 billion. To change that, Clinton sent Congress a comprehensive two-step game plan. Step one was a short-range package to stimulate the economy and accelerate its climb out of the previous recession by expanding unemployment insurance and increasing investments in short-term public works projects. Step two was a long-range plan to restore consumer and investor confidence, and strengthen long-term economic performance by getting the deficit under control and enhancing investments in education, science, and national infrastructure.

CLIMBING OUT OF THE DEFICIT DITCH

To fix the deficit problem, while making room for needed long-term investment in education and science, Clinton proposed a $500 billion deficit reduction package. He proposed to cut more than $200 billion out of lower priority programs and blend those cuts with added revenue—raised primarily by modestly increasing the top income tax rate that applied only to the top 2 percent of earners. The only income tax increase in Clinton's tax package was on income above $100,000. Clinton did have one modest increase that affected people making less than $100,000. It was an energy tax—a BTU equivalent tax aimed at raising revenue and promoting energy conservation at the same time. Overall, every ten dollars in deficit reduction was to be achieved by matching every five dollars in spending cuts with five dollars in tax hikes. Of every five dollars on the tax side, $3.75 was to be paid by those making $100,000 a year or more. Only $1.25 was to be paid by people making less than $100,000.

Those making less than $30,000 would have paid less or remained at their existing level. To pass the package, Clinton had to overcome the fierce opposition of Senate Republicans and some of the very same southern Democrats whose votes for Ronald Reagan's irresponsible tax bills had made possible the string of runaway deficits in the 1980s.

The most troublesome of the southern Democrats was David Boren of Oklahoma. Boren had voted for Reagan's 1981 budget, which had exploded the deficits, but he now expressed alarm that Clinton's modest, short-term economic stimulus package would increase deficits, ignoring the fact that the long-term deficit reduction in the Clinton package made up for the short-term bubble many times over. But Boren's real target was Clinton's BTU tax. Boren represented Oklahoma, and Oklahoma was dominated by oil. As a substitute for the BTU tax, which was an attempt to encourage energy efficiency, Boren proposed a cap on entitlement spending. That would have been a much sweeter deal for domestic oil producers who would not be paying the tax and it shifted billions of dollars from low-income elderly and working poor to the oil industry. The main defense of the Clinton package was that the lion's share of tax hikes would have been paid for by those making over $100,000, but the GOP demagogued the BTU tax and made it sound as though it would result in a huge hit on the middle class. That was nonsense, but it obscured our ability to show that the middle class was being protected in the overall package.

The press loved Boren; every time he was interviewed he would attack his own party's plan, so he turned up regularly on the Sunday talk shows. Boren and his allies shredded Clinton's package and proposed an approach that had the effect of shrinking the hit on high-income taxpayers by $40 billion and shifting the increase to those below them on the income scale. When Clinton's opponents finished their filibuster, about the only thing left of Clinton's BTU tax was a proposed 4.3-cent gas tax increase.

When I saw the direction things were going, I urged Clinton to completely drop the energy/gas tax. I told the White House that there was no substantive reason to keep it because a 4.3-cent gas tax was so small it would have absolutely no effect on energy consumption. "The only thing that damned nickel does at this point is to obliterate your ability to say that there is nothing in the tax package that hits workers under $100,000 in income," I told Clinton. "That gas tax is nothing but a political nuisance that gets in the way of your message that you are not raising middle-class taxes." But Clinton decided to keep it in order to avoid editorial criticism from those papers who bought into the symbolism of a gas-tax hike as a good government cause. I thought then, and still do, that it was a silly decision, which had unacceptably large negative consequences for Clinton's ability to win the budget debate.

As the debate progressed, Republicans fought the package furiously. When the final House vote on the package came late in the evening of August 5, 1993, no one knew how it would turn out. As the House vote clock ticked through the fifteen minute roll call, I stood in back of the chamber with Peter Barca, a newly elected Democrat from Wisconsin's First Congressional District, who knew when he cast his vote, he might be ending his career. "I have no choice," Peter said. "These bastards really want to bring down anything in order to win. I just couldn't live with myself if I voted with such destructive people," he told me. The bill passed by an excruciatingly close 218 to 216 margin. One vote less would have doomed it. Not a single Republican voted for the plan. The GOP leadership uniformly predicted the package would not only cause an economic recession but an explosion in both unemployment and the federal deficit. Newt Gingrich announced, "I believe this will lead to a recession next year. This is the Democrat machine's recession, and each one of them will be held personally accountable" (House press gallery, August 5, 1993). Dick Armey thundered, "Clearly, this is a job-killer in the short run. . . . The deficit will be worse. . . . The impact on job creation is going to be devastating" (CNN interview, August 2, 1993). John Kasich, the GOP Budget Committee ranking member made two wrong calls in one week. On July 28 he said, "This plan will not work. If it was to work, then I'd have to become a Democrat" (CNN). On August 3 he said, "It's our bet that this will come back here next year and try to help you when this puts the economy in the gutter" (Cong. Record). Phil Gramm predicted, "We are buying a one-way ticket to a recession" (Cong. Record August 5, 1993). Never in the modern history of Congress was a party leadership so uniformly wrong about something so important. Instead of the economic disaster they predicted, the United States was about to experience eight years of unparalleled prosperity. When the final vote came in the Senate, the victory margin was the same as it had been in the House—one vote—with not a single Republican voting to help out.

After the House vote that night, I took a long walk around the Capitol grounds in the reflected light of the magnificent dome, enjoying the soft summer evening and thinking how much things had changed since Reagan's 1981 budget victory. In 1981 the Democrats had been on the defensive, badly split, with fifty-nine Democrats voting to jump off the supply-side cliff. Countless Republicans and Democrats had told me during the ensuing twelve years after the 1981 vote that they knew they should have voted differently in 1981 but

Reagan had been "too popular to resist." I knew how they had felt—at the time Reagan's budget passed, almost 70 percent of the people in my district favored his plan.

For twelve years, under Reagan and Bush, the economic debate had been dominated and intellectually corrupted by the relentless Republican mantra that regardless of circumstances, the budget deficit could be brought under control by cutting taxes. Of course, shortly after passage of the Reagan plan, David Stockman revealed that cutting the deficit was not the real game plan. He explained that the GOP game plan had been to peddle whatever economic theory was necessary in order to reduce the amount of taxes that the most well-off citizens in the country had to pay to support the government. Despite the fact that Congress had cut Ronald Reagan's budget in seven of the eight years he was president, despite the fact that Reagan and Bush had never proposed a balanced budget, despite the fact that the Senate had been controlled by Republicans in six of the eight years that Reagan was president—despite all that, the Republicans had relentlessly pounded home the idea that they bore no responsibility for the last twelve years of Reagan-Bush deficits! Twelve years later under Clinton's leadership, some of the same Democrats who had voted for Reagan's 1981 package, like Dick Gephardt and the two Texans Charlie Stenholm and Marvin Leath, cast their votes to end the Reagan free lunch and began to drag the country out of the ditch they had helped put the country in back in 1981. Years later, Marvin Leath told his Texas colleague that the biggest mistake of his life had been his vote for the Reagan tax bill in 1981 and his best vote had been twelve years later to correct it. Stenholm said the same thing. So did Gephardt.

Throughout the 1980s I had seethed with anger, seeing the damage done to the country by twelve years of irresponsible fiscal policy and misplaced spending priorities. But on that night, after Clinton's budget repair package passed, that anger left me. I was proud of the role I had played in helping lead the fight against those disastrous 1981 actions and in fighting to change them over the next twelve years. I was also proud of Tom Foley, Dick Gephardt, and Dave Bonior for the skillful job they did in pushing Clinton's courageous budget through to passage. It had taken trillions of dollars of additional debt, Fritz Mondale's defeat, and Bush's retreat on his taxation promise before the problem became so obvious that Clinton had the elbow room to act. But act he had, and so had we.

Two years later, House Democrats paid a high price for their courage. When the vote was taken we knew that a good dozen or more of our colleagues from marginal districts were likely to face defeat, in large measure because of that vote. In fact, that vote was a key reason that we lost control of the Congress. But as I walked around the Capitol grounds that night, I didn't think about the downside. I was just immensely relieved and proud that the most fiscally irresponsible chapter in the modern life of our country was over. I never dreamed that eight years later George W. Bush would send the country careening into the same deficit ditch that we had worked so long and so hard to climb out of.

Health Care

In my mind, Clinton's forceful and courageous action in reversing twelve years of Republican fiscal recklessness alone would have marked him in history as a significant president. But Clinton wanted to take on two huge additional challenges: welfare reform and health care.

The question was which should come first. In the internal caucus debate, I came down on the side of those who believed we should tackle health care first. Health-care reform would be the toughest fight of the Clinton presidency, and the best chance of doing it right was to get it done before the 1994 congressional campaign season hit us. The issue was so vital to so many groups with big money—the insurance industry, the medical profession, and the pharmaceutical industry—that if the debate slipped into the campaign season, we would be swamped by a tidal wave of special-interest spending.

Clinton was convinced to move first on health care and then take more time to fashion a program to, as he said, "end welfare as we know it." In retrospect I now believe we made the wrong tactical choice. Tough as I thought the health-care fight would be, it wound up being even tougher. I now believe we would have had an easier time of it if we had first tackled welfare reform. In the minds of many Americans, the welfare system was a frustrating symbol of sloppy government. Public cynicism about lax enforcement of welfare laws was so pervasive that welfare had become a poster child for the antigovernment movement throughout the country. Many hard-working Americans grudgingly recognized their obligation to help their less fortunate neighbors, but they did not want to be taken advantage of, and they believed that government was simply not careful enough with their money when it was handing out welfare benefits.

The health-care debate also involved a clash of perceptions about the ability of government to organize any complicated enterprise. What I recognize now that I did not sufficiently appreciate then is if we could first have brought some discipline to the welfare system, we would have demonstrated the kind of mental toughness and commitment to the work ethic that would have enhanced our credibility in the health-care debate. That might have made it easier for conservatives in our caucus to vote with us on health care. As events unfolded, we might have passed a welfare bill that was much less harsh than the one that finally passed. But the way it turned out, we had very little leverage in the welfare debate because the subject was dealt with *after* the Republicans seized control of the Congress in 1994. Clinton wound up buying into a far less merciful and thoughtful welfare package than might have been necessary had we tackled the issue in 1993.

In September 1993 Clinton introduced his health-care plan. Debate in the caucus centered around three different approaches. Some, like Jim McDermott of Washington, wanted to push for a single-payer, government-run program, similar to Canada's system. Others, like California's Pete Stark and Henry Waxman, wanted to build on the existing Medicare system by expanding Medicare for everyone. The third option was to build on the existing employer-based system by requiring most employers to provide health insurance to their employees and providing government subsidies to help small businesses pay for a plan or enter a broader pool plan. Clinton took the unusual step of putting his wife, Hillary, in charge of a task force, staffed by Ira Magaziner, to develop the administration's plan. For months it seemed inevitable that some kind of major reform would pass, but two bold actions by the opposition changed the equation.

In the early stages of the controversy, debate on the issue had occurred in the context of a widespread belief that a crisis of availability and affordability was building in the health-care arena. But Bill Kristol, former vice president Quayle's chief of staff, changed the dynamic by widely circulating a memo urging Republican leaders to "just say no" by "denying that there was a crisis." "Change the terms of the debate; challenge the basic assumption that lies behind Clinton's effort—i.e., that there is a health care crisis," Kristol counseled. You could feel the momentum slow down after that memo. The other killer stroke was the decision of the American Insurance Institute to run its now famous "Harry and Louise" TV ads. The ads, featuring a fictional couple, Harry and Louise, conveyed the impression that Clinton was going to take away peoples' choice of doctors and ration health care. In fact, much of what those Harry and Louise ads predicted would happen to health care if Clinton's plan passed, did happen after its defeat: higher costs, people squeezed by HMOs, more and more decisions about treatment made by HMOs or insurance company bureaucrats rather than by patients' doctors. With the defeat of Clinton's reform efforts, the private sector players would work their wonders, unfettered by government. They produced the very reality they had warned against but delivered by their own hand, not Clinton's.

During the debate, I did work with a local insurance company—Wausau Insurance—on one issue. Wisconsin had long provided a well-run and effective workmen's compensation program. That was due in no small measure to the leadership that Wausau Insurance had provided through the years in making that program one that was supported by business and labor alike. I worked out an understanding with Democrats on the Ways and Means and Commerce Committees that whatever reforms were adopted as they affected workmen's compensation would not disrupt successful state programs like Wisconsin's.

The debate was so rancorous, the stakes so high, the resistance so wily and tenacious that the struggle lasted well into 1994. The fight finally ended in the Energy and Commerce Committee. Committee chair John Dingell, whose father had sponsored a national health insurance plan when he served in Congress during the Truman era, desperately trolled for votes to move the Clinton plan out of his committee. He needed to have the votes of two holdouts, Jim Cooper of Tennessee and Jim Slattery of Kansas, in order to get the bill out of committee and into the Rules Committee where it could be refined, but neither man gave Clinton the vote he needed and the effort died—the biggest single failure of the party and the administration during Clinton's presidency.

More than any other event in the years that I had been in Congress, that loss devastated me. Just as the AMA had done in 1948 when it blocked Harry Truman's first effort to pass national health insurance, the insurance industry and other big-business special interests had again blocked Clinton's effort to add the United States to the list of civilized countries that did not ration health care on the basis of ability to pay. That defeat demoralized Democratic voters throughout the country and was largely responsible for the low Democratic turnout that helped turn the Congress over to Republican hands in November 1994. But before that happened, my life changed in a major way.

CHAPTER 18

༡

The Chairmanship

For all of my years in Congress, the Appropriations Committee had been led by aged southern conservatives. From 1969 until 1982 the committee had been chaired by George Mahon, a conservative pillar of the Texas Democratic Party. He was widely respected throughout the caucus and the House, but no one would have ever mistaken him for a midwestern Progressive. When Mahon finally retired in 1978, he was succeeded by Jamie Whitten of Mississippi. When it came to agriculture or public works programs, Whitten was a New Deal spender and an activist, but on many other issues Jamie was a typical southern conservative. His main concern was protecting Mississippi farmers and that required, among other things, that he fiercely resist the environmental movement's calls for reduced use of pesticides. Like so many other "Sons of the South," he came to Congress as an avowed segregationist. As times changed on racial issues, so did he. "I haven't changed," Jamie often said. "It's just that the times have changed, and I've adjusted to change."

Whitten was a close-to-the-vest southern traditionalist, one who played no major role in the broad scheme of things. Through his staff he simply presided over the committee, tried to keep the appropriations train running on time, and provided little real leadership, except on issues dear to rural Mississippi. Under Whitten the committee drifted. It did its job of producing appropriations bills but in a largely routine way. Jamie's health began to fade in 1992, and within months he was moved by the caucus to chairman emeritus status because he was no longer capable of handling the demands of the committee.

Bill Natcher of Kentucky was the next in line to take his place. Natcher had a reputation for orthodoxy and rectitude. He was often put in the chair when difficult bills were on the House floor because he knew House rules and ran a fair, tight ship during debate. Bill, in his eighties like Jamie Whitten, was past his prime and would do little to sharpen the committee's approach to issues. He would move the bills, but there would be no identifiable sense of direction that guided them. That bothered me because the Gingrich-led hard-liners were taking an ever more strident and partisan approach to appropriations issues, and I felt the Democratic response was tepid and casual. Natcher became chairman in 1993, but before long he too began to wilt. In 1994, when Congress returned to Washington after the January recess, it was obvious that Bill was going downhill fast. Once again, the committee would soon need a new chairman.

Next in line of succession was Neal Smith of Iowa, another old-school appropriator who was quite comfortable in the traditional, conservative ways of the committee. He had a perfectly decent voting record and had been a strong voice on food safety issues, especially meat inspection, but I felt that in terms of strategic planning, public debate, and energy he was no match for what the Republicans were throwing at us every day. Newt Gingrich, Bob Walker, and dozens of others were politicizing every issue in sight, including appropriations issues, and I saw no evidence that Neal was prepared to deal with that. A lot of others on the committee felt the same way.

Vic Fazio was a Californian with a keen sense of the mood of the House and one of the best and most thoughtful legislators I had ever served with. With Natcher failing, I raised with him the desirability of challenging Smith. Without hesitation he said, "David, Neal is not up to the job; you have to do it." I talked to Martin Sabo, who was less sure than Vic but after some consideration said, "Go for it." The most intense encouragement for me to take on the fight came from several of the women on the committee, especially Rosa DeLauro of Connecticut and Nancy Pelosi of California, both of whom were energetic progressives with a solid, modern grasp of national and congressional politics. I loved them for their decency and for their conviction.

Nancy represented Phil Burton's old San Francisco district but also had strong roots on the country's other coast. Her father, Tom D'Alesandro, and her brother, Tommy Jr., had both served as mayor of Baltimore. Nancy was a superb politician who understood both urban machine politics and mainstream progressive issue-driven politics, and she was one of the people I considered to be the conscience of the Democratic Party. After college, she married a Californian, Paul Pelosi, an investment banker, moved to San Francisco, raised four kids, and involved herself in California politics. She became state chair of the California Democratic Party and in 1986 served as finance chairman of the Senate Democratic Campaign Committee that helped take back the Senate for the Democratic Party.

Rosa was a fiercely energetic political activist who, before she went to Congress, had been the driving force behind Emily's List, a national organization that raised money to help finance female candidates for congressional races. Elected to Congress from Connecticut in 1990, she was married to Stan Greenberg, Clinton's lead pollster. Together, Rosa and Stan were a superb one-two political punch. Even standing alone, Rosa was a formidable force with a fierce commitment to social justice.

"Dave," Rosa told me, "Newt and the boys are coming at us with long knives. We simply can't afford to have the most important committee in the Congress led by someone who is not ready to take them on at all levels. You've got to run." Nancy said virtually the same thing. "David, you must run," she said. "Of course, I am for you. What do you want me to do to help?" Within days they were joined by a third female appropriator, Nita Lowey from New York, who served with Nancy and me on the Foreign Operations Subcommittee. I was confident that with Nancy, Rosa, Nita, Vic, and Martin in my corner, I would have instant credibility across a broad range of the caucus.

Then I went to see Dick Gephardt. "Dave, a political firestorm is coming. We need every cylinder firing. I'll help you in the Steering Committee when the time comes, and I will talk to Tom," Dick told me. I was confident Foley would be with me, but also knew that Foley would be officially neutral and noncommittal as long as it was not clear to the caucus that Natcher was out of the picture. If a replacement for Natcher needed to be selected, the first required step was to win the blessing of the Democratic Steering and Policy Committee. Under the rules I had a right to challenge him in a head-to-head contest.

Natcher, who was then eighty-four, entered the hospital on February 4. He returned to the Hill the next week but was clearly fading fast. With both Whitten and Natcher largely immobilized, the committee was adrift. Fred Mohrman, the staff chief, tried to hold things together, but nothing was happening. On February 14, *Roll Call,* the Capitol Hill newspaper, carried a story by Mary Jacobi saying that a race between Neal Smith and Dave Obey was imminent.

Tom Foley knew the committee situation had to be resolved because the time for appropriations bills to hit the floor was just around the corner. But he was determined to treat Natcher with consideration and dignity, and made clear to Smith and me that he would not act until it was clear to all that Natcher could no longer do the job. On Tuesday, March 1, the House cancelled its votes to prevent Natcher from missing a vote while he was being treated in the hospital. On Wednesday, dressed in his familiar three-piece suit, he was wheeled in to the House chamber on a gurney to cast four votes. But on March 3, after having cast 18,401 continuous votes without a miss since the day he first entered the chamber on January 21, 1954, Bill Natcher finally broke his perfect career-long string, missing four votes as he lay in his hospital bed at Bethesda Naval Hospital. It was now time for Foley to act.

For three weeks I had been talking with every Steering Committee member except those I knew to be committed to Smith. I needed 18 votes in the 34-member Steering Committee and 132 votes from the 262-person Democratic caucus in order to win. For nearly ten days my count on the Steering Committee was stuck at fourteen, but then the votes slid my way. Martin Frost, a wily and savvy Texan who was a key man on the Rules Committee, had been an early commitment. My count got to seventeen votes before Natcher missed his vote. Within two days, the commitments fell into place. When Steny Hoyer, who had a reputation for being a good but cautious vote-counter, finally committed to me, I knew we had the Steering Committee. Going into the vote, my count showed at least 23 votes to 9 for Smith with 2 uncertain. Before the balloting on March 21, Foley announced that when the count got to 18 for any of us he would halt the vote. And indeed, he stopped the balloting when my count hit 18 with Neal trailing with 7. The battle now turned to the caucus.

My campaign steering committee met almost daily. It was organized by Scott Lilly, who had taken over DSG after Dick Conlon was killed, and by Joe Crapa, my chief of staff. We organized our vote-seeking whip operation by state, class, committee, and caucus subgroup. We used the same system we had used in the Budget chairman race, ranking every member of the caucus by number: "1" meant that person had personally told me that he or she would support me on each and every ballot until we had won and that commitment had been verified by at least two other people; "2" meant that I felt, after talking to them, that they were leaning to me, likely to vote for me, and had given the same impression to at least two other whips; "3" meant we did not know where they were going to wind up; "4" meant we thought they were likely to go to south even if some of them had indicated they were open to my candidacy; and "5" meant we thought they were lead-pipe cinches for Smith.

Members of Congress hate caucus elections more than almost anything else except certain political defeat. Members do not want to hurt or anger other members so if they are not for you, they try to mask that fact. To avoid that deception, we checked and cross-checked members in every possible way. We assigned members from each state to check out other members from their state delegation. We assigned members of each committee to check other members of that committee and subcommittee. We got to such a level of detail that we figured out who sat next to each other in committee and subcommittee, and we had them double-checking their seat mates. We had members who had been elected in the same year checking members from their own incoming class. We had members of caucus subgroups like the Blue Dogs, the Hispanic caucus, and the Black caucus scout out other members of that same group. Before it was done, each member had been checked and cross-checked at least six different ways. As soon as a member would tell me or one of the whips working for me that they would vote for me, I would send them a note saying, "Thank you for your commitment in our conversation yesterday [or in their conversation with member X yesterday] that you will be voting for me on every ballot. I appreciate your support more than you can possibly know, and I will be counting on it."

Our biggest problem was that the Smith campaign framed our campaign as an all-out attack on the seniority system. They said we were asking people to vote against a perfectly decent human being (they were right, he was) who had served his time and deserved a shot at the chairmanship. Our response was that they were right, Neal was a perfectly decent human being and a good Democrat, but larger issues were at stake, and we needed a more imaginative, energetic approach that would wage a more aggressive fight for progressive priorities.

During the first stage of the race, the hardest nut to crack was the Black caucus. Blacks had been victimized by discrimination for so long that they looked around for all the protection they could find. A number of senior members (Bill Clay and Charlie Rangel were the most vociferous) felt that the rigid adherence to the seniority system was the only way to assure that blacks would not be passed over for chairmanships as they rose on the committee seniority lists. The three people who gave me the most help in breaking into that caucus were Cynthia McKinney and John Lewis of Georgia, and Al Wynn of Maryland. The second group that was hard to target included the more senior members of Appropriations led by Jack Murtha, who for ideological and institutional reasons did not want to see the seniority system lose an ounce of power, and who felt more comfortable with Neal Smith's style and philosophy than with mine. The third layer of opposition was a cluster of senior members who resented my challenge to the seniority system because they themselves were at the top of the seniority list on their own committee and did not want to encourage opposition in their own bailiwicks. And some of them honestly felt that once seniority was abandoned, it would be a dog-eat-dog world, and committee elections would degenerate into personal popularity contests. My response was that the best way to preserve the seniority system was to recognize that the caucus needed to face the fact that there were a few occasions that cried out for exceptions. If it didn't, the pressure for change would become so great, as more and more committees became dead cylinders under weak leadership, that it would, out of frustration, disregard the entire system.

My strongest support, after the women on my committee, came from the newest members of the caucus. I urged them, when they were sounding out other members, to "please refute any charge that we were trying to break the seniority system." I urged them to frame it as respectful recognition that, in this case, a rare exception was required. By March 5, we had over fifty-six members working as my whips, and we told the press that we had at least 150 commitments. We did, but Smith's forces didn't believe it. Going into the vote our count was holding at 150 or better. Smith's campaign claimed 137 votes. When the nominating speeches were over and the votes were counted, our numbers held. The final vote was 152 for Obey and 106 for Smith. That vote made me the youngest chairman of Appropriations since the election of James W. Good of Iowa in 1919.

Immediately after the vote, Vic Fazio and I and several others stepped outside the caucus to field questions from the press. The feeling was unbelievable. Twenty-five years earlier I had joined the committee as its most junior member. For many of those years, until I became chairman of Foreign Ops, even though my party ostensibly controlled the committee, I had felt like an outsider. Now, finally, I was chairman and was in a position to shape appropriations priorities for the entire House.

I was determined to take control of the committee immediately and end the turmoil that had consumed it for months. Fred Mohrman, the staff director, had done everything humanly possible to hold things together for Natcher and the old order, but he responded to my win, which I knew he did not welcome, as a consummate professional. He understood that I had to make a change in staff leadership. He came to me with an offer to resign so that I could clear the decks and name my own man as staff director. He offered to stay for a few months to give us time to make the transition to a new team. I'm sure he was concerned that I would dump a lot of the old staff and install my own people, but that is not what I wanted.

The Appropriations staff was unique in the House. They were strongly apolitical, the closest thing to the British civil service system that could be found in the Congress. Many of them were conservative, but that did not bother me. They were extremely talented and dedicated and knew how to pay attention to detail. I knew I could not produce results without them. I wanted to put Scott in charge so that I had someone compatible whom I could trust to move the committee forward in the direction I wanted to go.

My next task was to say goodbye to Bill Natcher. Mike Stephens, the chief clerk of the Labor-H Subcommittee had an intimate, almost father-son relationship with Natcher. Mike called and suggested that Bill would like to see me. The next day Mike and I drove to Bethesda. I was stunned at how frail he looked. Thin and pale in his hospital gown, he received me graciously. Out of courtesy to him, the caucus had elected me "acting" rather than permanent chairman, but Bill knew the score. "Dave, you will make a fine chairman," Bill said. He told me he understood why the caucus had to do what it did. I told him the caucus loved him and that he should be proud of his service to the country. His frail hand reached out to mine one last time, and I left. A week later he was gone.

My first job as chairman was to take control of the process. I knew that Democrats and Republicans alike on the committee were wondering how I would operate. The first thing I did was to sit down with Scott to go over the staff situation. Scott told me that we had one vacant slot. Terry Peel and I thought we needed to make a goodwill gesture to the Republican minority and Scott agreed, so I called Joe McDade, the ranking GOP member from Pennsylvania, and told him that we would transfer that slot to the minority and that he should hire whomever he wanted. He used that slot to hire Jim Dyer who, for the next ten years, would most ably serve as the Republican staff director.

My next job was to try to get the subcommittee bills moving. To do that, I had to assign specific spending levels to each of the thirteen subcommittees under the procedures laid out in the Budget Act. Under the process, the full Appropriations Committee was assigned an overall spending limit for all appropriations (called the 302a allocation). Once that was done, I had to divide that number into thirteen separate parts for each of the thirteen Appropriations subcommittees (called the 302b allocation). That action defined appropriations priorities for the year, and it was crucial. In the past, that allocation had been made solely by the Appropriations chairman. Scott and I wanted to change that. I called Joe McDade and said, "Joe, if you would like, I'd like to sit down with you and work out a bipartisan 302b allocation. You and I might disagree about the funding details within each of the thirteen appropriations, but I'd at least like to try to work out an agreement about how much money should be in each of those bills." Joe was delighted. We sat down, and for the first and only time in the history of the Budget Act, agreed on bipartisan subcommittee allocations. That proved to be a key decision. It was the main reason that our committee was able to put every single appropriations bill on the president's desk before the beginning of the new fiscal year—the only time *that* had happened since 1948.

My next action was to bring in all thirteen of the GOP ranking members to the chairman's office for a talk about how we should proceed. I badly wanted to send a signal to all of them that, while I had strong priorities, I wanted to work with both sides of the aisle. As we sat around the great table in the committee's Capitol office, I told them, "Look, I know we'll first have to define our differences, but then I hope we can resolve a lot of them." I was astounded when one of them said, "You know, this is the first time I have ever seen the chairman's office." I was flabbergasted. I knew that the old guard that had run the committee had played the game close to the vest, but I never fully understood that even senior Republican members had experienced the same frozen-out feeling that we younger, more junior Democrats had felt on our side of the aisle. When I heard that comment, I immediately decided to try to change the vibes. I called Mel Laird and told him how stunned I was to hear that GOP members had felt as shut out as we had been. "Mel," I said, "I want to hold a reception in your honor in the chairman's office; would you come?" "Of course!" he answered. Several weeks later we invited a large cadre of members into the Appropriations office for a party. Mel loved the committee and it showed that night. I was surprised to find out that so few younger GOP members knew Mel, even though he was an institution.

We got the committee off to a good start. Taking over midway through the cycle, I could work no miracles, but we did bring a new, more open style to the committee operations. We were probably the only major power center in the House that got our work done without a huge amount of Sturm und Drang. Scott and I were determined to blow away any stereotype that we were liberals who could not cut waste. We produced bills that cut or eliminated some 123 different programs. We worked night and day. Our hardest job was to overcome the Senate roadblocks to enable conference committees to finish their work. Finally, on the last evening of the fiscal year, at about 8 p.m., I went down to the White House for Clinton's signing of the last appropriations bills—just under the wire.

The committee had finished our part of the job, but on other fronts chaos was reigning. Bill Kristol's line-in-the-sand memo counseling the Republican leadership to "just say no" on health-care reform had galvanized the GOP into across-the-board resistance to all of Clinton's initiatives. One of his key proposals, the crime bill, had been hung up for months.

Clinton, being from Arkansas, a rural state, should have known that loading down his crime bill with a gun-control provision would cost him crucial support from rural House members. Tom Foley tried to warn him as did some of the rest of us, but the administration ignored the argument. That decision blocked Clinton's crime bill for a long period. The twin failures of the health-care and crime-control package created the impression with Clinton's working-class base that he could not deliver. The crime bill finally passed but only after an enormous fight that further split Democratic voters.

As the election approached, Newt Gingrich and Dick Armey put together a scheme called "The Contract with America," built around promises to cut taxes, cut waste (read Medicare), and scale back government. The plan didn't add up—just as Reagan's hadn't twelve years earlier—but for those who noticed (because of the way it was packaged) it created the vague impression of coherence. Two weeks before the election, I told Tom O'Donnell, Dick Gephardt's staff chief, that I really believed we could lose the House. By election day I was sure of it.

PART 5

∽

PRIORITIES AND PRESIDENTS

CHAPTER 19

❧

Gingrich Takes Over

On election day in 1994, Clinton's popularity rating stood at 29 percent in my district. Election night was long and hard, and Democrats lost fifty-two seats. Even the Speaker, Tom Foley, fell to an opponent who pledged to limit himself to three terms, a pledge he later cynically abandoned. Dozens of Republican members came to office promising to leave within six years. The Democrats' forty-year reign in the House was over. Bill Clinton now faced a Republican Congress, and we faced a new world in the minority.

Gingrich wasted no time in reorganizing. First, he aggressively took away the institutional tools of the new minority by changing the rules to put the Democratic Study Group out of business. Newt recognized that much of the intellectual center of the party lay not with the committee structure but with the ability of members to pool their resources to obtain research independent of party leadership. Accordingly, he pushed through rules changes to prevent members from pooling office research to pay for DSG staff help. That effectively killed the DSG and several other useful organizations on both sides of the aisle. Newt understood that information was power, and he wanted us to have as little of it as possible.

Bob Livingston of Louisiana was slated to take over my Appropriations chairmanship. Bob had been my ranking GOP member on the Foreign Operations Subcommittee for years, but now the shoe was on the other foot. We were poles apart philosophically, but he was a good man who cared about the Congress as an institution and about the committee as a key instrument of that institution. The day quickly arrived when it was time for me to turn over the chairman's office to Bob. I hated the thought. I had worked for twenty-five years to climb to the top of the committee ladder and even then, in the end, I had to stage a revolt to take over the chair. Now it was gone. I sat down in my chair behind the desk, spun around to look once more out the window down the Mall toward the Washington Monument, and turned back to the desk to perform one last task. I reached into my briefcase and pulled out a quart of scotch, which was Bob's favorite. I put it in the bottom right-hand drawer and laid a note on the desk. "Bob, no one should inherit an empty desk," I wrote. "Good luck." I walked out the door of H216, which was just a few feet off the House floor, turned, walked down the hallway, and made my way up the flight of stairs to the third floor, took out my new key, and walked into H323, my new minority committee office. H323, a corner office overlooking the Mall, had been Joe McDade's Appropriations ranking minority office and Silvio Conte's before him. It would now be my operations center for the next twelve years—the planning room for the loyal opposition.

FROM FOREIGN OPS TO LABOR-H

Along with the change in office space came a change in legislative focus. As the ranking Democrat on the committee, I had voting membership on every subcommittee. I would have the responsibility of responding to GOP appropriations initiatives across the board, but I was also taking on another new subcommittee responsibility. Neal Smith had gone down in the November election and that meant that the ranking spot on Labor-H was vacant. For ten years my primary subcommittee responsibility had been to chair the Foreign Operations Subcommittee, but it was clear that, on appropriations issues, the major Republican challenge on the committee would come against many of the education, health, and worker protection programs that were central to a just society. I wanted to be in the best position to quarterback our response, so I made the switch to Labor-H.

GOP MACHETE

Within weeks of the GOP ascent to power, Livingston walked into committee with a $17 billion rescission package. He pulled out a machete, waved it above his head, and said he was going to carve up government waste and red tape. What he called red tape and waste turned out to be a whole range of education, health, and social services programs, including $6 billion in education cuts and a $1.3-billion cut in the Low Income Home Energy Assistance Program (LIHEAP), the program that helped low-income seniors and working families to pay their home heating bills, so they did not have to choose between heating their homes and eating.

Conservative Republicans had a thing about LIHEAP. At the height of the energy crisis in the late 1970s, at the suggestion of Elliott Fiedler, then my legislative director, Ed Muskie and I had persuaded the Appropriations Committee to start the program. We had had a lot of help from northeast Republicans like Sil Conte, but conservative ideologues saw it as just another welfare program and tried to do it in. When Livingston came after the program, Rosa DeLauro and I worked quietly with several northeast Republican appropriators and were able to save it.

With that change, the GOP passed its $17 billion cutback package, but Clinton vetoed their meat-ax approach. The GOP followed that with a sweeping environmental deregulation package, a wish list of special-interest gifts put together by Tom DeLay and lobbyists from a who's who of corporate America. Next came a budget resolution designed to find the money to pay for huge tax cuts for the richest by cutting $270 billion out of Medicare, $163 billion out of Medicaid, and billions of dollars from other crucial appropriations.

The Republican blueprint called for cutting $25 billion from elementary and secondary education over seven years. Another $5 billion was to be taken out of higher education. They also loaded up the bills with dozens of provisions, which gutted law after law protecting workers, consumers, and the environment. On the appropriation bill for EPA they included seventeen different provisions hamstringing EPA's efforts to control polluters. Those provisions gutted toxic-emission controls for refineries and cement kilns, allowed more raw sewage to be dumped into public waterways, weakened wetlands protections, and waged other far-reaching attacks on government's ability to protect the public from pollution. Lou Stokes, the ranking Democrat on the subcommittee, and I lost our initial effort to knock out those special-interest items from the EPA appropriations bill, but we teamed up with Sherry Boehlert, a moderate New York Republican, and finally won with the support of 163 Democrats and 63 Republicans.

The GOP budget game plan was to slash funding anywhere they could until they had enough room to pass their giant-size tax cuts—especially capital gains tax cuts that were targeted largely at the most prosperous constituents. In countering that effort, a huge tactical difference began to develop between the White House and House Democrats, and I was in the middle of it.

Clinton had a hard choice to make. Gingrich and the GOP believed they had the upper hand and could force Clinton to sign their kind of budget. Clinton knew the old political adage, "You can't beat something with nothing." He believed it was necessary for Democrats to join in the call for balancing the budget so that we would be on stronger ground in debating how to balance it. Dick Gephardt and I and others agreed, but the key issue was timing. Polling data showed that more than 50 percent of the American people did not yet realize that the GOP balanced-budget scheme was based on huge cuts in Medicare. Most Americans still did not know that Gingrich's budget aimed to slash Medicare by $270 billion and use $245 billion of those cuts to pay for tax cuts—cuts that would give over half the benefits to the tiny minority of Americans making more than $100,000 a year. We believed that if Clinton spent three more weeks using the White House megaphone to drive that point home, 15 to 20 percent more Americans would get the message, and that would give us more negotiating room and help assure a more favorable outcome. We believed we had an understanding with Clinton that we would all, for the moment, continue to focus on the GOP plans for Medicare. But with practically no notice, Clinton went off on his own, prematurely dropped his focus on Medicare, and switched to his balanced-budget theme before the public had adequate information about the implications of the GOP budget for Medicare. Gephardt and I were furious. It was clear that Clinton believed we had no choice but to follow his lead.

Medicare was not the only problem. From my perspective as the Democrat's top appropriator, I was also concerned that Clinton would lead us into a deal that we could not live up to because it would be based on a false promise to cut domestic appropriations far more deeply than the House would accept. I did not want Democrats to buy into an appropriations deal that I could not deliver. With the phone ringing off the hook from press people wanting me to comment on Clinton's shift, Scott and I decided to issue a statement that would send a message to the White House about the depth of our anger at Clinton's unilateral change of plans, a message that we would not accept that kind of unilateral action without raising hell. We wanted the statement to bite and knew it would—if it rang true on Clinton's reputation for bobbing and weaving. The statement I issued said, "I think most of us learned some time ago that if you don't like the president's position on a particular issue, you simply need to wait a few weeks."

The White House reacted to my statement with anger. "Jesus," one top staffer called to complain to Scott Lilly, "Obey couldn't have found a statement that stung us more." I told Scott to tell him that I said, "I know, that's why I said it," and that I would not be a willing partner in peddling budget bull-gravy, and that I would not bite my tongue if we were double-crossed or triangulated again without notice. As I expected, broad sections of the press didn't get it. A number of Hill reporters, such as Gloria Borger of *U.S. News* and Joe Klein of *Newsweek,* and most of the Washington pundits and editorial writers insisted on describing our reaction to Clinton's move as a reaction against his decision to support a balanced budget. They never figured out—and to my knowledge, haven't to this day—that Dick and I knew we needed to stake out support for a balanced budget, but that the issue was over timing—how much time was needed to build public understanding of the GOP plans for Medicare cuts—and over whether decisions should be made cooperatively or unilaterally by the White House.

By the last week of September, the end of the fiscal year, only two of the thirteen GOP appropriation bills had become law. The Budget Reconciliation Bill, which contained the tax cuts and the cutbacks in Medicare/Medicaid that were designed to pay for those tax cuts, was still being held close to Gingrich's vest. In September we agreed to a six-week temporary continuing resolution to keep the government open while negotiations continued. Livingston again demonstrated Republican antagonism to the LIHEAP program by initially demanding that funding for it be eliminated in the continuing resolution. He finally backed down on that demand, and the deal was done.

One month later the *Washington Post* reported that Gingrich, in a closed-door briefing with an insurance group, had made clear his disdain for traditional fee-for-service Medicare. In exploring Newt's two-step strategy for dealing with it, he was quoted as saying, "Now, we don't get rid of it in round one because we don't think that is politically smart, and we don't think that that's the right way to go through a transition. But we do believe it's going to wither on the vine." When the press reported those comments, some Republicans claimed that he was just talking about getting rid of the Health Care Financing Administration, not Medicare, but, given Newt's track record in trying to privatize Medicare and Social Security, we didn't buy the disclaimer for a minute. The same day, Senate GOP majority leader Bob Dole told another private group that he was proud of his 1965 vote against creating Medicare in the first place and said, "I was there fighting the fight against Medicare because we knew it wouldn't work." Gingrich was still eager to manufacture a crisis by using the threat of a government shutdown to put Clinton in a box and force him to sign Newt's Medicare/tax cut scheme. One week later, a tragedy struck that demonstrated the clear difference between real problems and manufactured ones.

RABIN'S ASSASSINATION

The last time I had seen Yitzhak Rabin in Washington, he closed the door to his hotel room, shooed people out, and said two things to me. The first was,

"David, please don't let Israel's well-meaning friends convince Congress to take away your country's ability to deal with the PLO. If they do, then there will be no one left but Hamas, and we will all be lost." Then he said, "My second request is this: Please help keep AIPAC off my back. I don't need them to conduct negotiations with your government. I'm a big boy. I'm perfectly capable of doing that myself."

In those closing days of 1995, the authority for the United States to continue dealing with the Palestinian Authority was scheduled to expire. In mid-October, Lee Hamilton came to me and said he was going to ask unanimous consent to extend the expiring authority. To our consternation, Michael Forbes, a backbench Republican from New York, made clear his plans to object. No doubt he expected to be a hero to militant segments of the American Jewish community. When I heard of Forbes's intentions, I grabbed Gingrich on the House floor and said, "Newt, you can't let this happen. It will hurt the peace process. You can't let Likud politics take over the House floor." Newt turned to me, looked straight into my eyes, and said, "Dave, you need to understand. I'm Likud; I'm Likud." I was appalled.

Two days later, on November 4, Rabin was assassinated by a young Israeli militant who was bitterly opposed to the Israeli-Palestinian peace process. It should not have been surprising. Israel had been in turmoil. Militant right-wing Israeli politicians and rabbis had been spouting vicious anti-Rabin rhetoric for months, zealously describing Rabin as an enemy of the State and the Jewish people. Driven by the concept of "DinRodef"—the idea that if a Jew becomes a grave threat to the Jewish state, it is defensible to kill him—some were even beginning to carry placards reading "Death to Rabin." "Bibi" Netanyahu, a Likud-coalition opponent of Rabin, had addressed a large rally at which a coffin labeled with Rabin's name had been carried aloft by the crowd. In their revealing book *Murder in the Name of God: The Plot to Kill Yitzhak Rabin*, Michael Karpin and Ina Friedman reported that Israeli security people had gone to Netanyahu, told him of their concern about the possibility of assassination, and asked him to cool his rhetoric, but Netanyahu had declined. Two days after my confrontation with Newt on the House floor, after addressing a massive outdoor peace rally in Israel, Rabin was gunned down. Until that moment, no Israeli political leader had ever been assassinated. Now, sadly, Israel had joined the United States and the rest of the world in losing the innocent belief that "it can't happen here."

I was at home in Wausau when I heard the news. I was heartsick. I had known Rabin for twenty years and had come to respect and admire him. His loss was a monumental tragedy. My favorite Israeli politician was Shimon Peres, a superbly eloquent and imaginative pioneer for peace, but I knew that Rabin had been the one man in Israel who was seen as being tough-minded enough to negotiate an acceptable deal with the Palestinians. I phoned my office immediately to find out what the funeral arrangements were and caught the first plane back to D.C. After the ceremony we immediately headed back to Washington to resume the "yinging" and "yanging" of the budget.

GINGRICH SHUTS DOWN THE GOVERNMENT

In Washington, Rabin's death had produced two changes. The first was that Forbes and Gingrich were now willing to let legislation go forward to continue the American relationship with the PLO. The second was a change in who held the whip hand in budget negotiations.

After the Rabin assassination, Newt wasn't calling himself Likud anymore. At least he didn't want to be caught acting like Likud. Now Rabin was a martyred hero and Newt and many others who one week earlier had demonstrated no interest in helping Rabin were anxious to avoid any association with the hard-line mind-set that had taken Rabin down. Suddenly, Gingrich was only too happy to allow legislation extending the authority for a continued relationship with the PLO to pass, but while Newt was mellowing out for the moment on the Middle East, he was throwing a hissy fit on budget negotiations.

We had returned from Rabin's funeral to face the pending expiration of the continuing resolution. To force Clinton's hand, Newt turned that possibility into a reality and engineered his long-threatened government shutdown. Americans visiting the nation's capital suddenly discovered that the Washington Monument and other tourist attractions were closed. Unbelievably, Gingrich was quoted as saying that he was justified in allowing the shutdown to occur because President Clinton had insulted him with poor seating arrangements on Air Force One on the return flight from Rabin's funeral. For the next three days, Newt's pout was the talk of the country.

I thought the incident perfectly captured Newt's split-level personality. Newt was as bright and facile as anyone I had ever dealt with in politics, but at the same time he was a man of monumental self-centered immaturity. In an instant, his "I'm-going-to-hold-my-breath-and-turn-blue" posture had radically changed the dynamics of budget negotiations. Newt had personalized the dispute and turned a gigantic fight over national priorities into something spectacularly petty. Literally overnight the public rallied to our side of the issue, and after three days of incredibly tone-deaf performances, Newt and his allies sued for peace. The only question was how high a price they would pay to get it.

In round-the-clock negotiations throughout the weekend, with Leon Panetta, representing the White House, Mark Hatfield and Bob Byrd on the Senate side, and Livingston and me on the House side, we worked with party leaders to tie down the details. On Sunday evening, we passed a one-day funding bill to open the government Monday morning, and on Monday, November 20, Livingston and I brought to the floor an agreement that kept the government open until the final version of the budget could pass in early 1996.

In January Clinton invited me to be part of a delegation to Bosnia to inspect the conditions faced by U.S. troops performing a peace-keeping role in the Balkans after years of ethnic conflict. Ten days after returning from Bosnia, Livingston, Hatfield, Byrd, Panetta, and I signed off on another temporary continuing resolution to keep the government open again until March 17. Finally, on April 25, the seven-month appropriations standoff ended. We passed a package heavy-laden with compromises, but we had made the Republicans pay a large price for the cuts they tried to make in Medicare, education, health, science, and environmental programs—and we had largely held our ground.

In the most tumultuous year since 1981, I had been at the center of the struggle. On the essentials, we had protected most of what we cared about. In the end, the agreement did not include Gingrich's sweeping attack on Medicare. It cut $23 billion in appropriations, but it did so without slashing education, job training, and the environment. We restored 90 percent of the Republican cuts in education, 70 percent of their cuts in training, and 80 percent of the funds they had cut from clean water and clean air programs. It also did not include the GOP attack on the enforcement of labor laws, which protect workers from abuse at the bargaining table and in the workplace. There would be no crippling of the National Labor Relations Board, no handcuffs placed on government's obligation to strengthen health and safety protections for workers on the job. Moreover, we had blocked Republican efforts to require workers to take comp time rather than overtime pay they were due. And the reward for our efforts? We got to do it all over again the next year.

The appropriations battles for the next year were much tamer. The GOP's tail feathers had been singed by the public reaction to their recklessness. Chastised by their near-death experience in confronting Clinton on the government shutdown, Gingrich and the GOP pulled back. Now, presidential politics dominated the year. When Bob Dole won the GOP nomination in August,

Clinton was riding at 55 percent in the polls. In November, when Clinton clobbered Dole, the Democrats picked up a handful of House seats, and my margin against the same opponent I had faced two years earlier increased to 14 percent. The following year, with the 1996 presidential election behind them (and without the moderating influence of Bob Dole to hold them back), the House GOP reverted to their earlier aggressiveness.

MORE ROUNDS IN THE BUDGET FIGHT

In August 1997, after weeks of intensive negotiations, Clinton reached a tentative budget agreement with congressional Republicans, but because it was again laced with phony assumptions about the next five years, I confronted Erskine Bowles, Clinton's staff chief, in a Democratic caucus and called the deal a "mini public fib" if not an outright lie. The agreement promised to cut spending by $260 billion over five years and cut taxes by $95 billion, including a cut in capital gains. I warned the caucus that it was a fib on three fronts.

First of all, the administration and the GOP leadership sold the deal to the press and the public as a deficit-reduction package with tax and entitlement cuts thrown into the mix. But in fact the skids were greased for the five-year deal by actually *increasing* rather than decreasing spending by $11 billion in the first two years it was in effect. That meant that the deficit for those two years would actually be larger than it would be if the Congress simply did nothing! But then the deal reversed field and pretended that in the following three years, Congress would suddenly and miraculously find the determination to vote for significant appropriations cuts. I knew that wouldn't happen and so did the administration.

The second fib was that the bill assumed $115 billion in Medicare cuts. I simply did not believe those cuts could or would occur without harming Medicare. "These cuts will never be delivered by either party," I told the caucus and the press.

The third fib was that the tax component of the package was fair, even though it contained a capital gains tax cut from 28 percent to 20 percent. With the inclusion of that provision, I knew that if distribution tables for the tax package were produced, they would show the tax benefits heavily targeted to the most well-off taxpayers. In past tax debates, we had used distribution tables—produced by Wendell Primus, the brilliant staffer on the Joint Tax Committee—to show the unfairness of the GOP plans. Now our own Democratic administration was declining to publish them because they would show a similar upper-income bias in the administration's deal. If we were to have tax cuts, I wanted a package that directed more of the relief to middle- and lower-income taxpayers, but the leadership of both parties chose not to advertise the impact of the cuts, and the deal held.

I was one of only eighty-five House members (and one of only fifty-two Democrats) to vote against the deal. Within the Democratic caucus, I felt a special obligation to insist on a fair distribution of tax burden: after the 1994 election debacle, Dick Gephardt and his top assistant, Tom O'Donnell, had asked Scott Lilly and me to take charge of economic and political research for the House Democratic Policy Committee. In that capacity, we had produced another policy report updating our earlier Joint Economic Committee paper on the distribution of wealth in the U.S. economy.

The new study focused on the fact that over a period of thirty years, America had gone from being the Western industrialized society with the smallest gap between the superrich and the poor to the society with the largest. Most of that transformation was due to the invisible hand of market force inevitability, but it had been magnified by conscious policy choices of government— aided and abetted by political investments of the reigning American economic elite. The report demonstrated that we had already experienced thirty years of class warfare—and the middle class had lost!

The report showed that the full magnitude of the wealth gap in this country had not been fully appreciated by large segments of the public or the press. Even before the huge run-up of wealth on Wall Street in the 1990s, on the investment side of the ledger, the financial wealth of the richest 500,000 families in the United States had grown from $2.5 trillion to $5 trillion in 1989. Those families could have paid off the entire national debt and still would have owned 10 percent more wealth than they did in 1983! Yet, on the worker side of the ledger, average hourly wages of American workers, adjusted for inflation, had declined from $12.85 in 1978 to $11.46 in 1996. From the end of World War II through 1979, the benefits of productivity increases had actually trickled down to America's workers. Eighty percent of productivity gains had been passed on to workers in the form of higher wages. But after 1979 trickle-down stopped working, and only 25 percent of productivity gains had gotten through to workers.

Our report recognized that market pressures, including globalization of the marketplace, had contributed to these trends, but it drove home the point that those pressures were magnified and abetted by government policies that actually weakened forces in the economy that might have helped redress those imbalances. Those policies included:

- Driving down the minimum wage
- Gutting and marginalizing the ability of workers to organize and unionize
- Crippling government regulation of business practices that weaken smaller economic players
- Pursuing tax policies that added to the stacked deck against those whose incomes came only from wages
- Skimping on economic investments in education, training, and health care that could help counterbalance the negative aspects of globalization
- Fashioning trade agreements that aggressively focused on the need to protect investments abroad but tepidly defended workers' wages at home

The report also described the widespread network of supposedly independent public policy research organizations. Foundations, such as the Heritage Foundation, the Richard Mellon Scaife Foundation, the Smith Robertson Foundation, the John Olin Foundation, the Bradley Foundation, the Coors Family Foundation, and the Koch Family Foundation, had been built over the previous thirty years by the right-wing economic elite; they produced supposedly independent academic research, which promoted policies that would intensify those right-wing trends.

These foundations and many others continually pumped out papers trying to justify government policies that would deregulate corporate America and facilitate the massive shifting of income and wealth up the income scale, all in the theory that dollars placed in the hands of the investor-class elite would eventually trickle down to everybody else.

We catalogued the actions of the foundations and families that were pouring resources into such Washington think tanks as Heritage, Cato, and others, which had produced ready-made action plans for Republicans since Ronald Reagan's election in 1981. Because of their sweeping influence, and because of the reluctance of the "New Democrat" wing of the Democratic Party to focus on equity issues, I felt that unless I raised the issue during Clinton's consideration of the new budget deal, few people would. Throughout the year, we used the report to buttress our position on budget negotiations and to put pressure on the administration and the GOP.

Since the electoral disaster of 1994, the Clinton administration and congressional Democrats had battled back from the edge of oblivion. Clinton had fought his way back to a 55 percent approval rating in the polls and experienced an easy victory over Bob Dole in 1996 by pushing a moderate response to Gingrich's extremism. Under those circumstances, given the need for Clinton to hold the middle ground in the political debate, I had not expected him to be on the cutting edge of economic equity issues, but someone needed to be. Having produced so many reports over the previous decade on the growing gap in wealth and income, I felt I was in the best position to do so. As the top Democrat on Appropriations, I was obligated to fight for honest budget numbers and enlightened funding priorities. Without them, federal investments that would be hit the hardest—except for Medicare—were those that were central to the committee's responsibility. During the negotiations I kept asking, "How can you say these numbers add up?"

In the end, for both parties the political convenience of fudging the numbers was too much to overcome, and the deal was sealed. It was based on many false assumptions and questionable promises. I didn't like it, but it was the best Clinton thought he could do.

Clinton's premature compromise on the Medicare message two years earlier finally extracted a price in the $115 billion cut that Congress adopted for Medicare. I felt bad about it but had done everything I could do to prevent it. It was far better than the $270 billion Newt had tried to extract, and I knew that in future years those cuts would be scaled back even further. We had done the best we could do, and much of what we valued had survived. Three more years of budget negotiations between Clinton and the Congress were still ahead of us, but before they unfolded, we were to endure a six-year GOP-driven soap opera that focused the nation on the sideshow of Bill Clinton's sex life.

CHAPTER 20

Impeachment Again

In all of my experience in politics, I have never seen so many people in one political party demonstrate so much poisonous ill will toward a president as Washington-based Republican elites showed against Bill Clinton. Over the previous twenty-five years, many Republicans came to believe that they had an almost permanent lock on the White House. When Clinton won, their shock was intensified by their personal disdain for him. As wary as Clinton had been about much of the Washington political establishment when he was elected, he probably underestimated the zeal with which his political opponents would pursue any course to turn the "infidel" out of the White House. Their dislike of Clinton was not just political; it was cultural and personal, rooted as it was in their disdain for his past relationships with women, their anger at his antiwar activities during the Vietnam War, and their determination to defend the privileged ground occupied by the economic elite they represented.

I first realized just how determined some Republicans were to destroy Clinton when deputy White House counsel Vince Foster was found dead by U.S. Park Police on the George Washington Parkway. Foster had come to Washington from Arkansas with the Clintons. He was known to be unhappy about life in Washington, and after an investigation, police ruled his death a suicide. But Clinton-haters in and out of Congress raised the specter of foul play, even murder. Rep. Dan Burton of Indiana was so daffy about it that he even tried to conduct his own madcap ballistic experiments by firing bullets into melons in his backyard. For the next four years, the case was dragged through the newspapers until the original police judgment of suicide was affirmed by (of all people) the man who was to spend almost six years of his life trying to destroy Bill Clinton, independent counsel Kenneth Starr.

Washington Republicans used the Foster death to resurrect rumors and innuendo about an Arkansas land transfer years earlier in which the Clintons had played a part. They succeeded in pressing attorney general Janet Reno into naming an independent counsel, Robert Fiske Jr., to investigate the Clintons' involvement. Months later, Fiske was abruptly dismissed by the U.S. Appeals Court judge David Sentelle, a partisan crony of right-wing GOP senator Jesse Helms. Fiske was replaced by Kenneth W. Starr, a prissy and zealously ideological former U.S. solicitor under Ronald Reagan and George Bush. Starr's attention ricocheted from Clinton's real estate transactions to his past sex life, then to an investigation of Clinton's new sexual involvement with a White House intern, Monica Lewinsky.

Ironically, four years later, on the first day of House impeachment hearings, Starr announced that he had decided against prosecuting Clinton on the very issue he was first hired to investigate—the Arkansas Whitewater land deal—because of the insufficiency of evidence. Up to that point, $40 million and four years of the country's time had been consumed in order for Starr to bring impeachment charges for activities related to private sexual acts committed by the president that hadn't even occurred when Starr was appointed in the first place. If that doesn't meet the definition of a prosecutorial fishing expedition, I don't know what does.

When Starr presented his report to the Congress, even though it was discussed in graphic detail in the news media, the guidelines announced by Speaker Gingrich prevented its discussion in specific terms on the House floor. Five days after the report was issued, I expressed my frustration about the over-reaching nature of the Starr report. Because of Gingrich's ruling, in a speech I delivered on the House floor, I was required to omit specific references to the report from my verbal statement on the floor. But I got around that restriction by issuing to the press the full text (with the censured portions in italics and the delivered portion in regular type) of what I would have said on the floor had I not been blocked by Gingrich's ruling. In response to the Republican's pious press statements about the president's morality, I said, "The Ten Commandments represent a guide for living and for the treatment of others. God did not give them to us to provide a road map for human beings and politicians to destroy each other. . . . Mr. Starr's active advocacy of impeachment, going so far as to draw up potential articles of impeachment is, as the *Washington Post* has said, an 'arrogant' act that claims for Mr. Starr a responsibility that is solely the prerogative of Congress. Mr. Starr's job is to lay out the facts in 'Joe Friday style'—as Mr. Starr himself has on occasion pointed out. It is not to reach a conclusion about what actions Congress should take. That is *our* job."

Public reaction to the Starr report was clear. Americans did not in any way appreciate the president's personal conduct, but they clearly felt this issue did not rise to the level of an impeachable offense: they wanted the Congress to drop it and move on. Most Americans believed that the GOP had over-reached, and they voted accordingly. Democrats had been widely expected to lose seats in the November election; instead, we picked up two seats. Still, Gingrich refused to get the message. Driven by Tom DeLay's relentless hatred for Clinton, he blocked what was the clear preference of the House at that time—to approve a motion of censure for Clinton's lack of truthfulness before the Grand Jury, a middle ground between impeachment and exoneration, and then move on.

As the storm was building I received a phone call from Clinton. He asked me where I thought things stood and what I thought the House would do. I told him I thought it was "not unlikely" that the House would impeach him and that the only way that might be stopped would be with a congressional resolution of censure, but that it would be hard to get. The only way a cen-sure motion might be accepted was to force the GOP to choose between their desire to take him down and their desire to avoid another four or eight years of a Democratic presidency. I told Clinton that if he privately raised the pos-sibility of resigning, that very act might force the Republicans to contemplate the prospect of having to run the next presidential campaign against Al Gore as an incumbent president. I was pretty sure the GOP would do almost any-thing to avoid that outcome and predicted that the GOP might be pulled toward the censure compromise.

Clinton clearly did not want to go down that road, but I felt I owed him my honest judgment that such an approach might be the only way he could prevent impeachment by the House. I didn't expect Clinton to consider that route—I had raised it as an "out-of-the-box" possibility that he should weigh—and Clinton soon adopted an all-or-nothing strategy, which the Re-publicans made clear they also preferred. Unless Clinton co-opted them, the ball was in the GOP's court, and they zealously proceeded down impeach-ment alley.

On December 19, the House approved two impeachment articles by votes of 228 to 206 and 221 to 212. It defeated the other two articles. Two days earlier, I had issued a statement announcing how I would vote. As usual, the House GOP leadership had rigged the outcome by denying those in the House who disagreed with their plans the opportunity to offer an alternative to their impeachment articles—in our case, a motion to censure instead of to impeach. In my statement I said:

The tool of impeachment was inserted in the Constitution to protect the country from irreparable harm, not to punish the president. Under our system of government, the proper institution to punish the president if he has violated the law is the court system (a legal institution) not the Congress (a political institution). . . . Whether the president has or has not committed perjury in legal proceedings is a technical, legal question that can be decided by a jury and a judge in our court system at the proper time. But there is no question that the president has misled the country and the Congress. That is unacceptable; but in my view, it does not rise to the level of an impeachable offense because the lie was essentially about sex, not about public acts. If the House ignores that distinction it fails in its obligation to put the president's acts in perspective. It will also fail to be fair if it treats the president differently from the way it treated Speaker Gingrich just two years ago when the Speaker was found guilty of not telling the truth to the House. In that case, the Speaker was not removed from office. He was not even censured. He was reprimanded and then re-elected to the Speakership by the Republican House majority.

For the House Republican leadership to, in effect, predetermine the outcome of this vote by refusing to allow a similar conscience vote on censure in this instance is a massive failure of fairness. If the House leadership can only win this vote by denying any alternative, it will have failed the country as much as Bill Clinton has.

After the House vote, the impeachment soap opera shifted to the Senate where both impeachment articles would eventually be defeated. But before that chapter could unfold, the House experienced yet another shock.

LIVINGSTON BECOMES A VICTIM

A decade earlier Newt Gingrich had brought down Speaker Jim Wright over what had initially been a minor scandal about violating the House rules on a book royalty deal. Now Gingrich had—unbelievably—ensnared himself in a much bigger book royalty deal. He had signed a six-figure deal with Rupert Murdoch, the international media zillionaire who had often concluded book deals involving large amounts of cash with the families of government leaders in other countries, such as China and Great Britain, where Murdoch wanted to do business. Gingrich had then compounded his problems by misleading the House Ethics Committee investigation about his manipulation of tax rulings. Newt was forced to publicly admit that he had dishonored the House by submitting "inaccurate, incomplete, and unreliable statements" to the Ethics

Committee investigating his use and abuse of tax exemptions. In a last-minute compromise to avoid censure, Gingrich had agreed to a reduced penalty, "a reprimand," and a $300,000 fine. Weeks later he announced he was leaving the Speakership and that he would be departing the House at a later date.

When it became clear Gingrich was likely to be pushed out, Bob Livingston jumped into the race to succeed Newt and within days had rounded up enough votes to be the next Speaker. I was delighted at the prospect because I thought Bob would be a principled leader who could drain off the poison and restore a sense of mutual respect in the institution. I also had a good working relationship with him and was confident we could continue that relationship. After the election, Bob was treated by everyone as the "Speaker-in-Waiting," but in the wake of House impeachment activities, stories of an extramarital affair surfaced, and Bob shocked the Capitol by announcing his own resignation from Congress.

I could not believe it. The frenzy that had enveloped Clinton had now devoured Livingston, my friend and one of the most decent, courageous, and honorable people in the House. I was in the Speaker's Lobby talking with reporters when word came to me that Bob had just made his resignation announcement on the House floor. "Oh my God, no!" I told the gaggle of reporters when they informed me of what Livingston had just said. It was beginning to look like the Salem witch trials, with no end in sight for the politics of personal destruction. I loved the House but could not bear to witness the cascading of events transforming the institution from an arena for the exchange of ideas to a poor imitation of a Roman coliseum where the blood sport was the devouring of reputations. Those weeks were probably the low point of my life in the House. The place had become a snake pit.

Washington was in a frenzy, and it was not a pretty sight. One week later the Republicans named Dennis Hastert of Illinois as their new Speaker. Hastert, a former high school wrestling coach, with the physical appearance of a burly, quiet, ambling bear, had been a lieutenant of Tom DeLay, the GOP whip. During the tumultuous last days of Gingrich, both Dick Armey, the GOP floor leader, and DeLay had been part of an aborted coup attempt. Armey did not have the horses to succeed Gingrich or Livingston, and DeLay was shrewd enough to recognize that he, like Newt, was too radioactive politically to accept a position as visible as the Speakership. In a display of self-evaluation and discipline rare in politicians, he decided to stay in the background, out of the spotlight, and told Hastert, "You're it." In sharp contrast to Gingrich, Hastert gave the GOP a softer, teddy-bear image. It was a smart public-relations move. But meanwhile, in true circus fashion, the show had to go on, and the Senate impeachment trial continued. One day after Hastert was elevated to the Speakership, the Senate trial of Clinton began. It continued for more than five weeks, until on February 12, 1999, the Senate turned down both impeachment charges. It was finally over, but it had done its damage to both parties.

Clinton's entire presidency had been diminished and robbed of its potential by six years of enervating attacks. Gingrich had destroyed his own utility as a leader by his pettiness and ruthlessness. Bob Livingston had become the latest victim in the cynical use of private conduct to destroy public lives. On a personal level I regretted Bob's action most of all; we were polar opposites in our political views, but we had developed a close working relationship after nearly two decades of Appropriations Committee work and were true friends.

In the tumult and chaos that surrounded the Livingston resignation, Jim Sensenbrenner, my Wisconsin colleague, observed in an interview with the *Milwaukee Journal* that public office could not be reserved for saints. "Anyone who serves in pubic office is a human being and subject to the same failings all of us are subject to," he told Frank Aukofer. "Maybe there are some people, particularly in the electronic news media, who ought to realize that the last perfect human being died two thousand years ago." I couldn't have said it better myself.

CHAPTER 21

༠

In the Trenches
with Clinton

In 1999, after eighteen years of digging out from Reagan-induced deficits, the performance of the economy (coupled with the long-term impact of Clinton's 1993 budget package) was moving the country away from triple-digit deficits toward a string of significant surpluses. Clinton and the Democrats hoped to use part of those surpluses for modest additional investments in education and health care, and use the rest to pay down some of the national debt so that the country would be better positioned to meet the pressures that the retirement of the baby-boom generation would place on the federal budget. The Republicans, however, couldn't leave well-enough alone. They were still hell-bent on using inflated predictions of future surpluses as an excuse to pass gargantuan tax cuts that would gobble up those surpluses. They would then be able to use the existence of the new deficits as an excuse to again push for cuts in Medicare, Medicaid, and other domestic programs, and to make a run at radically altering Social Security through a variety of privatization schemes.

The only reason the Republicans could vote for large tax cuts was because their outlandish economic assumptions allowed them to pretend that they were paying for them with projected surpluses, which in realty, under their program, would never exist. After passing their "Let's pretend!" tax cuts, the GOP again pleaded poverty because of those same revenue reductions; they proceeded to vote out of committee a Labor-Health-Education Appropriation bill that contained so many breathtaking gimmicks and which cut Clinton's education budget so deeply that they could not get the votes to pass the committee bill on the House floor. Over the following weeks, we went through the familiar arguments and counterarguments. When we finally got to conference with the Senate, the White House underestimated the strength of its own bargaining position. Congressional Republicans overestimated theirs.

I remember one late afternoon meeting in the Senate Appropriations Committee room when Arlen Specter and Tom Harkin, representing the Senate subcommittee, sat down across the table from John Porter and me. Specter and Harkin had produced a much more moderate bill than had the House GOP. Specter put on the table an offer for education that was roughly equal to the administration's request. He expected resistance from Porter, but not from me. He wanted a quick agreement; I didn't. I thought the longer the issue hung out, the better deal we could get for education. When I rejected his offer as insufficient, he exploded, "My God, I'm offering you the administration's level. You mean to say that's insufficient?" "That's exactly what I mean," I replied. He was furious, and I could tell Tom Harkin thought I was overplaying our hand. But it worked. We had to buck up the White House on two occasions in meetings in Dick Gephardt's office, but in the end, the conference produced a bill that was $1 billion *above* Clinton's for education and $2.4 billion *above* the original GOP House position. We had won major gains for the administration initiatives to reduce class size and increase investments in after school centers, teacher training, Title 1, and many other key activities.

The next year, Clinton's last, the House GOP marked up a Labor-H bill that again turned a cold shoulder to the president's education initiatives, cutting his request by $3 billion. Clinton had again focused on two areas in particular, reducing class size and improving teacher quality. We believed that the number-one concern of most parents was that their child be educated in a safe and decent, well-equipped school, in a class small enough to receive individual attention from a well-qualified teacher. The bill produced by the GOP committee largely dismantled Clinton's initiatives. The GOP conferenced the bill among themselves in July but avoided bringing it to the floor: the GOP leadership wanted to shield members from an internal caucus fight about going on record for such deep education cuts just before an election.

In September Dick Gephardt hosted a Democratic strategy meeting on appropriations, with the focus on the Labor-H bill. Representing the White House was John Podesta, Clinton's chief of staff, and Jack Lew, the budget director. When I told the group that I thought we ought to push for at least $6 billion more than the legislation the House Republicans had produced, they responded with skeptical chuckles. But Gephardt and I believed that with the election just around the corner, we could press our advantage to the hilt and get a strong deal for education. If Gore were elected, we would already be starting from a healthy base in putting together the following year's education budget, and if we lost the White House, which was beginning to look likely, it would be our last chance to strengthen those initiatives in a meaningful way. Podesta and Lew agreed to try.

For the next week, meeting in the Senate Appropriations Committee room, we pushed hard. Late in the evening, we reached agreement after a long, rough negotiation between Ted Stevens, Byrd, Young, Porter, and me. As the last items were being tied down, Stevens produced a satisfied smile and a bottle of Merlot, and we sealed the agreement with a toast. The agreement went far beyond restoring the $3 billion the House GOP had cut out of Clinton's education request. It provided $3.4 billion *above* Clinton's request and $6.3 billion *above* the original House GOP bill for education programs. But when the House GOP right wing saw the deal, they rebelled. Tom DeLay got the GOP to put a hold on the agreement. When Gore lost in November, we lost much of our bargaining power, but not all of it. Not by a long shot.

In December, at the Republicans' insistence, the agreement on education was cut back by $1.4 billion. Even with that change, we still wound up $2 billion above Clinton's and $4.9 billion above the original House GOP bill! And we had saved:

- An historic $1.2 billion to repair five thousand crumbling school buildings, a Clinton program that the House GOP bill had tried to kill
- A robust $1.6 billion to support thirty-seven thousand new teachers in order to reduce large classes in grades one through three, an initiative that had been dismantled in the House GOP bill
- An additional $661 million over the House GOP bill for academic tutoring for low-income children, increasing total funding for Title I grants to schools to a record $8.6 billion
- An additional $246 million over the House GOP bill to provide a record $846 million for after school services for 1.2 million children
- A $850 million increase over the House GOP bill for education services for children with disabilities, raising the federal contribution to special-education costs to a record $6.3 billion—about $1.1 billion more than the amount Clinton had requested
- A $3,750 maximum Pell scholarship for low-income college students, $250 more than the House GOP bill and the largest increase in the history of the Pell Grant program

It had been a wild eight-year run, but it had been worth the fight.

WHAT WE GAINED FOR EDUCATION

In the six-year period from fiscal year 1996 to 2001, we had succeeded in raising investments in education by some $16 billion above the level that would have resulted had the House GOP had been left to its own devices. I was proud that I had pushed the Republicans—and sometimes the White House—so hard that we had even been able to provide funding $3 billion above the levels requested by the Clinton White House. Despite our minority status, we had dragged House Republicans kicking and screaming from a position that in 1995 had demanded the elimination of the Department of Education to their acceptance of our demands to increase investments in education from $24 billion to $42 billion over eight years.

Despite the deep partisan divide on the value of federal support for education, John Porter and I were able to strengthen investments in Comprehensive School Reform (CSR)—through which schools that wanted to try to emulate research-based models for raising student performance would receive the guidance and planning help to do so. The CSR was generated by Scott Lilly and Cheryl Smith, my incredibly able and thoughtful education specialist on the Labor-H Subcommittee, working with the New American Schools Corporation (a group led by business leaders like David Kearns, former CEO of Xerox and former deputy secretary of the U.S. Department of Education). We were able to raise the funding for the initiative from $148 million in FY 1998 to $260 million by FY 2001, providing help to more than four thousand schools around the country.

Skeptical conservatives launched an attack on the initiative on the House floor during debate on the FY 1998 Labor-HHS appropriations bill. However, a compromise was ultimately brokered by Bill Goodling, the former Republican representative from Pennsylvania, who was familiar with the "Success for All" comprehensive school reform model developed by Robert Slavin at Johns Hopkins University and understood what John Porter and I were trying to accomplish.

We had also begun the process of increasing funding for Small School Reform. For a generation, the nation had pushed consolidation of high schools to create larger and larger comprehensive institutions. But new research seemed to indicate that the high schools that worked best were those with between six hundred and eight hundred students. For many students, high schools had become so big, so impersonal, and so remote that students and teachers had lost effective contact with each other. Cheryl and Scott showed me the research, which suggested that downsizing high schools or creating smaller learning centers might indeed eliminate a sense of student isolation and improve student performance. In the last two years of the Clinton administration, we had been able to nearly triple the funding for the program to $125 million, which helped nearly 750 large, comprehensive high schools to reorganize. Bill Gates, the founder of Microsoft, had become so enthusiastic about downsizing giant high schools that his foundation had invested about as much in the effort as the entire United States government.

We also achieved some worthwhile gains outside the area of education. In the aftermath of Clinton's failure to pass health-care reform, David Reich, my versatile Appropriations staffer on health and tax questions, led our effort to work with Donna Shalala to find ways to increase access to health care for the poor through a variety of ad hoc approaches. We raised funding for community health centers by 55 percent over that same six-year period and began the process of doubling research funding for NIH over a five-year period. We were also able to provide broader access to desperately needed dental care for thousands of additional Americans and to significantly expand help for the millions of American children suffering from depression, both of which were high priorities of mine. It had been a fight worth waging.

In the teeth of GOP efforts to eliminate LIHEAP, we had preserved it. Although we had been able to turn back Republican assaults on Labor Department programs that protected workers on the wage-and-hours, collective-bargaining, and pension-protection front, we experienced some setbacks on labor law. Being in the minority had not been as enjoyable as being in the majority, but sometimes the fights you won in the minority were more precious because of the magnitude of the potential damage to people you are trying to protect if you lose.

Throughout his presidency, Clinton had been a much higher maintenance president than any of us had imagined when he walked into the White House eight years earlier. But as he left, I knew we would miss having someone in the White House whose instincts were clearly on the side of social justice rather than social Darwinism, who had a deep belief in the social gospel and the message of the Sermon on the Mount, and whose veto power could increase our leverage to do good and prevent damage. His triangulation efforts after the Republicans took power had driven us to distraction, but at least on the basics, his heart was in the right place, even if he frequently gave away too much of his tactical advantage and did too little to prepare for the day when he would be gone and the people he cared about would need more friends in Congress.

CLINTON'S TRADE LEGACY

One issue on which I wish Clinton had provided greater clarity of leadership was trade. He correctly understood that economic globalization was a reality that could not be wished away, but from the start, he had been boxed in by his predecessor. George Bush had negotiated the North American Free Trade Agreement (NAFTA) with Mexico, and Clinton was stuck with the responsibility for pushing it through. Clinton went through the motions of trying to obtain sidebar understandings on environmental standards and workers rights, but he basically treated the issue as window dressing. That remained the case in the trade area for most of his presidency. Only in the last year, when anti-globalization demonstrators in Seattle and Washington hit the streets to voice their discontent about the injustice that often accompanied new trade rules, did he seem to take a more sensitive interest in the impact of trade agreements on lower-wage workers. Those demonstrations turned violent and, in the process, destroyed any chance that they would make a legitimate point, but the controversy compelled me, as a committed internationalist, to get a few things off my chest on the subject.

Years earlier, when the House debated NAFTA, the justification for NAFTA being put forward by both Clinton and Gingrich was that while the United States might indeed lose jobs to Mexico because of NAFTA, they would be low-wage jobs, and that those low-wage workers could be retrained, and the United States could concentrate on high-value-added jobs. In my capacity as JEC chair, I had the staff analyze conflicting studies of the impact of NAFTA on American jobs and wages. I then gave a floor speech predicting that when the time came to provide help to those displaced low-wage workers, the conservative free marketers in the Congress would stop short of providing sufficient resources to actually help the workers and that there would be no follow-through. That's exactly what happened. Once NAFTA was passed, the GOP majority gave only lip service to job training, and I struggled to find the resources in the budget for it.

After the Seattle and Washington demonstrations in 2000, I gave another speech saying that if free trade supporters wanted to avoid a class-based polarization of the country on the issue, they needed to deal with legitimate concerns about the social consequences of their position. On May 19, 2006, in a speech titled "Who Are the True Dinosaurs on Trade?" I observed:

> The Washington political establishment is looking down its collective elitist nose at those of us who are saying no to legislation that would provide permanent

most-favored-nation trading status for China. In their newspaper columns and at their cocktail parties they tut-tut that those of us raising a challenge to that legislation are simply trying to stop the economic progress that comes from globalized trade and are, therefore, hopelessly old fashioned. The fact is just the opposite. . . .

The issue here is not really China. China just happens to be the country that triggered this debate. The issue is whether America's policymakers, who have helped magnify the income gains of the most well-off in our society by squeezing the economic positions of the most at-risk families, will recognize their moral obligation to change course. The issue is whether those in this society—the investing class, the managing elite, the venture capitalists, the multinational corporations who have so much to gain by further globalization—will be willing to see a tiny fraction of that increased wealth used to help those who will otherwise be caught in the prop wash of their incredible prosperity.

When a doctor administers cancer-fighting drugs, he knows that he must also deal with the side effects of those drugs or his patient will not be able to tolerate the drug and will die. Isn't that just as true of the negative side effects of globalization on the lower-paid, under-skilled workers caught in the wake of economic change?

Demonstrators in Seattle and Washington may have aimed their protests at some of the wrong targets, but that should not obscure the injustice that produced those demonstrations. As Barney Frank has said, "the choice is not between isolation and integration, but between a global new deal and a global extension of the trickle-down theory."

Those who want us to approve their rules without first changing the rules of the trading game that contribute to this injustice are the true troglodytes and dinosaurs.

I had not expected to change any minds, and I didn't. I believed then and I believe even more strongly today that the worst example of American myopia on trade is the case of China. The U.S. trade deficit with China when Clinton took office was $18 billion. When he left office it had grown to $84 billion. Today it stands at over $200 billion, and it is rising.

Globalization of the economy is unavoidable, but if it is used in the twenty-first century to eliminate or minimize the gains that were made by workers in the twentieth century, public anger surrounding the trade issue will bitterly divide this country and will produce a destructive backlash that damages our ability to promote legitimate trading activities. In his last months in office Clinton seemed to recognize that, but it was too late for him and Al Gore.

The U.S. government's refusal to deal with that reality has been a huge policy failure. Over the next twenty years no foreign policy issue will be more important to the United States than the question on how to manage China's transition from a Third World, third-level economic and military power to the largest economy in the world. China has hundreds of millions of workers who are willing to produce any product at a price so low that no industrialized country's workers will be able to compete. This threatens to destroy the foundation under workers' wages, which has been at the core of U.S. prosperity and civil peace for two generations. The United States simply cannot allow China to continue to manipulate its currency in a manner that gives them a 30 percent price advantage in selling anything that we also seek to sell in the marketplace. We must find ways to prevent a centralized economy from pretending it is participating in the world marketplace as a real market economy.

Unless we want to experience a huge public backlash against trade, we simply must take action in the public sector to provide decent education opportunities, decent housing, and decent affordable health care to workers who would otherwise bear the full burden of competing with China, while others in the economy would avoid any share of that burden whatsoever. The United States has two challenges in dealing with China in the new century. One is to manage China's military growth in a way that does not turn tensions into crisis. The second is to manage China's economic growth in a way that allows the Chinese to improve the lot of their people without manipulating currency, exchange rates, and international trading rules in a way that destroys the ability of American workers to sustain the gains in wages, working conditions, and benefits that have been so hard won in the last seventy years. If this society does not find ways to compensate workers for the losses that result from the manipulation of the pressures of globalization by weaving safety nets under workers' wages and pensions, we will most certainly disintegrate into two different Americas, and the promise of the American dream will be gone for more than half of our population. That unhappy result will be harder to prevent, because Al Gore won the 2000 vote but lost the 2000 election to George W. Bush.

❧

CHAPTER 22

Bush II

No president I have ever served with has surprised me as much as George W. Bush. The way he came to office—selected rather than elected, the first president since 1876 to come into office knowing that more Americans voted for his opponent than had voted for him—led me and a lot of other Americans to the reasonable conclusion that he might, at least occasionally, try to govern through conciliation rather than confrontation. That was certainly the impression Bush gave the nation as he campaigned with his promise "to change the Washington way of confrontation," his reference to the need to reach bipartisan consensus, and his calls for a "more humble" foreign policy. I couldn't have been more wrong.

I had had great respect for the president's father. He hadn't had a clue about what was happening to people in the economy, but he was a thoughtful, practical man who, with the exception of his comment after his debate with Geraldine Ferrarro when he was Ronald Reagan's running mate ("I kicked a little ass tonight.") and his Willy Horton ad against Governor Dukakis, had a track record of demonstrating respect for his opponents. But it soon became clear his son was all big business. It took no time at all for Bush's approach to demonstrate that he would preside over the most unabashedly right-wing, pro-big business administration since William McKinley.

The clearest early indication was the list of people Dick Cheney appointed to the administration's energy transition team. Bush was straight out of the Texas oil crowd, and that group was given immense access to the inner circle of the new administration. Of sixty-three people appointed to the energy transition team, fifty were from energy corporations like Enron, Halliburton, and others of the same ilk. Only one was from a public interest group and one from an energy conservation group. The transition team was a clear signal that this would be an administration of big energy, by big energy, and for big energy.

TEXAS AS A MODEL

I had expected Bush to be a somewhat more conservative president than his father—he had after all grown up in Midland, Texas, rather than in Connecticut, and it showed. But by every action he took—on taxes, budgets, energy policy, government regulation, and environmental protection—he signaled he would be a radically conservative not moderate, confrontational not conciliatory, chief executive. In an insightful *Washington Post* column, Harold Meyerson wrote of the starkly different worldviews of two Texas presidents— Lyndon Johnson and George W. Bush. Meyerson noted that LBJ, as a protégé of FDR, was appalled by the rural poverty he saw in his own Texas neighborhood and tried to use government to do everything it could to raise Texas to national standards. In contrast, Bush seemed to want to do just the opposite. His program appeared to be designed to strip the role of government *down* to Texas standards, that Texas seemed to be the prototype for the kind of society Bush believed in, "with no income tax, few unions, low benefits, and little regulation of corporate powers." Meyerson observed that Texas leads the nation in senior citizen poverty and has the largest percentage of uninsured in the nation. "Texas had created an ownership society that excluded more Americans than any other state."

BACK INTO THE DEFICIT DITCH

The issue that most defined Bush and most infuriated me was taxes. From the day he took office he was hell-bent to reverse Clinton's hard-won gains on the fiscal front by cutting huge amounts from the nation's revenue base, without giving Americans a hint of what the consequences would be for our ability to make long-term economic investments, deal with huge remaining holes in the nation's safety net, or strengthen the system of hard-earned retirement benefits for working Americans. He proposed a $1.6 trillion ten-year tax cut based on the same false assumptions about mythical surpluses that congressional Republicans had used in their tax bills during the Reagan and Clinton eras. Telling the public that we could expect to see $6 trillion in surpluses the next ten years, Bush pushed the old-time GOP religion of free-lunch tax cuts that his father had denounced as "voodoo economics." With some modification, House Republicans bought the pitch. Bush suffered a temporary delay when

Vermont senator Jim Jeffords left the GOP, became an Independent, and voted with the Senate Democrats to give control of that body back to the Democrats by one vote—but within a month Bush got what he wanted. I focused my efforts on raising as much Cain as possible about the effect GOP tax policy would have on issues and programs within the jurisdiction of Appropriations.

When you are in the minority and the other team has the votes, you cannot very often measure your efforts by your victories. You recognize that in the short run you are going to lose whatever battles you are fighting. But it's important, even in the act of losing, to define differences in such a way that the public can understand the consequences for themselves and the country if their leaders make the wrong choices. If Bush was determined to spend every dollar on the table in tax cuts, then I wanted people—the Congress and the public alike—to understand what the tradeoffs were, and what they would be losing on the education and health-care fronts.

To give people an idea of what other trade-off decisions could be made between the president's tax proposals and other national priorities, David Reich, Cheryl Smith, Scott Lilly, and I put together a series of proposals to illustrate better uses for some of that money. We started with an educational alternative that focused on raising the quality of teacher training, which could be financed by limiting to the size of the tax cuts that Bush was proposing for persons who made over $200,000—those in the top two income-tax brackets. But the Republicans were determined to avoid votes on any such trade-offs and continually used House rules and the budget process itself to prevent the House from voting on such amendments. During the August recess, I spent much of my time talking with constituents about those trade-offs.

CHAPTER 23

9/11:
The World Changes

The summer of 2001 had been wonderful, much of it spent at our remodeled northwest Wisconsin cottage in Rusk County. Joan and I had two straight weeks there—our longest uninterrupted peaceful vacation time since we had taken our sons to Glacier National Park in 1983. The two weeks before the break had been killers. Because nights were short and sleep scarce, I badly needed the August recess to recharge my batteries, and for several weeks I did. In the middle of August, Scott Lilly reported to me on a classified briefing that he had received from the CIA. "The agency says that communications traffic has picked up considerably. They don't know whether something will happen here or abroad, but they think some kind of hit is coming." I asked Scott to let me know if any other information surfaced. I finished the recess by participating in the Merrill and Wausau Labor Day parades and returned to Washington rested and refreshed. The first week back started slowly, but that changed dramatically on an early Tuesday morning in September.

At 8:30 a.m. on September 11, Democratic members of the Appropriations Committee had gathered in Dick Gephardt's Capitol office to discuss the overall budget situation. About 8:55 Scott Lilly passed me a note saying that Gephardt's staff had just heard that a plane had hit the World Trade Center in New York. I leaned back and asked if the September 11 date had any special significance to any terrorist group. Ten minutes later, Scott whispered, "It's not one plane, it's two." Dick immediately turned on the TV, and the meeting broke up. We knew then that the world had changed.

Scott and I left Gephardt's office and hurried toward the Appropriations Committee office off the House floor to check in before we headed down to H140, where we were scheduled to mark up the defense appropriations bill. One of the issues to be discussed was an effort to move $640 million out of the missile defense account, money that had not been used, and move it to accounts aimed at dealing with terrorism. As we reached the Speakers lobby, just off the House floor, a lobby clerk told us, "The Pentagon has just been hit. We are under orders to evacuate the building. They are saying that a plane is in the air headed toward the Capitol." As Scott and I walked into the committee office, we could see through a window that smoke was rising from the city skyline across the Potomac. It was true; the Pentagon itself was under attack, and we expected to be next. The committee clerk told us the Department of Defense meeting was off, and we needed to clear out. As we stepped out into the hall, a herd of grim-faced, tense young House pages filed hurriedly out of the House chamber and headed for the elevators to take them down to the subway, which would in turn take them to the basement of the Rayburn House Office Building and away from the Capitol.

Scott headed to the Longworth building to make sure our committee staff had heard the news and had been evacuated, while I hurried to Rayburn to make sure my personal staff was out. We planned to regroup at the Democratic Club, about two blocks from the Capitol, to figure out what to do next. It was impossible to get an elevator because everyone was trying to get out of the building, so I went to the stairwell and ran up the stairs to my third-floor office. When I got to the office, most of the staff was still there watching events on TV. I ordered them out of the building. Next, I phoned Joan to make sure she had heard the news—she hadn't—and to ask her to call Craig and Doug. Then I left, thinking that any moment we were going to be hit.

When I got to the club, it was closed. People in an office next door invited us to come in to watch the events with them and to use the phones. For the next two hours, we alternately watched the horror on television and tried to get information on the phone from the White House, the CIA, and other information sources. At that point, after the bridges across the Potomac had emptied, I drove over the Fourteenth Street bridge and up the George Washington Parkway past the Pentagon, and worked the phone from home.

A UNITED RESPONSE

The next morning, we were told that the White House was planning to ask for an unlimited amount of money for an unlimited period of time for any items whatsoever that they could tie in any way to a response to terrorism. My immediate reaction was that such carte blanche would be an unwarranted and unprecedented abdication of Congress's power of the purse.

Scott and I met with Bill Young and his staff chief, Jim Dyer, to voice our concerns about a congressional blank check. They agreed. By evening, they had decided to prepare an alternative that would provide an immediate $20 billion on a no-questions-asked basis. I told Young that I still regarded that as a huge abdication of Congress's responsibility and would not support it.

The next morning, the Speaker called a meeting in his office, and after some discussion asked Young and me and our Senate counterparts, senators Robert Byrd and Ted Stevens, to hammer out a proposal by the end of the day. The four of us met in S128, the ornate Senate Appropriations Committee room on the first floor of the Capitol. Both New York senators, Chuck Schumer and Hillary Clinton, had been pushing the president for a specific amount of money as a down payment on the huge rebuilding job ahead for New York City. At about 4:30 p.m. we finally agreed on a four-step proposal:

1. The first $10 billion would be made available to the president to finance any emergency response he felt appropriate, subject to consultation with Congress. In practice that meant the top congressional leadership and the Appropriations Committee leadership would be briefed on the details.
2. The second $10 billion would be made available subject to a requirement that the president submit his plans for the money to Congress and that Congress have fifteen days to review them and suggest alternatives to the president. In my view this was *crucial* to maintaining the ability to force agencies to listen to congressional concerns and suggestions.
3. The last $20 billion would be provided through the regular appropriations process. The administration could request but Congress would have to approve the funding in future appropriations bills—the normal order of business.
4. Within that $40 billion three-step total, $20 billion would be committed to response-and-reconstruction efforts in New York, Virginia, and Pennsylvania, the three crash sites.

Jim Dyer called OMB to tell Mitch Daniels what we had agreed upon. Jim reported back that Daniels's response was that it sounded reasonable to him, and he would tell the president. Just as Jim finished reporting, a Capitol cop burst into the room and told us to evacuate the building because a lock on a basement door seemed to be altered and they were worried about a bomb. We spilled out onto the east grounds of the Capitol and began working our cell phones. When we were finally given the all clear to reenter the building, I headed to HC5, a nondescript, windowless room in the Capitol basement, to brief the Democratic caucus.

At the caucus, scores of members buttonholed me to express their consternation at the idea of voting a blank check. Most were reassured when I explained how we had modified the administration's original plans. After cooling down the caucus, I went up to H218, the Appropriations Committee room, to see how soon we could have the first draft ready for the floor. But instead of being handed a copy of the language reflecting our agreement, I was given a copy of new language that was being suggested by the White House—language that departed sharply from the agreement we had reached just two hours ago. The language again gave the president carte blanche authority to spend $20 billion any way he wanted. I immediately told Bill Young that there was no way I was going to accept an unraveling of the agreement we had just worked out. I hurried down to Gephardt's office to tell him that it looked like the administration was backing off the agreement, but Dick was not in his office. Ironically, he and Speaker Hastert had just gone out on the lawn to tell CNN how pleased they were that we appeared to have reached a bipartisan agreement. Dick's staff called the Speaker's office and told them I was raising hell because of the new language. One of the Speaker's staff said, "We don't blame Obey for being mad—it looks like a deal-breaker to me."

Then we got word that I was to come to an emergency meeting in the Speaker's office. At about 9 p.m. we walked into the Speaker's meeting where Young, Byrd, the Speaker, Tom Daschle, and Harry Reid, the majority leader and majority whip, had already gathered. To my surprise, we were joined by Don Nickels, the Senate GOP whip who had been a constant thorn in the side of Senate majority leader Trent Lott; Pete Domenici, the Budget Committee ranking member; and my old nemesis Phil Gramm.

For the next four hours we went round and round the table. I mostly listened while Gramm, Nickles, and Domenici raised one challenge after another to the deal. They seemed to have three objections. First, they objected to the size of the package and wanted it renegotiated to suit GOP conservatives. Nickels spoke as though Democrats had pumped up the package. I responded that when Byrd and I began negotiating, we were proposing an immediate $5 billion package in contrast to the administration's open-ended, unlimited proposal. Then Gramm and Nickels objected to the size of the New York piece. Gephardt and I pointed out that the president himself had agreed to that $20 billion in conversations with senators Clinton and Schumer. It was determined that since more money would eventually be needed, the number would stand.

Dick Armey raised concerns about the second $10 billion being subject to what is known as the notification process. Under that process, money is appropriated, but the administration must notify the Appropriations Committee of their specific plans, and if the chair and the ranking member of the committee or subcommittee disapprove of a particular proposal, the administration informally agrees to modify its approach. Dick made a snide remark that the process "gave an awful lot of power to four people"—referring to Byrd, Stevens, Young, and myself. The Republican right wing in the House for years had found fault with the process, claiming that it gave Appropriations leaders too much power. I turned to Armey and said, "Dick, I'll make you a proposition—if you want to include a provision in this package that eliminates the notification process across the board I will support it. You act as though that process is an enhancement of congressional power and committee power. In fact, it is just the opposite." "Without it," I explained to Armey, "the executive branch would have to submit detailed plans for the spending of every dollar, and once Congress had appropriated the money, the administration would have no flexibility whatsoever to move money around." To my great surprise, Tom DeLay, the House Republican whip, who almost without exception has been aligned against me and the things I held dear for as long as he had been in Congress, turned to Armey and said, "That's exactly right, Dick." That ended the argument, especially because Bob Byrd had previously stood hard and fast against the idea of reneging on the previous agreement.

Then I turned to the Speaker to deal with the demands coming from Gramm and Nichols.

> Mr. Speaker, everyone says that at this moment we need unity and I agree with that. But at a time of crisis, there are two kinds of unity. One is the unity that papers over honest differences and is imposed in the passion of the moment. The other is the kind that comes from listening to each other and taking into account and reconciling honestly held differences. The first kind of unity lasts only as long as the passion. The second lasts as long as it needs to. We want unity, but one that reasonably respects the needs of the president for fast action and the obligation of Congress to retain the power of the purse. Outside of the power to investigate, the Congress has only two powers that really count in the end. The first is the power to make war; the second is the power of the purse. Like it or not, the last thirty years of changing technology and the acceleration of decisions that are required, it is the president in the real world who decides how and when the trigger is pulled. We can try to prevent that power from being eroded further, but our ability to do so is increasingly diminished. That makes it all the more important for Congress, as a coequal branch of government, to protect our constitutional obligation to control the power of the purse. That is the last power we have to preserve American liberty.

After several others had commented, the Speaker cut in and said that he believed the agreement—except for language changes that we had agreed upon to clarify some questions raised by Gramm—should stand. As Nickels and Gramm fought their rearguard action, it became clear to me what they were really after. They wanted to use the emergency supplemental to make future appropriations decisions subject to procedural roadblocks, which could be raised on the Senate floor through points of order. Their targets were Bob Byrd and Ted Stevens. It became obvious to me why Ted Stevens wasn't at that meeting that night. He had no intention of supporting their demands, and figured he ought to stay out of the line of fire and let others like Byrd, Young, and me shoot them down. About 12:45 a.m., the Speaker said, "We are going to stay here until we have this tied down." Tom Daschle then made a concession to Gramm on a modest procedural point, and the steam went out of the mini-rebellion. As I walked out of the room I thought to myself that the Speaker had played an indispensable role in pushing the group to a final conclusion. He had listened to what everyone was trying to say. If he had not been in the room, the meeting would have descended into ideological hairsplitting within GOP ranks. I admired the steady hand he had applied to the situation.

The next morning, Young and I brought the agreement to the floor and it passed unanimously. But before the evening was over, another group tried to claim almost one-third of the $40 billion we had appropriated. The GOP chief deputy whip Ray Blunt, Tom DeLay, and Don Young, the chair of the Public Works Committee, and my good friend, Jim Oberstar, his Democratic counterpart, tried to bring to the floor a proposal to divert at least $12 billion of the money we had appropriated earlier that day to provide an emergency bailout of the airline industry, which had been hit hard by the DOT order on 9/11 to ground every plane in America until safety could be assured.

Bill Young and I saw three problems with that. First, the money we had appropriated was not for that purpose. Second, there had been no reasonable review of actual industry needs—several airlines had been near bankruptcy before the terrorist attack because of economic mismanagement and other corporate problems. Third, while billions were being requested to shield investors from losses, nothing whatsoever was being provided for the twenty thousand airline workers who had also been crunched by the industry shutdown and laid off.

Don Young tried to get the bill brought up by unanimous consent. Bill Young and I both recognized that some kind of aid to the airline industry was essential because the aftermath of 9/11 had ruined their balance sheets, and the country certainly could not afford a collapse of the industry. We teamed up on the floor to raise a series of questions that needed to be answered before $15 billion of taxpayers' money was given away. The floor was in total confusion, but our litany of questions helped members on both sides of the aisle to understand why the proposition should be delayed until both the administration and Congress could review it. I knew that Lloyd Dogget of Texas was eventually going to object to the bill's immediate consideration, but I wanted to get on the record the legitimate reasons for taking the weekend for those questions to be answered. After we laid out the questions, Dogget did object, which stopped consideration until the House could gain enough information to deal with the issue the following week.

The airlines were mad as hell. They thought that in the panic of the moment no one would have the guts to get in the way of their power play. Even before September 11, Continental Airlines, which was headquartered in Dogget's home state, had been planning to lay off thousands of workers because the company was near a second bankruptcy. Immediately after Dogget's objection, the company president announced the layoff of thousands of workers, but in a cynical twist, inserted a note along with the worker's pink slips telling them they were being laid off because of Dogget's action. It wasn't true. Most of the layoffs had been in the works before 9/11, but it helped coerce Congress into passing a similar bill a week later. That bill was exhibit A in how the Congress often sets one standard for the investor class and another for the working class. It provided billions to bail out the industry, but not one red cent to help the workers who had lost much more than their investment— they had lost their jobs.

Eight days after September 11, Bill Young and I went up to ground zero in New York to get a firsthand understanding of the damage as well as a classified briefing from the FBI Anti-Terror Unit in New York. Because planes weren't flying, we made the trip by Amtrak. On the way up we got a taste of things to come when Amtrak officials briefed us on the cost of their own security needs. The numbers were mind-boggling, but they were just a fraction of the costs that would hit us within days.

ANTHRAX

On October 18, Capitol Hill was shut down after an envelope containing anthrax powder was mailed to Senate Democratic leader Tom Daschle's office. Anthrax spores were found in Daschle's office and Russ Feingold's office next door. They were also detected in the Longworth House Office Building and several federal mail-handling facilities in Washington. The Speaker ordered the House shut down over a long weekend until the nature of the anthrax threat could be determined. Scott and I decided that since we could not get into our offices, we ought to use the time to talk with intelligence and security agencies like the CIA, NSA, FBI, HHS, and CDC to get a better understanding of what they needed from Congress after the initial $40 billion to deal with the threat of terrorism. We called Bill Young and Jim Dyer to suggest we do it together, and they readily agreed.

Scott, Jim, and I arranged three full days of briefings so that we would have a clear understanding of the needs and concerns of the agencies most responsible for future security action. We started with the NSA in Fort Meade, Maryland. The NSA coordinates, monitors, and analyzes all U.S. global electronic intercepts. That briefing was followed by a session with the CIA to get a fuller picture of worldwide intelligence gathering activity and their detective efforts to piece together how the disaster had happened, where Bin Laden could be reached, and where our future vulnerabilities might lie. Then came a long session with the FBI task force organized to find the perpetrators and analyze where further terrorist sleeper cells might be hiding. One investigator told us, "I can't sleep at night. Every night I think: 'If we could just find one more piece I might be able to prevent another disaster.'" After that came sessions with HHS and CDC to get a full picture of the threats to public health and the government's ability to deal with those threats. Those meetings were followed by other staff briefings with Immigration and Customs. I met with Dick Gephardt, told him what Young and I were doing, and warned that we would need billions more to begin to deal with the nation's most serious security gaps. Especially high on our list of concerns were a number of threats to our own security agencies. "I'll back whatever you think is necessary," Dick said and volunteered that he would ask the president to sit down with appropriators to hear our concerns.

STIFFED AT THE WHITE HOUSE

What Bill and I had expected was that when the DoD appropriations bill was reported to the full committee, he and I would offer a bipartisan emergency supplemental to address security measures at our own security agencies, expand the capacity of the FBI, Coast Guard, Immigration, Customs, Energy Department, and the Army Corps of Engineers to patrol and inspect our borders and ports, and protect nuclear weapons facilities, nuclear power plants, and the nation's system of locks and dams, and finally, accelerate our efforts to prevent nuclear material in the former Soviet Union from falling into the hands of rogue nations and terrorists. On the Senate side our opposite members—Ted Stevens and Bob Byrd—mapped similar plans. We wanted to sit down with the president and Mitch Daniels, his OMB director, and lay out our concerns and reasons for wanting additional funding.

I looked at the preliminary list of options being developed and told Scott to knock off every program, no matter how deserving, if we didn't need to launch it immediately. Then I told him to cut our bottom line in half so there could be no doubt that what we were recommending constituted true emergencies.

BUSH STONEWALLS HOMELAND SECURITY

When the president walked into the Cabinet Room, it was immediately obvious to me that it was going to be a political rather than substantive meeting because none of the president's substantive people—Cheney, Justice Department, FBI, Immigration—were there. But his political people, led by advisor Karl Rove, were.

Bush sat down and said, "Thank you for coming. I understand some of you want to spend more money on homeland security than we are asking for. My friend, Mitch Daniels from OMB, tells me that we have asked for all that we need. I'll ask him to walk you through the numbers, but I want you to know if you appropriate one dollar more than we asked for, I will veto the bill. I'll now call on Mitch to explain." After Daniels had walked briefly through the administration's budget request, Bush said, "I'll now take four or five comments and then I'm out of here for another meeting." Young and I exchanged quick glances and shook our heads.

Bush first called on Bob Byrd, who vented his views about relationships between the executive and legislative branches of government. Next Bush called on Ted Stevens who told Bush, "Mr. President, it's important for you to understand that all the dollars we are thinking about providing are on a contingency basis, which means that, for each item, if you don't sign an emergency designation, the money for that item can't be spent." It was obvious from Bush's reaction that that had not been explained to him. Then Bill Young was called on, and he tried to make the same point and urged the president not to get into a veto mode on something that we were trying to keep bipartisan. Then Bush called on me.

> Mr. President, you've been blunt, and so I will be blunt as well. In the thirty years
> I have been coming down here this is the first time I ever heard a president say

his mind was closed before the subject was even opened. You say you will veto whatever we send you if it is one dime above what you asked. I'm sorry to hear that because the four of us here are trying to put together a package of security measures that are distinctly bipartisan. I know you are being told that we are putting together a list of items that is porked up, the way that Congress often reacts. Well, Mr. President, I want you to know that if you can find a single item of pork in the bill that Bill Young and I are putting together, I'll eat this table. I am confident that if you would have your staff sit down with ours, you will have no objection with three-quarters of these items, and whatever items you do object to we will drop. Mr. President, OMB tells you that they do not need the money that we're talking about, but I want to ask you about four instances where we have been told by your own agency people that federal installations themselves are at risk of a terrorist attack. I want to ask you if you have been briefed about any of them. If you have, I want to know what you've been told because I know what I've been told, and it scares the hell out of me.

I then described four classified cases of extreme vulnerability that had been the highest concern of security experts in the agencies we had talked with and asked Bush if he had been briefed on any of them. If he had been, he gave no evidence of it. His body language, eyes darting around the room, glancing over his left shoulder, made clear to me that he hadn't.

I tried to make one last point with Bush. I told him of the FBI agent we had talked with who had told me about his inability to sleep because of his desperate hope to find one more clue that would put the puzzle together. Bush's response was "Thank you for coming." He then took a couple of brief comments from others, said he had to leave, and the meeting was over. So much for give-and-take discussion. As we walked out of the meeting I turned to Dick Gephardt and said, "Dick, that man is a walking, talking security risk. He doesn't know enough about homeland security issues to be using a veto threat on anybody. I can't believe we're even having an argument about this."

Back on the Hill, the GOP leadership quickly ordered the Rules Committee not to allow my amendment incorporating the Young-Obey list to be offered. After some behind-the-scenes maneuvering, the Republican leadership prevailed and adopted a rule that prevented the House from even voting on my homeland security package. I knew the Senate would not roll over as easily because Byrd would fight, and Senate rules provided much greater opportunity to obtain consideration of amendments. Byrd also lost the initial battle in the Senate but was able eventually to squeeze billions more into the package. In conference, Byrd, Young, Stevens, and I put our staff chiefs into a room, and in a matter of days we agreed on a $2.7 billion homeland security add-on . . . and the president reluctantly signed it.

The White House was not alone in resisting added resources for homeland security. So was the highest law enforcement official in the land. One day before the United States was attacked by Al-Qaeda, John Ashcroft met with his staff in a planning meeting to determine Justice Department priorities for the following year. In that meeting Ashcroft specifically declined to list anti-terrorism as an agency priority, saying that he preferred to focus on such issues as drugs. Ashcroft later tried to deny the episode when I questioned him about it in an Appropriations hearing, but spreadsheets and other documents had been leaked to us, which made it clear that despite concerns expressed by his staff, antiterrorist activities were not on Ashcroft's radar screen.

Throughout Bush's first term, it continued to be incredibly difficult to persuade the administration to provide sufficient homeland security budgets. After we had won that first fight to add $2.7 billion over the president's objection, I thought it would be easier to follow through with more aggressive funding the next time around. But the following year the tug of war repeated itself.

Changing the Homeland Security Boxes

Of all the issues I have dealt with in my years of congressional service, none has baffled me as much as the resistance to bipartisan congressional efforts to invest more in homeland security demonstrated by the Bush administration.

Our frustrations deepened the following year when the president, in effect, pocket-vetoed security add-ons that were a fraction of what we needed. While we were trying to add money to help first responders and local communities upgrade their training and equipment, working to strengthen customs and immigration screening along the Canadian border, and struggling to strengthen our ability to inspect cargo containers in vulnerable ports across the nation, the administration's focus turned instead to reorganizing the homeland security bureaucracy.

Not long after 9/11, Joe Lieberman introduced legislation to reorganize the executive agencies that dealt with homeland security by creating a cabinet-level Department of Homeland Security. At first the idea appealed to me, but the more we analyzed it, the more Scott Lilly, Beverly Pheto, my Homeland Security expert, and I concluded that reorganization was almost peripheral to our main security problems. For months the administration resisted Lieberman's proposal, but, in the end, I believe they simply got tired of having to resist a popular idea and switched their position from resistance to advocacy.

In the House, Dick Armey was named chair of the special committee to deal with the reorganization effort. On January 17, 2002, Young and I outlined our concerns in testimony before Armey's committee. Our main concern was that under the guise of reorganization, the administration was proposing massive changes in budgeting that would remove too many congressional checks on agency funding. The White House proposed that the administration be given authority to spend millions of dollars appropriated to the agencies involved in any way it chose, without any consultation with Congress. It proposed to allow the administration to terminate any program or activity in any agency within the department and to spend those funds on any activity within the department *without regard to existing law or acts of Congress.* The administration also requested authority to sell assets without prior approval and use the proceeds of such sales for any purpose the administration desired. To my pleasant surprise Dick Armey, who was occasionally quite good on matters of civil liberties and congressional power, agreed with us and indicated that the language that both Bill Young and I opposed would be changed. Armey was as good as his word, and that major problem was resolved. That left three remaining problems with reorganization.

The first issue was whether it was in the interest of the country to reorganize in the middle of a war against terrorism. "There was a reason that the Department of Defense was not reorganized in the middle of World War II," I told the Armey committee. "We recognized that we needed to win the war first and reorganize the bureaucratic boxes later." I was concerned that if we threw a reorganization at operatives in the field who were already strung out trying to track down Al-Qaeda, they would spend the next year finding their desks, determining who their new boss was, what channel of command they had to report through, and getting the phone and computer systems up and running. Two full years later the chaos afflicting the new agency would vividly demonstrate the validity of those concerns. More than 20 percent of key positions would remain unfilled and the agency would still not have managed to publish an agency phone directory.

The second problem was that the administration's reorganization proposal destroyed FEMA, the Federal Emergency Management Agency. FEMA, whose mission was to prepare for and provide help to areas afflicted by natural disasters, had a long history of impotence and incompetence. Often staffed extensively by political appointees, it had a far from successful track record in dealing with natural disasters. The agency experienced a dramatic turnaround when Bill Clinton appointed James Lee Witt as its director. Witt professionalized the agency and turned it into one of the great success stories of the

Clinton administration. Witt was alarmed that the reorganization structure would bury FEMA in the bowels of a huge new Homeland Security agency bureaucracy, destroying its ability to respond to natural disasters with nimble efficiency. I fully agreed with Witt and sent a letter to every member of the House urging them to heed the concerns expressed in a letter from Witt, which I also circulated. In my letter I asked members to keep several things in mind when they voted.

> While FEMA is an agency that most people do not think about most of the time, it can be the most important agency in the federal government at particular points in time. This is true on a nationwide basis when the country grapples with how to help the victims of a recent disaster. It is far truer when a disaster hits your home state, and you bear some responsibility for the quality of the federal response.
>
> The individual broadly viewed as the spark plug that turned FEMA around, James Lee Witt believes that it would be a huge mistake to put the disaster response function of FEMA into the new department. That would "diminish the focus of the department and dismantle what only recently has become a successful and vital agency."

Witt's letter, which I circulated to every House member, warned that

> Reorganizations of FEMA, within the past year, are leading down a path that is recreating that previous imbalance. FEMA's new Office of National Preparedness has already taken many staff from the Disaster Response and Recovery and Mitigation Directorates. In a further diluting of mission, all responsibility for disaster training has been placed under FEMA's U.S. Fire Administration.
>
> In the atmosphere of the past year (including the period prior to September 11) the devotion to terrorism planning has already affected the FEMA mission. All the momentum for pre-disaster mitigation work with communities has been lost. Folding FEMA into a homeland or national security agency will seriously compromise the nation's previously effective response to natural hazards.

The Congress paid no heed. Americans in Louisiana, Mississippi, and Alabama would pay a heavy price for the reorganization four years later when Hurricane Katrina smashed New Orleans and the Gulf Coast to smithereens. President Bush appointed a person to head FEMA whose only qualification when he first joined the agency was that he was the college roommate of the previous director. The agency, buried in the new Department of Homeland

Security bureaucracy, performed with stupefying sluggishness because it had been hollowed out by the loss of many career employees and was left in the hands of people who did not know what they were doing.

The third problem with the homeland reorganization scheme was even more basic. Before reorganization, 133 agencies, boards, and commissions had something to do with homeland security. "What this plan does," I told the committee, "is to take 22 of those 133 agencies, call them the Homeland Security agency, and leave 111 others outside the tent—and among those 111 are the two agencies most deeply involved in conducting the war on terrorism— the CIA and FBI." It was my view that someone operating out of the White House, as Governor Ridge was before reorganization, would have more clout in making these agencies work together than would a separate cabinet agency. I knew it was of no use to talk about substantive details like that because political considerations seemed to be driving the whole discussion. And I still felt the important question was the astounding lack of resources being provided to deal with the problem, not the agency organizational tables.

In frustration, I delivered a speech to the National Press Club that outlined the inadequacies to the administration's response. I pointed out that less than 2 percent of cargo containers in our nation's ports were inspected, that the main deterrents to crossing the Canadian border in some sections were rubber traffic cones, that while airline passengers were patted down and inspected before boarding, cargo in those same planes often was not. I pointed out that while Bush had held a press event touting a new system of cargo inspection by the customs department, he had pocket vetoed the funding to make that system a reality.

In the midterm election, the Republican campaign apparatus got away with murder on the homeland security issue. George Bush had originally opposed the entire idea of reorganizing the homeland security bureaucracy, and had strongly resisted the Lieberman bill, but halfway through the debate they flip-flopped and endorsed the proposition. When the vote on final passage came in the Senate, Max Cleland of Georgia voted against the reorganization bill for many of the same reasons I did. Incredibly, the Republican campaign apparatus and Saxby Chambliss, Cleland's opponent, scurrilously used the vote to attack his patriotism even through Cleland had left two legs and an arm on the battlefield in Vietnam, and they defeated him. That personal attack will go down in history with Nixon's campaign against Helen Gahagan Douglas and Joe McCarthy's attacks on General George Marshall's patriotism as among the most despicable in modern American politics. Cleland had been right to oppose the plan, and so had I.

Today, the security gaps I described in that press club speech have been only marginally closed. It is common knowledge in Washington that the gargantuan Homeland Security Agency is a mess. The intelligence community has also been reorganized, but the result is that those now providing the president with his daily intelligence briefing are not those directly involved in obtaining that intelligence. So the president has one more filter between him and those in the intelligence community with the most direct knowledge of what is really going on in the covert world. And tax cuts for the wealthy are still pushing every other consideration—including homeland security—to lower positions on the Bush administration's priority list, with the exception of paying for the most costly military misadventure since Vietnam: our attack on Iraq.

CHAPTER 24

Misled into War

George H. W. Bush was a creation of World War II. He saw the rise of Imperial Japan and Nazi Germany, and witnessed their fall. He watched the rise of Soviet power and presided over its fall. His whole foreign policy experience was the product of a world that taught daily lessons about the necessity for cooperation, alliances, and common purpose. He gathered around him people who understood those nuances of an effective policy. But his son saw things quite differently, and from his first months in office it showed. That was doubly surprising, because during the campaign, he had spoken of a need for an American foreign policy that walked "more humbly" through the world.

The operating style that Bush brought to world affairs was anything but humble. Unlike his father, he had almost no foreign policy experience. Unlike his father, who surrounded himself with skilled and thoughtful negotiators like Admiral Brent Scowcroft, Jim Baker, and Larry Eagleburger, this Bush—at the suggestion of Dick Cheney—brought in hard-nosed advocates like Donald Rumsfeld and hard-line academics like Paul Wolfowitz, Elliott Abrams, and Richard Perle. They believe in doing things their own way, and they have little patience with people with a more subtle worldview.

One exception was Bush's selection of General Colin Powell as secretary of state. Powell's approach to leadership has often reminded me of Eisenhower, though on a more modest scale. Ike had held in his hands the responsibility for the lives of millions and had been made more thoughtful by the experience. In Vietnam and in the first Iraq war, Powell had the same experience, but in a much more limited way. As the coordinator of an alliance of members who shared the same goals but not always the same perspective, Ike had the responsibility to lead, not just through direction but through negotiations and compromise. Powell had had similar experiences, but they were experiences that had required the ability to persuade as much as the ability to dictate. As a result, Powell was almost alone in the councils of the Bush administration.

I had known Bush's national security advisor, Condoleezza Rice, since we had both attended Aspen Institute conferences on the Soviet Union in the early 1990s. She was well known in academic and political circles where she was viewed as reasonable and bright, and I very much liked her and respected her ability. Her presence in the Bush inner circle, however, was due more to Bush's personal comfort with and confidence in her than to her deep strategic insight.

Even before Bush took office, there was talk of his wanting to right a wrong by finishing what his father had left undone in Iraq. Neoconservative advisors like Perle and Wolfowitz were known to have a strategic view of the Middle East that called for taking a hard line with the Palestinians while changing the regime in Iraq and perhaps even Syria and Iran. In the early months it was just talk. But early on, Bush demonstrated his willingness to follow a unilateral rather than multilateral approach to foreign policy. First, he announced the United States was scuttling the global warming treaty. Anyone with a clue knew the Kyoto treaty was not going anywhere unless it asked countries like China to make some of the long-range cutbacks in climate-changing emissions, which the treaty required of more developed countries. But instead of saying, "Look folks, this treaty needs to be renegotiated," the administration unilaterally rejected it. Then they walked away from the ABM treaty with the Russians and gave the impression that they would do the same with the nuclear test-ban treaty.

The events of 9/11 changed almost everything in U.S.-allied relations. Allies and former enemies alike expressed deep sympathy with us, and a worldwide conversation began about how to moderate hatred and put terrorism back in a corner. A few disgruntled enemies relished our shock and loss, but the majority of the world sympathized with us. There has probably never been a time in our history when the nations of the world felt more warmly toward the United States. But today much of that sentiment has dissipated, largely due to the way Bush misled us into war in Iraq.

From the beginning, the Bush administration left no doubt that irrespective of world opinion, we were going after Iraq. The world community could understand why we would go after Al-Qaeda because that's who attacked us, and that is why so many nations supported our operation against Al Qaida and the Taliban in Afghanistan. But despite claims of linkages from the Pentagon and the White House, the rest of the world understood, even if a lot of Americans didn't, that it was Al-Qaeda, not Saddam Hussein, who had hit us on 9/11.

Nine years earlier Bush I had brought the Congress along every step of the way on the first Iraq war. The intelligence briefings we received fully backed up virtually everything we were told by the White House at that time. In contrast, Bush II had a few similar meetings with us on Iraq, but the discussions were essentially cheerleading sessions, and on several occasions the president turned the meeting quickly over to others, something I hadn't seen since Reagan's day.

Nine years earlier, in the debate before the first Gulf War, I raised a series of questions that needed to be answered before we sent troops into the field. I asked whether we had commitments from the Saudis and other Arab countries to provide postwar economic assistance to the poorest Arab countries in the region in order to ease the economic and social conditions that could lead to revolutions. I wanted to know whether the Arab countries were willing to do more than hold Arafat's coat, letting him negotiate with the Israelis without any of the sovereign Arab countries throwing their own political weight behind the peace process. I asked what measures were being taken to attack the core economic and political problems in the Middle East so that we would not be viewed as buttressing unresponsive and corrupt regimes in the region, making us the target of even more resentment. But almost a decade later, very little has been done by any Arab government, by Israel, or by us to change the nature of the Middle East or the nature of societies within the Arab world. When the 9/11 attack came, I viewed those who died in the World Trade Center, the Pentagon, and the downed plane in Pennsylvania as the last casualties of the first Iraq War. They were the victims of Al-Qaeda's twisted resentment about the continued presence of U.S. troops in the Arab and Muslim world long after the war was over.

When the House vote finally came on attacking Iraq, I voted against giving the president a blank check to go to war. As an alternative, I voted to give him the authority to attack *if* we had the backing of our UN and NATO allies. If that support was not forthcoming, the resolution I voted for required the president to come back to Congress for another vote, so we could judge at that time whether the evidence required us to act.

I voted that way for many reasons: First, I agreed with the thoughts of the president's father several years earlier in explaining why he had not occupied Baghdad. Bush I said that

[if America tried] to eliminate Saddam, extending the ground war into an occupation of Iraq . . . we would have been forced to occupy Baghdad and, in effect, rule Iraq. The coalition would instantly have collapsed, the Arabs deserting it

in anger, and other allies pulling out as well. Under the circumstances, there
was no viable "exit strategy" we could see, violating another of our principles.
Furthermore, we had been self-consciously trying to set a pattern for handling
aggression in the post–Cold War world. Going in and occupying Iraq, thus
unilaterally exceeding the United Nations' mandate, would have destroyed the
precedent of international response to aggression that we hoped to establish.
Had we gone the invasion route, the United States could conceivably still be an
occupying power in a bitterly hostile land. It would have been a dramatically
different—and perhaps barren—outcome.

I couldn't have said it better myself.

Second, I was not convinced by the intelligence briefings that Saddam was
the imminent threat to the United States that the White House and DoD
were making him out to be. He might be in the future, but I thought that we
had more time. Based on the administration's briefings, I did believe Saddam
probably had—or was close to—a chem and bio program. But we were told
by the CIA that Saddam would *most likely* use those weapons if we attacked
Iraq. I did not believe he was anywhere near a nuclear capability, and I was
bothered that the administration, in its comments to the public, often left the
impression that when they were talking about "weapons of mass destruction"
they were really talking about nuclear weapons.

Third and most important, while I knew the State Department had been
drawing up plans for a postwar Iraq for over a year, there was little evidence
of the detailed planning by the Defense Department and the White House
that would be necessary to make the aftermath of the war a success.

I had no doubt that our military attack in Iraq would go well and publicly
said so. After all, when you spend $400 billion on defense and the other guy
spends $10 billion, I think you're going to win. But the real question we kept
asking was, "What about afterwards?" Would we have sufficient forces to
pacify the territory? Would we really be able to avoid protracted, day in and
day out guerilla sniping by remnants of Saddam's regime and by the terrorists
who would gravitate to Iraq because of the war? Would we be able to persuade
the Sunnis to work with us in trying to achieve "democracy" in Iraq when they
saw that Shiites made up three times the population that they did and that
"One man, one vote" would mean that their Shiite enemies would control
the country for the first time in modern history? How could we convince the
Sunnis to work with us under those circumstances? Would our attack turn
Iraq into a terrorist magnet, a motivator, and a training ground for a whole new
cadre of terrorists? Would our attack on Iraq wind up providing an enhanced

long-term opportunity for Iran to take advantage of a political vacuum in Iraq and thereby expand its influence in the region? In fact, wasn't Iran a bigger potential threat to Israel's interest and our own than was an Iraq that had been substantially weakened since the last war? Were we really letting ourselves in for a commitment of U.S. troops acting as an occupying force in Iraq for a decade or more? Would we be stuck with the whole financial and manpower cost? Was our army large enough to effectively handle the postwar pacification task, given other potential flashpoints around the world? Would such an attack risk destabilizing the entire region?

When General Shinseki, the army chief of staff, told us that we would probably need 200,000 troops to pacify Iraq after the war, Rumsfeld came down on him like a ton of bricks. "No, no, no, many fewer," he said. Rumsfeld's deputy, Paul Wolfowitz, ridiculed Shinseki's estimates, saying he found it "unimaginable" that more troops would be required after the war to keep the peace in Iraq than had been required to conquer Iraq in the first place. Events have proven Shinseki right and Rumsfeld and Wolfowitz spectacularly wrong. But Shinseki paid a price for honestly answering our questions. The Pentagon announced his successor as army chief months before they needed to, effectively making him a lame duck; when he retired fourteen months later, Rumsfeld sent no one to Shinseki's mustering out ceremony—a shameful way to treat a great patriot who had been wounded twice in Vietnam.

Lack of logistical planning and preparation for pacification showed up in critical ways. The first Gulf War had been a triumph of brilliant logistics. After that war, we were briefed in Kuwait by General Schwarzkopf, and he introduced us to Lt. General William "Gus" Pagonis as "the real hero of this war." He had been in charge of logistics and by all accounts had done his job brilliantly. That pattern of logistical excellence did not repeat itself this time around.

During and after the attack on Iraq, our troops experienced significant shortages—shortages that were not reported to Congress until Jack Murtha discovered them on one of his trips to Iraq. Forty thousand GIs were sent to Iraq without the proper ceramic inserts for their body armor. Large numbers of Humvees were not equipped with the under-body armor to protect occupants from roadbed explosions. Troops were given inadequate numbers of electronic jammers to intercept the electronic signals that remotely detonated bombs and land mines. Many GIs told me that months after the war, our troops still had not been given access to pure drinking water. Some told me that during the war they often had only one meal a day because of insufficient MRE deliveries to the front.

After the occupation, the shortage of troops on the ground had become apparent, with devastating consequences for our ability to pacify the country in the months that followed. When Shinseki told us that 200,000 troops would be needed to handle the aftermath of the war, Rumsfeld had raised the roof and lowered the estimates. But three months after the war, we had 147,000 troops there and needed more. The Pentagon could not provide proper troop rotation after the war was over without issuing stop orders that held Reserve and Guard personnel in service long after they were entitled to go home. That meant that for those who were held beyond their expected tour of duty, the country had effectively reinstated the draft.

Throughout the operation, Richard Perle and Paul Wolfowitz had been extremely critical of the intelligence information being provided by the Defense Intelligence Agency (DIA) and CIA. It was then discovered that in Rumsfeld's attempts to obtain intelligence information more in keeping with the administration's hopes and expectations, he had established a separate intelligence group within the DoD to feed him information and evaluations, outside the reach of the CIA and separate from the DIA, which had been established by Congress within his own department. I requested that the Appropriations Committee begin a staff investigation of that action. I was supported by Bill Young and Jack Murtha, but the committee chairman, Jerry Lewis, blocked the request.

In contrast to CIA and State Department analysts who demonstrated a degree of skepticism about Iraq's weapons of mass destruction capability, Cheney, Wolfowitz, Perle, and Rumsfeld seemed to eagerly swallow the predictions of Ahmad Chalabi and his followers that "we would be greeted with open arms" and that we could easily establish a new governing authority that would put Iraq on the way to producing a reasonably reliable democracy. There was only one problem—Chalabi had not lived in Iraq in forty years and was regarded by many in the CIA as being unreliable. Instead of our troops being welcomed with open arms, they were met with closed fists. Years after Bush, dressed in a custom-fit flight suit, landed on an American carrier under a large banner that read MISSION ACCOMPLISHED and declared that military action was over, American GIs were still dying—victims of sniper fire, rocket attacks, ambushes, and other nasty surprises organized by remnant allies of Saddam and terrorists who had flocked to Iraq after the war. Events later demonstrated that established intelligence agencies like the CIA missed the mark widely in overstating Saddam's capability to produce and deliver weapons of mass destruction. But across the board, they were never in accord with the rosy assertion that we would be received in Iraq with little opposition once the occupation began.

Because I had lost all faith in their competence and in their ability to convince the world to trust American leadership after the Iraqi mess, in September of 2003 I became the first member of Congress to call for the resignation of Rumsfeld and Wolfowitz. In a letter to the White House I argued that "the assessment that the civilian leadership of the Pentagon passed on to their subordinates that the Iraqis would welcome us with open arms was not in fact the assessment of any established U.S. intelligence agency." I had not called for their resignation because I disagreed with their policy in Iraq (although I did). I did so because I thought that policy had been pursued with such unilateral belligerence and incompetence that America's capacity to lead the world on this issue had been nearly obliterated. Indeed, I was convinced that the "I'm smarter than you are and I will do whatever I want come hell or high water" attitude of the civilian Pentagon leadership would make it almost impossible for the administration to succeed in its mission.

Bush's go-it-alone determination also meant that the Iraqi population's acceptance of our troop presence in their country was much more reluctant than it could have been because we did not benefit from the aura of operating under international auspices. It meant that in addition to the $300 billion deficit that we were already running in the U.S. budget, we would shell out at least $500 billion for the war and its aftermath. And the strain on our budget was matched by the pressure on our military forces.

Because of the administration's miscalculations, the United States found itself in danger of stretching the military to the breaking point. I was told by career military leaders that the regular army was not large enough to do the jobs it could be asked to do if another crisis popped up in the world, but Rumsfeld would not admit it. We were also told that the Pentagon's claims that they were rapidly training large numbers of Iraqis to take over military and policing duties were highly exaggerated, based as they were on dubious definitions of training, but Rumsfeld would not admit that either. I was convinced that the arrogance of the civilian leadership at the Pentagon was exceeded only by their capacity for misjudgments. Several highly ranked officers told me that not since Robert McNamara had they seen such arrogance on the part of the Pentagon's civilian political leaders.

In April of 2004 we learned that the strain imposed on our military was far worse than any of us had imagined. The administration's desperate desire to gain information that would enable it to keep the Iraqi insurgency under control led to numerous acts of torture and other grotesque human rights abuses that were carried out by U.S. personnel at the Abu-Ghraib prison in Iraq. Follow-up investigations showed that the problem was not isolated and was not just confined to Abu-Ghraib; similar abuses had occurred in hundreds of instances in Iraq, Afghanistan, and in the U.S. compound at Guantanamo Bay in Cuba. The *Washington Post* reported that the White House counsel, the CIA, and the top civilian and military Pentagon leadership had been involved in meetings or in the production of memos authorizing the use of dogs, painful shackling, simulated drownings, and other illegal conduct that had led, in numerous cases, to death. As Pamela Constable, deputy foreign editor at the *Washington Post* pointed out, "More than thirty people have died in American custody overseas, and others have been secretly shipped to foreign countries which had been condemned by the U.S. government for practicing torture. . . . One . . . was a shy Afghan taxi driver who died in American custody after being hung by the wrists, choked in a hood, and forced to roll back and forth kissing his captors boots before he died."

No serious investigation of top administration officials ever took place. The "rap" was pinned on a few lower-ranking soldiers. The fact that the White House counsel, Justice Department, the secretary of defense, General Miller, Lieutenant-General Ricardo Sanchez, top CIA leadership, and other higher-ups had at one time or another defended our right to proceed *outside* certain norms of the Geneva Convention was conveniently swept under the rug. In the process, America lost something special. We lost the ability to claim that we were living up to our ideals. Our image as the world's greatest and most civilizing democratic power suffered enormous damage in the arena of world opinion. In the process we also weakened our ability to prevent U.S. military personnel from being tortured if they fell into enemy hands. Emotions that inflamed the Muslim world and the disgust generated elsewhere would inevitably make it more difficult to prevent such abuses from being directed against our own servicemen and women. The administration tried to question the patriotism of those of us who raised these questions, but professional military men understood that we raised issues about those operations to protect the safety of our own troops. Because of that controversy, I was especially pleased to receive, with Bill Young, Legislator of the Year awards from the U.S. Army Association for our efforts to provide adequate equipment for our troops and adequate financial compensation for the sacrifices that so many in uniform will make.

In the end, the Bush II administration had used bad information and misinformation to mislead us into the dumbest, most misguided and unnecessary war since 1812. As of today, our misadventure in Iraq has lasted longer than our involvement in World War I. And American families are still paying the ultimate price. We are indeed, in the words in the old Pete Seeger refrain, bogged down "knee deep in the big muddy," and much of the Muslim world hates us.

In floor debates, committee hearings, and speeches around the country and in my own district, I have made all these points over and over again. I have pointed out that while President Bush, Vice-President Cheney, and officials like Rumsfeld, Wolfowitz, and Perle liked to view themselves as being tough-minded realists, in reality they were zealous romantics who made Woodrow Wilson look like Clemenceau by comparison. Their arrogance, their misuse of the powers of office, their refusal to accept any kind of checks and balances, their refusal to listen to dedicated intelligence professionals who were saying "No, wait a minute. Listen!" have made them the most dangerous American leaders since Richard Nixon. Once again American GIs have paid with their lives for the self-important dreams of the civilians who lead this country. In the administration's rush to war, Congress did not meet its responsibilities to ask the right questions and neither did the press. In fact, large segments of the press whooped the country to war as irresponsibly as William Randolph Hearst did before the Spanish-American War.

Today, one of the most frustrating questions I keep getting is, "Well, Congressman, if you were so opposed to the war, what is your plan for getting out?" My response is, "You know, sometimes in life if you make a really bad mistake, there's no good way to repair it." America's situation in Iraq reminds me of the story about Eddie Stanky, the old New York Giants second baseman in the 1950s. Leo Durocher, the Giants manager, was hitting ground balls to his infielders in spring training practice, and Stanky muffed two in a row. Durocher grabbed the glove, trotted out to second base, and said "Here, Stanky, I'll show you how it's done." But the first ball hit to Durocher, he dropped. In exasperation, Durocher turned to Stanky and said, "Damn it, Stanky! You've got second base so screwed up nobody can play it!" Today, picture Iraq as second base and George W. Bush as Eddie Stanky, and you've got the picture.

That's a funny story, but what is happening to our troops in Iraq isn't funny, and today, years after the first American died while we were preparing to go into Iraq, Americans in uniform are still paying the price for their commander in chief's hubris. And there is no good way out. No matter what course the administration pursues, we will not have brought real democracy to the Middle East, but we will most certainly have contributed in a major way to the destabilization of the region and the strengthening of Iran, the region's country that is most in our interest to contain.

Our best chance of salvaging anything out of this mess is to pursue a variation of a proposal by Zbigniew Brzezinski's, President Carter's former national security advisor.

1. Make clear we have no plans for permanent bases in Iraq.
2. Insist that all parties agree to establish a coalition government within a matter of weeks.
3. Encourage the new Iraqi government to ask us to leave.
4. Set a target date for ending our occupation of Iraq.
5. Have Iraq convene a conference of all regional powers to work out a regional understanding of mutual relationships after our departure.
6. Help establish a donor's conference to agree on a long-term plan of reconstruction.

That approach may or may not work. The odds against anything working are high—but it is probably our best hope.

PART 6

OTHER BATTLES

CHAPTER 25

❧

Hell-Bent on Deregulation

Four months after Bush took office, the economy began to sag. Unemploy-ment continued to rise until, three years after he moved into the White House, not a single new job had been created. By August of 2003, the economy had in fact lost more than three million jobs. Bush completed his first term with the worst record of job creation for any president since Herbert Hoover. He came within a whisker of being the first president since Hoover to preside over a net job loss during the course of his four-year term. With the stagnation of the economy came the collapse of the public's confidence in the corporations that employed them, as well as the government that was supposed to protect their interests from manipulation by the corporate whales of the American economic system. Names that had seemed models of corporate excellence like Enron, Arthur Andersen, and Merrill Lynch now became synonymous with corporate excess, betrayal, conflict of interest, and fraud. And as repeated sto-ries of corporate recklessness and greed unfolded, investors lost their savings, and workers lost their jobs and pensions. Once again, as in the 1980s during the S&L scandal, Americans began to ask, "How did all this happen?"

To answer that question I issued a report on August 29, 2002, titled *The Republican Agenda and the New Corporate Abuse,* an analysis that traced the two-decade-long drive to systematically turn government regulators of corporate power from watchdogs into lapdogs. It documented the systematic deregula-tion of the economy that had taken place since the late Carter years. It showed that beginning with the election of Ronald Reagan, the capacity of government agencies to protect investors, depositors, consumers, workers, and responsible corporations from manipulation of the marketplace had been systematically eroded. That report documented that the deregulation binge came in two stages: first, with the election of Ronald Reagan in 1980; second, with the GOP takeover of Congress in 1994 and the ascension of Newt Gingrich and Tom DeLay to leadership in the House. It described the deregulation recipe that had been precooked for the incoming Reagan administration by the Heritage Foundation and a network of radically conservative foundations. Since Goldwater's defeat in 1964, these foundations had been marshaled to develop a political climate that would strip government of the power to regulate abusive corporate power. It documented the sustained twelve-year assault by the GOP on the web of regulation that protected our health and safety at work, preserved the purity of our air and water, provided financial protection for pensions and investments, and created the economic stability that is enhanced by healthy oversight of the most powerful elements in corporate America. That assault had been renewed under George W. Bush.

From 1980 on, the protective capacity of the antitrust division at the Department of Justice and the Federal Trade Commission was being shrunk at the same time America experienced the greatest wave of mergers and corporate acquisitions in the nation's history. The staff of the Consumer Product Safety Commission (CPSC) was cut in half by Reagan.

In February 1981, Reagan, by executive order, dramatically centralized control over the agency rule-making process. He designated OMB, under David Stockman, as the central agency to review regulations. The Office of Information and Regulatory Affairs (OIRA) used its enhanced powers to override decisions by federal agencies and give big business off-the-record opportunities to reargue battles they had previously lost at the agency level.

CRIPPLING WORKER PROTECTION

The clearest example of the Reagan administration's neglect of its responsibility to protect the health and safety of workers—and the one I was most deeply involved in fighting—had been the antiworker agenda advanced by Thorn Auchter, appointed by Reagan to head the Occupational Safety and Health Administration (OSHA). In Reagan's first two years, despite strong protests from Billy Ford and me, OSHA failed to tighten standards for a single cancer-causing chemical to which workers are exposed—despite overwhelming evidence indicating the necessity for action on a variety of workplace chemicals. While it was well known that asbestos was a much bigger danger than anyone had thought, OSHA reduced the number of workplace air samples for asbestos by 70 percent between 1979 and 1983 and delayed tightening up regulations for asbestos use for two years. During this time, OSHA did nothing to protect workers from such cancer-causing compounds as ethylene oxide, ethylene dibromide, benzene, and formaldehyde, despite the fact that 100,000 workers were dying and 240,000 became disabled each year due to occupational diseases caused by exposure to toxic substances on the job.

In March of 1983, I confronted Auchter in a tense hearing in the Labor-H Subcommittee. Under Auchter's direction, OSHA's Washington office had just revised standards that were supposed to guide OSHA's regional offices in determining which companies should be at the top of their list for worker health and safety inspections. Under those standards, the Denver regional office put together its inspection priority list. Several workers had been killed in accidents at a Coors operation, and under the new guidelines one of the sites at the top of the list for inspection was a Coors plant. When the inspection took place, the Coors operation complained to Auchter's office, and pressure was brought to bear on the Denver region to back off. We were alerted to the episode by whistle-blowers within OSHA. When the OSHA Washington office learned that I had internal documents outlining its actions and intended to closely question them at their budget hearing, Auchter showed up at the hearing with his own video camera; I grilled him for almost an hour. That night we were told by sources within OSHA that a videotape of my questioning of Auchter was on its way to the Coors operation.

Even when OSHA did act (as when it published the Health Communication Standard in 1983), the standard was limited to manufacturers and required such minimal steps as warning labels on containers and worksheets. There was no requirement for medical monitoring or periodic medical examinations. And it wasn't until the courts ruled in 1987 that the requirement was extended to employers *other than* manufacturers. When OSHA revised their standards to comply with the court ruling, the regulations were rejected by OMB, which claimed that the revised disclosure requirements were not necessary to protect employees. It took a 1990 Supreme Court ruling, which ruled that OMB had no authority to block the OSHA regulations, to get workers the minimal protections that they needed and deserved.

The assault on America's regulatory structures continued through the Bush-Quayle administration. The principal tool was the President's Council on Competitiveness, created by executive order in January 1989 and chaired by Dan Quayle. George Miller, Billy Ford, and I regularly clashed with the council because it met and acted in secret, created another layer of bureaucracy to systematically undermine health and safety regulations, and was difficult to reach because it operated within the bureaucratic structure of the White House. It was especially active on matters affecting the environment, including Clean Air Act emissions regulations and wetlands. The deregulatory binge intensified after the GOP took control in 1995 and was applied across the board to agencies such as the Securities and Exchange Commission and other corporate watchdogs.

Repeatedly since 1995, House Republicans voted to pass appropriations bills that cut the SEC budget below the president's request. In most of those years, progressive Democrats worked to restore some of the funds, but we fought a losing battle. That meant that while the workload was exploding, the ability of the SEC staff to keep up with that workload was undermined. The percentage of all corporate filings reviewed by the agency declined dramatically, from 21 percent in 1991 to about 8 percent in 2000. Is it any wonder the Enrons of this world were convinced they could get away with anything?

~

CHAPTER 26

Environment under Assault

The most fundamental bond between us as biological organisms is through the air we breathe, the water we drink, the land we walk. The most basic test of our respect for one another is the way we meet our stewardship responsibilities to the environment that sustains us all.

The purpose of government regulation is not to harass legitimate entrepreneurs; it is to protect them from those who seek illegitimate advantage—not just for the individual good of the vulnerable but for the common good of us all. In a democracy, it is the politicians who are charged with the responsibility to keep those rules straight and fair. When they fail in function, they fail in their fundamental obligation. Growing up in the Wisconsin River Valley, I encountered on a regular basis visible examples of how government had failed that fundamental test.

As a college student working summers at Brokaw paper mills, I observed firsthand the junk that the paper industry poured into the Wisconsin River—a clear example of how the taxpaying public was indirectly subsidizing the industry. Every gallon of sulfite liquor pumped by a paper mill into the river represented a shifting of costs from industry to nature and to the broader society. I also saw how industry fouled the air at the expense of others every time I visited my Grandma Chellis on Wausau's Third Avenue. If we wanted to sit on the porch swing, we had to take rags and wipe down the furniture to clean up the silica dust that poured from 3M smokestacks two blocks away and coated everything in the neighborhood, including people's lungs. Seeing all that as an idealistic teenager, I vowed that if I could ever do something about it, I would. My election to Congress meant that I not only had an opportunity to do something about it but had an obligation.

I entered the Congress at a time when environmental consciousness was reaching a high-water mark. In the Senate, Gaylord Nelson, Ed Muskie, Scoop Jackson on the Democratic side, and Bob Stafford on the Republican side had built a bipartisan coalition of environmental visionaries that began to wipe away decades of environmental neglect. They were blessed with a team of House allies led by Mo Udall, Phil Burton, Henry Reuss, Paul Rogers, and a host of others. Together they legislatively surrounded the Nixon administration and took step after step to strengthen the whole ethic that defined our stewardship responsibilities to our natural surroundings. A wave of legislation, including the Clean Water Act, the Clean Air Act, the Wilderness Act, Strip Mining Reform, National Environmental Policy Act, the Endangered Species Act, the Wild and Scenic Rivers Act, and the Environmental Education Act, was reshaping the public policy landscape. Those measures represented great steps in the effort to take back our rivers, our streams, and the very air that we breathe from the industries that had abused them.

As a junior member of Congress, I initially had little role in that battle, except to join the hallelujah chorus, but I did so with gusto. But soon my co-sponsorship of legislation banning DDT caused me to run afoul of Jamie Whitten. Whitten had chaired the Appropriations Agriculture Subcommittee almost since the founding of the Republic. When Rachel Carson published her landmark book *Silent Spring,* which alerted the nation to the loss of song-birds because of the effect of DDT, Jamie lent his name as the author of record to a book ghostwritten in response by scientist flacks for the chemical industry. When he discovered I had introduced legislation banning the use of DDT, Jamie never missed a chance to let me know that he thought Gaylord Nelson was an idealistic meddler and that I was ill advised to follow his lead. Because of his determined actions to resist any effort to limit pesticide use or encourage the development of alternative methods of pest control, Jamie became a prime target of environmentally conscious members of the House. After the Watergate revolution brought fifty-one new Democrats into the House following the 1974 elections, Eddie Boland and I worked out an arrangement to preserve Whitten's Agriculture chairmanship, but only as part of a compromise that removed a number of environmental agencies from the jurisdiction of his subcommittee.

With Reagan's election in 1980, the White House was antagonistic to most of my conservation and environmental values; worse yet, my friend and mentor, Gaylord Nelson, the greatest voice in Washington for an enlightened and balanced environmentalism, was defeated for reelection in the Reagan landslide. The golden age of pioneering action on conservation and environmental issues was behind us, but I found that there were still opportunities to do things that enhanced and preserved Wisconsin's outdoor resources. I was able to pass legislation adding Long Island to the Apostle Islands National Lakeshore. When Northern States Power decided to divest itself of extensive unspoiled land holdings in the Chippewa Flowage (the Big Chip) in Sawyer County, I got the money in the federal budget to enable the state to buy it and to preserve it for future generations. Bill Proxmire and I had also worked out an agreement with Senator Bennett Johnston that removed northern Wisconsin from the list of potential sites for the burial of nuclear waste. In addition, I also continued on a regular basis to obtain funds to expand and extend Wisconsin's system of Ice Age National Trails. And I was able to secure funds to build the Chippewa Moraine Ice Age Trail visitor's center and the Lake Superior Great Lakes Visitor Center.

When George H. W. Bush followed Reagan into the White House, he produced a record on the environment somewhat more moderate than Reagan's. But Clinton and Al Gore brought several world-class environmental leaders back into the agencies—Katy McGinty at OMB, Bruce Babbitt at Interior, Deborah Williams (who handled Alaskan issues for the Interior Department), Mike Dombeck at the U.S. Forest Service (Dombeck was a Hayward area boy who got his degree at UW–Stevens Point). Together they made a gutsy team, and that gutsiness was reflected at the very top by Clinton himself. Through a series of executive orders and other actions before he left office, Clinton preserved more acres of national land treasures—such as the desolately beautiful Grand Staircase–Escalante National Monument—than any president since Teddy Roosevelt. But when the GOP took over Congress in 1995, Tom DeLay organized a who's who alliance of anti-environmental special interests that had been waiting for twenty-five years for the opportunity to exterminate a whole range of environmental regulations.

For the rest of the Clinton years, the GOP majority mounted a relentless effort to scale back environmental protections. Ted Stevens, the top Senate Republican on Appropriations, was constantly pressing to minimize federal protection on a whole set of Alaskan issues—timber cutting in the Tongass, roads in Denali, drilling in Anwar, to name just a few. Meanwhile, DeLay and his allies launched far more sweeping attacks. Each year, working with Clinton in conference, we beat most of them back. And in one area we actually made a significant step forward.

Over the years, numerous environmental groups had become frustrated with a twenty-year lag in funding for the Land and Water Conservation Fund. During the Eisenhower administration, the Congress had passed the landmark

Tidelands Oil legislation, under which a specific portion of revenues from the sale of U.S.-owned offshore oil deposits to energy companies was to be deposited into a new Land and Water Conservation Fund. Through the years dollars built up in the fund, but many of those dollars were not appropriated to enable the program to reach its full potential. To remedy that shortfall, in 2000 a broad coalition of environmental groups wanted to take a second run at establishing a requirement that all money in the fund be spent. The bill gained wide support and passed the House 315 to 102, but then got hung up in the Senate because of the furious opposition of western senators who wanted no part of additional land-acquisition programs. The controversy spilled over into the Appropriations Committee.

I wanted to break through the logjam but did not want to make the program an entitlement because, if we did, dozens of other groups would want to turn other parts of the budget into entitlements. But I did want to substantially increase funding levels. After weeks of yinging and yanging, Norm Dix and I on the Democratic side and Ralph Regula on the Republican side reached a compromise with the Clinton administration; we set up a six-year schedule for greatly expanding funding for such projects and attacking the huge maintenance backlog at national parks. Roger Schlickheisen of Defenders of Wildlife described the agreement as being "a giant leap forward . . . an historic funding package that would help protect the last vestiges of open space wildlife habitat and wild lands across the country before they are lost forever."

For two years, the agreement held. But in 2003 North Carolina's Charlie Taylor, the new GOP chairman of the Interior Subcommittee, broke the agreement. To my surprise Regula, who had shaken hands on the original agreement, didn't lift a finger to save it. The next year Taylor further cut programs under the agreement to $880 million, in comparison to the $1.6 billion scheduled under the agreement. Republican backsliding meant that over the last five years the program had been shortchanged by $2 billion. Shortly after Dix, Regula, and I had reached agreement on the added conservation funding, the Wilderness Society presented me their Ansel Adams award for lifetime conservation achievement. When the organization first informed me of the award, I thought that they had chosen me because of my work on that agreement, but they told me that it was really more because of the ongoing fights I had waged against Tom DeLay's repeated efforts to cut back on environmental protections. The award read, "You have repeatedly thwarted those who sought to achieve by procedural legerdemain what they could never achieve in open debate." One incident on the House floor several years earlier illustrates just how contentious my relationship with DeLay had been.

CHICKEN BLANK

On April 9, 1997, I had been working in my office with the TV on low so I could monitor the House floor. I noticed that my friend George Miller of California was in a heated exchange with Tom DeLay, so I turned up the volume. George had been speaking in favor of campaign finance reform; he was using the widely reported planning session that DeLay had organized several years earlier, after the Republican takeover, to establish a strategy for a wholesale rollback of environmental regulations and laws as an example of why reform was needed. DeLay jumped into the debate by asserting that Miller's claim that he had worked hand-in-glove with special-interest lobbyists was off base. Miller was right: for several years I had kept on my desk a masterful article by Michael Weiskoff and David Maraniss in the *Washington Post,* which described in detail the very meeting that DeLay was denying. The article, dated March 12, 1995, began: "The day before the Republicans finally took control of Congress, Representative Tom DeLay strolled to a meeting in the rear conference room of his spacious new leadership suite on the first floor of the Capitol. The dapper Texas congressman, soon to be sworn in as House majority whip, saw before him a group of lobbyists representing some of the biggest companies in America. . . . He could not wait to start on what he considered the central mission of his political career: the demise of the modern era of government regulation." It went on to say, "Since his arrival in Washington a decade earlier, DeLay, a former exterminator who made a living killing fire ants and termites on Houston's wealthy west side, had been seeking to eradicate federal safety and environmental rules that he felt placed unnecessary burdens on businesses." I knew the article was correct because, that same year, I had led the fight, along with Lou Stokes, against DeLay's efforts to attach seventeen anti-environmental riders to the HUD EPA appropriations bill.

When DeLay brazenly denied Miller's charge, I grabbed the article from my desk and sprinted to the floor. When I reached the House chamber I was recognized by the presiding officer. The following exchange took place as reported in the *Congressional Record:*

MR. OBEY: Mr. Speaker, I was in my office when I saw the incident that just occurred on the House floor involving the meeting that was discussed by the gentleman from California, which he indicated had taken place in the Majority Whip's office. The Majority Whip has said that the newspaper article to which the gentleman from California referred contained no names of lobbyists. I have in my hand, as a Senator from my own state used to say, a copy of the article in question, and if my colleagues examine the text, there are the names of seven lobbyists listed.

MR. DELAY: Mr. Speaker, would the gentleman yield and read those names?

MR. OBEY: I would be happy to allow the gentleman to read the names. I am not going to mention the name of any person on the floor who is not here to defend himself.

MR. DELAY: Mr. Speaker, will the gentleman yield?

MR. OBEY: Mr. Speaker, I will not yield further, not at this time. The gentleman can come here and read the names. I would ask unanimous consent again to be allowed to place this in the *Record* so that the names can be in the *Record*.

SPEAKER PRO TEMPORE: Is there objection to the request of the gentleman from Wisconsin?

MR. DELAY: I object.

MR. OBEY: I thought the gentleman would.

SPEAKER PRO TEMPORE: Objection is heard.

MR. OBEY: I thought the gentleman would. I find it interesting that the truth is being suppressed on the floor of the House in the name of the rules of the House. . . .

. . . Mr. Speaker, the gentleman from Texas [Mr. DeLay] has asked why I do not want to read the names of the lobbyists in the article. It is very simple. They are not Members of the House and they cannot defend themselves. He can, and he ought to. I would suggest that if he wants to discuss these names, I am happy to discuss them with him publicly or privately any time.

When my time expired and the exchange was over, I took the article from the well of the House where I had been speaking and walked over to the Republican leadership table where DeLay was standing and said, "Here, Tom, you can read the names if you want to." DeLay moved toward me, eyes flashing, jabbed his forefinger into my chest and said, "You chickenshit, you chickenshit." The force of his pressing on my chest moved me backwards. As Tom took another step toward me and again raised his hands to my chest, I said, "Tom, don't do this, don't do this."

The press the next day reported that he had shoved me. I told them I really didn't think Tom had tried to shove me, that his fingers had just pressed against my chest forcefully and that I had stepped back to give Tom time to think and cool down. The incident ended when a DeLay staffer pulled him back away from me. Several reporters who had not seen the incident tried to reconstruct it the next day.

The only reporter who was in the House gallery to witness the event was Adam Clymer of the *New York Times* and not surprisingly his was the most accurate account. In describing our confrontation on the floor the next day, Clymer's article noted, "Mr. Obey walked over to Mr. DeLay and held a photocopy of the article out to him. Mr. DeLay poked at the article with his finger, and then shoved Mr. Obey with both hands. He also shouted at Mr. Obey that his tactics amounted to chicken droppings. Scott Hatch, an aide to Mr. DeLay, intervened and led his boss off the floor."

In the *Washington Post,* John Yang's article noted, "One month to the day after the House civility retreat ended in Hershey, Pa., House Majority Whip Tom DeLay (R-Tex.) and Rep. David R. Obey (D-Wis.) engaged in an animated discussion that ended with DeLay shoving Obey. A DeLay aide led his boss away before Obey could offer a rebuttal."

A reading of the article that caused DeLay to erupt makes clear why he did not want to have attention drawn to it. The portions of the article that I had circled and outlined so many months ago read in part as follows:

In fact, as outlined that day in DeLay's office by [a] lobbyist for energy and petrochemical interests who served as the congressman's initial legislative ghost-writer, the first draft of the bill called for a limited, 100-day moratorium on rulemaking while the House pushed through the more comprehensive anti-regulatory plank in the Contract. . . . But his fellow lobbyists in the inner circle argued that was too timid, according to participants in the meeting. Over the next few days, several drafts were exchanged by the corporate agents. . . .

As the measure progressed, the roles of legislator and lobbyist blurred. DeLay and his assistants guided industry supporters in an ad hoc group whose name, Project Relief, sounded more like a Third World humanitarian aid effort than a corporate alliance with a half-million-dollar communications budget. . . . On key amendments, the coalition provided the draftsman. And once the bill and the debate moved to the House floor, lobbyists hovered nearby, tapping out talking points on a laptop computer for delivery to Republican floor leaders. . . .

DeLay described his partnership with Project Relief as a mode for effective Republican lawmaking. . . . Turning to business lobbyists to draft legislation makes sense, according to DeLay, because "they have the expertise." . . . At the Jan. 3 meeting in DeLay's office, [a] lobbyist for some of the nation's largest motor fleets, criticized [the] draft because it excluded court-imposed regulations. He volunteered to do the next draft and came back with a version that addressed the concerns of his clients. [He] removed the threat with a stroke of his pen, extending the moratorium to cover court deadlines. . . . [A] lobbyist for [chemical company] had a different concern: He wanted to make sure the moratorium would not affect new federal rules if their intention was to soften or streamline other federal rules. . . . According to participants, a Project Relief lobbyist was given the names of 72 Democrats to target.

What DeLay's long involvement in anti-environmental efforts demonstrated and the *Post* article reflected is that through the 1990s, the bipartisan commitment to the environment, which had been the hallmark of Congress in the 1970s and 1980s, had been steadily eroded.

Even in the Reagan era, when GOP senator Bob Kasten chaired the Senate Foreign Operations Subcommittee and I chaired the House subcommittee, we had disagreed on so many other foreign policy issues, but we had managed to work together in a bipartisan partnership to pressure international financial institutions like the World Bank into paying more attention to the environmental consequences of their Third World economic development projects. But over three decades, as the Republican Party changed, the bipartisan coalition that had sustained environmental progress had been reduced to tatters on all but a few issues. Three developments had brought about the change:

1. Unlike the heady days when Gaylord Nelson founded Earth Day and it seemed like there was so much to do, by the twenty-first century many people began to take environmental protection for granted and vigilance was lost. Some environmental groups had become more preachy and less operational, which made them more ineffective. Often some of them seemed more at war with each other than was the case in the 1970s. And some have become so purist and rigid in their approach that they have lost the coalition-building skills that are necessary to be effective in an era of adversity.

2. The Republican Party itself had changed. The backbone of the GOP a generation ago had been the Midwest and the Northeast, which meant that those regions sent their fair share of moderate or progressive Republicans to Congress. But by the twenty-first century, three rounds of reapportionment had moved the Republican Party center of gravity to the South. Those southern Republicans were much more conservative than their midwestern and northeastern predecessors, which meant that there were very few moderate Republicans left in the House.

3. As the role of money in politics had increased, so had the pressure for the political system to respond to big business and the result had been bad news for the environment.

What must be understood is that DeLay was not just a one-man environmental extermination squad. He was the visible manifestation of the reality that an alliance of highly organized, highly ideological, and deeply self-interested termites had for years been gnawing away under the surface at the ethic that has been the foundation of government's regulation of corporate power. Environmental deregulation has been just one example of their long-term goal—nothing less than the across-the-board gutting of the regulation of corporate America. That development has been reinforced by the concentration of power in the Congress as it has not been seen since the days of "Czar Cannon" (Joseph Cannon, the legendary Speaker of the early twentieth century who ruled the house with an iron fist), and it has been lubricated by money.

~

CHAPTER 27

Limiting Money
in Politics

When I was first elected to the legislature, I spent a grand total of $1,168 to be elected, and I beat a twenty-year incumbent in the process. When I was first elected to Congress, I was outspent roughly $75,000 to $55,000, and my opponent was the Walter Cronkite of Northern Wisconsin politics—the news anchor of the dominant TV station in the district. In both cases, my victories demonstrated that an effective candidate could be outspent and still win. I have always believed that the fewer dollars in politics, the more likely it is that the electoral outcome will be decided by the clash of ideas rather than the clash of bank accounts.

In the early 1970s, in the wake of Richard Nixon's money-laundering campaign scandals, I voted for the new changes in campaign laws that were supposed to reform politics. That law, pushed principally by my friend and hero Mo Udall, tried to limit both the amount of money that could be contributed to candidates and the amount they could spend. But in the now infamous *Buckley vs. Valleo* decision, the Supreme Court shredded many of those restrictions—especially limits on what could be spent. Congressional candidates were then forced to compete under what was left of the congressional reforms. The court decision created a huge opportunity for candidates and parties to easily dance around the provisions of the law. The practical result was that limits on campaign spending were obliterated because the court virtually equated money with speech under the First Amendment to the Constitution. Subsequent rulings by the courts and by the Federal Elections Commission also unleashed a flood of money into the coffers of both political parties from sources never contemplated by the Congress.

When Congress passed that reform legislation in the 1970s, we thought we were creating a system that would limit the amount that could be contributed to $2,000—from any source. We thought we were forbidding contributions from corporations and union general treasuries alike. But court decisions and Federal Election Commission rulings so warped congressional intent that contributions of $50,000, $100,000 and $200,000 in "soft dollars" became commonplace. Further rulings also allowed special- and single-interest groups to directly spend large amounts of money on ads, which were clearly meant to get around the law. Congress had clearly intended to create a system under which any money spent in a campaign was channeled through the campaign treasury of the individual candidates or party committees; however, subsequent court and agency rulings meant that any organization could go to a TV station and plunk down a small fortune to pay for ads attacking an opposing congressman or senator with no questions asked. As long as they did not utter the magic words "vote for" or "vote against," interest groups were permitted to buy as many ads as they wanted, right up to election day.

The public would never know who paid for these ads because they could call themselves the "Citizens for Sweetness and Light" and never have to disclose who paid for them. In one election, a medical lobby group spent $100,000 trashing Rep. Pete Stark of California; as chair of the Health Subcommittee of the Ways and Means Committee he hadn't done their bidding on health care. Under the new reality created by these court decisions, with no limits on what can be spent by an alienated special-interest group, members of Congress now found themselves on a money-raising treadmill, constantly trying to increase the amount of money in their campaign coffers in order to avoid being suddenly blindsided by big-money, special-interest ad campaigns.

In the late 1970s, working with Common Cause, Rep. Tom Railsback, a moderate Republican from Illinois, and I tried to reinstate reasonable limits. We focused our efforts on capping a candidate's spending and limiting contributions by political action committees (PACs) through a voluntary system of partial public finance for candidates who agreed to abide by the limits. They were voluntary limits because court rulings had forbidden mandatory restrictions. Our bill, which passed the House but died in the Senate, focused on PAC contributions because, in those days, PACs seemed to be the greatest source of new money in the system. But gradually, over time, as court and agency rulings produced a whole different set of problems, I came to believe that PAC contributions posed a much lesser threat to the public interest than did the huge $100,000 to $200,000 gifts to both parties by big business and other special interests and large individual contributors. Those large individual contributors indeed push political parties and the entire political system to the right, toward the moneyed interests and away from the interests of regular working people.

Dan Rostenkowski used to say that effective campaign reform legislation could not be achieved without a Constitutional amendment. I once thought that he was saying that just to stall reform efforts, but I came to believe that he was right. Before 1994, no soft money existed in congressional campaigns, but in 1994 Newt Gingrich's operation raised $25 million in soft money and took over the House. In 1996 both congressional party committees competed aggressively for soft money. Today, hundreds of millions of dollars find their way into congressional campaign efforts—money that is unregulated and unidentified. In the process, the system is put at an even greater distance from the reach of average citizens.

In 2003 my Wisconsin colleague, Russ Feingold, along with John McCain, successfully pushed through Congress new legislation that placed strict limits on soft money, and that legislation has largely been upheld by the U.S. Supreme Court. I applaud that action, but even though the bill is an improvement over the old way of doing things, there are still too many ways that huge contributions can be anonymously funneled into special-interest efforts to influence elections on the sly.

In 2005 Congress was hit with another scandal in which Jack Abramoff, a crony of Tom DeLay and the Republican establishment, pleaded guilty to massive violations of lobby law in which he had manipulated huge amounts of money—including campaign contributions. With little expectation that Congress would do anything soon on the subject, I drafted and introduced radical campaign finance reform legislation that eliminated all private contributions in House general election campaigns. Eight Democrats—Barney Frank, Henry Waxman, Rosa DeLauro, Bob Filner, Steve Israel, Jim McGovern, Tim Ryan, and Pete Stark—joined me in the effort.

The bill created a grassroots Democracy Fund into which citizens could contribute any amount in order to take their government back from special interests. To finance those campaigns, the FEC was authorized to conduct a major advertising campaign from January 1 to April 15 of each year, alerting the public to the existence and purpose of the fund. Citizens could make voluntary contributions when they filed their tax returns, which would not add to the deficit because these contributions would be a "check up" not a "check off." That is, they would be *in addition* to taxes already owed, not a deduction. Because costs vary widely from district to district, the fund would deposit in an account for each district an amount based on median family income in each district.

Money would be distributed to candidates in each district based on their party's performance in the last two elections. Skeptics objected, pointing out that incumbents would get more funding than nonincumbents. My response pointed out that we had earlier suggested an equal distribution to each candidate, but opponents countered then that such a distribution formula would artificially create support for candidates, which did not reflect actual district sentiments. In 90 percent of the nation's congressional districts, our formula would provide significantly more funding for challengers than does the existing system.

Under the plan, third-party and independent candidates could obtain funding either through a formula based on the performance of such candidates in the previous election, or through a petition system that would demonstrate whether they were serious challengers or simply nuisance candidates with little public support. State and national parties would be able to provide a modest amount of assistance to candidates. All other independent expenditures would be banned outright and the only spending that would take place would be through each candidate's campaign committee—all this in order to end the fraudulent pretense that the "Citizens for Sweetness and Light" who were spending thousands of dollars in television ads were not trying to influence the outcome of the election.

To encourage the courts to uphold the plan, the act contained a congressional finding that the limitations in the bill were required to preserve the integrity of the electoral process. If the courts overturned those limitations, then the bill contained provisions for expedited congressional consideration on a Constitutional amendment that would allow the implementation of those changes. It also contained a sunset clause in case the proposition turned out to be a horrible idea.

The bill is based on the belief that elections, in a democracy, should be almost sacred events. More than anything else in this society, they should be public events, not private battlegrounds. For those who say that public financing of elections would be too expensive, I say that nothing costs the public more than the existing system in which private interests contribute private money to try to bend public policy to the will of those same private, well-heeled interests, with all too frequent success.

Public financing may seem a radical departure from today's system, but the very idea of representative democracy itself is the most radical idea in modern history—the idea that all citizens are free and equal, and need not see their interests sacrificed to the most financially powerful among us. In *Buckley vs. Valleo*, the Supreme Court was profoundly wrong when it equated money with speech under the First Amendment. In a democracy, the speech that should count is not speech borne on the wings of money, but speech borne on the strength and quality of ideas.

Until the courts finally recognize that the amount of money a group is willing to spend should not determine how well their speech can be heard, the public interest will struggle to have its voice heard above the din. The price this nation has paid for the existing campaign finance system is the continued growth in the gap between the richest of our citizens and everybody else. Fewer than one out of every thousand American citizens gave a contribution of more than $200 to a presidential candidate for the 2000 election. Without fundamental reform that I am afraid only a Constitutional amendment would allow, public policy will continue to deliver the most to those who financially invest the most to determine that policy. That is why I continue today to press for passage of total public general election financing in House campaigns.

In September of 2005, Tom DeLay was indicted by a Texas grand jury for allegedly engaging in a conspiracy to illegally funnel corporate money into campaigns. That event, and the indictment of several people around him, finally drove him to announce his resignation from Congress in April of 2006. Under American law, he is entitled to a presumption of innocence until proven guilty in a court of law. But even if he is found innocent of the charges in the indictment, the way he has used his power to build an interlocking relationship between K Street special-interest lobbyists and his own party caucus, and the way he has threatened lobbying groups who do not play ball by hiring Republicans to run their trade associations and pacts, is a demonstration of just how corrupted the system has become. E. J. Dionne of the *Washington Post* wrote that the importance of the Tom DeLay case goes beyond the narrow facts of the legal case in question. It lies in the fact that DeLay "was a pioneer in something entirely new; a fully integrated political apparatus that linked Republican Party committees, lobbyists, fundraisers, corporations, ideological organizations, and the process of governing itself. There was a candid shamelessness, even genius, about how the operation worked. Traditional limits on what was permitted in politics were dismissed as the obsessions of squishes and goo-goos, a term coined long ago to deride advocates of good government."

Jacob Hacker and Paul Pierson, authors of *Off Center: The Republican Revolution and the Erosion of American Democracy,* stated:

> DeLay is one of the most important architects of this new power structure, but he's not essential to its continuance. Grover Norquist—head of the conservative group Americans for Tax Reform and another key GOP power broker—recently joked that if a bus ran him over, someone else could easily step into his place and assume his role and relationships. Some might see this as false modesty, but Norquist is right.

The same conclusion applies to DeLay. His role is crucial not because of who he is but because of where he sits—at the intersection of money, organization. and influence.

That's why after DeLay's indictment, I updated and reintroduced my legislation to eliminate *all* private money in congressional elections. I am confident that I will be called naïve, but in reality the truly naïve are those who do not see the urgent need to take this radical step. Bob La Follette would understand why. Discussing his early service in the House of Representatives from 1885 to 1891, La Follette wrote, "I have endeavored . . . to show how in those days the concentration of private interests of all sorts overwhelmed Congress. . . . Even then the two diametrically opposed ideas of government had begun a death grapple for mastery in this country. Should government be for the benefit of private interests . . . or shall government be for the benefit of the public interest. This is the simple issue involved in the present conflict in the nation." Anyone who believes it is any different today has simply not been watching. And anyone who understands how much congressional decision making has been centralized and removed from public view also understands how those changes have made it easier for special interests to prevail.

The strength of Congress as an institution has been rooted in the ability of individual members to specialize and, over time, develop a degree of expertise that enables a serious member to compete on even terms with any agency head. That combination of tenure and specialization has allowed Congress to develop institutional expertise on almost any subject. Legislating at its best includes utilizing that knowledge within the context of an overall program guided by party leadership. A legislative product defined and driven in top-down fashion by party leaders, with no input from members with substantive expertise in the field, is not a program—it is political dogma. A legislative product that is simply the sum of individual initiatives by committees with specialized expertise is also not a program—it is simply a rote response to rampant undirected individualism.

The job of good legislative leaders is to enrich party programs with the specialized knowledge of the most informed and thoughtful members. That blending of the political and the substantive, that blending of power and knowledge, that mixing of top-down direction with bottom-up knowledge of detail and consequences is necessary to produce a useful product that will survive its first contact with real-world challenges.

When I came to Congress, committee chairs had too much power and too many individual members acted like one-man bands. The committees operated almost as independent fiefdoms. Many of the changes we adopted in the 1970s were designed to create a better balance between the centralized power of the leadership and the independence of committees. That balance showed in the relationship I had with my party leadership in the ten years I chaired the Foreign Operations Subcommittee, and during the time I chaired the full Appropriations Committee. In that time not once did my party leadership order me to do anything. If they wanted something to happen, they would call me, describe their goals, and ask if I thought their concerns could be accommodated. Often, they could be. If I did have an objection, we would work things out, or the idea would be dropped. But in the last twelve years, under Gingrich and even more under Hastert, decision making has been centralized in the leadership to an overwhelming degree.

The Republican leadership has regularly held House floor votes open for long periods—sometimes hours—until they could break enough arms to turn defeats into victories. They have arbitrarily changed the text of legislation reported by committees without a vote and then refused to allow roll calls on efforts to restore the original committee text. In addition, they have often inserted many pages of legislation into conference reports without a vote of approval by the conference committee. In December of 2005, to restore a better balance between centralized leadership power and committee and individual member expertise, Barney Frank, David Price, Tom Allen, and I introduced a fourteen-point House rules reform package to prevent the House leadership from manipulating the legislative process to achieve passage of legislation about which individual House members and committees would often be less aware than would the well-connected lobbyists who had worked to put them there. Old Bob La Follette would understand why.

PART 7

SUMMING UP

CHAPTER 28

❧

Presidents

Our founding fathers believed they were establishing Congress as the primary power in American government. Indeed, the first article of the Constitution describes the shape, nature, and power of the Congress. But through the years, especially in the twentieth century, power has flowed to the presidency, and presidents have come to dominate events. I've often asked myself how I would rank the presidents I have known. After much thought, I surprised myself with the answer.

I have served with seven presidents. My dear friend, Senator Robert Byrd, would correctly insist that I say "with" rather than "under" because Congress and the presidency, under the Constitution, are indeed coequal branches of government.

Of those seven presidents I have concluded that the best *for the country* was Gerald Ford. That conclusion surprises me because he was, after all, an accidental president who was never elected and who served less than three years. Selected to be vice president by Richard Nixon when Nixon's vice president, Spiro Agnew, resigned in disgrace, Ford became president when Nixon resigned in the wake of Watergate. During his presidency no great measures became law. Why, then, do I rank him as the best? Because, on his watch, he did the two great things that the country needed most.

First, after the deep scars of Watergate, Gerald Ford healed the nation. By the very example of his decency, humility, sense of duty, balance, and fairness, he healed the country and contained the tide of cynicism that was Richard Nixon's legacy. He was the very model of civility, and through his conduct he restored America's confidence in the decency of our system of government. Second, he pardoned Richard Nixon. By doing so, he helped move Nixon off stage and allowed the country to focus on the future rather than the past. Yes, that was in the interest of his Republican Party, but it was also right for the country. I opposed it at the time, but I was wrong. His action was intensely misunderstood, but as much as was possible, it got rid of Richard Nixon. Ford endured immense criticism for it, but I do not believe, as conventional wisdom holds, that it led to his defeat in 1976. Ronald Reagan and the Republican right-wing ideologues did that—making Ford look weak with their constant drumbeat of criticism. Presidents are defined not just by themselves but by their circumstances. We can ask no more of any leader than to measure up to the largest challenges of his time. Ford did that. By that standard, I would rank him number one.

Ford died the day after Christmas, 2006. About a year before he died, Ford paid us a visit on the House floor. When I told him that I was writing a book in which I would say that he was the best president I had worked with, he grinned, put his hand on my shoulder, and said, "Slim pickings, wasn't it, Dave."

Who would rank second? That is a hard call between Jimmy Carter and Bill Clinton, in part because they were so different.

Both men were highly intelligent policy wonks. Both accomplished one great thing. Clinton reversed the fiscal recklessness of the Reagan era and returned the nation to fiscal rationality, and in the process he restored the confidence that was so essential to economic prosperity. Carter, in an intensely personal tour de force, brought together two traditional Middle East adversaries, Menachim Begin and Anwar Sadat, and against all odds forged the Camp David peace accords between Egypt and Israel. I do not know when peace between Israel and the Arab world will finally come, but when it does that event will be regarded as the turning point in the process.

Carter's presidency was done in by external events over which he had little control—the rise of rampant inflation generated by exploding interest rates after the second energy crisis, and the relentless day-in and day-out media hype of the Iranian hostage crisis. In contrast, Clinton was not brought low by external events. He was instead brought low by the internal chaos in the Democratic Party on issues like health-care reform and crime, and by his own personal recklessness that made him vulnerable to a barrage of personal attacks from his adversaries. Neither of those events would have been weighty enough to seriously wound any of Clinton's postwar predecessors, but Clinton was the first president since Herbert Hoover to preside in an era when America was without an effective external enemy. With the Soviet Union gone, no nation posed a serious military threat to us. In the absence of external pressures, the voting public felt much freer to "take a flyer," on less weighty concerns and candidates. Issues that would have seemed like irritants in the context of the Cold War took on larger scale and weight in its absence.

During the Cold War, before the Soviet collapse, any administration that presided over healthy economic growth and avoided major foreign policy setbacks would have been hailed as a rousing success. But with external consequences diminished and economic prosperity taken for granted, the risk of paying an external price for internal chaos seemed small. Consequently, as Clinton's personal indiscretions came to light, he was judged by a tougher standard than his predecessors—especially by the press. The new casualness produced almost weightless politics and trivia geared to a 24/7 news cycle in which personality and personal performance were much more center stage. Politics and journalism took on a new sense of inanity.

In the end, I would give Clinton a slight edge over Carter for the same reason that I ranked Ford number one—Clinton, too, faced up to the most crucial obligation of his presidency. In Clinton's case, rescuing the nation from the disastrous fiscal legacy of Ronald Reagan. It was an excruciatingly difficult task and one that was a major reason we lost control of Congress, but again, it was the right thing to do. Clinton also had the courage to confront the moral disgrace of the United States of America being the only industrialized country in the world to have no room in the inn for more than forty million American men, women, and children who have no health insurance. In that effort he failed, but he did so in a great cause, driven by the conscience of a good heart, and I honor him for it.

So who ranks after Clinton and Carter? The choice there is easy—George Bush I over Ronald Reagan by a dozen lengths.

George H. W. Bush was a man of decency who surrounded himself—at least on the foreign policy front—with quality people. With the help of people like Jim Baker, Larry Eagleburger, and Brent Scowcroft, he responded to the downfall of the Soviet Empire with reasonable skill. Unlike Carter, he was lucky enough, with the collapse of the Iron Curtain, to be on the receiving end of good news, and he did nothing major to screw it up. He showed a strong sense of duty in doing everything possible to push the Middle East peace process forward—at considerable political risk to himself. Most important, in the 1990 budget deal, after one false start, his administration began the process that Clinton so courageously carried out—that of getting a handle on the national deficit.

His problem was that he never really had a clue about what was happening to common ordinary people in the economy. In spite of that, he probably would have won his fight for reelection against Clinton in 1992 if Ross Perot and Pat Buchanan hadn't split the GOP base and created an opening for a Democratic candidate. Bush's handling of Iraq was far superior to his son's performance because he always recognized that there was a larger context in which that war needed to be conducted. He *built* an alliance rather than fragmenting it. He was a man who understood the world and in dealing with it made no major mistake. That is no small accomplishment.

After George Bush, the rating job gets really difficult. Ronald Reagan was a disastrous president. His reckless supply-side economic elixir tripled the nation's debt. Bush I was right the first time when he labeled it "voodoo economics." Reagan's fiscal irresponsibility was so breathtaking that the country ran up more debt on his eight-year watch than it had incurred under all previous thirty-nine presidents combined. His policies contributed more to the widening gap between rich and poor than any president in modern history . . . until George W. Bush came along. But that wasn't the worst of it. The worst aspect of Ronald Reagan's presidency was this: he convinced the country that *government was the people's enemy.* It was under Reagan's relentless antigovernment mantra that our government was stripped of so much of its power to prevent the powerful from trampling the weak. It was Ronald Reagan who succeeded in changing the country's mind-set from "We're all in this together!" to "Every man for himself!" In any normal historical time frame, that action alone would be enough to assure his selection as the worst president for the country of the last thirty-six years, but this has not been a normal time frame.

In our time we have been "blessed" with the likes of Richard Nixon and George W. Bush, and when it comes to damaging the country, they are in a league of their own! Which of these two would I rate as having done the most damage to the county? When I first began writing this book I fully expected it to be Richard Nixon, but that was before I had much time to see Bush II in action. At first blush, Nixon would seem to be an easy call, and if anyone wanted to insist that his sins against public trust and the Constitution itself were unparalleled in their venality, I would not strenuously disagree. After all, Nixon's career was rooted in red-baiting smears of decent public servants— sort of a junior league Joe McCarthy.

He also was one of the originators of the "who lost China" war cry in the 1950s, which helped disarm this country by depriving it of crucial expertise about China in the highest councils of our government. He made it dangerous to think truthful thoughts about the weaknesses of our ally, Chiang Kai-shek—weaknesses that made a communist takeover of that country almost inevitable. The resulting lack of expertise in the highest councils of government, and the paranoia generated by the whole "who lost China?" crowd, helped make America less than prepared to understand the true intentions of the Chinese during the Korean War, which led to the loss of thousands of American lives. Certainly Nixon damaged the country by relentlessly using the "Soft on Communism" label to undercut those in the Truman administration who, after all, had designed what proved to be the successful long-term strategy for the containment of communism by the United States and our allies. And who can seriously argue that Nixon's paranoia did not create, in fact demand, a mind-set within his administration that defined opponents as enemies and political opponents as targets for domestic espionage? And who can deny his willingness to use the most intimidating arms of government—the FBI, the IRS, and other federal agencies—to snoop on and intimidate those who legitimately and honorably represented opposition points of view? No doubt, his lies about Vietnam were at least as damaging to the country as were Lyndon Johnson's. And certainly Nixon's two-year-long strategy of lying to the public about his, up to then, unsurpassed abuses of government power did more damage to the American system than any president since the Confederacy's Jefferson Davis.

And yet there are aspects of Nixon's substantive record that work in his favor. He did propose a welfare plan, which, had it not been defeated by an alliance of opposites (the Far Left and the Far Right), could have led this country into a more humane repair of the system. His Family Assistance Plan could have limited the prosperity gap that later developed between the nation's rich and poor. Moreover, Nixon did propose a health-care reform plan, which if adopted would have resulted in many fewer Americans living without health insurance than is the case today. And it is also true that he acquiesced in the environmental reforms passed by Congress.

Finally, Nixon did lead a policy reversal that sought to undo some of the damage to U.S. foreign policy toward China that he himself had caused earlier in his career, unlike Bush II's refusal to admit error in Iraq—or in any other area. Similarly, with Henry Kissinger at his side, Nixon sought to "manage" our relationship with the Soviet Union, and that made the world safer in the nuclear age than it would have been without detente. In short, he was a serious and knowledgeable person. Some of those policy achievements do to some extent counterbalance the profound damage Nixon's viciousness did to this country and to the political system that drives it. That is why I am left with the judgment that Nixon may in some ways be surpassed by the present occupant of the White House in comparative damage done this country.

I reach that conclusion for a number of reasons. Like Jerry Ford, Bush II came to the presidency under a special set of circumstances that should have led him to reach out to the opposition and the majority of the country who had voted for his Democratic opponent. Instead, he purposely pursued a governing strategy that was precisely the opposite. It aimed at dividing rather than uniting the country. That is a terrible thing for the president of the United States to do.

After the trauma of 9/11, he did one fine thing. He reassured the country that those who attacked New York and the Pentagon, and tried to hit the U.S. Capitol, would fail in their efforts to cripple America at home and around the world. But even in the wake of that tragedy, in dealing with the home-front response to the attack, he offered the back of his hand rather than welcoming bipartisan initiatives to strengthen our home-based response to the new threat. In the wake of the crisis on which he chose to define his presidency, he repeatedly resisted making the investments needed to shore up our homeland defenses, a decision that bordered on willful negligence. And months later, even though 90 percent of the members of both parties in both Houses voted for legislation to make our borders, ports, communities, and air transportation more secure by increasing Homeland Security funding, George W. Bush effectively vetoed expenditure of those funds.

Across the board, at the very moment in the nation's history when he could have been hugely successful in pursuing a bipartisan attack on the nation's largest problems, he chose instead to polarize and divide the country on virtually every issue he confronted by pursuing a highly political and zealously ideological agenda. When the nation desperately needed resources to pay for his war of choice, to shore up Social Security and private pensions, to repair the nation's education system, and to close the holes that were allowing millions of Americans to slip through our health-care system, Bush purposefully and relentlessly stripped the cupboard bare.

His "My way or the highway" mind-set demonstrated that he was determined to advance his uncompromising agenda.

- On the home front, that agenda focused on reversing the most successful policies of the previous decade. Bush reversed and repudiated the responsible Clinton budget actions that had turned record deficits into real surpluses.
- He gleefully reversed tax policy that had narrowed the gap between the haves and the have-nots, in the process obliterating the first government surpluses in a generation and plunging the country into unparalleled new indebtedness with the addition of almost $3 trillion to our nation's debt.
- On education he insisted that reform preceded new investment and then, when he got his reforms, declined to put the check in the mail.

- On health care he brought to an end the effort to double National Institutes of Health research and did virtually nothing significant to ease the plight of forty million Americans who cannot experience the benefits of that research because they have no health insurance.
- On prescription drugs for seniors he cynically blocked a comprehensive drug benefit under Medicare by pushing a piecemeal and haphazard plan that was a bonanza for pharmaceutical companies because it specifically prohibited the government from negotiating lower drug prices.
- On the environment he found ways on issue after issue to scale back the federal government's commitment to make the nation a cleaner, healthier, and more beautiful place.
- His most significant contribution to civil liberties was to appoint the most authoritarian attorney general in the postwar period.

Virtually every economic policy change he pursued sent the same message that Ronald Reagan had sent twenty years earlier: "Communitarian values out; rampant individualism in!" And with his reelection, he set about trying to dismantle Social Security, the most successful domestic program in almost a century. At every turn, his policies have given the most help to those who need it least and the least help to those who need it most. He has waged class warfare on all but the wealthiest and has replaced the values of the social gospel with the values of rampant individualism and social Darwinism. And his message to our allies and the world was the same. In international as well as domestic affairs, ideology has driven facts, rather than the other way around. The message he sent to the world has been: "I decide; you follow!" Bush entered the presidency in an era of Western international cooperation, but within a year transformed it to one of confrontation and belligerence. The result? General James Jones, commander of NATO, recently declared that U.S. influence in the world had declined to a fifty- to seventy-five-year low.

As the only superpower in the world, the United States has a larger stake in stability and cooperative working relationships than does any other nation. It was, after all, America that, in the aftermath of World War II, designed the network of international institutions—the IMF, the IFIs, NATO, and the UN—that helped to regularize relations between nation states, institutions in which the United States is far more dominant than any other country. Yet the Bush administration has recklessly taken actions that erode the sense of cooperation and stability buttressed by those institutions. His administration unilaterally announced its intention to wipe away the ABM treaty, the Global Warming treaty, the Nuclear Test Ban treaty. It unilaterally declared that it would wage preemptive war in Iraq under the misleading banner of anti-terrorism, even though the administration's own intelligence could not demonstrate in any way that Iraq was connected to Al-Qaeda's 9/11 attack on our country.

Bush led the nation into war on the flimsiest of intelligence, and when the information that was used to drive the nation to war was found to be wildly off the mark, the administration questioned the patriotism of those who challenged the misuse of that information. In doing so, it disregarded the hard-nosed judgments that our military leadership had reached about what would be required to stabilize Iraq in the aftermath of that war. That action has now cost more than three thousand American lives and many more than seventeen thousand wounded. While draining the treasury of more then $400 billion, George W. Bush has mired us in a quagmire that will hold us captive for years to come. Iraq has become for America what Afghanistan was decades earlier to the Soviet Union. And in its zeal to stretch the limits of international law, the Bush administration has blundered into allowing the United States to appear to be apologists for torture and abuse, in stark contrast to the values we have cherished for so long—an action that has increased the risks of American soldiers encountering the same treatment.

In short, this sad record leads me to the conclusion that, despite Richard Nixon's malevolence, George W. Bush has indeed been the worst president for this country. He has, at every turn, divided our country, not because he needed to but because he *chose* to, as part of a deliberate strategy to win election. Internationally, he has proven himself a dangerous romantic whose policies have left us more isolated from our allies than at any time in my lifetime. In the process he has raised the world's level of anti-American hatred to a height never before seen. That is a legacy totally at odds with American interests and American values, one that will hurt this country for years to come. The administration has moved from the position in which it was the recipient of the sympathy and goodwill of the world after 9/11 to a government that is widely seen as willful, arrogant, and recklessly bent on destroying the structure of international law that, for almost sixty years, the United States had taken the lead in building.

And perhaps most damaging, the Bush administration has elevated the pursuit of money in politics to its highest place in American history. No administration has more openly or more proudly paraded to the nation its zeal in raising millions of dollars in fundraising. Much more than any other administration in modern history, it has made clear its determination to use money to drive out any other factor in American elections. Bush's cronies readily admit their intention to drown out any other form of political speech with speech that is paid for with money. As never before, they have made clear their intention to make real the aphorism that "money talks."

Aided and abetted by its political allies in and out of Congress, the Bush administration has sought to turn the political system over to the modern-day equivalent of the nineteenth-century robber barons. By doing so, it has helped to make both parties more beholden to the most powerful elements in our society. Through its actions, the administration has done more than any administration in a century to remove government from the reach of average working Americans. Almost in amazement, therefore, I reach the conclusion that the actions of the Bush administration are even more corrosive to the health of America's economy and democracy, in the long run, than the actions of Richard M. Nixon.

The Bush administration has been at least as destructive to of the long-term health of American democracy as Nixon's, but without any of the policy actions that leavened to some degree the perniciousness of the Nixon conspiracy. While it has mouthed religious pieties, its policy prescriptions have cynically gone counter to the message of the social gospel, leaving us the saddest of legacies by any president in the postwar period. Instead of following Hubert Humphrey's challenge to comfort the afflicted and afflict the comfortable, George W. Bush has raised doing the exact opposite to a high art form, not only weakening American society but destroying its standing in the world in the process.

❧

CHAPTER 29

Values

One of the great ironies of my life is that despite its deep influence on my actions in public life, I have had a rocky—and sometimes painful—relationship with the most authoritarian faction in my own church.

My first public disagreement with them came during my service in the Wisconsin legislature. A Madison monsignor chastised me and a number of other Catholic legislators for declining to acquiesce in his demand that we vote to make contraceptives illegal in Wisconsin. He suggested that any Catholic who did not do so was "failing his church." When the subject was debated in the state assembly, I argued that the laws that we passed applied to people of *all* religions, not just my own, and that Catholic Church officials were overstepping their bounds when they tried to dictate a "Catholic outcome" to any question affecting people of all religions and people of no religion. I pointed out that Cardinal Cushing of Boston had remarked, during a similar controversy in Massachusetts, that a Catholic did not need the added crutch of civil law to support his own beliefs in a matter of conscience. The monsignor was outraged, but the contentiousness passed.

The next conflict occurred with our efforts to pass a fair housing law to outlaw racial discrimination in housing. The leading opponent of that legislation was the Wisconsin Realtors Association, and the state president of that association was Bob Viele, a realtor from my hometown. My strong support of that bill created considerable tension between Viele and me because he was my boss. My job in the state legislature paid only $3,600 per year, and when the legislature was out of session, I augmented that income with a real estate broker's license: I worked out of Viele's office.

The open housing bill was not popular in my district, and I received a mountain of organized mail against it. As I reviewed that mail, I was appalled to discover that I had received more letters from clergymen against the bill than I had received in support of it. Only three Catholic priests had written me on the subject—one for the bill and two against it. When I publicly remarked about my disappointment that Catholic and Protestant clergy alike had been more active against the legislation than for it, I was angrily told by a local priest that my statement was "disrespectful" of the Catholic Church. I did not think so. I thought I was making a simple observation of fact.

Since my election to Congress I have voted on many issues that are related in one way or another to "Catholic values." In the vast majority of cases, a comparison of my voting record and the position statements by the Catholic bishops would seem to indicate a reasonable level of agreement on issues ranging from economic justice, the rights of workers to organize, expanding educational opportunities, expanding affordable health-care coverage, and strengthening international food-aid programs, to opposing unnecessary wars and opposing the death penalty. For ten years I was the House leader in pushing through Congress the ultimate life legislation, the foreign assistance bill that expanded funding for child survival programs, child health and education programs, and childhood immunization programs in the Third World, where one of every five children dies before the age of five—all programs that have saved the lives of millions of children.

The one issue that has caused tension with the Catholic hierarchy has been the issue of abortion. The idea of abortion has always repelled me, and I have agreed with Church teachings that abortion is generally immoral and represents a tragic failure. That is why I have repeatedly led the fight for federal budget priorities that strengthen funds for programs that could help convince young pregnant mothers, often unmarried, to complete their pregnancies rather than seeking abortions—real life programs such as adoption assistance, domestic abuse prevention, expanded maternal and child health care, expanded child care, strengthened job training, and mental health counseling. I have also felt, and have publicly so stated, that the court decision in *Roe v. Wade*, which set different rules for different stages of pregnancy, would need to be modified over time as advances in medical science make it possible for a fetus to survive at earlier stages of development.

But I have also adhered to the obvious principle that what I thought to be immoral and what I thought should be specifically outlawed by statute were sometimes two different questions. So for years I tried to think my way through the various abortion-related issues as they came before me. In that effort I have been guided by the principle stated by John Cardinal Newman, quoted in 1968 by Cardinal Ratzinger (now Pope Benedict XVI) of Germany,

that "above the pope as an expression of the binding claim of church authority stands one's own conscience, which has to be obeyed first of all, if need be,
against the demands of church authority."

When the issue of federal funds for Medicaid abortions first arose in the
1970s, I opposed legislative efforts to prohibit poverty-level women from obtaining abortions under the Medicaid program because I felt it denied to poor
women something that the courts had declared to be a constitutional right.
But it soon became obvious to me that funding for all kinds of health and
education programs would be blocked if a compromise was not reached on
the issue, so I accepted the language of the Hyde Amendment, which denied
federal funding except in the cases of threat to the mother's life. And when
health-care delivery changed with the rise of HMOs, I worked with Nita
Lowey, Henry Hyde, and Frank Monahan, of the U.S. Catholic Bishops, to
try to find a compromise in applying the Hyde Amendment to HMOs in the
same way that it had been applied to fee-for-service medicine.

I was not comfortable with the unfairness or the legality of denying exceptions in cases that threatened the mother's health, but I felt that, to achieve
the greatest good for the greatest number, the compromise was necessary to
break the legislative logjam in providing increased federal funding for other
programs for the poor. Yet, I consistently declined to support a constitutional
amendment to outlaw abortion—on separation of church and state grounds.
It was, and is, my firm belief that if such an amendment were to become law,
it would result in massive disregard of the law and a weakening of support
for all law. That was certainly the case before *Roe v. Wade,* when, in spite of
the then current law, thousands of illegal abortions were performed each year,
often under circumstances that threatened women's lives and left many of
them unable to have children in the future. Because of my position, a number of antiabortion groups have attacked me through the years.

At the same time, on numerous occasions, I have also antagonized freedom-
of-choice groups on the other side of the issue. When I chaired the Foreign
Operations Appropriations Subcommittee, I helped fashion a provision that
reduced the U.S. contribution to the UN population program by the amount
of money that the UN spent in China. I did so because of the Chinese policy
of forcing women to have abortions after they have given birth to one child.
That infuriated some abortion-rights advocates.

After dealing with the issue for almost thirty years, I have virtually given up
talking about it because it has become almost impossible to have a rational,
civil conversation with so many groups on either side of the issue. Each side
seems to feel morally superior to the other, and so many on each side seem to

firmly believe that people on the other side are either ignorant or evil. Each
side has objected to even the smallest departure from its own orthodoxy, and
each seems more interested in enforcing down-the-line, rigid adherence to its
viewpoint rather than allowing room for nuance.

Three years ago, after more than a decade of equilibrium, the issue mani-
fested itself in a new way, with a new confrontation over partial-birth abortions. Again, I made neither side happy, because I did what I was supposed
to do: I used my own judgment to try to sort out the nuances of the issue. I
supported a ban on the practice (which upset the freedom-of-choice groups)
but also supported an amendment that made an exception for cases when the
health of the mother might be seriously impaired: I thought that *without* such
an exception the courts were likely to rule such a limitation unconstitutional
and strike it down. That position did not satisfy either side.

The abortion issue has immersed me and every public figure who has dealt
with it in a dilemma far broader than the issue of abortion itself. That conflict
is rooted in the fundamental question of how public officials should apply
their private and personal religious and moral principles to their public responsibilities in a democratic society, which has reached no consensus on many of
the questions involved. In situations like that, in a democracy, the question is
not "What is the policy?"; rather it is "Who decides?"

Through the late 1980s and 1990s, the issue arose in more and more instances, and the debate became more polarized and nasty. In the 1990s, at a
time when several workers at abortion clinics had been shot, one antiabortion
organization placed on its website pictures of a number of members of Congress, with a target superimposed over each face—implying that those officials
should be eliminated (and I don't mean politically). More recently, the issue
has been further complicated by the rise of stem cell research, which produces
lifesaving arguments on either side of the issue. I have tried to work my way
through these issues by asking, not just what I believed but what I thought
was achievable, enforceable, and sustainable in a democratic, pluralistic society. I know that some people hate that term, but that is what our society is,
and neither wish nor demand will change it. In each case, I tried to apply my
judgment and my conscience to specific circumstances that were often complicated, with competing sets of equities on both sides. Several years ago, the
issue took on a new dimension.

My congressional district covers more than one-quarter of the land area of
the state of Wisconsin. It is split between two Catholic Church dioceses. The
southern part of the district is part of the LaCrosse Diocese, which is governed
from LaCrosse, Wisconsin, a city some sixty miles away from my district. The

northern part of my district falls within the Superior Diocese and is governed from Superior, Wisconsin. The bishop of LaCrosse was Raymond Burke, a hard-line conservative who had spent years in the Vatican as a canon lawyer but had little pastoral experience. He rapidly established himself as one of the most zealous right-wing bishops in the church. He demonstrated his deep and zealous conservatism when he objected to parishioners supporting Crop Walk because 1 percent of the dollars in that operation went for family-planning purposes. On another occasion he also raised strong concerns about children reading Harry Potter books.

In December 2002, with no prior notice of dissatisfaction on his part, I received a letter from Burke in which he chastised me for my votes on several abortion-related issues, and without having heard one word of rebuttal, asserted that my positions were "gravely deficient." Throughout the year we exchanged several private letters on various aspects of the issue. Each of his letters became more authoritarian in his demand that I conform to his judgment on how Catholic doctrine dictated I should vote on such issues as stem cell research, medical collective bargaining, the use of military hospitals, and the UN population program. When I replied to him that I respected his right to tell me at any time how he believed I should vote, just like any other citizen, but that I objected to his assertion that he had a right to dictate my vote, he replied, "It is not I who dictate to you, but the Magisterial teachings of the Church."

During Burke's years as bishop, I had met him only once, at my home parish, St. Anne's, where we had, at most, a three-minute conversation about the history of the parish. I had been following the bishop's activities and those of one of his close associates, Arthur Hippler, in the diocesan newspaper. I had seen Hippler's columns suggesting, among other things, that the progressive income tax was immoral because it was too burdensome on the wealthiest and productive members of society. I had also seen the bishop's speech in my hometown assuring Catholics that they need not agree with the pope's opposition to the Iraq War. It was vividly apparent that the bishop and Hippler were both politically and ideologically hard right conservatives.

Since the bishop began his first letter to me by indicating that he had already concluded my voting record was in error, rather than by asking about my reasoning for the votes in question, it was obvious to me that he intended to provoke a confrontation. That confrontation came to a head in November 2003 when he wrote me a letter threatening to use his ecclesiastical authority to punish me if I did not conform my voting record to his views. In his next letter, he informed me that he was taking action to deny me the privilege of receiving the Eucharist. He took the same action against two Democratic state legislators from my district—one of whom was just recently elected and had yet to cast a single vote on the legislation that concerned him.

The bishop began his correspondence with me on a "confidential" basis, and I respected that confidentiality in my responses to him. But within days of his last letter to me, newspapers reported the bishop's action. At the same time, my office received a number of form letters from the Milwaukee area, far from my district, which contained paragraphs that were virtually identical to the language of the bishop's letter to me. That indicated to me that the bishop's office—or someone familiar with it—had leaked the bishop's actions to the organization that was behind those letters.

Then came the announcement that Burke had been promoted to archbishop of the St. Louis Diocese. Within days of his moving to St. Louis, the archbishop gratuitously announced that if John Kerry came to St. Louis and attended Mass he would be denied Communion—and that elevated the issue to the national level. Cardinal McCarrick of Washington, D.C., was appointed chair of a task force of the American Council of Catholic Bishops to try to establish a consensus on how the bishops should relate to public officials on matters of faith. All of these developments occurred in the midst of another raging controversy: the manner in which the church hierarchy had handled and sheltered pedophile priests over the past two decades.

When the bishop's office made public the action he had taken against me I issued a statement saying,

> I have said on many occasions that I agree with the Catholic Church about the undesirability of abortion, but this country is not exclusively Catholic. Bishop Burke has a right to instruct me on matters of faith and morals in my private life and—like any other citizen—to try to persuade, not dictate, how I vote on any public matter. But when he attempts to use his ecclesiastical position to dictate to American public officials how the power of law should be brought to bear against Americans who do not necessarily share our religious beliefs on abortion or any other public issue, he crosses the line into unacceptable territory. The U.S. Constitution, which I have taken a sacred oath to defend, is designed to protect American citizens from just such demands. The U.S. Constitution says, "Congress shall make no law respecting an establishment of religion, or prohibiting the free exercise thereof." That means that in an American Democracy no one, not a public official and not a bishop, gets to impose by law his religious beliefs on people of other religions who do not necessarily share those same beliefs.

When contacted by the press, a spokesman for the bishop said that not only was I out of line, but that women who used contraceptives should also not present themselves for Communion.

Over the next few weeks, as my dispute with Burke became more widely known, I was encouraged by a number of priests to write an article for the Jesuit magazine *America* outlining my beliefs about how I, as a public official who happened to be a Catholic, applied my religious views to public life. I had been thinking about that question for almost forty years since John F. Kennedy's declaration of conscience speech in 1960. That article appeared in August 2004 issue of *America*. It is important to me because the question of how public officials should and should not apply their religious views to matters of public law will be at the center of national debate for the remainder of my lifetime. Along with a speech I gave at the University of Wisconsin on March 27, 2004, commemorating the one-hundredth anniversary of the university's Political Science Department, it is one of two statements that I have written in my public life that comes closest to summing up my core beliefs. Together, they make clear exactly what I believe and why I believe it.

In the *America* article I stated:

> I very much regret the fact that the bishop saw fit to take the course of action he has chosen. But I make no apology for insisting that the bishop distinguish between his right to try to persuade me on how to vote on any issue and his right to dictate my vote. . . .
>
> I believe that if the full texture and context of all my legislative actions were to be reviewed—and given the fact that at least one hundred members of Congress have voting records more at variance with church wishes than my own—I firmly believe that Bishop Burke's action says much more about him than it does about me.
>
> The basic problem is that I remain a John Courtney Murray kind of Catholic, while Bishop Burke is not. Murray was the key American theologian who advised the American Catholic bishops during the deliberation of the historic Second Vatican Council convened by Pope John XXIII.

I pointed out that in his book *We Hold These Truths: Catholic Reflections on the American Proposition* (1960), Murray discussed the right and the obligation of legislators to reserve to themselves prudential judgments about what was enforceable through law in a multireligious society—a society that does not just guarantee majority rights but also *guarantees* the rights of minorities against the majority. Murray wrote: "It is not the function of the legislator to forbid everything that the moral law forbids, or to enjoin everything that the moral law enjoins."

A few months after my article was published, the magazine's editor, the Reverend Thomas Reese, was pushed out of his job. One of the four reasons given for his removal was that he printed my article. Like Father Langer before him, he was a victim of ideology. His offense was that he thought that Catholics were adult enough to hear both sides of any argument.

Two thousand years ago Christ said, "Render unto Caesar the things that are Caesar's and to God the things that are God's." That is what we do—all of us—public official and private citizen alike, as we distinguish between the religious and the secular. For all of my public life, my official actions have occurred in the context of my religious beliefs. But it is also true that my religious beliefs are applied in the context of my official responsibilities.

Under the Constitution, I have the obligation to make that distinction, and that is what I have tried to do in my forty years of public service on a whole range of issues that have a moral dimension. It would have been much easier not to do so. It would have saved much wear and tear politically and emotionally, but my conscience would not allow me to disregard that distinction, and I make no apology for it. As a rather well-known figure in religious history once noted when he nailed his Ninety-five Theses to the church door: "Here I stand, I can do no other."

WISCONSIN VALUES

At about the same time that my dispute with the bishop surfaced publicly, I was invited to return to the University of Wisconsin to deliver a luncheon address at a two-day symposium celebrating the centennial of the University of Wisconsin's Political Science Department. When I first received the invitation I was inclined to turn it down because I was preoccupied by my dispute with the bishop; but the more I thought about it, the more I saw it as an opportunity to sum up my core beliefs and acknowledge what the Wisconsin La Follette tradition and the university itself meant to me. I accepted the invitation and had a wonderful time, listening to panel discussions, renewing old acquaintances with long-since retired professors, and enjoying the camaraderie of other alumni such as Chris Bury of ABC News, Rita Braver of CBS, Bob Barnett, the well-known Washington lawyer, and many others. In a luncheon speech to the alumni and political science students, I told the audience:

I'm grateful for all those memories and for the substantive grounding the university gave me to prepare me for my congressional responsibilities. But the grounding I received from the university was not just because of the courses I took. It was also because of the spirit, the philosophy, the progressive mind-set that defined the university and set it off as something special in the American experience. You simply cannot live in Wisconsin and go to the University of Wisconsin without recognizing the centrality of the La Follette progressive tradition that is at the heart of Wisconsin history and the linkage the university has with that tradition.

The greatest public servant Wisconsin ever produced was Robert La Follette. Before La Follette led his Progressive revolution, Wisconsin's politics was owned lock, stock, and barrel by the railroads, the mining companies, and the timber interests. Government was geared to promote the welfare of those engaged in the production of wealth. The interest of the working class was an afterthought. La Follette changed all that—aided and abetted by the university. La Follette changed the focus of Wisconsin government from enriching the few at the expense of the many to enriching the few *by enriching* the many.

What I learned here that inspired me is that while La Follette and other Progressive reformers like George Norris and Theodore Roosevelt were regarded as secular men, they really were at the moral core of a movement that had deep roots in the Jewish prophetic tradition and the Christian social gospel, which implied that there were certain norms of decency that must be the objectives of political choices in a democracy. That tradition was rooted in the belief that politics must be more than merely transactional. It must be more principled than "who gets what." That it could and should be, as Bill Moyers has said, transformational—that it must try to "even the starting gate so that people who are equal in humanity but not in resources have a reasonable opportunity to pursue a full and decent life."

I closed by saying:

Now, I'm sure that some of you may strongly disagree with the thrust of what I have said today. That's okay. As Will Rogers observed, "If two people agree on everything, one of them is unnecessary." That difference would probably be rooted in the fact that we follow different philosophers. Some of you may follow Plato or Aristotle or even Ayn Rand, God forbid. But my favorite philosopher is Archy the Cockroach. Archy was a character invented by a writer by the name of Don Marquis in the 1920s. He was supposedly a poet who had died and had come back to life in a body of a cockroach. He lived in a newspaperman's office and every night would crawl out of the woodwork, climb onto the type-writer, dive head first on the keys, and leave little messages, which would appear in the newspaper the next day. He had a thought for every occasion. One of the things he said was this:

> did you ever notice that when
> a politician does get an idea
> he usually gets it all wrong

But my favorite was this:

> im too small to feel great pride
> and as the pompous world
> goes by i see things from
> the underside

Like Archy, I try to see life from the underside. I make no apology. I learned it here!

These two incidents—my confrontation with the bishop and my speech at the University of Wisconsin—highlight the values that have driven me in my years of public service. I have not always applied them correctly, but Lord knows I've tried.

What was I trying to say in those two statements? What would my friend Archy see as he looked at life from the underside? He would see how typical working families are struggling to keep their heads above water. He would see how desperately so many American families are struggling to give their kids an opportunity to grab a middle-class life while the opportunity for that lifestyle appears to be getting smaller before their eyes.

He would tell us that the struggle is not just about living standards, but about life itself. He would understand—and hope that we would—that if a young pregnant woman or a poverty-level couple had no education, no job, no decent housing, and no health-care coverage, then they have no incentive to complete a pregnancy and every incentive to end it because in that situation, all too often another baby is seen as an unbearable burden rather than an indescribable blessing. And at that point, in those conditions, all the lectures in the world from bishops or congressmen simply don't cut it. That is why federal budgets that pay for tax cuts for millionaires with budget cuts in education, Medicaid, child care, and health care are not just unfair; they are immoral. And, yes, they are anti-life! That is why some things as arcane as the way the congressional budget process works to avoid rather than force political accountability for inhumane budget choices are not just unfair; they are destructive of the very values we supposedly stand for.

Today the Congress, in the wake of the Abramoff lobby scandal, is engaged in another debate about ethics. My old House colleague Otis Pike made an observation during the Reagan years that rings as true today as it did when he said it:

> You can talk about ethics forever and pass more rules and reveal yourselves until all of your and your spouse's finances, food, drink, sex, religion, clothing, vacations, and the hours and minutes and places of your arising and retiring are public records, you will never be held in high regard or deemed ethical while you say you can't balance a budget unless a constitutional amendment makes you; while you accept gloriously optimistic economic projections rather than deal with real ones; while you write a Gramm-Rudman bill and then spend days finding ways to get around it; while you let one man make $550 million a year while thousands sleep in the streets.

So what is our challenge? Until government makes policy choices that provide a *New* New Deal to American workers, we will continue to erode our values and the quality of life that should be within the reach of every American. Americans still like to believe in the American dream, to see themselves as part of the middle class. But more and more, each day, as political leaders make choices that redistribute income up, rather than down, the ladder, as the forces of globalization weaken the safety net under the American worker, as the shrinkage of the labor movement further weakens the floor under American wages and family income, life from Archie's view of the underside is becoming more and more a struggle.

From the end of the Great Depression through the end of World War II, a larger and larger share of American workers were working their way into the middle class. By the end of that war, only the poorest fifth of American workers were earning too little to have a taste of the middle-class life. Since the early 1970s, however, rising family income has not kept pace with rising family expenses. As a result, today, the bottom two-fifths of American workers are no longer within reach of a middle-class existence.

Harvard law professor Elizabeth Warren has done the best and clearest job of expanding and refining the analysis of wealth and income data that Scott Lilly and I had reported on the 1980s and early 1990s. She demonstrated that in real terms, after adjusting for inflation, the American male worker precisely in the middle of the income stream, with half earning more and half earning less, is making no more than he did thirty years ago. His reality is that for thirty years, in terms of real income, he has been standing still. Warren showed, as we did in our JEC reports ten and fifteen years earlier, that all of the gain that the American working family in the exact middle of the income stream has experienced over the last generation has come about because a second family earner has entered the workplace. But in real terms, that family of four is no better off because all of the increase in income from a second family paycheck has been devoured by rising costs of items such as health care, child care, housing, and transportation. And as tax burdens have been shifted down the income scale and from corporations to individuals, the tax burden on that family in the middle has also risen.

Warren further points out that, contrary to the American myth, families today are more vulnerable to economic shock than they were a generation ago. Thirty years ago, if someone in the family fell ill for a long period, someone (usually the wife) was home to take care of them. Not so today, with two people in the workforce. Thirty years ago, when women were still at home, if the husband lost his job, it was possible to bring some emergency income into the house by sending the woman into the workplace, but today with husband and wife already employed, there is no extra worker in the family who can augment family income in a crisis. With strains like that on the American family, family savings rates have dropped from 10 percent of income a generation ago to near zero today. In short, American families are working overtime to hang onto a middle-class lifestyle. They work harder, work more hours, and take shorter vacations than comparable families in almost every other industrialized country, all to give their kids a chance to stay in that middle class.

Housing costs in many neighborhoods are exploding because parents are willing to pay exorbitant prices to live in a neighborhood where the schools are excellent, not mediocre. Those same parents are seeing college costs rise farther and farther beyond their reach. The college board has just announced that in the last four years alone the cost of attending a four-year public university has risen by $3,100. At the same time, the major student-aid program for students from low-income families has shrunk so markedly that it pays for only 32 percent of college costs compared to the 70 percent it covered thirty years ago.

Under these conditions, when Congress votes to pay for tax cuts for people making more than a million dollars with budget cuts in education, Medicaid, low-income housing, and job training, it is not just making an accounting decision. It is making a values decision that has a profound effect on families struggling to do the right thing. When politicians choose to pay for huge tax breaks for people with estates of $7 million or more by cutting Social Security guarantees to workers who earn $30,000 a year, it is not just making accounting decisions. It is consciously deciding that it will make the lives of many people of limited means more miserable in order to make a few extremely fortunate people exceedingly comfortable.

And when Congress is called back into session by Tom DeLay and Co. to demand that the feeding tube for Terri Schiavo, paid for by Medicaid, be reconnected, but then votes to cut $10 billion from Medicaid, making it more difficult for thousands of people to afford any health care at all, has it really made a moral decision? Not in my book. My whole public life has been one long protest against that kind of indifference.

In February 2005, I received a letter from Bishop William Skylstad, chairman of the Catholic Bishops Conference, asserting that budgets were moral documents and urgently asking that Congress make budget choices to help people in the margins of life. He was right. He got it! That is what Bob La Follette understood. That is what Archy understood. That is what the social gospel and the Wisconsin Progressive tradition are all about. Every day I have spent in public life, I wish that I had been able to do a better job carrying that message.

SUMMING UP

So how do you sum up a public life? On a famous day in 1939 in Yankee Stadium, Lou Gehrig said, "Today I consider myself the luckiest man on the face of the earth." If *I'm* not the luckiest man on earth, I come awfully close.

I imagine that many people look at presidents, senators, and congressmen, and think they were born that way. The truth is so much different. All but a handful started anonymously, growing up in regular families with all the problems that families face in life. Each made his or her own way with a combination of luck and determination. Each brought his or her experiences and values to bear on the decisions and activities that are associated with public life.

As did so many others, I started as a shy boy from a troubled family of modest means. Sometimes, in spite of myself, I was taught by people, first the nuns and then the public school teachers, who at critical times salvaged me, inspired me, and opened my mind to the possibilities of life. I was lucky enough at an early age to find a life partner who has made all the difference. She has given me two fine sons who today share and live the same values that first drove me to public service. They have, in turn, been blessed with two loving wives who also share those same values. Joan and I have known what it is to lose a child, and we have, I believe, been made wiser and more appreciative of life by the experience. And for the last four years, we have been issued into the wonderful world of grandchildren.

My election to the state legislature was due not to any purposeful plan but rather to someone else's suggestion. Before I left the legislature, I was honored by my colleagues as their deputy floor leader and was privileged to work with two governors of conscience, as well as legislators of both parties who took their responsibilities seriously, worked together, and produced legislative landmarks in the fields of civil rights, education, conservation, and transportation.

I was privileged to be elected the nation's youngest member of Congress when a fine and decent public servant, Mel Laird, resigned his congressional post to assume one with even higher responsibilities. In that people's arena I was taught and guided by men of honor and skill: Gaylord Nelson, Bob Kastenmeier, Henry Reuss, Bill Proxmire, Bill Steiger, Mo Udall, Carl Albert, John Dingell, Dick Conlan, Jim O'Hara, Dick Bolling, Otis Pike, John Moss, Abe Mikva, Tip O'Neill, Dick Conlon, and many, many others. I have had the privilege of working for and with four of the greatest men in American history who *never* became president—Hubert Humphrey, Mo Udall, Fritz Mondale, and Dick Gephardt. How much happier the country's history would have been had any or all of them won.

I have been given the privilege by my constituents of being one of the 10,561 people who, in our history, have served in the House of Representatives, and I have the extraordinary privilege of having served longer than all but twenty-five of them.

As I have learned, more and more responsibility fell my way.

- Writing a new code of ethics for the House (Gaylord Nelson did the same for the Senate)
- Chairing the Foreign Operations Subcommittee, which for ten tumultuous years helped manage our relationship with a changing world
- Chairing the Joint Economic Committee, which gave me the opportunity to learn the workings of the world's economy and our own
- Serving as a key House spokesman and strategist for my party on the three issues closest to my heart—education, health, and worker protection
- Serving as chairman, then ranking Democrat, then chairman again on the Appropriations Committee, at the center of Congress's debate on national priorities

Those positions of influence were not important in and of themselves. Their importance was in what they have enabled me to do on the many issues that affect the corners of people's lives.

I have been given the opportunity by my constituents to work on so many problems that affect us all. We have lost at least as often as we have won. That sometimes haunts me because the needs are so great and so urgent. But I take comfort in the knowledge that even Babe Ruth struck out fourteen hundred times.

The hope of every public servant, certainly every member of Congress, is to make at least a small difference in the life of the nation and in the lives of the people and the communities of the district he or she represents. I cannot possibly begin to describe the satisfaction I derive from the knowledge that I have been able to use my position in Congress to do just that, across a whole range of activities—economic development, education, transportation, community development, environmental protection, housing, health care, law enforcement, and the like. Whatever the project, I can remember the people who worked with me to make these things happen, and I can see that a public life can make a difference.

During my time in Congress, according to the Library of Congress, I have served with 1,608 different members of the House. On April 4, 2005, I became the longest serving member of Congress in Wisconsin history. Through every one of those more than thirty-eight years I have done my best to meet my responsibilities in a manner consistent with my own values—values rooted in the Catholic social gospel and Wisconsin's La Follette Progressive traditions. I have made mistakes along the way, more than even my most vociferous political opponents know, but I've done my best. But that is not the end of the story. There is so much more to do.

Several years ago, in his autobiography, former governor Tommy Thompson claimed that he and his conservative allies were the true, modern-day inheritors of the La Follette Progressive tradition. That claim is preposterous. In fact, the Thompson administration in Wisconsin, and the Reagan and Bush administrations nationally, restored to economic and political ascendancy the very economic elites that La Follette fought all of his life. If he were alive today, La Follette's mission would be to:

- Restore the principle that America will go to war only as the last option, not the first
- Restore the principle that we will conduct ourselves as a nation in full and willing compliance with, not above or in contravention of, international law

- Lead the world toward accepting and embracing, rather than avoiding, our stewardship responsibility to the planet's environment that sustains us all
- Deliver on the promise contained in the Pledge of Allegiance to make America a nation that provides "liberty and justice for all," not "for almost everybody"
- Fight to strengthen economic justice by pursuing policies that narrow rather than widen the gap between the haves and have-nots of society
- Resist those who, in the name of unthinking globalization, would allow multinational corporations to obliterate the economic gains that workers have fought so hard to establish and maintain for the past two generations
- Restore a modicum of democracy in the way the Congress does business by curbing the arbitrary abuse of power by congressional leadership that until this year so sadly defined "the People's House"

La Follette would tell us that we must make certain that access to affordable health care is recognized as the right of every American man, woman, and child. We must transform "equal access to education" from a slogan to a reality. We must not allow rampant individualism to destroy Social Security, the greatest social insurance program the country has ever known. We must not ignore our responsibility to make crucial investments in education, health, science, and community infrastructure that are necessary to enable America to reach its full economic potential for coming generations.

I have, I hope, become somewhat wiser as I have learned new things along the way. I no longer trust government's ability to directly run many things as I did when I was young. But even more passionately than when I first entered public life, I believe government must be strong enough to be an effective referee, a fair umpire capable of knocking the rough edges off capitalism, just as an umpire can curb a bully on the ball diamond, to keep the big boys honest and protect the weak from being crushed or bloodied.

Since 9/11, America has been told that the number-one threat to the nation's future is terrorism. That is simply not true. Certainly, terrorism is indeed a serious threat that must be contained, but the greatest threat to a strong and decent future for America is indifference—the indifference that still threatens American families with inadequate education for their children, inadequate access to affordable and comprehensive health care, inadequate protections for pensions earned with a lifetime of hard work, and water and air that threaten the health of our children.

We can all do some things alone as individuals to make life better for ourselves, our family, our friends, and our neighbors. That is what personal responsibility is all about. But for most important problems facing this country we need effective government. There are those in society—and they are in the ascendancy today—who detest the very idea of relying on government. I know. I talk with them every day. But FDR was right when he said, "Better the occasional faults of a government that lives in a spirit of charity than the consistent omissions of a government frozen in the ice of its own indifference." If I could leave one message for today's young people it would be this: "Give a damn! Crusade against indifference!"

A decade ago Rep. Henry Reuss, one of the finest public servants Wisconsin or the nation has produced, said at a commencement speech at the University of Wisconsin–Milwaukee:

> Pericles was right when he told the Athenians that the citizen who takes no part in public affairs is not merely unambitious but useless. If you will combine the private aim of getting ahead in life with the public pursuit of justice, you will help restore the essence of democracy—informed and lively participation by its citizens. And that can produce a government which feels compelled neither to do everything nor to do nothing.

We must fight to open wide the door of opportunity for every man, woman, and child in this great country. The most important victories are those that are still to be won!

Epilogue

After six long years of George W. Bush's presidency and after a decade-long abuse of power by Republican congressional leaders (personified by Tom DeLay's operating style), in November of 2006 the American people decided they had finally had enough.

Public frustration and disillusionment about the fruitless war in Iraq, the unconscionable widening of the income gap—with CEOs of major corporations being paid as much in one day as their employees earned in a year—and a steady drumbeat of news stories about congressional corruption and abuse of power finally produced a long overdue political explosion. On November 7, 2006, the American people decided to put in place some checks and balances to restrain President Bush. That election produced a Democratic majority in the House of Representatives for the first time in twelve years. In the Senate, Democrats were given a majority by the slimmest of margins— one vote. Two days after the election Donald Rumsfeld resigned as Secretary of Defense.

With that election, I have once again assumed the chairmanship of the House Appropriations Committee. That election has given me an opportunity to pursue a different set of priorities than Congress had pursued over the last decade. The election meant that Nancy Pelosi would become the first woman Speaker of the House in history. She had an ambitious reform agenda and in the weeks after the election I worked with her on two fronts.

On the ethics front, she pushed through a package that included a number of reforms originally drafted by Barney Frank, Dave Price, Tom Allen, and me that banned lobbyists or their employers from having anything to do with congressional travel, banned extraneous material from being inserted into conference reports without a specific vote of the conferees, and required any member asking to earmark appropriated funds for specific projects in his or her district to certify that the requesting member did not stand to gain financially from the earmark.

To strengthen congressional oversight of administration intelligence activities, we announced the creation of a special hybrid appropriations panel composed of members appointed by the Speaker from the Select Committee on Intelligence and the Appropriations Committee. The purpose of the panel was to force better cooperation between, and stronger oversight by, the committee that authorized intelligence activities and the committee that funded those activities.

We also took action to change congressional spending priorities. In 2006, the Republican congressional majority had completed action on only about half of the year's budget. They had passed the defense and homeland security appropriations but had completed action on none of the domestic appropriations. All but one of the bills had been passed by House Republicans, but their Senate GOP counterparts had delayed action because they did not want to defend cuts in education, health, the environment, and science before the election.

After the election, the Republicans gave up on passing any of them and instead passed a stopgap short-term resolution continuing almost all funding at previous year's levels until February 15, 2007. To clean up the mess, Senator Byrd and I worked with Pelosi and the new Senate Majority Leader, Harry Reid, to put together a yearlong continuing resolution that would make as many adjustments as possible to prevent agency layoffs or furloughs, reshaping priorities as much as possible within the overall spending limits established by the previously passed Republican budget resolution. We also announced that we would suspend all new earmarks for a year until we could reform the earmarking process to prevent it from being abused by members such as Randy "Duke" Cunningham, who had just been convicted of bribery for accepting huge payoffs in return for budget earmarks he had obtained in the intelligence and defense budgets.

On January 31, 2007, the House passed the new continuing resolution, which froze most programs at previous year's levels, cut about sixty others, and used roughly $17 billion made available by those actions to significantly change budget priorities. We added $3.6 billion dollars to help 325,000 veterans to receive better health care. We added $500 million to improve military housing and $1 billion to help military personnel and communities to adjust to the base-closing process that was occurring around the country. We added $500 million to strengthen the FBI and local law enforcement.

In education, we provided $615 million to help more than five million college students by expanding the Pell Grant program, increasing the maximum grant for low income students by $260 dollars.

In science, we provided a $620 million increase for medical research grants at the National Institutes of Health, reversing a two year decline in new research grants.

In health, we added $200 million to expand community health centers, to help 1.2 million Americans to gain access to health care. We also provided $1.4 billion more to expand our global efforts to combat HIV/AIDS, tuberculosis, and malaria.

The Republican leadership of the House strongly opposed our efforts, but in the end fifty-seven rank and file House Republicans voted with us, enabling the bill to pass by greater than a two-to-one margin. What a difference one election had made. We were only four weeks into the new congressional session but we had been able to reshape budget priorities in a significant way without spending more money than the Republicans had intended.

An even bigger example of how much difference the election had made is the way the House responded in March to President Bush's supplemental budget request for an additional $100 billion dollars to pay for the costs of the Iraq War. Presidents often ask for supplemental funding requests to cover the costs of unexpected emergencies, such as those that stem from hurricanes or severe drought. But George Bush had turned the process on its head by funding the war through a series of partial-year supplemental requests that had the effect of obscuring the full-year costs of the war.

In February, Bush sent the Congress his new fiscal year 2008 budget, which squeezed out and short-changed many crucial long-term investments in education, health, science, and the environment that were important to the future economic and social strength of the country. In addition to his regular defense spending request he used the device of yet another supplemental budget request to ask for almost $100 billion in extra funding for the war.

Since the war began, the Congress had responded in rubber stamp fashion, but with the new election, Democrats moved from minority to majority status in the House. That gave us our first chance to try to use a presidential request for funds to change the course of American policy in Iraq. When Congress first gave Bush the authority to attack Iraq in October of 2002, as the minority party, Democrats had been able to muster only 133 votes against the proposition. But our new status as the majority party gave us an opportunity to gather 218 votes to take the first step toward ending our military involvement in what had clearly become an Iraqi civil war. At the same time

Bush sent down his budget request, he announced that he was intensifying our efforts in Iraq (what he called a surge) by sending thousands of additional troops.

Speaker Pelosi, Jack Murtha, Ike Skelton (the new chairman of the Armed Services Committee), and I held a series of meetings with other key members to fashion a response. Murtha designed an approach that would allow that surge to proceed only if the president could certify that each additional unit sent to Iraq would be able to meet specific standards of military readiness. His plan ran into major resistance in our own caucus from two sources. Conservative members resisted because they worried the requirements might be too tough. Liberals expressed unhappiness because the approach was largely focused on the surge, but did not deal with the broader question of getting our troops out of a civil war. I agreed with Murtha's efforts, but it was clear that the approach had to be broadened in order to generate the support we needed.

Rob Nabors, my Appropriations staff chief, and I worked with the Speaker's staff to fashion a set of performance benchmarks to be applied to Iraqi performance. We tied those benchmarks to a flexible timetable for repositioning our troops out of Iraq by August 2008. Through a series of meetings adjustments were made until we had an approach that made sense on the ground in Iraq and had a chance to gain the support we needed to pass it in the House. We felt that what was important was not so much the specific language of the proposal, but the message it would send to Iraqi politicians that they needed to reach a political settlement.

We met with fierce opposition from the White House and from the most conservative and the most liberal members of our caucus for opposite reasons. For almost a month we worked to produce enough converts to reach the magic number of 218 votes that was needed for passage. The bill that I sponsored and managed came to the floor for two days of debate starting on Thursday, March 22. Just before the bill came to the floor, our caucus had a meeting with Zbigniew Brzezinski, President Carter's National Security Advisor, a strong proponent of what we were trying to do.

At 8:30 Friday morning, our caucus met one last time to enable us to make a final push for support from still wavering members. As the meeting drew to a close, Nancy Pelosi praised Ike Skelton and Jack Murtha on the military aspects of the package. She then paid tribute to my efforts. As the caucus rose to give me a standing ovation, I shouted, "I don't want your applause; I want your damned votes!" Everyone laughed, and we headed for the House chamber for the last two hours of debate.

After often impassioned debate, the vote finally came and the bill passed by the narrowest of margins—218 to 212. A switch of three votes would have doomed it: 216 Democrats and 2 Republicans (Wayne Gilchrist of Maryland and Walter Jones of North Carolina) voted for it and 198 Republicans and 14 Democrats voted no. The final Democratic votes against it were evenly divided between the most conservative and the most liberal of our caucus.

The effort that had gone into eeking out our victory was immense. Nancy Pelosi—on the phone and in face to face encounters in her office—pulled people along one by one. Jack Murtha and I worked more closely than we had in our entire careers in the House. The rest of the Democratic leadership—Steny Hoyer, Jim Clyburn, Rahm Emmanuel, John Larson, Rosa DeLauro, George Miller, and many others—begged and persuaded reluctant colleagues to come along. What Nancy and I found especially frustrating was that even though the Bush White House and the Republican Party were vehemently opposed to our actions, several groups of far left antiwar protesters were targeting us for demonstrations and sit-ins at my offices and at Nancy's home. I told the press that their actions were akin to someone on a football team trying to sack their own quarterback.

In the end, every single new Democrat brought to the House by the 2006 election voted with us—a stark demonstration of the fact that elections do make a difference and that American citizens can change the direction of their country. The battle is still not won. As this is written, the fight to change American policy in Iraq moves to the Senate where Democrats hold only a one vote margin. Because Senate rules require sixty, not fifty-one, votes to shut off debate on matters such as this, in practical terms we are ten votes short of being able to put many of these issues on the president's desk without substantial Republican help.

Our narrow margin of control, especially in the Senate, will severely limit our ability to rein in the president on the international front before he does even more damage to America's military and to America's place in the world. And it will also significantly limit our ability to change national priorities here at home. But we now have a renewed opportunity to try. The nation expects us to make the most of it.

Index